Lecture Notes in Computer Science 3489

Commenced Publication in 1973
Founding and Former Series Editors:
Gerhard Goos, Juris Hartmanis, and Jan van Leeuwen

George T. Heineman   Ivica Crnkovic
Heinz W. Schmidt   Judith A. Stafford
Clemens Szyperski   Kurt Wallnau (Eds.)

Component-Based Software Engineering

8th International Symposium, CBSE 2005
St. Louis, MO, USA, May 14-15, 2005
Proceedings

 Springer

Volume Editors

George T. Heineman
WPI, Department of Computer Science
100 Institute Road, Worcester, MA 01609, USA
E-mail: heineman@cs.wpi.edu

Ivica Crnkovic
Mälardalen University, Department of Computer Science and Engineering
Box 883, 72123 Västerås, Sweden
E-mail: ivica.crnkovic@mdh.se

Heinz W. Schmidt
Monash University, School of Computer Science and Software Engineering
Wellington Road, Clayton VIC 3800 , Australia
E-mail: Heinz.Schmidt@csse.monash.edu.au

Judith A. Stafford
Tufts University, Department of Computer Science
161 College Avenue, Medford, MA 02155, USA
E-mail: jas@cs.tufts.edu

Clemens Szyperski
Microsoft
One Microsoft Way, Redmond, WA 98053, USA
E-mail: cszypers@microsoft.com

Kurt Wallnau
Carnegie Mellon University, Software Engineering Institute
Pittsburgh, Pennsylvania 15213-3890, USA
E-mail: kcw@sei.cmu.edu

Library of Congress Control Number: Applied for

CR Subject Classification (1998): D.2, D.1.5, D.3, F.3.1

ISSN	0302-9743
ISBN-10	3-540-25877-9 Springer Berlin Heidelberg New York
ISBN-13	978-3-540-25877-3 Springer Berlin Heidelberg New York

Springer is a part of Springer Science+Business Media

springeronline.com

© Springer-Verlag Berlin Heidelberg 2005
Printed in Germany

Typesetting: Camera-ready by author, data conversion by Boller Mediendesign
Printed on acid-free paper   SPIN: 11424529   06/3142   5 4 3 2 1 0

Preface

On behalf of the Organizing Committee I am pleased to present the proceedings of the 2005 Symposium on Component-Based Software Engineering (CBSE). CBSE is concerned with the development of software-intensive systems from reusable parts (components), the development of reusable parts, and system maintenance and improvement by means of component replacement and customization. CBSE 2005, "Software Components at Work," was the eighth in a series of events that promote a science and technology foundation for achieving predictable quality in software systems through the use of software component technology and its associated software engineering practices.

We were fortunate to have a dedicated Program Committee comprised of 30 internationally recognized researchers and industrial practitioners. We received 91 submissions and each paper was reviewed by at least three Program Committee members (four for papers with an author on the Program Committee). The entire reviewing process was supported by CyberChairPro, the Web-based paper submission and review system developed and supported by Richard van de Stadt of Borbala Online Conference Services. After a two-day virtual Program Committee meeting, 21 submissions were accepted as long papers and 2 submissions were accepted as short papers.

We are grateful for the assistance provided by the organizers of the ICSE conference, in particular the General Chair, Gruia-Catalin Roman, and the Workshops and Co-located Events Co-chair André van der Hoek. We also wish to thank the ACM Special Interest Group on Software Engineering (SIGSOFT) for their sponsorship of CBSE 2005. The proceedings you now hold were published by Springer and we are grateful for their support. Finally, we must thank the many authors who contributed the high-quality papers contained within these proceedings. As the international community of CBSE researchers and practitioners continues to grow, we expect the CBSE Symposium series to similarly attract widespread interest and participation.

March 2005   George T. Heineman
Worcester, MA
USA

Organization

CBSE 2005 was sponsored by the Association for Computing Machinery (ACM) Special Interest Group in Software (SIGSOFT). CBSE 2005 was a co-located event with the 27th International Conference on Software Engineering (ICSE 2005).

Organizing Committee

Program Chair   George T. Heineman (WPI, USA)

Steering Committee   Ivica Crnkovic
                         (Mälardalen University, Sweden)
                       Heinz W. Schmidt
                         (Monash University, Australia)
                       Judith A. Stafford (Tufts University, USA)
                       Clemens Szyperski (Microsoft Research, USA)
                       Kurt Wallnau
                         (Software Engineering Institute, USA)

Program Committee

Luca de Alfaro	University of California, Santa Cruz, USA
Rob Armstrong	Sandia National Laboratories, USA
Uwe Aßmann	Dresden University of Technology, Germany
Jakob Axelsson	Volvo Car Corporation, Sweden
Mike Barnett	Microsoft Research, USA
Judith Bishop	University of Pretoria, South Africa
Jan Bosch	Nokia Research Center, Finland
Michel Chaudron	University Eindhoven, The Netherlands
Ivica Crnkovic	Mälardalen University, Sweden
Susan Eisenbach	Imperial College London, UK
Wolfgang Emmerich	University College London, UK
Dimitra Giannakopoulou	NASA Ames, USA
Richard Hall	LSR-IMAG, France
Dick Hamlet	Portland State University, USA
George T. Heineman	WPI, USA
Tom Henzinger	EPFL, Switzerland and UC Berkeley, USA
Paola Inverardi	University of L'Aquila, Italy
Bengt Jonsson	Uppsala University, Sweden
Magnus Larsson	ABB, Sweden
Kung-Kiu Lau	University of Manchester, UK
Nenad Medvidovic	University of Southern California, USA
Rob van Ommering	Philips Research, The Netherlands

Program Committee (cont.)

Otto Preiss   ABB Corporate Research Centers, Switzerland
Ralf Reussner   University of Oldenburg, Germany
Douglas Schmidt   Vanderbilt University, USA
Heinz W. Schmidt   Monash University, Australia
Jean-Guy Schneider   Swinburne University of Technology, Australia
Judith A. Stafford   Tufts University, USA
Kurt Wallnau   Software Engineering Institute, USA
Dave Wile   Teknowledge, Corp., USA

Co-reviewers

Eddie Aftandilian   Xiaohong Jin   Joachim Parrow
Mikael Åkerholm   Merijn de Jonge   Corina Pasareanu
Somo Banerjee   Hugo Jonker   Paul Pettersson
Steffen Becker   Thomas E. Koch   Roshanak Roshandel
Dirk Beyer   Emanuel Kolb   Chris Sadler
Egor Bondarev   Sten Löcher   Johanneke Siljee
Ivor Bosloper   Rikard Land   Marco Sinnema
Guillaume Brat   Ling Ling   James Skene
Reinder J. Bril   Markus Lumpe   Antony Tang
Arindam Chakrabarti   Frank Lüders   Faris M. Taweel
Robert Chatley   Wolfgang Mahnke   Perla Velasco Elizondo
Sybren Deelstra   Sam Malek   Björn Victor
Viktoria Firus   Antinisca Di Marco   Erik de Vink
Kathi Fisler   Chris Mattmann   Lucian Voinea
Eelke Folmer   Hailiang Mei   Anders Wall
Johan Fredriksson   Raffaela Mirandola   Zheng Wang
Esther Gelle   Johan Muskens   Wang Yi
Falk Hartmann   Martin Naedele   Yang Yu
Mugurel T. Ionita   Ioannis Ntalamagkas
Vladimir Jakobac   Owen O'Malley
Anton Jansen   Fernando C. Osorio

Previous CBSE Workshops and Symposia

7th International Symposium on CBSE, Lecture Notes in Computer Science, Vol. 3054, Crnkovic, I.; Stafford, J.A.; Schmidt, H.W.; Wallnau, K. (Eds.), Springer, Edinburgh, UK (2004)

6th ICSE Workshop on CBSE: Automated Reasoning and Prediction http://www.sei.cmu.edu/pacc/CBSE6. Portland, Oregon (2003)

Previous CBSE Workshops and Symposia (cont.)

5th ICSE Workshop on CBSE: Benchmarks for Predictable Assembly
http://www.sei.cmu.edu/pacc/CBSE5. Orlando, Florida (2002)

4th ICSE Workshop on CBSE: Component Certification and System Prediction.
Software Engineering Notes, 26(10), November 2001. ACM SIGSOFT Author(s):
Crnkovic, I.; Schmidt, H.; Stafford, J.; Wallnau, K. (Eds.)
http://www.sei.cmu.edu/pacc/CBSE4-Proceedings.html. Toronto, Canada,
(2001)

3rd ICSE Workshop on CBSE: Reflection in Practice
http://www.sei.cmu.edu/pacc/cbse2000. Limerick, Ireland (2000)

2nd ICSE Workshop on CBSE: Developing a Handbook for CBSE
http://www.sei.cmu.edu/cbs/icse99. Los Angeles, California (1999)

1st Workshop on CBSE
http://www.sei.cmu.edu/pacc/icse98. Tokyo, Japan (1998)

Table of Contents

Extra-Functional System Properties of Components and Component-Based Systems

Components at Work

Performance Prediction of J2EE Applications Using Messaging Protocols

Yan Liu, Ian Gorton

National ICT Australia (NICTA),
1430, NSW, Australia
{jenny.liu, ian.gorton}@nicta.com.au

Abstract. Predicting the performance of component-based applications is difficult due to the complexity of the underlying component technology. This problem is exacerbated when a messaging protocol is introduced to create a loosely coupled software architecture. Messaging uses asynchronous communication, and must address quality of service issues such as message persistence and flow control. In this paper, we present an approach to predicting the performance of Java 2 Enterprise Edition (J2EE) applications using messaging services. The prediction is done during application design, without access to the application implementation. This is achieved by modeling the interactions among J2EE and messaging components using queuing network models, calibrating the performance model with architecture attributes associated with these components, and populating the model parameters using a lightweight, application-independent benchmark. Benchmarking avoids the need for prototype testing in order to obtain the value of model parameters, and thus reduces the performance prediction effort. A case study is carried out to predict the performance of a J2EE application with asynchronous communication. Analysis of the resulting predictions shows the error is within 15%.

1 Introduction

Many software component models utilize synchronous communication protocols, such as Enterprise JavaBeans (EJB) based on RMI, and RPC-based CORBA or COM+ components. Synchronous communication dictates that the client process blocks until the response to its request arrives. More loosely coupled software architectures can be constructed using asynchronous invocations. These place an intermediary messaging service between the client and server, decoupling their execution. In addition, asynchronous invocations are desirable for applications with high performance and scalability requirements. For these reasons, component technologies have been integrated with messaging protocols to support the development of applications with asynchronous architectures.

Messaging services are implemented by message-oriented middleware (MOM), such as Microsoft MSMQ, IBM WebSphere MQ, CORBA Notification Services and Sun's JMS (Java Messaging Service). JMS is a Java interface specification, which provides a standard way for Java applications to access enterprise messaging infra-

G.T. Heineman et al. (Eds.): CBSE 2005, LNCS 3489, pp. 1-16, 2005.

structure. MOM typically supports two forms of messaging: point-to-point (PTP) and publish/subscribe (Pub/Sub). In the PTP model, the message producer posts a message to a *queue*, and the message consumer retrieves the message from the queue. In the Pub/Sub model, a message producer publishes a message to a *topic*, and all consumers subscribing to the same topic retrieve a copy of the message. MOMs also define a set of reliability attributes for messaging, including non-persistent or persistent and non-transactional or transaction queues [18].

A component-based application using messaging protocols hence exploits an asynchronous, queue-based communication paradigm. It must also address additional architectural considerations such as the topology of component connections, message persistence and flow control. All of these factors can heavily influence the resulting application's performance [18].

However, the choice of application architecture must to be made early in the application life cycle, long before substantial coding takes place. Unwise decisions at design-time are often very difficult to alter, and could make it impossible to achieve the required performance level once the system has been delivered [5][6]. Consequently, the designer needs to be able to predict the performance of asynchronous components, working from an abstract design but without access to a complete implementation of the application.

Our previous work in [9] develops an approach to predicting the performance of only synchronous J2EE applications from design-level descriptions. The contribution of this paper is the extension of our approach to predict the performance of applications comprising both synchronous and asynchronous communications. This is achieved by modeling the component infrastructure that implements the messaging service. We then execute benchmarks to obtain values of model parameters associated with the performance characteristics of the underlying component infrastructure and the messaging service. We validate our approach through a case study, in which we compare predicted versus actual performance of an example application.

2   Related Work

Our previous work in [9] integrates analytical modeling and benchmark testing to predict the performance of J2EE applications using EJB components. A case study showed that without access the application source code, prediction can be accurate enough (prediction error is below 15%) to evaluate an architecture design. However, this work only addresses synchronous communication between components.

Performance modeling is a useful approach for performance analysis [16]. Traditional performance modeling techniques can be manually applied to applications based on Message-Oriented Middleware (MOM). [17] analyzes a multilayered queue network that models the communication between clients and servers via synchronous and asynchronous messages. [11] applies a layered QNM for business process integration middleware and compares the performance for both synchronous and asynchronous architectures. However, explicit values for performance parameters are required to solve these models, such as the CPU time used by each operation.

However, such performance parameters cannot be accurately estimated during an application design. A common practice therefore is to build a prototype and use this to obtain measures for the values of parameters in the model. For a complex application, this is expensive and time-consuming. Progress has been made to reduce the prototyping effort with tool support for automatic generation of test beds [1][3]. Although prototype testing can produce empirical evidence of the suitability of an architecture design, it is inherently inefficient in predicting performance as the application architecture inevitably evolves. Under change, the test bed has to be regenerated and redeployed, and the measurement has to be repeated for each change.

In related research towards software performance engineering, many approaches translate architecture designs mostly in United Modeling Language (UML) to analytical models, such as Queuing Network models [7], stochastic Petri nets [14] or stochastic process algebras [2]. In these approaches, the application workflow is presented in a sequence or state diagram, and a deployment diagram is used to describe the hardware and software resources, their topology and characteristics.

Importantly however, the component infrastructure and its performance properties are not explicitly modeled. These approaches therefore generally ignore or greatly simplify the details of the underlying component infrastructure performance. As a result, the models are rather inaccurate or non-representative. [8] developed a simulated model of CORBA middleware but the work is specific to threading structure of a CORBA server. Hence, little work has been done to develop an engineering approach to predict during design the runtime performance of messaging applications.

3   Major Performance Factors of J2EE Applications

J2EE includes several different component types, including EJB. EJB components act as servers and execute within a component container. A request to an EJB is passed through a method invocation chain implemented by the container and finally reaches the EJB method specified in the request. The invocation chain is used by the container to call security and transaction services that the EJB methods specify.

The container provides the hosting environment for EJBs and manages their lifecycle according to the context information of the request. The container also coordinates the interaction between EJBs and other J2EE services and facilities access to external data source connection pools. To improve performance and scalability, the container is multi-threaded and can service multiple simultaneous EJB requests. Multiple instances of threads, EJBs and database connections are pooled to provide efficient resource usage in the container. Incoming requests are queued and wait for a container thread if none are available from the fixed size thread pool.

Concurrent EJB requests experience contention at three points inside the container. These are during request dispatching to an EJB, during container processing and during access to external data sources. As a result, apart from the underlying hardware and software environment, the performance of a deployed J2EE application depends on a combination of the following factors:

- behavior of its application-specific EJB components and their interactions;
- particular implementation of the component infrastructure, or container;

- selected configuration settings for the container (e.g. thread pool size);
- attribute settings of both the application components (e.g. the persistence attribute of EJBs) and the infrastructure components (e.g. the transaction isolation level of the container);
- simultaneous request load experienced at a given time by the application [5].

Integrating a JMS messaging service with EJB components introduces further performance considerations. These include the topology of component connections, message persistence needs, and flow control. For instance, non-persistent messaging has better performance than persistent messaging [18]. However persistent messaging creates an application that is guaranteed not to lose messages, and hence is more reliable. For an architect, the ability to quantify this performance/reliability trade-off without building each solution is desirable, as is determination of the level of performance that the overall system provides under load.

4 The Performance Prediction Approach

A performance prediction approach for J2EE applications with messaging protocol needs to encompass the following three aspects. First, the performance model should explicitly represent the component container, the MOM service and their communication with application components. Second, the service time of a request depends on the container and MOM attributes. For example, in MOM-based applications, the setting of a messaging attribute is an architectural design decision and the effect on performance should be modeled as a function of the messaging attributes of interest. Third, an application-independent performance profile of the container and the MOM infrastructure is required. This is because the container and message server implementation and the operating system/hardware platform must be taken into account to be able to make accurate application performance predictions.

The relationship between the performance model and the component container performance profile for a selected architecture model are represented as a performance prediction framework in [9]. In this framework, a queueing network model (QNM) P models the component infrastructure by identifying the main components of the system, and noting where queuing delays occur.

An architect has several alternatives to fulfill the same functionality using EJB technology. For example, a server side EJB component can be made either stateless or stateful, simply by setting an attribute. Each architecture alternative impacts the service time of the component container. Therefore the component architecture model f^A is a function of the service time of the components participating in an architecture A. The output of f^A is the input to P.

Performance profiles are required to solve the parameter values of the performance model. They are obtained from benchmarking measurements. The benchmark application differs from an application prototype in that the business logic of the benchmark is much simpler than a prototype. The operations of the benchmark are designed simply to exercise performance sensitive elements of the underlying component container. The aim is to determine the performance profile of the container itself, and not to evaluate the overall application performance (the traditional aim of benchmarking).

By using a simple benchmark application, we can remove any unpredictability in performance due to application business logic.

The model is finally populated using the performance profile and used for performance prediction. This approach enables performance prediction during the design of software applications that are based on a specific component technology.

A comprehensive description of this approach can be found in [9][10]. It is designed to support the following use cases during performance engineering:

- Support efficient performance prediction under architecture changes where components are added or modified.
- Capacity planning of the system, such as predicting the average response time, throughput and resource utilization under the expected workload.
- Reveal performance bottlenecks by giving insight into possible flaws in architecture designs.

The requirements of this approach are:

- Ensuring a reasonable level of accuracy for performance prediction. According to [12] (page 116), prediction error within 30% is acceptable.
- Cost effective. The approach must be faster than prototyping and testing.

5 The Performance Model

A performance model should capture the component container behavior when processing a request from a client. For this reason, we focus on the behavior of the container in processing EJB method invocation requests. As EJB containers process multiple simultaneous requests, the threading model utilized must also be represented. The QNM in Fig. 1 models the main infrastructure components involved and their interactions.

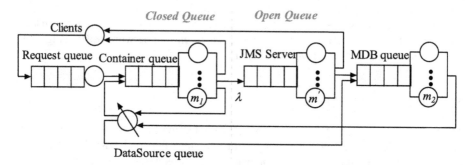

Fig. 1. The QNM model of a J2EE server with a JMS Queue

The model comprises two sub-networks, a closed and an open QNM. A closed QNM is appropriate for components using synchronous communication, as component containers employ a finite thread pool that effectively limits the maximum requests active in the server. An open QNM models asynchronous communication as a component container sends a message to a JMS queue, and the message is forwarded to a message driven bean (MDB) to process the business logic.

In the closed model, application clients represent the 'proxy clients[1]' (such as servlets in a web server) of the EJB container. Consequently, a client is considered as a delay resource and its service time equals the *thinking* time between two successive requests. A request to the EJB container is interpreted and dispatched to an active container thread by the request handler. The request handler is modeled as a single server queue with no-load dependency. It is annotated as *Request queue* in the QNM.

The container is multi-threaded, and therefore it is modeled as a multi-server queue with the thread capacity m_1 and no load dependency. It is annotated as *Container* in the QNM. The database clients are in fact the EJBs that handle the client request. Database access is therefore modeled as a delay server with load dependency. Its active database connections are denoted as k in the QNM, and the operation time at the database tier contributes to the service demand of the *DataSource* queue.

In the open model, asynchronous transactions are forwarded by the container to a queue managed by a JMS server. The JMS server is multi-threaded, and has a threshold for flow control to specify the maximum number of the messages pending in the JMS server. Assuming that the arrival rate of requests is a Poisson distribution with rate λ requests per second and the service time is exponential, we can model the JMS server as an $M/M/m'/W$ queue, where m' is the number of JMS server threads and W is its flow control threshold.

A message is subsequently removed from the queue by a MDB instance, which implements the business logic. MDBs are asynchronous message-handling façades for data access carried out in entity beans. MDB instances are also managed by the EJB container and are associated with a dedicated server thread pool. So the *MDB* queue is modeled as a load-independent multi-server queue.

The implementation of an EJB container and JMS server is complex and vendor specific. This makes it extremely difficult to develop a performance model that covers all the relevant implementation-dependent features, especially as the EJB container source code is not available. For this reason, our quantitative model only covers the major factors that impact the performance of applications, and ignores many other factors that are less performance sensitive. Specifically, we do not currently consider workloads that include large data transfers. As a result, the network traffic is ignored and the database contention level is reduced.

5.1   The Architecture Model

The task of solving the QNM in Fig. 1 involves obtaining the service demand of each queue. We need to calibrate the component container that will host the alternative designs in order to obtain the service demands of each request on each queue.

The service demand of the *Request* queue equals the service time of a request being accepted by the server and dispatched to the *Container* queue. It can thus be considered as a constant. The *Container*, *DataSource*, *JMS* and *MDB* queues are responsible for processing the business logic and this comprises the majority of the service demands on these queues.

---

[1] As opposed to clients driven by human interaction, proxy clients such as servlets continually handle requests that arrive at a web server.

Fig. 2 shows the state diagram for processing transactions in an EJB container. The container has a set of operations that a request must pass through, such as initializing a set of container management services, invoking the generated skeleton code for a bean instance, registering a transaction context with the transaction manager, finalizing a transaction and reclaiming resources.

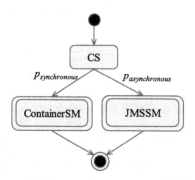

Fig. 2. Overall state diagram of the J2EE server

These container operations are identical for all requests, and the service time can again be considered constant, denoted as T_0. For convenience, these states as a whole are referred to as a composite, CS. Synchronous transactions are processed by the *Container* queue, modeled as a compound state machine *ContainerSM* with a probability $p_{synchronous}$, while asynchronous messages are posted to the JMS server, modeled as a compound state machine *JMSSM* with a probability $p_{asynchronous}$. *ContainerSM* and *JMSSM* are further decomposed into models of different component architectures. The service times of operations in *Container*, *DataSource*, *JMS* and *MDB* queue are modeled as f_c, f_d, f_j and f_m respectively.

From the above analysis, we know that f_c and f_d are determined by the component architecture in *ContainerSM* (e.g. optimizing data access to an entity bean by different cache management schemes). The comprehensive architecture models are developed in [9][10]. The models for container managed persistence of entity beans are listed below as an example:

$$f_c = hT_1 + (1-h)T_2 \tag{1}$$

$$f_d = T_{find} + T_{load} + pT_{store} \tag{2}$$

- h is the entity cache hit ratio;
- p is the ratio of operations updating entity data;
- T_1 is the service time for the container to access the entity data in its cache;
- T_2 is the service time of the container to load/store an entity bean instance from/to disk;
- T_{find} is the service time of identifying the entity instance by its primary key;
- T_{load} is the service time of loading data from the database into the entity bean cache;
- T_{store} is the service time of storing updates of an entity bean data.

For each business transaction, the necessary behavioral information can be extracted from design descriptions, such as use case diagram, and sequence diagrams [9][10]. This must capture the number and type of EJBs participating in the transaction, as well as the component architecture selected. Therefore for each transaction r the service demand at the *Container* and *DataSource* queue can be calculated as

$$D_{r,Container} = T_0 + \sum_{each \cdot bean} f_c \qquad (3)$$

$$D_{r,DataSource} = \sum_{each \cdot bean} f_d \qquad (4)$$

The execution demands of a message façade for entity beans in the *MDB* queue is exactly the same as the session façade for entity beans in the *Container* queue. Therefore the service demands of the *MDB* queue can be modeled in the same way, namely:

$$D_{r,MDB} = T_0 + \sum_{each \cdot bean} f_c \qquad (5)$$

In this paper we assume the JMS server is co-located in the same container with the EJB components to minimize communications overheads. The JMS queue used to communicate between components can be configured as persistent or non-persistent, depending on the reliability requirement of the application. In this paper, we consider the following messaging attributes:

- Non-persistent messages: Messages are not persisted in the JMS.
- Persistent messages with *cache-flush*: A message is first copied into memory and then flushed to the disk. The transaction cannot be committed until all of writes have been flushed to disk.
- Persistent messages with disabled *cache-flush*: *Disabled* means that transactions complete as soon as file store writes are cached in memory, instead of waiting for the writes to successfully reach the disk.

Fig. 3 shows the *JMSSM* decomposition for these messaging attributes. For non-persistent messages, the message is delivered directly. For persistent messages with the *cache-flush* setting, the message is copied to memory and then written to a file store. The XA transaction manager forces a two-phase commit if there is more than one transaction participant. When *cache-flush* is *disabled*, the transaction ends once the message is cached and the message is persisted to the file store in a background thread. The following parameters in Table 1 are necessary for calculating the *JMSSM* architecture model in equation (6)-(8) for three messaging attributes.

$$f_j^{non-persistent} = T_{Jsend} \qquad (6)$$

$$f_j^{cache-flush} = T_{Jcache} + T_{Jwrite} + T_{Jxa} + T_{Jsend} + T_{jJremove} \qquad (7)$$

$$f_j^{disabled} = T_{Jcache} + T_{Jxa} + T_{Jsend} \qquad (8)$$

Note that $f_j^{disabled}$ is calculated along the branch consuming the least service time in Fig. 3 (c). The service demand of a JMS server queue with a specific messaging attribute is:

$$D_{jms} = f_j \qquad (9)$$

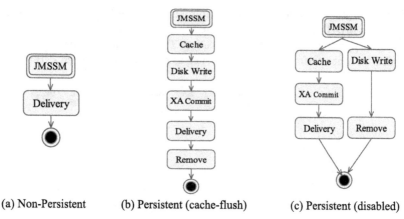

(a) Non-Persistent   (b) Persistent (cache-flush)   (c) Persistent (disabled)

Fig. 3. The JMS sub-state machine decomposition

Table 1. Parameters of JMSSM architecture models

T_{Jcache}	The service time of copying a message into memory
T_{Jxa}	The service time of an XA transaction commit
T_{Jwrite}	The service time of writing a message to disk
T_{Jsend}	The service time of sending a message to its destination
$T_{Jremove}$	The service time of removing the message from its persisted list

6 Benchmarking

Benchmarking is the process of running a specific program or workload on a machine or system and measuring the resulting performance [15]. In our approach, benchmarking is used to provide values for certain parameters in the performance models that are used for prediction.

6.1 Benchmark Design and Implementation

The key innovation of our modeling method is that we model the behavior solely of component infrastructure itself, and augment this with architecture and application-specific behavior extracted from the application design. This implies that the benchmark application should have the minimum application layer possible to exercise the component infrastructure in a meaningful and useful way. Component technologies leverage many standard services to support application development. The benchmark scenario is thus designed to exercise the key elements of a component infrastructure involved in the application execution.

We have designed and implemented a benchmark suite to profile the performance of EJB-based applications on a specified J2EE implementation. The implementation of the benchmark involves a session bean and an entity bean. The benchmark scenario is shown in   Fig. **4**. In order to explore the JMS server and MDB container's performance profiles, a new scenario is introduced in Fig. 5, which involves a JMS queue and a MDB object. Table 2. lists the J2EE services and design patterns used by each transaction in the benchmark application. The benchmark scenario can easily be extended for other performance profiles, such as creating/removing an EJB instance.

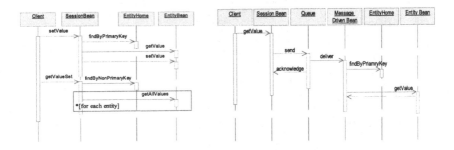

Fig. 4. The basic benchmark scenario   **Fig. 5.** The benchmark scenario with JMS and MDB

The benchmark suite also comprises a workload generator, monitoring utility and profiling toolkit. A monitoring utility is implemented using the Java Management Extensions (JMX) API. It collects performance metrics for the application server and the EJB container at runtime, for example the number of active server threads, active database connections and the hit ratio of the entity bean cache.

Table 2. J2EE service and design pattern usage matrix

Transaction	J2EE service	Design Pattern
setValue	EJB 2.0 (stateless session bean, entity bean with container man-	Session façade, service locator, read mostly
getValueSet	aged persistence), container managed transaction, JNDI, security	Session façade, service locator, read mostly, aggressive loading
getValue	Above services and JMS, MDB	Message façade, service locator, read mostly

A profiling toolkit *OptimizeIt* [13] is also employed. *OptimizeIt* obtains profiling data from the Java virtual machine, and helps in tracing the execution path and collecting statistics such as the percentage of time spent on a method invocation, from which we can estimate the percentage of time spent on a key subsystems of the J2EE server infrastructure. Profiling tools are necessary for black box COTS component systems, as instrumentation of the source code is not possible.

The benchmark clients simulate requests from proxy applications, such as servlets executing in a web server. Under heavy workloads, this kind of proxy client has an ignorable interval between two successive requests. Its population in a steady state is consequently bounded[2]. Hence the benchmark client spawns a fixed number of threads for each test. Each thread submits a new service request immediately after the results are returned from the previous request to the EJB. The 'thinking time' of the client is thus effectively zero. The benchmark also uses utility programs to collect the measurement of black-box metrics, such as response time and throughput.

Table 3. Hardware and software configuration

Machine	Hardware	Software
Client	Pentium 4 CPU 2.80 GHz, 512M RAM	Windows XP Prof. BEA WebLogic server 8.1,
Application and database server	Xeon Dual Processors, 2.66 GHz, HyperThreading enabled, 2G RAM	WindowsXP Prof. BEA WebLogic server 8.1, JDK1.4 with settings –hotspot, –Xms512m and –Xmx1024m. Oracle 9i

6.2 Measurement

The benchmark suite must be deployed on the same platform (both software and hardware) as the target application. In our case study, the benchmarking environment consists of two machines, one for clients, and the other for application and database server. They are connected by a 100MB Ethernet LAN. The hardware and software configuration is listed in Table 3. For the application and database server machine, *HyperThreading* is enabled, effectively making four CPUs available. Two CPUs are allocated for the application server process and the other two CPUs are allocated for the database server process.

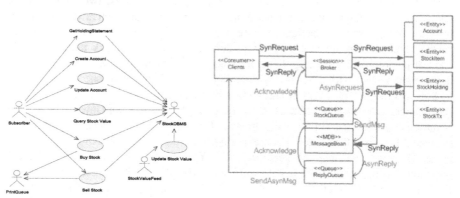

Fig. 6. Stock-Online use case

---

[2] A web server has configuration parameters to limit the active workload. For example, Apache uses *Max-Client* to control the maximum number of workers, thus the concurrent requests to the application server are bounded.

Each experiment has three phases, *rampUp, steadyState* and *rampDown*. The system is started and initialized in the *rampUp* stage for 1 minute. The system then transfers to *steadyState* for 10 minutes. Each experiment is run several times to achieve high levels of confidence that the performance difference between two runs under the same initialization conditions is not significant (below 3%). The values of parameters obtained from benchmarking are listed in Table 5. They populate the performance model we developed above with specific hardware/software configuration in Table 3.

Table 4. Default Stock-Online business models

Usage Pattern	Transaction	Transaction Mix
Read-only point (read one record)	Query stock	70%
Read-only multiple (read a collection of records)	Get stockholding	12%
Read-write (inserting records, and updating records; all requiring transactional support)	Create account	2%
	Update account	2%
	Buy stock	7%
	Sell stock	7%

7 Case Study: Performance Prediction of Stock-Online

Stock-Online [4] is a simulation of an on-line stock-broking system. It models typical e-commerce application functions and aims to exercise the core features of a component container. Stock-Online supports six business transactions, two of which are relatively heavyweight, write intensive transactions, and four others that are lightweight read or write transactions. Its use case diagram is shown in Fig. 6. The supporting database has four tables to store details for accounts, stock items, holdings and transaction history. The application transaction mix can be configured to model a lightweight system with read-mostly operations, or a heavyweight one with intensive update operations. The default transaction mix is listed in

Each experiment has three phases, rampUp, steadyState and rampDown. The system is started and initialized in the rampUp stage for 1 minute. The system then transfers to steadyState for 10 minutes. Each experiment is run several times to achieve high levels of confidence that the performance difference between two runs under the same initialization conditions is not significant (below 3%). The values of parameters obtained from benchmarking are listed in Table 5. They populate the performance model we developed above with specific hardware/software configuration in Table 3.

Table 4. Suppose that Stock-Online is to be implemented using EJB components. A common solution architecture is to use Container Managed Persistence (CMP) entity beans, using the standard EJB design pattern of a session bean as a façade to the entity beans. A single session bean implements all transaction methods. Four entity beans, one each for the database tables, manage the database access.

Buy and *Sell* transactions are the most demanding in terms of performance, each involving all four entity beans. For this reason, in our implementations *Buy* and *Sell*

transactions operate asynchronously[3], while the remaining short-lived transactions are always called synchronously. In this asynchronous architecture, the session façade EJB sends a request as a message to a JMS queue and returns immediately to the client. The queue receives the message and triggers the *onMessage* method inside a MDB instance. *onMessage* embodies the business logic and accesses the entity beans for data access. The Stock-Online architecture can be modeled using the QNM developed in Fig. 1, in which the stereotypes <<session>> and <<entity>> beans are included in the *Container* queue, <<MDB>> bean are included in the *MDB* queue and <<Queue>> is modeled as the *JMSServer* queue.

Table 5. Parameters from benchmarking

T_o	
	7.833
T_1	
	1.004
T_2	35.85
	6
T_{create}	0.497
T_{load}	0.215
T_{store}	0.497
T_{insert}	0.497
T_{Jxa}	10.97
	2
T_{Jsend}	0.929
$T_{Jwrite} + T_{Jremove}$	109.718
Cache hit ratio (h)	0.69

Table 6. Stock-Online service demands

Transaction, Queue	Service demand
All, Request	0.204
NewAccount, Container	34.726
NewAccount, DataSource	0.497
UpdateAccount, Container	35.777
UpdateAccount, DataSource	0.927
BuyStock, MDB	81.959
BuyStock, DataSource	2.780
SellStock, MDB	70.844
SellStock, DataSource	2.780
QueryStockValue, Container	19.641
QueryStockValue, DataSource	0.430
GetStockHolding, Container	76.708
GetStockHolding, DataSource	0.516
BuyStock and SellStock/JMS (non-persistent)	0.929
BuyStock and SellStock/JMS (cache-flush)	122.623
BuyStock and SellStock/JMS (disabled)	12.905

Assume Stock-Online is to be deployed on the platform described in Table 3. In order to predict its performance, we need to estimate the service demand of each transaction imposed on each queue in the QNM. As we have discussed, the necessary behavioral information of each transaction must be captured such as the number and type of EJBs participating in the transaction, as well as the component architecture selected. For example, the transaction to query stock value has read-only access to one entity bean *StockItem,* and we use the performance profile in **Table 5** to populate Equation (10), hence its service demand on the *Container* queue can be calculated as:

$$D_{QueryStockValue, Container} = T_0 + hT_1 + (1 - h)T_2 = 19.641 \qquad (10)$$

Table 6 lists the Stock-Online's service demand for each transaction in each queue using equation (3)-(9).

---

[3] This is exactly how online stock broking sites such as E-Trade operate.

7.1 Predicting Performance for Different Messaging Attributes

With the benchmark results, the performance model can be populated with perform-ance profiles, and solved to predict the performance of Stock-Online with the three different messaging quality of service attributes. The arrival rate of requests for the open QNM depends on the throughput of the application server sending asynchro-nous *Buy/Sell* requests, while the load imposed on the *DataSource* queue by the open QNM affects the response time of the closed QNM. The overall model is solved itera-tively between the two QNMs using the Mean Value Analysis (MVA) algorithm.

In order to validate the accuracy of these predictions, Stock-Online has been im-plemented and deployed. A workload generator injects six types of transactions into the Stock-Online application. The response time and throughput of both the EJB server and the JMS server are measured for a range of client loads.

Fig. 7 and 8 show the predictions for response time and throughput, respectively. Most prediction errors are less than 10% and the maximum error is within 15%. The predictions demonstrate that throughput achieved with the cache flush disabled option for persistent messages is approximately 96% of that achieved by non-persistent mes-sages. Hence these two architectures are comparable in term of performance. This is verified by measurement of the Stock-Online implementation, where the cache flush disabled option provides 95% throughput of non-persistent messaging.

Persistent messages with *cache-flush* are much slower, because of disk write op-erations. We predict that the performance of *cache-flush* message persistency de-grades approximately 28%. The actual measures show that performance degradation is approximately 32%. Hence the case study demonstrates that our approach is accu-rate enough to support messaging architecture evaluation in terms of performance.

Buy and *Sell* transactions have higher service demands than the others transactions. Dispatching them to the JMS server reduces the load in the EJB server. Therefore the average application response time is smaller than the JMS server with MDB. This can also be observed from our predictions.

8 Conclusions

In this paper, we present an approach for predicting, during the design phase, the performance of component-based applications with both synchronous and asynchro-nous communications. It combines analytical models of the component behavior and benchmark measurements of a specific platform. The case study is a J2EE application using the JMS API. Our approach is applied to predict the performance of three dif-ferent MOM QoS attributes and two entity bean cache architectures. Without access to the application source code, the error of prediction is below 15%.

Currently, predictions are carried out manually. However it is possible to automate much of the process by leveraging research in the software engineering community. For example, the benchmark application can be generated and run automatically using the tool developed by Cai at el. [1]. An on-going research project is to automatically generate the performance model and the benchmark suite from a design. Also more evidence is required that the approach is broadly applicable and scalable. To this end we are working to (1). Apply this approach to other middleware platforms, such

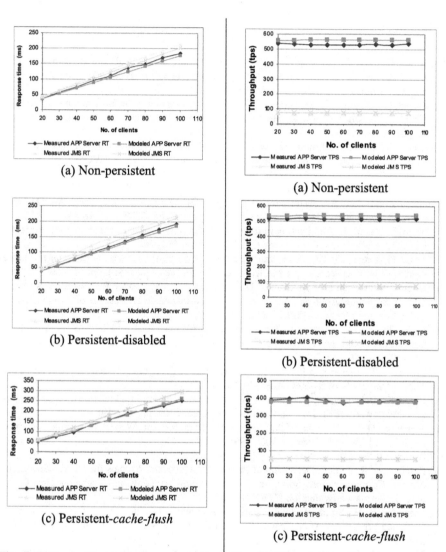

(a) Non-persistent

(a) Non-persistent

(b) Persistent-disabled

(b) Persistent-disabled

(c) Persistent-*cache-flush*

(c) Persistent-*cache-flush*

Fig. 7. Response Time with three messaging attributes (measured vs. predicted)

Fig. 8. Throughput with three messaging attributes (measured vs. predicted)

as NET and CORBA; (2) Test the approach on more complex applications; and (3) Design software engineering tools that hide the complexity of the modeling and analysis steps in our performance prediction approach from an architect.

References

[1] Cai, Y.; Grundy, J.; Hosking, J.: Experiences Integrating and Scaling a Performance Test Bed Generator with an Open Source CASE Tool, Proc. IEEE Int. Conf. on Automated Software Engineering (ASE), September, 2004.

[2] Canevet, C.; Gilmore, S.; Hillston, J.; Prowse, M.; Stevens, P.: Performance modeling with UML and stochastic process algebras. *IEE Proc. Computers and Digital Techniques*, 150(2):107-120, 2003.

[3] Denaro, G.; Polin, A.; Emmerich, W.: Early Performance Testing of Distributed Software Applications. Proc. Int. Workshop on Software and performance (WOSP), pp. 94–103, January 2004.

[4] Gorton, I.: Enterprise Transaction Processing Systems, Addison-Wesley, 2000.

[5] Gorton, I. and Liu, A.; Performance Evaluation Of Alternative Component Architectures For EJB Applications, IEEE Internet Computing, vol.7, no. 3,2003, pp.18-23.

[6] Gorton, I.; Haack, J.: Architecting in the face of uncertainty: an experience report, Proc. 26th Int. Conf. on Software Engineering (ICSE), pp. 543- 551, 2004.

[7] Gu, G. P.; Petriu, D. C: XSLT transformation from UML models to LQN performance models, Proc. Int. Workshop on Software and performance (WOSP), pp. 227-234, 2002.

[8] Harkema, M.; Gijsen B.M.M.; Mei, R.D.; Hoekstra, Y.: Middleware Performance: A Quantitative Modeling Approach, Proc. Int. Sym. Performance Evaluation of Computer and Communication Systems (SPECTS), 2004.

[9] Liu, Y.; Fekete, A.; Gorton, I.: Predicting the performance of middleware-based applications at the design level, Proc. Int. Workshop on Performance and Software Engineering (WOSP), pp 166-170, 2004.

[10] Liu, Y.: A Framework to Predict the Performance of Component-based Applications, PhD Thesis, University of Sydney, Australia, 2004.

[11] Liu, T.K.; Behroozi, A.; Kumaran, S. A performance model for a business process integration middleware, IEEE Int'l Conf. on E-Commerce, 2003, pp. 191-198.

[12] Menascé, D.A.; Almeida, V.A.F.; Capacity Planning for Web Performance, Metrics, Models, and Methods. Prentice-Hall, 1998.

[13] OptimizeIt Suite, http://www.borland.com/optimizeit/

[14] P. King and R. Pooley: Derivation of Petri Net Performance Models from UML Specifications of Communications Software, Proc. Int. Conf. on Tools and Techniques for Computer Performance Evaluation (TOOLS), 2000.

[15] Saavedra, R. H., Smith, A. J.: Analysis of benchmark characteristics and benchmark performance prediction, ACM Transactions on Computer System, vol. 14, no. 4, pp. 344-384,1996.

[16] Simeoni, M.; Inverardi, P.; Di Marco, A.; Balsamo, S. Model-Based Performance Prediction in Software Development: A Survey. IEEE Transactions on Software Engineering, vol. 30, no. 5, pp 295-310, 2004.

[17] Sridhar R., Perros, H. G.: A multilayer client-server queueing network model with synchronous and asynchronous messages, IEEE Trans. on Software Engineering, vol. 26, no. 11, pp. 1086-1100, 2000.

[18] Tran, P.; Gosper, J.; Gorton, I.: Evaluating the Sustained Performance of COTS-based Messaging Systems, in Software Testing, Verification and Reliability, vol 13, pp 229-240, 2003.

EJBMemProf – A Memory Profiling Framework for Enterprise JavaBeans

Marcus Meyerhöfer and Bernhard Volz

Friedrich-Alexander University of Erlangen and Nuremberg
{Marcus.Meyerhoefer,sibevolz}@immd6.informatik.uni-erlangen.de

Abstract. Deriving resource properties of components such as memory consumption is a requirement for the specification of non-functional properties of software components, enabling developers to make a selection among components not solely based on their function. In this paper we present a profiler for Enterprise Java Beans components that has been specifically adapted to the characteristics of such components. It facilitates focussing on the component concept whithout getting caught up in the details of the objects that actually constitute a component and offers several views concerning what to attribute to the memory consumption of a component. Our implementation is based on JVMPI and uses filtering inside the agent to generate the component profiles.

1 Introduction

The application of component-based software engineering (CBSE) to industrial software development has risen with the propagation of mature component models in the last years, especially on the server side. CBSE offers many advantages, among them reuse of pre-existing, well-tested solutions or increased productivity through developing a new software application by combining existing components. Therefore, nowadays, one major task in developing software is to select appropriate components often written by different vendors. Such a selection process is obviously first of all based on the functional specification a component has to fulfill, but finally non-functional properties (NFPs) [1] are even more important, because if an application exhibits unacceptable performance, consumes too much resources or does not scale well, it might be of no use. Because of that, NFPs should be considered in the development process from the beginning and a developer should be able to choose among components based on non-functional constraints (e.g. run-time or resource consumption). Moreover, to have precise information about the non-functional properties of the selected components is a necessary prerequisite to estimate the non-functional behaviour of the application before it is actually built. In this paper we introduce the architecture and concepts of a memory profiling environment for components following the Enterprise Java Beans (EJB) specification [2].

In the COMQUAD project[1] we have implemented a memory profiling solution for EJB components enabling us to measure the memory consumption of EJBs, with the

---

[1] "COMponents with QUantitative properties and ADaptivity" is a project funded by the German Research Council (DFG FOR 428). It started October 1, 2001, at Dresden University of Technology and Friedrich-Alexander University of Erlangen and Nuremberg.

G.T. Heineman et al. (Eds.): CBSE 2005, LNCS 3489, pp. 17–32, 2005.

long-term objective to generate a specification that includes such resource properties [3]. The profiler was designed to measure EJBs in an isolated environment, as we are interested in precise data and this requires the use of an event-based technique, which has a significant overhead not tolerable in production environments. In this paper we argue that most current profilers lack specific support for EJB profiling and we present our solution offering four different views on memory consumption of an EJB. Furthermore, we show different techniques for memory profiling and explain why we chose a Java Virtual Machine Profiler Interface (JVMPI) [4] based approach. Applying several filters inside the profiler agent adapted to the characteristics of EJBs, we are able to focus the profiling process on these software components. After giving some impressions of the performance of our current prototype, we conclude with a discussion of the specialities as well as drawbacks of our proposed solution.

2   Related Work

There exist several approaches to determine the amount of resources a Java application comsumes; however, the most common one is the usage of a profiler to gather detailed information about memory and CPU consumption[2]. Especially for Java a lot of solutions exist, both commercial and open source ones. Most of them have similar properties: they are based on JVMPI or, additionally, on some kind of proprietary bytecode instrumentation and mainly differ in their frontends. Most of them count the number of objects allocated, as well as classes loaded, and some are able to apply basic text based filters in their frontends. Unfortunately, they are usually bound to their frontend application and no API is supplied that would enable to integrate the profiling agent into our own solution. At the beginning profiling solutions were only available for regular Java applications and they did not offer specific support for multi-tiered enterprise applications. Basically, a component-oriented application developed using Enterprise Java Beans can be profiled with such a tool as well, but the user will be distracted from the EJBs he is interested in. This is because the profiling will not only show the EJB invocations, but the whole runtime infrastructure, including the application server, as well.

The *Optimizelt Profiler Enterprise Edition 6* from Borland [5] is thought to be a performance monitor for J2EE applications. But memory is not specified on basis of components but on the basis of objects that have been allocated. Through the frontend, the user can filter the incoming data retrieved by the profiling agent by applying a simple text filter, which does not allow the identification of objects created dynamically by an application server during the deployment phase.

The *JProbe* analyser suite [6] is able to set up filters based on an EJB jar file, that is the classes and interfaces contained in that archive. These filters are later used to retrieve the objects related to an EJB instance, but JProbe does not differentiate between two EJBs: memory allocation data and the memory consumption is displayed in the same window. In order to separate different EJBs from each other, the profiling process

---

[2] Some profilers have additional capabilites, e.g. they allow for the analysis of lock contention. As we are only interested in memory consumption we will focus only on that aspect.

must be done repeatedly, with the filter being parameterized not to choose all classes/interfaces from an EJB archive but only those related to the EJB of concern. The filtering also includes instances of classes dynamically created at runtime but an exact identification of them is missing: e.g the dynamic proxies generated during EJB deployment inside the JBoss[3] server are simply named as $ProxyNN where NN is a positive integer number.

JProfiler 3 from ej-technologies [7] also supports filters being able to cope with dynamically generated classes but the filter process itself is based on a name comparison of a type name and filter string, which causes all proxy classes—such as those of the JBoss application server—to be accounted for the memory consumption and not only those of the profiled EJB. Additionally the profiler does not separate different EJBs—all data validated through the filter definitions is displayed instead.

Most of the open source solutions do not offer as sophisticated interfaces as commercial ones do: *HProf* [8] is a sample implementation of a profiler provided by Sun Microsystems and lacks special support for J2EE. The latest version already employs the JVMT interface for collecting data by bytecode instrumentation. For earlier versions of the JDK a version using the JVMP interface is still available. Memory allocation data of this profiler contains the instance count for classes and the memory amount consumed by these instances. The Heap Analyzer Tool (HAT) facilitates the creation of HTML pages from the binary files written by HProf. The JBoss-Profiler [9] is a profiler agent based on the JVMPI and AOP developed by JBoss, but it seems to be in a very early stage and apparently does not recognize Enterprise Java Beans. It generates compressed logfiles, which after the profiling run can be parsed by a separate web application.

In addition to the profiler agent implementations introduced above there are several academic frameworks, based on JVMPI as well as on bytecode instrumentation. Dmitriev [10] describes the application of dynamic bytecode instrumentation support of the experimental profiling system JFLUID to the selective profiling of Java applications. Based on the capability of a special virtual machine, enabling code hotswapping of running methods, the tool uses automatic call graph revelation to instrument dynamically only the methods of interest. Obviously, this technique aims at selective CPU profiling of only code parts of interest, instead of profiling the whole application, but could be applied to selective memory profiling as well. The evaluation shows that although partial profiling provides a considerable reduction of overhead, the absolute overhead can easily reach more than 100 per cent. For larger applications like J2EE Dmitriev argues that the overhead becomes acceptable, as benchmarks show substantially lower overheads ranging from 2 to 12 per cent. The dynamic bytecode instrumentation approach is already available for production use in the NetBeans environment as a profiler plugin [11], but its frontend only displays the overall memory consumption of the VM at present.

Reiss and Renieris [12] describe a three-layer architecture to generate Java trace data based on JVMPI. The profiler agent *TMon* creates output streams for each thread. The frontend *TMerge* merges several streams providing consistency and uniqueness and generates a comprehensive trace file. Analysis and visualization is provided by *TFilter*,

---

[3] http://www.jboss.orghttp://jboss.org

depending on the data from TMerge. Because there is no filtering inside the first layer, the TMon agent, they have generated more than 1.6 GB data for a 25 seconds run of an unnamed server application [12, ch. 4]. The aim of this approach is not to filter, but to collect as much data as possible for later program visualization. Therefore, a later publication [13] discusses several interesting methods to compress the data by different encoding techniques, like run-length encoding, grammar-based encoding and finite state automata encoding which might be useful for our profiler as well.

The *Java Performance Monitoring Toolkit* (JPMT) [14] supports event filtering at run-time. It offers event-driven measurement as well as time-driven measurement. The authors do not consider a component concept in general or EJBs in particular, but nevertheless, they describe the modification of bytecode in order to insert callbacks to the profiler agent into classes of interest during the class loading event handling. An adaption of that approach could allow efficient filtering for EJB method entries, in order to activate and deactivate memory profiling selectively at EJB method entry and exit to reduce the overhead of filtering necessary with JVMPI solutions.

Form denotes a framework [15] for building tools for dynamic analysis and profiling of Java code in general and can be adapted to the EJB component model. It is based on a three-tier architecture, consisting of profiler agents to collect all available data through JVMPI events and send these to the additional middle-tier, the controllers. Controllers collect the data from one or more agents and provide support for filtering, applying two filter stages: the first is used to create a mapping from an incoming event to interested views, the second stage decides which event is sent and which not, based on include- and exclude filters. The regular frontend tier of usual profiling systems is called views, which re-use the controllers and agents through an interface. Multiple views can be attached to one controller and each view can analyze a different scenario, e.g. one is interested in time spent in certain methods while the second analyzes the memory consumption. Obviously, in that architecture the agents must deliver everything they can catch which leads to a huge amount of collected data, but on the other hand, the agents are much simpler and just have to collect and transfer data.

3   Background and Environment

Before we introduce the concepts of our solution, we will explain some necessary background knowledge. We will give a deeper coverage of the JVMPI compared to the new JVMTI, because when we started our work JVMTI was still in an early stage[4] and the old standard is still suitable for memory profiling (see discussion in Sect. 4).

JVMPI Versus JVMTI With the publication of version 1.2 of the Java software development kit in 1998 the JVMP interface (JVMPI) [4] especially designed for profiling purposes was added to the standard and has since been widely used for the creation of profilers[5]. JVMPI incorporates an event-driven mechanism for the development of profiling software into the Java Virtual Machine (VM): there are more than 30 events

---

[4] Beta1 was not yet available.

[5] However, the status of that interface never changed from its initial "experimental" status.

defined, such as loading of a class into the VM, object allocation or object destruction. A registered profiler will be notified whenever an event of interest occurs. Although this interface is mainly based on events, the programmer is given the additional ability to perform instrumentation of the Java bytecode inside the profiler by reacting to an event that notifies the profiler about the loading of the bytecode for one class.

With the new version 5.0 (codename "Tiger") of the Java SDK, which has been released in autumn 2004, a new interface for profiling tools was introduced: the Java Virtual Machine Tool Interface (JVMTI) [16]. It combines the JVMPI and the Java Virtual Machine Debugger Interface[6] (JVMDI). The most important change of the new specification is that the event-driven mechanism of JVMPI are being superceded by a new profiling paradigm: the new architecture now relies on bytecode engineering. JVMPI and JVMDI will still be available in v5.0 but are marked as "deprecated" and will be removed sometime in the future.

Profiling Agents Profilers for the Java platform are generally split into two parts: the core part (called *profiler agent* or just *agent*) is implemented as a platform-specific library that is loaded by the VM into the address space of the profilee where it is able to collect data of interest; the second part is optional and usually responsible for the subsequent processing of the collected data. It might be very simple and just displays the data. Commercial solutions usually offer very sophisticated graphical user interfaces but also use the same split architecture. It is obvious that the profilers differ in their usability and the presentation of the gathered information; however, as the functionality of the agent is based on the standard JVMP interface the profiling possibilities themselves are quite similar.

Architecture of a JVMPI-Based Profiler The basic architecture of a profiler based on the JVMP interface can be found in [4]. In the subsequent section we will only highlight the core parts. A profiler agent written for the JVMP interface mainly consists of three parts: the first part is used to do necessary initialization (including activation of the events of interest), the second one for processing the incoming events and the last one for deinitializing the profiler agent when the VM process exits. The entry point JVM_OnLoad() is used for initializing the profiler agent. It is called sometime during the startup process when the VM has not been fully initialized yet. Its purpose is only to initialize the profiler agent; basically, it has to register a callback handler for incoming events and then enable the events of interest for the startup process. Registration of the central callback function (CF) for incoming events is easily done by setting a pointer to the callback function which has to suffice a given signature. The CF is usually a large switch construct using the supplied event type contained in the parameter of the callback function. According to the event type that parameter contains different information. It is important to understand that this event handler might be called by different threads and thus synchronization is necessary if the event handler itself accesses common data structures. When starting up, all events offered by the VM are disabled by default. In

---

[6] Another part of the former standards mainly adressing the support for debugging of Java software.

order to receive event notifications, the events of interests have to be enabled first. This is done for each event separately using the method EnableEvent(). The JVMP interface does not allow enabling/disabling of events globally as some events significantly reduce the speed of the profilee. One event especially interesting for startup and intialization of the profiler agent is the JVMPI_EVENT_JVM_INIT_DONE event as it signals the end of the initialization process of the VM to the profiler agent. After the signaling of that event it is safe to call certain JVMPI functions like CreateSystemThread() to create a new thread. Furthermore, now the events of interest to the profiler should be enabled, e.g. JVMPI_EVENT_CLASS_LOAD to retrieve information about classes and their load time or JVMPI_EVENT_OBJECT_ALLOC to be notified of object allocations.

4   Proposed Solutions

Before introducing our solution to EJB memory profiling we explain different possible techniques together with their advantages and disadvantages. This discussion also clarifies why we have chosen the event-driven approach.

Bytecode Instrumentation Bytecode instrumentation is a technique that applies manipulations to the Java bytecode in order to reach a specific goal. There are several libraries available (e.g. BCEL or JavaAssist) that support developers in modifying bytecode. There are many possible ways where such modifications can take place: they can be done statically prior to execution of an application or component or dynamically at runtime by using a custom classloader or using the profiling agent to apply them during class loading events. If this approach is to be used for memory profiling, the bytecode of a class would have to be manipulated such that it reports for instance the creation of objects to a specially designated listener or that it just counts class instances.

Obviously, among the advantages of bytecode instrumentation is the fact that it is a very generic approach that makes it possible to tune the profiling for different settings; for example, it is easy to only generate code for those pieces of the program that are of interest. This will usually result in faster profiling code as compared to solutions that have to profile all code or no code at all. Additionally, the profiler itself only has to display the values set by the injected bytecode and need not apply complex processing of the gathered data. On the other hand this is also the biggest disadvantage: all pieces that should be taken into account have to be instrumented. This means that the profiler might also have to take the classes of the JDK or third party libraries into account and all those classes have to be instrumented as well. Besides the rising complexity of instrumentation, now filtering, too, has to be done according to the classes instrumented.

As an example for this consider a class Foo with one method public void foo() which allocates several objects of type String. If the JDK class java.lang.String is instrumented, all allocations of String objects happening outside of the class of interest Foo will be taken into account, too. These "miss-generated events" then have to be filtered out—either by the injected bytecode or the profiler. Furthermore the class String might make use of other data types, which also should be taken into account if they have been created by a String object created by the method foo(). It is obvious, that if a profiler is interested in all memory transitively allocated by an object, filtering will be a major task beside instrumentation.

Event-Driven Approaches Another approach for profiling Java applications and EJBs is the solution offered by JVMPI, which is based on events: the virtual machine generates various events, e.g. at load time of a class, for object allocations or when an object is freed by the garbage collector. The advantage is obvious: code does not need to be changed and thus no unwanted sideeffects can make their way into a profilee. Every class and every object, allocated with the operator new, can be found by object allocation events. Local variables of primitive types are more complicated and are not part of the data provided with every single event.

The amount of data which can be collected by this approach is massive: if every single object allocation is taken into account this can exceed the megabyte limit within minutes, which is exaggeraged if a complex application like an application server is being profiled. Therefore, filtering all incoming events and removing the uninteresting ones is a major task in this approach. Another pitfall of event-driven approaches is the speed of the profilee: event generation inside the virtual machine does not depend on the actual profiling interests—they just happen for every single object allocation and thus filtering for the interesting events can become very expensive. In fact this is the major problem of event-driven profilers: having algorithms to sort out the unwanted events as soon and as fast as possible.

Static Analysis A completely different way is to analyze the bytecode or even the source code of EJBs in order to derive the necessary information. This approach is rather fast as it does not concern EJBs actually running in an application server. Even information about dynamically allocated resources could—theoretically—be extracted by taking into account which parameters might be passed on to a method exposed by an EJB. But this requires a lot of knowledge about the semantics of each method which might be rather hard to extract. The main advantage is that this method only gives information about the resources the EJB methods allocate and use: the part of the application server does not need to be filtered out separately—it is not included in the static analysis. On the other hand this might also be a disadvantage when choosing among different application servers, as they will usually differ in the amount of resources for hosting an EJB.

Statistical Methods Similar to the static analysis is a statistical approach. The profiler scans the objects of the Java heap and separates the objects of the application server from the ones belonging to a component. Doing this in regular intervals yields information about the living objects. This sampling-based approach is a well-known technique for CPU load profiling of a program (not by sampling the objects allocated, but the threads active), but it is a rather coarse way to find the allocated amount of memory: during the time the profiler is not sampling objects, the EJB might have allocated and freed resources. Generally, sampling techniques can not give the precision of event-based solutions as they sample the current state at discrete points in time; however, if the sampling interval is chosen correctly the overhead is lower as compared to event-based methods and that is why many commercial profilers offer sampling-based and event-based profiling side by side.

4.1 Profiling Enterprise Java Beans Components

As explained above there are various profiling techniques usable for Java profilers. In order to choose the most suitable method, it has to be clear what data to acquire: in the context of Java, memory profiling basically means gathering information about the life cycle of objects, e.g. when and where they have been created or when destroyed. Adressing EJBs, this topic gets more complicated: an EJB consists of several classes, which are themselves hosted inside an application server. Again, these classes might create further objects. Should they also be part of the memory allocation picture the profiler has to create?

Obviously, there is no general answer to those questions, as on some occasions for example the whole transitive memory consumption of an EJB is of interest while on others only the consumption of the EJB instance itself should be determined. Furthermore, it might even be interesting to have the infrastructure used by the application server accounted for the memory consumption—this then would allow us to compare certain application servers. In order to integrate all those viewpoints, we decided to have four different kind of views on the memory allocation data:

1. The *Restricted View* contains all objects that are instances of the classes contained in the archive of the profiled Enterprise Java Bean. This allows measuring only the objects of the EJB itself without any other infrastructure the EJB needs for providing its service.
2. The *EJB Center View* contains the Restricted View and additionally all objects created by the business and internal helper methods. This provides for a detailed view on how much memory an EJB consumes, where this memory is allocated and how much memory the EJB needs for providing its service.
3. The *Complete View* contains the EJB Center View and additionally all objects created by the application server that are used for hosting the profiled EJB.
4. The *Application Server Restricted View* contains only those objects created by the application server in order to host the profiled EJB. This view allows the comparison of application servers by different vendors as not the EJB itself is of interest but the internals of the application server.

Therefore, a memory profiler for EJBs should be able to generate output for each view. Considering the different possible approaches discussed at the beginning of Sect. 4 and taking into account that Java is an environment supported by a garbage collector and the profiler is interested in an exact memory consumption, the statistical and the static bytecode analysis approaches are not useful. Instead, an event-driven approach is chosen. The generation of the necessary events can either be achieved by bytecode instrumentation or by using VM-driven event reports.

In order to support all four views mentioned above, it is necessary to collect all objects the EJBs allocate during their lifecycle. Thus, it is better to rely on the event reporting mechanism of the Java Virtual Machine as otherwise the bytecode instrumentation approach would converge against the event reports in terms of performance, as filtering is needed as well. But, for compliance with future versions of the Java programming environment, the architecture of the agent should be designed such that the bytecode instrumentation approach can be implemented easily.

4.2   Searching the Needle in the Haystack: Filtering

In order to implement the different views described above a profiler agent has to subscribe to allocation events, which then will notify it of all objects created during the run of a profiled component-based application inside an application server. The main task of the profiler is filtering the incoming events. Doing so, it is necessary to know which objects have to be accounted for the memory consumption of a given EJB. Objects identified to be part of the EJBs memory consumption will be called "valid", the others "invalid", respectively.

The objects directly belonging to the EJBs can be detected by comparing the class of an allocated object with the classes of the EJB archive. All objects that are instances of a type contained in the EJB archive can be added to the memory consumption. The filter doing the class comparison will be called *class filter*[7].

Objects created by methods of the EJB can be found searching the call stack of an object allocation. If the call stack contains a method which is part of a type of the EJB classes, it again can be added to the memory consumption. This filter will be called *call stack filter*. Listing 1.1 shows which data can be retrieved by the class and call stack

```
   public class Foo {
2      public void foo () {
           byte aData [] = new byte [20]; // call stack filter
4      }
   }
6
   public class FooBar {
8      public static void main ( String sArgs []) {
           Foo oFoo = new Foo () ; // class filter
10         oFoo . foo () ;
       }
12  }
```

Listing 1.1. An example for the data the class and call stack filter can retrieve.

filters: it contains two classes Foo and FooBar. Foo should be considered a class of the EJB (all infrastructure belonging to the EJB has been left out for better readability) which provides one method foo (). This method allocates an array of byte values (line 3).

The class filter is parameterized such that it accepts objects of type Foo, the call stack filter such that it accepts objects created by methods of the class Foo. This adds the following objects to the memory consumption:

---

[7] The classes and interfaces an EJB consists of are given by the EJBs specific deployment descriptor which is contained in the archive.

- Line 9: the object oFoo is of type Foo and thus is validated by the class filter.
- Line 3: when the method foo() is called, it creates a byte array. This array aData is then validated by the call stack filter.

The class and call stack filters only accumulate the memory of objects directly related to the profiled EJB. The infrastructure[8] of the hosting application server is missed. In order to include it as well, a third filter called *inheritance filter* is introduced: an object is accounted for the memory consumption of the application servers part of the EJB if the object's class is, directly or indirectly, derived from a class of the EJB or implements an interface of the EJB—like the local-home interface. The class and inheritance filter can be applied during the load time of a class. The latter filter also covers classes that are dynamically created during runtime. This, however, makes it more difficult to retrieve information about a type, like which interfaces are implemented and of which super classes the class derives. Therefore, our solution applies a native library to parse the bytecode while the class loading event.

By implementing these three filters, all views on the allocation data mentioned in Sect. 4.1 can be retrieved as follows:

- The *Restricted View*: only the class filter is switched on.
- The *EJB Center View*: the class and call stack filters are parameterized.
- The *Complete View*: all three filters are active.
- The *Application Server Restricted View*: only the inheritance filter is used.

4.3   The Architecture of EJBMemProf

Our profiler *EJBMemProf* follows the canonical architecture of profilers for the Java environment and consists of two parts: the profiling agent as a platform specific library, which is responsible for collecting the profiling data and a frontend responsible for visualisation. The agent and its frontend are connected via a TCP/IP connection for bidirectional communication using a simple XML-based message format. The data collected by the agent is sent to the frontend as soon as possible. The order of events issued by the virtual machine is preserved by that communication and additionally, all data carry timestamps and sequence numbers to identify the times at which the events have been issued by the VM and their order.

Currently, the JVMPI-based agent runs under the Linux operating system with the Sun Java software development kit (JDK) version 1.4.2. As it is written completely in C++ and uses just open source libraries we expect the agent to be easily portable to other platforms. The frontend is written in Java and should run on any platform having a JRE version 1.5 available and the SWT GUI library (v3) installed.

Figure 1 gives an overview of the processing of incoming events and the internal structure of the profiling agent[9]. The core elements of the profiler are the central

---

[8] Such infrastructure could comprise dynamically generated proxy objects for an EJB.

[9] Please note that this figure shows only the main events necessary for memory profiling. There are some other events like initialisation of the VM or garbage collection runs the profiler has to register for as well; those events are left out for ease of presentation.

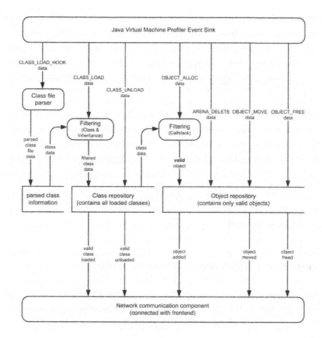

Fig. 1. The data flow inside the profiler agent.

dispatcher responsible for thread synchronization and passing the event to the corresponding handler methods, a class file parser and the several filter implementations which store information about classes and objects into repositories. Moreover, there are modules for writing log information and sending the relevant data to the frontend or receiving commands from it.

The events shown in Fig. 1 address the complete lifecycle of an object, that is allocation, its lifetime while being used and finally its destruction. Before an object is instantiated the very first time, the bytecode of its class has to be loaded. The process is interrupted by a CLASS_LOAD_HOOK event of the profiler which internally activates the class file parser to retrieve the implemented interfaces of the class loaded. At the time the VM loads a class a CLASS_LOAD event is issued. This triggers the generation of descriptive information inside the agent, which will be combined with the information gathered by the class file parser described above. Afterwards, the class and inheritance filters are applied, checking whether the loaded class is contained in the list of valid classes (class filter) to be profiled or whether the class derives from a given set of valid superclasses or implements at least one interface of a given set of valid interfaces (inheritance filter). Finally, the class information is stored and if the class is considered valid, an event report is sent to the frontend. After loading a class, it can be instantiated. The profiler then receives an OBJECT_ALLOC notification and has to check whether its class has been marked valid before. If not, the call stack filter has to search the call stack whether the object has been created in the context of a valid method. If valid, the information is stored and an event sent to the frontend.

It is a common misconception that there are no events addressing an object during its lifetime. Unfortunately, the virtual machine might move an object around in memory, caused by a garbage collector run. This changes the object id by which an object is identified. Therefore, the agent has to take care of OBJECT_MOVE events because the old id might be reassigned to either newly created objects or different objects moved by the virtual machine.

Finally, if an object gets destroyed an OBJECT_FREE event is raised. If the object has been tagged valid by the profiler, it has to update its data structures and notify the frontend. However, there is still another possiblity of freeing objects. The garbage collector can free a whole arena of memory, thus implicitly freeing all objects stored inside. Therefore, if an ARENA_DELETE event occurs the agent has to check its object repository for objects that were stored in the given arena. To be complete, classes can be unloaded by the virtual machine. The corresponding event CLASS_UNLOAD has to be handled by the agent as well.

4.4   Performance of the Enterprise Java Beans Profiler

Execution of additional profiling code always results in a loss of performance independent of the technique used to retrieve the data of interest. As already described in Sect. 2 this problem is common to all current profilers even if they apply sophisticated optimizations like JFluid [10]. We have conducted different measurements[10] to investigate the performance of our solution and to identify areas for further improvement. The test application was an MPEG4-compliant video codec consisting of about ten entity beans with different components closely interacting and using many objects as intermediate return value wrappers. This application, therefore, can be regarded as a real-life example exhibiting a worst-case like behaviour of the profiler. For the purpose of the measurements, we encoded a very short video sequence consisting of three pictures.

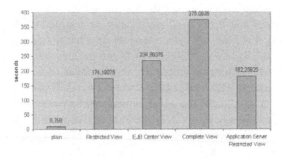

Fig. 2. Comparison of average processing times of XviD EJB.

---

[10] We used a PC with 512MB RAM, 800MB swap space and an AMD Athlon 1600 processor (1.4GHz). The machine was fitted with Gentoo Linux 2004.3 using the Linux Kernel 2.6.9. As application server JBoss 3.2.3 (default configuration as distributed with JBoss) was installed along with the Sun JDK v1.4.2.06. The frontend and profiler agent were running on the same machine.

We did not expect our solution to be low overhead, because JVMPI does only allow enabling object allocation events globally and therefore all incoming events have to be filtered, even if only a small amount actually matter. Additionally, both the special kind of filtering employed by the analysis of the call stack of each invocation and the need of synchronisation and context switching in a JVMPI-based profiler agent introduce a large amount of overhead.

Our expectations were met by the measurements: the startup time of the used application server JBoss is nearly doubled if the agent is attached (we measured the startup time ten times and took the average value; in the simple case the time is 52 seconds while it is 92 seconds with profiling). This is mainly caused by the interception of every class loaded and filtering it as described. The runtime overhead is even higher when profiling our demo application. A run of three images took about nine seconds without profiling and about 20 to 27 times that, depending on the kind of profiling view selected (see Fig. 2). However, if a component was invoked more often by a client, we were able to measure a significant decrease in overhead as the application server used object pooling. Generally, as expected, the overhead is mostly caused by object allocation events when the call stack filter is involved, which currently uses a simple string comparison-based implementation. Nevertheless, our prototype was able to cope with such a demanding application and several ways of possible improvement are currently under consideration. Besides that, our solution—as mentioned in Sect. 1—is targeted at a specific measurement scenario where such overhead is tolerable. Clearly it is currently not apt for use in productive environments.

4.5 Discussion

Our current implementation does not employ bytecode instrumentation for the generation of events. This is because, based on the four different kinds of view on the data, bytecode instrumentation offers no advantages when retrieving the memory allocation data. As shown in Sect. 4, many classes would have to be instrumented in order to generate data for all four views, but filtering the allocation data would still be needed. That would barely reduce the overhead of filtering. Furthermore, often EJBs of third party distributors have to be measured. Here, it is sometimes illicit to alter the code of a program as most vendors prohibit this in their license terms for a component. By not using instrumentation, no license regulation is violated. However, with the new JDK v1.5.0, the JVMP interface is marked as deprecated and superceded by a new instrumentation based one (see [16]); it is therefore important that the existing structure of the agent be easily re-usable and altered such that it can use the JVMTI as well. Anyhow, a lot of application servers still run with the older version 1.4.x and are able to use the JVMPI. Nevertheless, we already have a prototype profiler using the new interface and are planning to migrate our solution to this new technique.

The *EJBMemProf* memory profiler has been designed to work with the Enterprise Java Beans component model. To this end, the filters have been designed in such a way that they only generate data reports containing resources directly or indirectly related to one or more EJBs when parameterized correctly. As pointed out in Sect. 2, many profilers for the Java platform are readily available, but nearly all of them generate too much data which distracts the user from the actual EJBs of interest or are unable to distinguish between the resources only related to the application server, only related to one or more EJBs and that resources related to an EJB as well as to the application server. As our solution is specialized on EJBs, a minimum knowledge about the component is needed in order to do profiling at all. It is not necessary to know which classes are instantiated by one EJB as the filters are retrieving them automatically. The only information necessary is the set of classes and interfaces a EJB consists of, which can easily be extracted from the deployment descriptor.

Although the profiler focusses on EJBs and uses several filtering mechanisms, it still can, according to the parameterization of the filters, generate large reports for the frontend. This is why it is not uncommon for a more complicated scenario with several EJBs involved being profiled for a longer time, to generate two or more gigabytes[11]. As the network could be a bottleneck with such a huge amount of data, our prototypical implementation allows for the storage of the profiling data to a file on the server side. However, our current frontend holds all profiling data in memory as well—independent of whether it receives the data via the network or from a local file—which leads to high memory consumption on the client in such scenarios.

In contrast to that, the very detailed allocation data paves the way for extensive statistical calculations without specifying the kind of calculation and the data involved at the start of the profiling process: calculating, for instance, the amount of memory allocated by one specific method/object/EJB is simply a query on the data and doing the calculation again for a second method/object/EJB is just a repetition of the query with other conditions. Thus, it can be interesting to split the profiling process into two phases: in the first one all the data is collected and stored to files or in a database, which allows more complex queries on the gathered data. After the data collection has been finished, the data can be analyzed without having the profiler agent running on a system. This is not a novel approach as some profilers like the JBoss-profiler (see Sect. 2) use it to decouple the data collection process from the load generated by an analysis.

An interesting aspect of the proposed solution is the possibility to compare application servers of different vendors: the complete view is not restricted to the objects allocated by the EJB itself, but also reports those created by the application server for providing its service. Application servers might have implemented the EJB service differently. The memory used by these objects could also be accounted to the memory allocated by the EJB—that makes it possible to compare application servers. However, we did not exploit that possibility yet.

Considering the accuracy of our event-based solution, the profiler generally recognizes every object allocation reported by the VM through the OBJECT_ALLOC event. This does not cover objects allocated in native code which has been invoked through the Java Native Interface if these objects are not Java objects. But, on the other hand, there is no need to catch these allocations as the current version of the EJB specification (2.1) forbids loading a native library and calling native code from an EJB anyway, for its ability to compromise security (see chapter 25.1.2 of [2])[12]. Local variables of

---

[11] Profiling our MPEG4 component application with an input movie consisting of only three pictures generated already a file of size 2.6GB.

[12] If the profiler agent is interested in this memory, additional profiling techniques suitable for retrieving memory allocations from native code must be introduced. The filters cannot be pa-

primitive types like `int`, `float` or `boolean` are exempt from the object allocation event of the JVMPI. If a method uses the Java wrapper classes for the primitive types (e.g. `Integer` for `int`), these local variables are included. It is safe to state that every object is contained in the event for which the `new` operator is called to instantiate it. This definition includes arrays where the elements are of a primitive type like `int[]`.

If the profiling is done twice for the same EJB, the user may notice that not exactly the same memory consumption is reported—even if the EJB processed requests with the same data. As the Java environment uses a garbage collector, the point in time when objects are freed depends on the parameterization and the type of garbage collector of the JVM used. This causes the difference in the actual and maximum memory consumption values for two profiling sessions. As a result the value measured for the overall memory consumption for one scenario is not solely determined by the value of one single profiling session, but by a range measured for more sessions. The lower bound of this range is given by the lowest maximum memory consumption and the upper bound by the highest maximum memory consumption contained in the measurement series.

Regarding performance, we already discussed some areas of improvement, e.g. a more sophisticated string comparison algorithm in the call stack filter. Furthermore, as it is necessary to switch to JVMTI for the future anyway, there might be some performance gains because the costs for context switching between Java code and the C++ profiler agent code will be reduced significantly. But still, excessive filtering will be inescapable in the current architecture. Therefore, we currently consider an enhanced architecture where object allocation events—independent of whether generated by byte-code instrumentation or by an event based API—can be selectively enabled only when a thread enters an EJB and can be switched off again after it leaves it (see discussion in Sect. 2 addressing [14]).

5   Conclusion

In this paper we have described the architecture and implementation of an event-based memory profiler that has been specifically designed for Enterprise Java Beans components. Most current profilers for the Java platform either do not adapt to the specialities of component profiling—with the consequence that a user has to dig through a lot of data he is not interested in or is not able to interpret—or do not differentiate what should be presented to the user. Additionally, there is usually no API by which a different frontend could use a given profiling agent. After presenting several approaches to EJB memory profiling, we have argued that an event-based mechanism is necessary to offer a precise look at memory consumption. We have introduced four different views on the memory allocation of an EJB and have shown how these can be implemented by applying three different filter mechanisms inside the agent, with the advantage of significantly reducing the amount of data necessary to be transferred to a frontend. We have given a first impression of the performance of our prototypical JVMPI-based implementation and have identified the advantages as well as the drawbacks of our approach in the discussion.

---

rameterized such that they also include native objects (only if the profiler is not used with EJBs).

Basically, as the overhead of the profiler is still very high in complex scenarios, especially if the call stack filter is involved, a use in production environments is prohibitively expensive. This fact, however, is alleviated as we primarily designed our solution to be used in a stand-alone measurement environment targeted at the generation of a component specification including resource usage. As a next step we want to improve our implementation in order to reduce its overhead; ideally, a solution usable in production environments will result, which then could make it possible to check resource specifications of components at runtime or have the application server adapt to resource constraints. To achieve this, bytecode instrumentation will be a necessary technique to reduce context switches; but this has to be accompanied by selectively switching on and off the event-generation depending on the business method of interest of a component. Otherwise, the main task of a bytecode instrumentation approach will also be filtering again.

References

[1] Brahnmath, G., Raje, R.R., Olson, A., Bryant, B., Auguston, M., Burt, C.: A quality of service catalog for software components. In: Proc. Southeastern Software Engineering Conf. (Huntsville, Alabama, April). (2002) 513–520

[2] Sun Microsystems: Enterprise Java Beans Specification, Version 2.1. (2003)

[3] Röttger, S., Zschaler, S.: CQML$^+$: Enhancements to CQML. In Bruel, J.M., ed.: Proc. 1st Intl. Workshop on Quality of Service in Component-Based Software Engineering, Toulouse, France, Cépaduès-Éditions (2003) 43–56

[4] Sun Microsystems: Java Virtual Machine Profiler Interface. (1998) URL http://java.sun.com/j2se/1.4.1/docs/guide/jvmpi/jvmpi.html, downloaded at 2004-10-19.

[5] Borland: OptimzeIt Enterprise Edition 6 (2004) http://www.borland.com/optimizeit/.

[6] Quest Software: JProbe (2004) http://www.quest.com/jprobe/index.asp.

[7] ej Technologies GmbH: JProfiler (2004) http://www.jprofiler.com.

[8] O'Hair, K.: HPROF: A Heap/CPU Profiling Tool in J2SE 5.0. (2004) URL http://java.sun.com/developer/technicalArticles/Programming/HPROF.html, downloaded at 2004-12-18.

[9] JBoss.org: Jboss-profiler documentation (2004) URL http://www.jboss.org/wiki/Wiki.jsp?page=JBossProfilerDocumentation, downloaded at 2004-12-08.

[10] Dmitriev, M.: Profiling java applications using code hotswapping and dynamic call graph revelation. In: Proceedings of the fourth international workshop on Software and performance, ACM Press (2004) 139–150

[11] Netbeans.org: The NetBeans profiler project (2004) URL http://profiler.netbeans.org.

[12] Reiss, S.P., Renieris, M.: Generating Java trace data. In: Proceedings of the ACM 2000 conference on Java Grande, ACM Press (2000) 71–77

[13] Reiss, S.P., Renieris, M.: Encoding program executions. In: Proceedings of the 23rd International Conference on Software Engineering, Toronto, Ontario, Canada, IEEE (2001) 221–230

[14] Harkema, M., Quartel, D., Gijsen, B.M.M., van der Mei, R.D.: Performance monitoring of Java applications. In: Proceedings of the Third International Workshop on Software and Performance, ACM Press (2002) 114–127

[15] Sounder, T., Mancoridis, S., Salah, M.: Form: A Framework for Creating Views of Program Execution (2001) Drexel University, Departement of Mathematics and Computer Science.

[16] Sun Microsystems: The JVM Tool Interface (JVMTI). (2004) URL http://java.sun.com/j2se/1.5.0/docs/guide/jvmti/jvmti.html, downloaded at 2004-12-10.

Model-Driven Safety Evaluation with State-Event-Based Component Failure Annotations

Lars Grunske[1], Bernhard Kaiser[2], and Yiannis Papadopoulos[3]

[1]School of Information Technology and Electrical Engineering ITEE,
University of Queensland, Brisbane, QLD 4072, Australia
grunske@itee.uq.edu.au
[2]Fraunhofer IESE, Sauerwiesen 6, 67661 Kaiserslautern, Germany
bernhard.kaiser@iese.fraunhofer.de
[3]Department of Computer Science, University of Hull, HU67RX, U.K.
y.i.papadopoulos@hull.ac.uk

Abstract. Over the past years, the paradigm of component-based software engineering has been established in the construction of complex mission-critical systems. Due to this trend, there is a practical need for techniques that evaluate critical properties (such as safety, reliability, availability or performance) of these systems. In this paper, we review several high-level techniques for the evaluation of safety properties for component-based systems and we propose a new evaluation model (State Event Fault Trees) that extends safety analysis towards a lower abstraction level. This model possesses a state-event semantics and strong encapsulation, which is especially useful for the evaluation of component-based software systems. Finally, we compare the techniques and give suggestions for their combined usage.

1 Introduction

Safety critical systems are systems that pose potential hazards for people and the environment. Recently though, the ability to implement cost effectively complex functions in software has yielded a plethora of computer controlled safety critical systems in areas that include automotive electronics, aviation, industrial process control and medical applications. The safety assessment of such systems is currently performed using a range of classical techniques, which include Fault Tree Analysis (FTA), Failure Modes and Effects Analysis (FMEA) and Hazard and Operability Studies (HAZOPS) (for a review of these techniques the reader is referred to [2, 17, 28]). During the safety assessment process, a team of analysts manually applies a combination of these techniques to identify possible hazards, analyze the risk associated with these hazards, and devise strategies to mitigate the level of risk where this is necessary.

Although there are many commercial tools that automate the quantitative, mathematical analysis of such models, the construction of evaluation models and the overall application of hazard and safety analysis techniques remain manual processes, which are performed by expert analysts. For relatively simple systems, safety and reliability analysis is a manageable process, although fault trees and other analyses can rapidly

G.T. Heineman et al. (Eds.): CBSE 2005, LNCS 3489, pp. 33–48, 2005.

become very elaborate [2]. With increasing system complexity however, manual analysis becomes laborious, error prone and questions are therefore asked as to its applicability to complex technologies.

New computer-based systems deliver increased functionality on increasingly more powerful electronic units and networks. Such systems introduce new complex failure modes, which did not arise in older electromechanical designs. Such failure modes, for instance, include commission failures, i.e. conditions in which functions are being provided in the wrong context of operation (e.g. inadvertent and wrong application of brakes in a vehicle control system). As the density of implementation per electronic unit increases over time in such systems, and as functions are being distributed on networks of embedded components, the possibility of common cause failure and unpredicted dependent failure of critical functions caused by malfunction of non-critical functions also become greater concerns. Beyond those new safety concerns, difficulties are also caused by increasing scale and complexity. To deal with the complexity, new assessment processes are needed in the context of which composability and reuse of component safety analyses in the construction of system safety cases will be possible [25]. Such processes are also demanded by modern standards. The CENELEC railway standards [5], for example, introduce the concept of composable safety cases, according to which the *safety case* (i.e. the collective evidence of safety) of a system is composed of the safety cases of its sub-systems or components, which in theory could be certified independently. This type of composability in safety analysis is expected to bring similar benefits to those introduced by well-tested and trusted software *components* in general software engineering [25]. A body of work is already developing looking into techniques for specification and application-level reuse of component-based safety analyses. This paper reviews this work and proposes a new component-based safety evaluation model (State Event Fault Trees), which is appropriate for the representation and analysis of components and systems that exhibit probabilistic and deterministic behavior.

The rest of the paper is organized as follows: In Section 2, recently proposed techniques for safety analysis of component-based systems are reviewed. In Section 3, we introduce State Event Fault Trees (SEFTs), a new model for safety analysis and describe the proceeding of a component-based safety analysis with these SEFTs. The case study of a fire alarm system in Section 4 demonstrates application of SEFTs. Finally, we discuss the benefits, limitations and differences of the proposed techniques in Section 5, and we conclude and describe relevant future work in Section 6.

2   Safety Evaluation for Component-Based Systems: Earlier Models

To place the proposed work in context, this section reviews earlier work on safety evaluation of component-based systems. To deal with the modular nature of component-based systems, safety evaluation models also need to be modular and should be capable of describing the failure behavior of components with respect to all possible environments. A number of models have been proposed to meet these requirements. In this section, we examine three models, which we believe will help to illustrate the principle and value of modular safety analysis as well as the limitations of current work in this area. These models are: Failure Propagation and Transformation Notation (FPTN), tabular failure annotations in Hierarchically Performed Hazard Origin and Propagation Studies (HiP-HOPS) and Component Fault Trees (CFT).

2.1 Failure Propagation and Transformation Notation (FPTN)

The Failure Propagation and Transformation Notation (FPTN) described in [9] is the first approach that introduces modular concepts for the specification of the failure behavior of components.

The basic entity of the FPTN is a FPTN-Module. This FPTN-Module contains a set of standardized sections. In the first section (the header section) for each FPTN-module an identifier (ID), a name and a criticality level (SIL) are given. The second section specifies the propagation of failures, transformation of failures, generation of internal failures and detection of failures in the component. Therefore, this section enumerates all failures in the environment that can affect the component and all failures of the component that can effect the environment. These failures are denoted as incoming and outgoing failures and are classified by the failure categorization of Bondavalli and Simoncini [3] (reaction too late(tl), reaction too early(te), value failure(v), commission(c) and omission(o)). In the example which is given in Fig. 1 the incoming failures are $A{:}tl$, $A{:}te$, $A{:}v$, and $B{:}v$ and the outgoing failures are $C{:}tl$, $C{:}v$, $C{:}c$ and $C{:}o$. The propagation and transformation of failures is specified inside the module with a set of equations or predicates (e.g for propagation: $C{:}tl{=}A{:}tl$ and for transformation $C{:}c{=}A{:}te\&\&A{:}v$ and $C{:}v{=}A{:}t\|B{:}v$). Furthermore a component can also generate failures (e.g $C{:}o$) or handle an exiting failure (e.g $B{:}v$). For this, it is necessary to specify a failure cause or a failure handling mechanism and a probability. FPTN-Modules can also be nested hierarchically. Thus, FPTN is a hierarchical notation, which allows the decomposition of the evaluation model based upon the system architecture. If a FPTN-module contains embedded FPTN-modules the incoming failures of one module can be connected with the outgoing failures of another module. Such a connection can be semantically interpreted as failure propagation between these two modules.

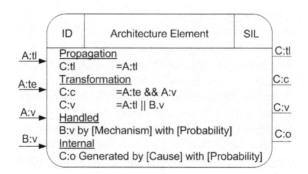

Fig. 1. Abstract FPTN-Module

2.2 Tabular Failure Annotations and HIP-HOPS (Hierarchically Performed Hazard Origin and Propagation Studies)

Building on earlier work on FPTN, Papadopoulos and McDermid proposed HiP-HOPS [19], a model-based semi-automatic safety and reliability analysis technique that uses tabular failure annotations as the basic building block of analysis at component level. In HiP-HOPS a structural model of the system (hierarchical if required to manage complexity) is first annotated with tables that contain formalized logical descriptions of component failures and their local effects. The annotated model is used as a basis for the automatic construction of fault trees and FMEAs for the system. Application of the technique starts once a concept of the system under design has been interpreted into an engineering model, which identifies components and material, energy or data transactions among components.

In HiP-HOPS, failure annotations at component level contain sets of logical expressions, which show how output failures of each component can be caused by internal malfunctions of the component and deviations of the component inputs. A technique called Interface Focused FMEA (IF FMEA) [18] has been proposed as a means of deriving such failure annotations. Analysts will typically apply this technique on components to identify plausible *output failures* such as the *omission, commission, value* (hi, low) or *timing* (early, late) failures at each output and then to determine the local causes of such events as combinations of *internal component malfunctions* and *input failures*. Once this analysis has been inserted into the model, the structure of the model is then used to automatically determine how the local failures specified in failure annotations propagate through connections in the model and cause functional failures at the outputs of the system. This global view of failure is captured in a set of fault trees, which are automatically constructed by traversing the model and by evaluating the local failure expressions encountered during the traversal. In HiP-HOPS, synthesized fault trees form a directed acyclic graph sharing branches and basic events that arise from dependencies in the model, e.g. common inputs. Thus, qualitative or quantitative analysis can be automatically performed on the graph to establish whether the system meets its safety or reliability requirements. In recent work [20], the authors also showed that the graph can be automatically reduced into a simple table, which is equivalent to a classical FMEA.

2.3 Component Fault Trees (CFT)

Component Fault Trees (CFTs) [12] are an extension of basic Fault Trees (FTs) [11, 26] to analyze complex component-based systems. This extension allows arbitrarily defining partial FT that corresponds to the actual technical components.

CFTs can be modeled and archived independently from each other, because they are encapsulated entities using input and output ports to connect the components. CFTs are treated as a set of propositional formulas describing the truth-values of each output failure port as a function of the input failure ports and the internal events. CFTs are acyclic graphs with one or more output ports. Each component constitutes a namespace and hides all internal failure events from the environment. Components may be instantiated several times and can be reused in other projects. Thus, all necessary preconditions for an application of safety analysis to component-based systems are fulfilled. Apart from the component and port concepts, CFTs are ordinary FTs and provide the same expressive power and analysis techniques.

Fig. 2 gives an example of a CFT and the hierarchical decomposition. The left CFT describes the failure behavior of the system, i.e. an instance of the top-level component-class C1. The system incorporates two instances Sub1 and Sub2 of another component type C2 as its subcomponents. On the higher hierarchy level, subcomponents are represented as black boxes that show only the ports, representing the external interface of the embedded CFT. As in UML, colons are used to separate instances from classes, e.g. Sub1:C2 denotes that Sub1 is a component (instance) of component-class C2. Note that the internal events Sub1.E1 and Sub2.E1 within the two subcomponents (not visible on top system level) are two distinct instances of: C2.E1 and thus independent events, while System.E1 is another distinct event and a common failure cause to both subcomponents.

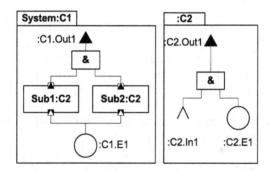

Fig. 2. Example of a Component Fault Tree

The application of CFTs for component-based systems is described in [10]. This includes the annotation of CFTs to components and a model-based construction algorithm of system-level CFTs (safety cases) based on the structure specification and the component fault trees of the used components. This construction algorithm is similar to the generation of fault trees in HiP-HOPS.

3   State Event Fault Trees

While the preceding section describes established and industry-proven component-based safety analysis techniques, this section presents a very recent technique, the State-Event-Fault-Trees (SEFTs). We first give an informal introduction and briefly describe the syntax and semantics of SEFTs. Then we summarize how to analyze hazard probabilities with SEFTs and present the application to component-based systems.

3.1 Informal Introduction and Syntax of SEFT

SEFTs are a visual model that integrates elements from discrete state-based models with FTs. The principal distinction from standard FTs is that states (that last over a period of time) are distinguished from events (sudden phenomena, in particular state transitions). The graphical elements are adopted from traditional FTA and from State-charts (or derived notations like ROOMcharts [24] or UML 2.0 State Diagrams) that are widely used in industry. An explicit event symbol is introduced and causal edges show cause-effect relations, connected by logical gates, as usual in FTA.

State transitions occur due to three different reasons: either the state changes de-terministically when a certain sojourn time in a state has elapsed, or it changes sto-chastically according to an exponential distribution of the sojourn time, or it changes because some other event caused, or *triggered* the state change. The latter relation between two events is denoted by a *causal edge*, which can be graphically distin-guished *from a temporal edge* that denotes the predecessor/successor relation be-tween states and events.

As in FTA, gates add logical connectors to the causal paths. The fundamental gates are AND, OR and NOT in their different variants. Semantically, SEFTs are an ex-tended state-machine model and no longer a purely combinatorial model as standard FTs are. Consequently, SEFT gates are typed in the sense that they have different semantics depending on whether they are applied to state terms or to event triggering relations. The shift from a combinatorial model towards a state-based model enables new kinds of gates (e.g. Duration gate, History-AND) and allows for a more formal definition of gates that have traditionally been used in FTA (e.g. Priority-AND, In-hibit). Similar to CFTs, SEFTs also extend the plain tree structure to Directed Acyclic Graphs (the same cause triggers multiple effects) and deal with repeated events or states correctly. Causal cycles without explicit delay are not allowed, because this would raise some semantic problems during analysis. SEFTs are structured by com-ponents. *Components* are defined as types (component classes) that can be instanti-ated as subcomponents in other components. Subcomponents appear as black boxes on the next higher level where only the ports are visible. This results in a component hierarchy, of which the topmost component is the system to be examined. Ports achieve information flow between components across hierarchical levels. To enforce consistency, we distinguish input from output ports and type ports as state ports and event ports. Examples can be found in the case study in Section 4. Event ports trans-fer triggering relations from one component to another, without backward conse-quences and without forcing synchronization of both components. The semantics of a state port is that the destination component has access to the information whether or not the state in the source component is active, again without the possibility to back-ward influence this state. A main difference to standard FTs is that states and events that appear in the model are not necessary failures; normal operational states can, in conjunction with other states or events, become safety issues upstream in the causal chain. The following figure sums up the graphical elements of SEFTs.

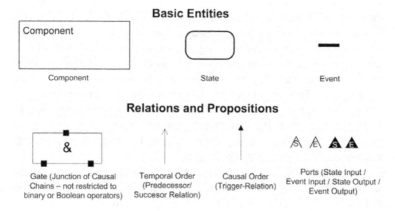

Fig. 3. Syntactic Elements of SEFT

3.2 Transformational Semantics and Analysis of SEFT with DSPNs

To analyze a traditional Fault Tree, the underlying Boolean formula is converted into a Binary Decision Diagram (BDD) [4]. Due to the state-based nature, SEFTs cannot be evaluated this way. Instead we propose a translation to Deterministic and Stochastic Petri Nets (DSPNs) [1] since DSPNs are a concurrent model possessing all needed kinds of transitions and provide analysis techniques for the properties we are interested in. Assuming some basic knowledge about Petri Nets we briefly point out the main features of DSPNs: DSPNs are a timed variant of Petri Nets, i.e. the (deterministic or probabilistic) time that a transition waits before firing after becoming enabled is explicitly specified in the model. There are three kinds of transition that differ by their way of firing: immediately after activation, after a deterministic delay (specified by an annotated time parameter) or after an exponentially distributed random delay (specified by an annotated rate parameter). Firing of transitions is atomic and takes no time. In the graphical representation, black bars depict immediate transitions, empty rectangles depict transitions with exponentially distributed firing time, and black filled rectangles depict transitions with deterministic firing time. Transitions are joined to places by input arcs, output arcs or inhibitor arcs. The latter forbid firing as long as the corresponding place is marked; whereas the other arcs are as in standard Petri Nets. Priorities can be attached to immediate transitions to resolve conflicts: the transition with the highest priority number wins. Alternatively, weights can be assigned to decide conflicts probabilistically. Places can have a capacity of more then one token and arcs can have a multiplicity of greater than one, but we currently do not exploit this property. We assume the underlying time scale to be continuous. Analysis of DSPNs has been described in [6] and several tools are available to apply it. We are using the tool TimeNET [29] from Technische Universität Berlin for analysis and/or simulation.

The translation of SEFT states and events to DSPN places and transitions is straightforward: each state is mapped to a place and each event to a transition. For ports and trigger relations, special DSPN structures are applied that inhibit backward influence. SEFT gates are translated as a whole by looking up the corresponding DSPN structure in a dictionary that has been introduced in [14]. An excerpt is given in Fig. 4. This figure also exemplifies the meaning of typed gates: the AND joining two states is distinct from the AND joining a state and an event, and so on. The graphical symbols for both the State/Event-AND and the State-AND are identical to the AND gate from traditional FTA, but a confusion is impossible due to the different type of one input port. This is comparable to method overloading in OO programming languages, where the arguments passed decide which actual function need to be executed. A central feature of SEFTs is that, in contrast to standard FTs, all events can occur more often than once, and repair or reset can be modeled. This is reflected in the DSPN structures chosen as gate equivalents.

In the figure, dashed places or transitions signify import places/transitions, i.e. references to places/transitions in other partial DSPNs. During flattening (integration of the partial nets), the import elements are merged with corresponding export elements by resolving a reference table.

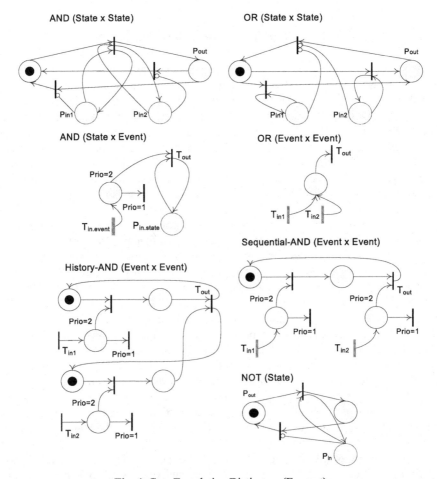

Fig. 4. Gate Translation Dictionary (Excerpt)

After states and events have been translated to places and arcs and after the partial DSPNs corresponding to the gates, the remaining steps of the translation are simplification, flattening and parameter translation. Flattening turns the hierarchical DSPN (due to the component structure) into one flat DSPN. Flattening is an automatic procedure, based on the unique IDs of the ports. This enables creating semi-automatic safety cases for component-based systems. The resulting flat DSPN can be stochastically analyzed and/or simulated with the tool TimeNET. The requested measure (e.g. average probability of a state term that is connected to an output port) must be translated into a measure that can be determined by the DSPN analysis tool (e.g. the marking probability for a place that corresponds to the system state of interest). Currently we start the analysis manually, but we are working towards an integrated solution, started from the GUI of our own tool ESSaRel [7].

3.3 A Safety Evaluation Method with SEFTs

The last two sections introduced SEFTs and gave a brief overview of their syntax, semantics and analyzability. Based on the foundation of SEFT we want to describe a methodology for model-based hazard analysis for component-based software systems. The underlying model is the architecture specification, which could be specified with an architectural description language (e.g., AADL[8] or MetaH[27]) or with the UML 2.0. This architecture specification is the basic construction plan of the system. It describes how the system or a component is decomposed into smaller components and which of them interact during the runtime of the system as well as which software components are deployed on which hardware platform.

The methodology for hazard analysis with SEFT can be structured into three phases. In the first phase, a SEFT must be manually constructed for each component-class instantiated in the architecture. This SEFT describes the behavior of the component on a low-level, i.e. referring to detailed states and events. This behavioral model can be derived from the model for the normal functional behavior, as specified in the system design phase. However, it is not the same as a functional model: it is reduced by details that are not relevant to safety and on the other hand, it may be extended by potential faulty behavior, which is of course not part of a functional model.

In the second phase, a SEFT is constructed for the entire architecture. All necessary details for this construction are contained in the architectural model and the SEFTs of the subcomponents. The algorithm for the construction first instantiates recursively all SEFTs of the subcomponents and connects the ports of two SEFT (in ports with out ports), if there is a dependency between the relating components. Then the algorithm creates ports in the SEFT if there is an unconnected port in the SEFT of a subcomponent.

The result of the previous phases is a SEFT for the complete system. This SEFT can be analyzed quantitatively to determine the probability of the relevant system failures or hazards. To do so, the analyst must further specify which output ports or which combinations of output failures lead to a hazard, which is preferably done using the Fault Tree modeling elements. Some output states or events are marked as the critical ones (hazards or system failures), of which the probability has to be calculated. Quantitative analysis is performed on the underlying DSPN. If the calculated hazard probabilities are lower than the tolerable hazard probabilities defined in the requirements specification, the system fulfils its safety requirements.

The benefit of this methodology is the tight coupling between the architectural model and the hazard analysis. Once the architecture or a SEFT of a used component is changed, a new SEFT for the complete system can be constructed and a new hazard analysis can be applied.

4   Case-Study

We exemplify the usage of SEFTs for safety analyses of component-based systems by the case study of a fire alarm system. We start our example by introducing the system components and environment and finally present the system model that shows the architecture and specify the hazard to be examined. For brevity, we do not explain the analysis of the example; this step can be found in [13,14].

The system consists of a software-implemented *controller unit*, a *smoke sensor* and a *sprinkler*. The hazard to be examined is the case that a fire breaks out and the *sprinkler* is not turned on within a given delay. The *fire* is an event that occurs in the *environment*; it is a particularity of the new SEFT method that system and environment are described in the same modeling technique and thus failure-on-demand situations can be modeled easily. The hardware components of the fire alarm system can fail; therefore, inspection and repair is foreseen on a regular basis and a hardware *watchdog* restarts the *controller* on a periodical basis.

The first component to be modeled is the *sensor* (Fig. 5, left side). It is modeled as a system with two states (*ready* and *defect*), one event input and one event output. If the input *fire breaks out* is triggered while the sensor is in state *ready*, the output *detect smoke* is triggered. If the sensor is in state *defect* while the *fire breaks out*, nothing happens at the output. The transition from the state *ready* to the state *defect* occurs probabilistically with a constant rate of $1/10^7$ hours. Like all figures in this example, this is a fictitious number; in reality, one would have to insert a number that has been derived from failure statistics, experiments or mathematical models. The way back from the state *defect* to the state *ready* corresponds to repair, which is also modeled by a constant rate as well, corresponding to the periodical visits of a service technician.

The *sprinkler* (Fig. 5, right side) is a component with three states: *ready*, *sprinkling*, *defect*. In this component, deterministic behavior (triggering) is mixed with probabilistic behavior (going to state *defect*). Again, failure and repair are modeled by constant rates. The transitions from *ready* to *sprinkling* and back are triggered transitions: it is the *controller* that commands start and stop of the sprinkling. The two event inputs *sprinkler on* and *sprinkler off* are technical interfaces in the sense that these are actually the spots where the *controller* interacts with the *sprinkler*, e.g. via an electrical line. The state output *sprinkling* is an interface to the environment; it does not correspond to a technical interface but represents that sprinkling is obviously visible to an outside observer.

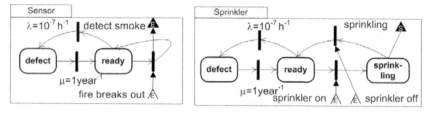

Fig. 5. SEFT of the Sensor and Sprinkler

The next part of the system is the *controller*; which is designed with software and hardware. The hardware has two states, *working* and *defect*. The transition from *working* to *defect* is again probabilistic with constant rate; it triggers the event output *hardware fails* that causes the software to enter the state of unavailable (*off*). The transition of the hardware back to state *working* is this time not a probabilistic one, but is triggered by a *reset* input that will later be connected to the *reset* output of a separate *watchdog* component. A *reset* of the hardware immediately triggers the reboot of the software. The software is modeled with three states: *off*, *ready*, *alarm*. Alarm is the state when the *sprinkler* is *turned on*. Entrance to this state triggers the *sprinkler on* output, leaving this state triggers the *sprinkler off* output. This state *alarm* is entered when the *detect smoke* input (connected to the *sensor* output) is triggered. The *sprinkler* operation is limited by the software controller to 120 seconds; this is denoted by a deterministic delay transition. There are self-transitions from the state *ready* and *alarm* that produce output *I am alive!* if the input *are you alive?* is received. The OR connection at the event output means (in FT notation) that the component can send the output *I am alive!* in both states.

The last technical component to be considered is the *watchdog* (Fig. 7, left side) – usually a highly reliable separate hardware timer. It is modeled as a component with two states, *ready* and *awaiting reply*, failure of the *watchdog* is so rare that it does not have to be modeled. Every 10 seconds the watchdog sends an event *are you alive?* to an output which will be connected to the input of the controller software with the same name. If the response *I am alive!* arrives from the software, the *watchdog* goes back to ready state for another 10 seconds. If the response does not arrive within 1 second, the watchdog triggers a *reset* of the controller hardware.

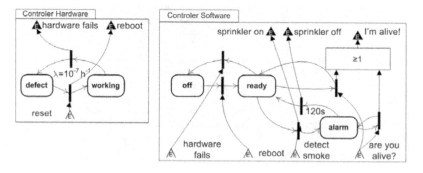

Fig. 6. SEFT of the Fire-Alarm Control System (Hardware and Software)

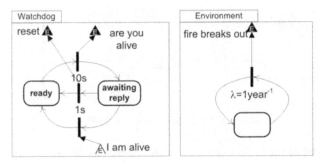

Fig. 7. SEFT of the Watchdog and Assumptions about the Systems Environment

The *environment* is modeled in Fig. 7, right side. It has just one state, which has no name. It signifies that probabilistically, with an assumed rate of once per year, a fire breaks out. The event output means that the beginning of the fire can be noticed by other components, particularly the sensor in our example.

The overall scenario including the FT for the hazard to be examined is shown in Fig. 8. The system components are connected to each other according to matching port names (not shown in the figure). In the upper part of the figure, the fault tree elements describe the hazard scenario: The hazard is the state that is present if the sprinkler is not enabled 10 seconds upon a fire breaks out. The probability of the hazard has to be calculated. The evaluation is as described in [14]: Translation of all components to a Deterministic and Stochastic Petri Net (DSPN), flattening of the component hierarchy and analysis and/or simulation using one of the existing DSPN tools.

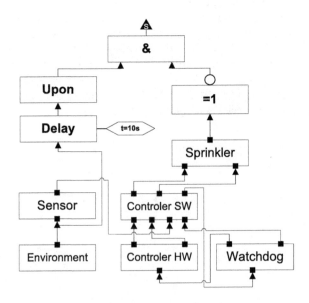

Fig. 8. Hazard Description: fire breaks out and the sprinkler is not turned on within 10s

5   Discussion and Comparison of the Different Modeling Techniques

So far, four different safety-analysis techniques for component-based systems have been introduced: FPTN, HiP-HOPS with their tabular annotations, CFTs and SEFTs. All of them have emerged during the last decade. They all have in common that they reflect hierarchical component and system structures and allow composing of the system safety case out of the safety models of the components. All of them allow probabilistic estimation of failure frequencies.

CFTs are closest to the traditional FTA technique. They introduce the port concept (input and output ports) and thus allow arbitrarily cutting a system into components and reusing the component models. Standard combinatorial FTs cannot handle time dependencies and order of events and durations (in contrast to SEFTs). The FT events can be low-level events or faulty states of components, but also general propositions on a higher level. CFTs by themselves do not provide help in finding appropriate failure categories.

HiP-HOPS and FPTN share the component and port oriented view of the system that CFTs offer. Both techniques offer guide words to failure identification and are focused on data flows, in particular the flow of failures. They also are unsuitable to model timing issues directly, but among the proposed failure classifications are key-words like "too early" and "too late" that allow expressing timing faults. While FPTNs are a graphical notation, failure propagation tables of HiP-HOPS are a tabular notation. Note, that this is merely an ergonomical issue: graphical notations are often easier to capture for humans, but large amounts of data are better collected and re-viewed in tables. There are other differences between the two techniques. In FPTN, a failure specification is developed in parallel to the system model while in HiP-HOPS failure annotations are only added to that model. Thus, in FPTN, special arrows are used to represent the explicit failure propagation between FPTN modules while in HiP-HOPS specified component failures propagate implicitly through deviations of material, energy or data flows in the model. In FPTN a number of predefined failure classes are only examined (provision, timing and value failures) while in HiP-HOPS analysts are free to define their own failure classes. To simplify the analysis and cap-ture common causes of failure, HiP-HOPS also allows simultaneous hierarchical annotation of the model at subsystem and component levels. Apart from these differ-ences, in their basic form FPTN and HiP-HOPS can be considered equivalent and can thus be applied in combination. A combination with CFTs is also possible, as CFTs could be used explain the different failure modes and their relations, provided that the failure inputs and outputs are named according to the FPTN / HiP-HOPS specifica-tions.

SEFTs are a new and quite different approach, because they model the system on a lower level. They introduce a more precise semantics and distinguish states from events. They mix fault tree notation elements with state-based modeling elements; their overall semantics is state-based. Thus they can model low-level behavior of (especially software) components well and can be seen as a contribution to fill the gap between safety analysis techniques and formal methods. The main difference to the former techniques is that SEFTs do not model failures and hazards, but behavior in general (although the analyst preferably models only those aspects of the behavior that have an influence on system-level failures or hazards). For instance, SEFTs do not express that an event occurs too late, but rather the time when it occurs. Only on a high level, upstream in the tree, the occurrence time of an event is compared to an acceptable delay or to another event and if the acceptable delay is exceeded, this constitutes a failure.

In summary, SEFTs work on a lower abstraction level and model more details, but this richness in detail can be a drawback when it comes to analysis performance (state explosion problem). Moreover, many of the needed detail information is only present at design or implementation stage of the system, while more informal considerations can be conducted from the earliest development phases. In practice, it is not possible to model very complex systems in all detail. A possible recipe for practitioners is to apply FPTN or HiP-HOPS on system level and to apply SEFTs on component level where the origin of some relevant behavior must be explained. For instance, an SEFT output indicating that some event occurs later than expected provides the probability of the "too late" failure mode in a FPTN.

6   Conclusion and Future Work

Hazard analysis techniques for safety critical systems are concerned with (1) identifying the causal relationships between elementary failure modes (causes) and system level hazards (effects) and (2) with a quantitative or qualitative evaluation of these relationships [9, 15, 22, 28]. Both tasks are currently performed using a range of classical techniques, which include Fault Tree Analysis (FTA), Failure Modes and Effects Analysis (FMEA) and Hazard and Operability Studies (HAZOPS). However, these techniques are not suitable to analyze component-based systems, because the underlying evaluation models lack of composability and the evaluation methods cannot deal with hierarchical component structures. New evaluation models (FPTN, tabular failure annotations in HiP-HOPS, CFT) have been proposed to allow hazard analysis for component-based systems. The semantics of these techniques is concerned with failure propagation or failure flow between components. These techniques are suitable to analyze high-level system structures at an abstract level. In this paper, we presented a new evaluation model called State Event Fault Trees, which has state-event semantics and is suitable to describe the stochastic behavior of a component on a low level, i.e. referring to detailed states and events. The state event semantics allows expressing facts that cannot be expressed in standard Fault Trees and many other safety analysis techniques (e.g. temporal order of events or duration). The state-event semantics is similar to the one used in behavioral modeling techniques in the design phase of software and hardware systems. Due to this compatible semantics, it is possible to integrate SEFTs with behavioral models of a component or even to derive them automatically. Additionally SEFT are strongly encapsulated (providing information hiding and strict interfaces) and typed (SEFT-components). As a result, safety cases can be composed hierarchically according to the component structure of complex systems.

For the techniques CFT and HiP-HOPS, tools are already available on a prototype level (e.g. UWG3 [7] supports CFTs or an extension of Matlab-Simulink support HiP-HOPS [21]). The integration of SEFTs into a usable tool is part of our current research. The platform is the project ESSaRel [7], a user-friendly Windows-based tool encompassing different modeling techniques has already been built within this project. In the end, we are working towards an integrated tool chain for safety and reliability analysis of embedded systems that enable the model-based hazard analysis. For further integration of safety analysis and systems modeling, we plan a filter to import models from CASE-Tools that can be integrated into SEFTs. As SEFTs are a state-based technique, performance issues have to be resolved in the future using suitable reduction and abstraction techniques. All mentioned techniques have been tried out in industrial environment, but a large body of experience is not yet available.

References

1. Ajmone Marsan, M., Chiola, G.: On Petri nets with deterministic and exponentially distributed firing times. European Workshop on Applications and Theory of Petri Nets 1986. Lecture Notes in Computer Science, volume 266, pages 132-145. Springer 1987
2. Birolini, A.: Reliability engineering: theory and practice, New York, Springer, (1999)
3. Bondavalli A., Simoncini, L.: Failure Classification with Respect to Detection, in: Predictably Dependable Computing Systems, Task B, Vol. 2, May (1990)
4. Bryant, R.E.: Graph-based algorithms for Boolean function manipulation. IEEE Transactions on Computers, C-35(8), Aug. (1986) 677--691
5. CENELEC: Railway applications The specification and demonstration of dependability, reliability, availability, maintainability and safety (RAMS), European Committee for Electrotechnical Standardisation, Brussels, Standard EN 50126, 128, 129, (2000-2002)
6. Ciardo, G., Lindemann, C.: Analysis of deterministic and stochastic Petri nets. In Proc. of the Fifth Int. Workshop on Petri Nets and Performance Models (PNPM93), Toulouse, France, Oct. 1993
7. ESSaRel: Embedded Systems Safety and Reliability Analyser, The ESSaRel Research Project, Homepage: http://www.essarel.de/index.html
8. Feiler, P., Lewis, B., Vestal, S.: The SAE Avionics Architecture Description Language (AADL) Standard: A Basis for Model-Based Architecture-Driven Embedded Systems Engineering. RTAS 2003 Workshop on Model-Driven Embedded Systems, 2003
9. Fenelon, P., McDermid, J.A., Nicholson, M., Pumfrey, D. J.: Towards Integrated Safety Analysis and Design, ACM Applied Computing Review, (1994).
10. Grunske, L.: Annotation of Component Specifications with Modular Analysis Models for Safety Properties, In Proceedings of the 1st International Workshop on Component Engineering Methodology, (WCEM 03), (2003), pp. 31-41
11. IEC 61025: International Standard IEC 61025 Fault Tree Analysis. International Electrotechnical Commission. Geneva(1990)
12. Kaiser, B., Liggesmeyer, P., Mäckel, O.: A New Component Concept for Fault Trees. in Proceedings of the 8th Australian Workshop on Safety Critical Systems and Software (SCS'03), Adelaide, (2003)
13. Kaiser, B.: Extending the Expressive Power of Fault Trees. Accepted for Publication of the 51st Annual Reliability & Maintainability Symposium (RAMS05), January 24-27, Alexandria, VA, USA

14. Kaiser, B., Gramlich, C.: State-Event-Fault-Trees - A Safety Analysis Model for Software Controlled Systems. In: Computer Safety, Reliability, and Security. 23rd International Conference, SAFECOMP 2004, Potsdam, Germany, September 21-24, 2004, Proceedings. Lecture Notes in Computer Science, Vol. 3219 2004, p. 195-209
15. Laprie, J.C.(ed.): Dependability: Basic Concepts and Associated Terminology. Vol.5, Dependable Computing and Fault-Tolerant Systems Series,Vienna: Springer (1992)
16. Meyer, B.: Applying design by contract. IEEE Computer 25, 10, (1992) 40-51
17. Musa, J.D., Iannino, A., Okumoto, K.: Software Reliability - Measurement, Prediction, Application, McGraw-Hill International Editions, (1987)
18. Papadopoulos, Y., McDermid, J.A., Sasse, R., Heiner, G.: Analysis and Synthesis of the Behavior of Complex Programmable Electronic Systems in Conditions of Failure, Reliability Engineering and System Safety, 71(3), Elsevier Science, (2001) 229-247.
19. Papadopoulos, Y., McDermid, J. A.: Hierarchically Performed Hazard Origin and Propagation Studies, SAFECOMP '99, 18th Int. Conf. on Computer Safety, Reliability and Security, Toulouse, LNCS, 1698 (1999) 139-152
20. Papadopoulos Y., Parker D., Grante C.: A method and tool support for model-based semi-automated Failure Modes and Effects Analysis of engineering designs, 9th Australian Workshop Safety Critical Programmable Systems (SCS'04), Brisbane, Conferences in Research and Practice in Information Technology, Vol. 38, Australian Computer Society (2004).
21. Papadopoulos, Y., Maruhn M.: Model-based Automated Synthesis of Fault Trees from Simulink models, Int'l Conf. on Dependable Systems and Networks, (2001), pp. 77-82
22. Pumfrey, D. J.: The Principled Design of Computer System Safety Analyses, Dissertation, University of York, (1999).
23. Reussner, R., Schmidt, H., Poernomo, I.: Reliability Prediction for Component-Based Software Architectures, Journal of Systems and Software, 66(3), Elsevier, The Netherlands, (2003) 241--252
24. Selic B., Gullekson G., Ward P. T.: Real-Time Object-Oriented Modeling. Wiley, New York, (1994)
25. Szyperski, C.: Component Software. Beyond Object-Oriented Programming. ACM Press/ Addison Wesley, (1998)
26. Vesely, W. E., Goldberg, F. F., Roberts, N. H.,. Haasl, D. F.: Fault Tree Handbook. U. S. Nuclear Regulatory Commission, NUREG-0492, Washington DC, (1981)
27. Vestal, S.: MetaH Programmer's Manual, Version 1.09. Technical Report, Honeywell Technology Center, April 1996.
28. Villemeur A.: Reliability, Availability, Maintainability, and Safety Assessment, John Willey and Sons, ISBN: 0-47193-048-2 (2000).
29. Zimmermann, A., German, R., Freiheit, J., Hommel, G.: TimeNET 3.0 Tool Description. Int. Conf. on Petri Nets and Performance Models (PNPM'99), Zaragoza, Spain, 1999

Optimizing Resource Usage in Component-Based Real-Time Systems

Johan Fredriksson, Kristian Sandström, and Mikael Åkerholm

Mälardalen Real-Time Research Centre,
Department of Computer Science and Engineering,
Mälardalen University, Box 883, Västerås, Sweden
http://www.mrtc.mdh.se
johan.fredriksson@mdh.se

Abstract. The embedded systems domain represents a class of systems that have high requirements on cost efficiency as well as run-time properties such as timeliness and dependability. The research on component-based systems has produced component technologies for guaranteeing real-time properties. However, the issue of saving resources by allocating several components to real-time tasks has gained little focus. Trade-offs when allocating components to tasks are, e.g., CPU-overhead, footprint and integrity. In this paper we present a general approach for allocating components to real-time tasks, while utilizing existing real-time analysis to ensure a feasible allocation. We demonstrate that CPU-overhead and memory consumption can be reduced by as much as 48% and 32% respectively for industrially representative systems.

1 Introduction

Many real-time systems (RTS) have high requirements on safety, reliability and availability. Furthermore the development of embedded systems is often sensitive to system resource usage in terms of, e.g., memory consumption and processing power. Historically, to guarantee full control over the system behavior, the development of embedded systems has been done using only low level programming. However, as the complexity and the amount of functionality implemented by software increase, so does the cost for software development. Also, since product lines are common within the domain, issues of commonality and reuse are central for reducing cost. Component-Based Development (CBD) has shown to be an efficient and promising approach for software development, enabling well defined software architectures as well as reuse. Hence, CBD can be used to achieve goals such as cost reduction, and quality and reliability improvements.

In embedded RTS timing is important, and scheduling is used to create predictable timing. Furthermore, these systems are often resource constrained; consequently memory consumption and CPU load are desired to be low. A problem in current component-based embedded software development practices is the allocation of components to run-time tasks [1]. Because of the real-time requirements on most embedded systems, it is vital that the allocation considers

G.T. Heineman et al. (Eds.): CBSE 2005, LNCS 3489, pp. 49–65, 2005.

temporal attributes, such as worst case execution time (WCET), deadline (D) and period time (T). Hence, to facilitate scheduling, components are often allocated to tasks in a one-to-one fashion. However, for many embedded systems it is desired to optimize for memory and speed [2], thus the one-to-one allocation is unnecessarily memory and CPU consuming.

Embedded RTS consist of periodic and sporadic events that usually have end-to-end timing requirements. Components triggered by the same periodic event can often be coordinated and executed by the same task, while still preserving temporal constraints. Thus, it is easy to understand that there can be profits from allocating several components into one task. Some of the benefits are less memory consumption in terms of stacks and task control blocks or lower CPU utilization due to less overhead for context switches. Different properties can be accentuated depending on how components are allocated to tasks, e.g., memory usage and performance; Hence, there are many trade-offs to be made when allocating components to tasks.

Allocating components to tasks, and scheduling tasks are both complex problems and different approaches are used. Simulated annealing and genetic algorithms are examples of algorithms that are frequently used for optimization problems. However, to be able to use such algorithms, a framework to calculate properties, such as memory consumption and CPU-overhead, is needed. The work presented in this paper describes a general framework for reasoning about trade-offs concerning allocating components to tasks, while preserving extra-functional requirements. Temporal constraints are verified and the allocations are optimized for low memory consumption and CPU-overhead. The framework is evaluated using industrially relevant component assemblies, and the results show that CPU-overhead and memory consumption can be reduced by as much as 48% and 32% respectively.

The idea of assigning components to tasks for embedded systems while considering extra-functional properties and resource utilization is a relatively uncovered area. In [3, 4] Bondarev et. al. are looking at predicting and simulating real-time properties on component assemblies. However, there is no focus on increasing resource utilization through component to task allocation. The problem of allocating tasks to different nodes is a problem that has been studied by researchers using different methods [5, 6]. There are also methods proposed for transforming structural models to run-time models [7, 8, 1], but extra-functional properties are usually ignored or considered as non-critical [9]. In [10], an architecture for embedded systems is proposed, and it is identified that components has to be allocated to tasks, however there is no focus on the allocation of components to tasks. In [9] the authors propose a model transformation where all components with the same priority are allocated to the same task; however no consideration is taken to lower resource usage. In [11], the authors discuss how to minimize memory consumption in real-time task sets, though it is not in the context of allocating components to tasks. Shin et. al [12] are discussing the code size, and how it can be minimized, but does not regard scheduling and resource constraints.

The outline for the rest of the paper is as follows; section 2 gives an overview of the component to task allocations, and describes the structure of the components and tasks. Section 3 describes a framework for calculating the properties of components allocated to tasks. Section 4 discusses allocation and scheduling approaches, while evaluations and simulations are presented in section 5. Finally in section 6, future work is discussed and the paper is concluded. Detailed data regarding the simulations can be found in [13].

2   Allocating Components to Real-Time Tasks

In RTS temporal constraints are of great importance and tasks control the execution of software. Hence, components need to be allocated to tasks in such a way that temporal requirements are met, and resource usage is minimized. Given an allocation we determine if it is feasible and calculate the memory consumption and task switch overhead. To impose timing constraints, we define end-to-end timing requirements and denote them transactions. Transactions are defined by a sequence of components and a deadline. Thus, the work in this paper has three main concerns:

1. Verification of allocations from components to tasks.
2. Calculating system properties for an allocation
3. Minimizing resource utilization

CBSE is generally not used when developing embedded RTS, mostly due to the lack of efficient mappings to run-time systems and real-time properties. One approach that allows an efficient mapping from components to a RTS is the Autocomp technology [14]. An overview of the Autocomp technology can be seen in Fig 1. The different steps in the figure are divided into design-time, compile-time, and run-time to display at which point in time during development they are addressed or used. The compile-time steps, illustrated in Fig 1, incorporate an allocation from the component-based design, to a real-time model and mapping to a real-time operating system (RTOS). During this step the components are allocated to real-time tasks and the component requirements are mapped to task-level attributes.

By combining the notion of transactions and the pipe-and-filter interaction model we get a general component model that is easy to implement for a large set of component technologies for embedded systems such as Autocomp [14], SaveCCM [15], Rubus [16], Koala [17], Port-based objects [18], IEC61131[19] and Simulink[20]. The component model characteristics are described in the section 2.1 and the task model characteristics are described in section 2.2.

2.1   Component Model Characteristics

In this section we describe characteristics for a general component model that is applicable to a large set of embedded component models. Both component and task models described are meta-models for modelling the most important

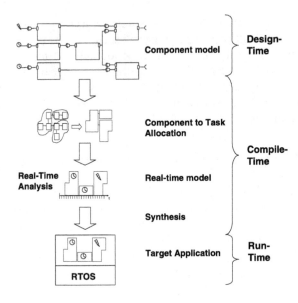

Fig. 1. Autocomp system description

attributes of an allocation between components and tasks. The component interaction model used throughout this paper is a pipe-and-filter model with transactions. Each component has a trigger; a time trigger or an event trigger or a
trigger from a preceding component. A component transaction describes an order of components and defines an end-to-end timing requirement. In Fig 2, the
notation of a component assembly with six components and four transactions is
described. The graphical notation is similar to the one used in UML.

The component model chosen is relatively straight forward to analyse and
verify. The pipe-and-filter interaction model is commonly used within the embedded systems domain. Many component models for embedded systems have
the notion of transactions built in; however, if a component model lacks the
notion of transactions, there are often possibilities to model end-to-end timing
requirements and execution order at a higher abstraction level. In general a system is described with components, component relations, and transactions (flow)
between components. The component model is described with:

Component c_i is described with the tuple $< S_i, Q_i, X_i, M_i >$, where S_i is
a signal from another component, an external event or a timed event. Q_i
represents the *minimum inter arrival time* (MINT) in the case of an external
event. It represents the period in the case of a timed trigger and it is unused
if the signal is from another component. The parameter X_i is the WCET for
the component, and M_i is the amount of stack required by the component.
Isolation set I defines a relation between components that should not be allocated. It is described with a set of component pairs $I =< (c_1, c_2), (c_3, c_4) >$
that define what components may not be allocated to the same task. There

may be memory protection requirements or other legitimate engineering reasons to avoid allocating certain combinations of components; for example, if a component has a highly uncertain WCET. The isolation set is indexed with subscripts denoting next inner element, i.e., $I_1 = (c_1, c_2)$ and $I_{12} = c_2$.

Component Transaction ctr_i is an ordered relation between components $N_i = c_1, c_2, ..., cn$, and an end-to-end deadline dc_i. The deadline is relative to the event that triggered the component transaction, and the first component within a transaction defines the transaction trigger. A component transaction can stretch over one or several components, and a component can participate in several component transactions. Component c_a should execute before component c_b and component c_b should execute before c_c to produce the expected results. The correct execution behavior for the set $N = c_1, c_2, ..., c_n$ is formalized by the regular expression denoted in (1).

$$c_1 \Sigma^* c_2 \Sigma^* ... c_n \qquad (1)$$

Where Σ^* denotes all allowed elements defined by N.

In a component assembly, event triggers are treated different from the periodic triggers as the former is not strictly periodic. There is only a lower boundary restricting how often it can occur, but there is no upper bound restricting how much time may elapse between two invocations. Thus, if an event trigger could exist inside or last in a transaction, it would be impossible to calculate the response time for the transaction, and hence a deadline could never be guaranteed.

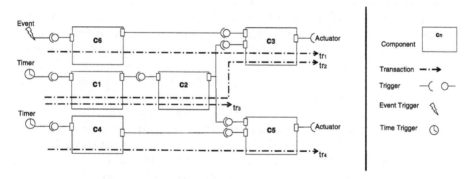

Fig. 2. Graphical notation of the component model.

2.2 Task Characteristics

The task model specifies the organization of entities in the component model into tasks and transactions over tasks. During the transformation from component model to run-time model, extra-functional properties like schedulability and response-time constraints must be considered in order to ensure the correctness of the final system. Components only interact through explicit interfaces; hence tasks do not synchronize outside the component model. The task model is for evaluating schedulability and other properties of a system, and is similar to standard task graphs as used in scheduling theory, augmented with exclusion constraints (isolation). The task model is described with:

System K is described with the tuple $< A, \tau, \rho >$ where A is a task set scheduled by the system. The constant τ is the size of each task control block, and can be considered constant and the same for all tasks. The constant ρ is the time associated with a task switch. The system kernel is the only explicitly shared resource between tasks; hence we do not consider blocking. Also blocking is not the focus of this paper.

Task t_i is described with the tuple $< C_i, T_i, wcet_i, stack_i >$ where C_i is an ordered set of components. Components within a task are executed in sequence. Components within a task are executed at the same priority as the task, and a high priority task pre-empts a low priority task. T_i is the period or minimum inter arrival time of the task. The parameters $wcet_i$ and $stack_i$ are worst case execution time and stack size respectively. The $wcet_i$, $stack_i$ and period (T_i) are deduced from the components in C_i. The $wcet_i$ is the sum of all the WCETs for all components allocated to the task. Hence, for a task t_i, the parameters $wcet_i$ and $stack_i$ are calculated with (2) and (3) .

$$wcet_n = \sum_{\forall_i (c_i \in C_n)} (X_i) \qquad (2)$$

$$stack_n = \forall_i (c_i \in C_n) max(M_i) \qquad (3)$$

Task transaction ttr_i is a sequence of tasks $O_i = t_1, t_2, ..., t_k$ and a relative deadline dt_i. O_i defines an ordered relation between the tasks, where in the case of $O = t_1, t_2$; t_1 is predecessor to t_2. The timing and execution order requirements of a task transaction ttr_i are deduced from the requirements of the component transactions ctr_i. The task transaction ttr_i has the same parameter as the component transactions ctr_i but $t_1, t_2,..., t_k$ are the tasks that map the component $c_a, c_b, ..., c_n$, as denoted in Fig 4. If several task transactions ttr_i span over the exact same tasks, the transactions are merged and assigned the shortest deadline. An event-triggered task may only appear first in a transaction. Two tasks can execute in an order not defined by the transactions. This depends on that the tasks have different period times, and thereby suffer from period phasing; hence transactions can not define a strict precedence relation between two tasks. Fig 3 is an execution trace that shows the relation between tasks and transactions. The tasks and transactions are the same as in Fig 4, left part.

3   Allocation Framework

The allocation framework is a set of models for calculating properties of allocations of components to tasks. The properties calculated with the framework are used for optimization algorithms to find feasible allocations that fulfil given requirements on memory consumption and CPU-overhead.

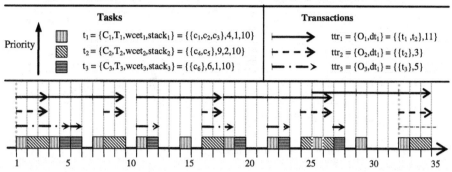

Fig. 3. Task execution order and task transactions.

For a task set A that has been mapped from components in a one-to-one fashion, it is trivial to calculate the system memory consumption and CPU-overhead since each task has the same properties as the basic component. When several components are allocated to one task we need to calculate the appropriateness of the allocation and the tasks properties. For a set of components, $c_1,...,c_n$, allocated to a set of tasks A, the following properties are considered.

- CPU-overhead p_A
- Memory consumption m_A

Each component c_i has a memory consumption stack. The stack of the task is the maximum size of all components stacks allocated to the task since all components will use the same stack. The CPU overhead p, the memory consumption m for a task set A in a system K are formalized in equations (4) and (5):

$$p_A = \sum_{\forall_i (t_i \in A)} \frac{\rho}{T_i} \tag{4}$$

$$m_A = \sum_{\forall_i (t_i \in A)} (stack_i + \tau) \tag{5}$$

Where p_A represents the sum of the task switch overhead divided by the period for all tasks is the system, and m_A represents the total amount of memory used for stacks and task control blocks for all tasks in the system

3.1 Constraints on Allocations

There is a set of constraints that must be considered when allocating components. These are:

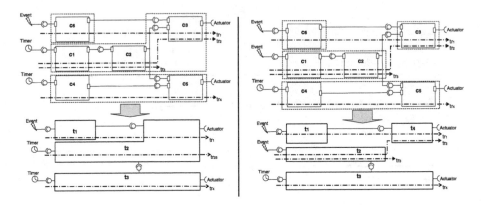

Fig. 4. Two allocations from components to tasks dependent on intersecting transactions.

- Component isolation
- Intersecting transactions
- Trigger types and period times
- Schedulability

Each constraint is further discussed below:

Isolation It is not realistic to expect that components can be allocated in an arbitrary way. There may be explicit dependencies that prohibits that certain components are allocated together, therefore the isolation set I defines which components may not be allocated together. There may be specific engineering reasons to why some components should be separated. For instance, it may be desired to minimize the jitter for some tasks, thus components with highly uncertain WCET should be isolated. There may also be integrity reasons to separate certain combinations of components. Hence it must be assured that two components that are defined to be isolated do not reside in the same task. This can be validated with equation (6):

$$Iso(a, b) : c_a \text{ has an isolation requirement to } c_b$$

$$\neg \exists_i (\forall_j \forall_k (c_j \in C_i \land c_k \in C_i \land Iso(j, k))) \tag{6}$$

Where there must not exist any task t_i that has two components c_j and c_k, if these components have an isolation requirement.

Intersecting Transactions If component transactions intersect, there are different strategies for how to allocate the component where the transactions intersect. The feasibility is described in equations 7 and 8. A component in the intersection should not be allocated with any preceding component if both transactions are event triggered; the task should be triggered by both transactions to avoid pessimistic scheduling. A component in the intersection of one time-triggered transaction and one event-triggered transaction can be allocated to a separate task, or with a preceding task in the time-triggered transaction. A component in the intersection of two time-triggered transactions can be allocated arbitrarily. In Fig 4, two different allocations are imposed due to intersecting event-triggered transactions. In the left part of Fig 4 there is an intersection between a time triggered and an event triggered transaction. Then the intersecting component c_3 is allocated to the task triggered by the time triggered transaction. In the right part of the figure, where two event triggered transactions intersect, the component c_3 is allocated to a separate task, triggered by both transactions.

$$T_E(tr) : \text{transaction is event triggered}$$
$$T_T(tr) : \text{transaction is time triggered}$$
$$P(a, b, d) : c_a \text{ is predecessor to } c_b \text{ in the set } N_d$$
$$X_a^{bc} = c_a \in N_b \wedge c_a \in N_c$$
$$Y_{ab}^{c} = c_a \in C_c \wedge c_b \in C_c$$

$$\neg \exists_i (\forall_j \forall_k \forall_l \forall_m (X_l^{jk} \wedge Y_{lm}^{i} \wedge T_E(ctr_j) \wedge T_E(ctr_k) \wedge (P(m, l, k) \vee P(m, l, j)))) \qquad (7)$$

$$\neg \exists_i (\forall_j \forall_k \forall_l \forall_m (X_l^{jk} \wedge Y_{lm}^{i} \wedge c_m \in N_k \wedge T_T(ctr_j) \wedge T_E(ctr_k) \wedge P(c_m, c_l, N_k))) \qquad (8)$$

Where there must not exist any task t_i that has two components c_l and c_m in a way that two component transactions ctr_j and ctr_k intersect in c_l, and c_m precedes c_l in the transactions ctr_j or ctr_k, if ctr_j or ctr_k are event-triggered.

Triggers Some allocations from components to tasks can be performed without impacting the schedulability negatively. A component that triggers a subsequent component can be allocated into a task if it has no other explicit dependencies, see (1) in Fig 5. Components with the same period time can be allocated together if they do not have any other explicit dependencies, see (2) in Fig 5. To facilitate analysis, a task may only have one trigger, so time triggered components with the same period can be triggered by the same trigger and thus allocated to the same task. However, event triggered components may only be allocated to the same task if they in fact trigger on the same event, and have the same minimum inter arrival time, see (3) in Fig 5. Components with harmonic periods could also be allocated to the same task. However, harmonic periods create jitter. Consider two components with the harmonic periods five and ten that are allocated to one task. The component with the period five will run every invocation, while the other component will run every second invocation, which creates a jitter; therefore we have chosen not to pursue this specific issue.

Schedulability Schedulability analysis is highly dependent on the scheduling policy chosen. Depending on the system design, different analyses approaches have to be considered. The task and task transaction meta-models are constructed to fit different scheduling analyses. In this work we have used fixed priority exact analysis. However, the model can easily be extended with jitter

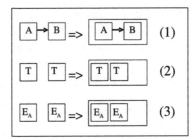

Fig. 5. Component to task allocation considering triggers.

and blocking for real-time analysis models that use those properties. The framework assigns each task a unique priority pre run-time, and it uses exact analysis for schedulability analysis, together with the Bate and Burns [21] approach for verifying that the transaction deadlines are met.

4   Using the Framework

An allocation can be performed in several different ways. In a small system all possible allocations can be evaluated and the best chosen. For a larger system, however, this is not possible due to the combinatorial explosion. Different algorithms can be used to find a feasible allocation and scheduling of tasks. For any algorithm to work there must be some way to evaluate an allocation. The proposed allocation framework can be used to calculate schedulability, CPU-overhead and total memory load. The worst-case allocation is a one-to-one allocation where every component is allocated to one task. The best-case allocation on the other hand, is where all components are allocated to one single task. To allocate all components to one task is very seldom feasible. Also, excessive allocation of components may negatively affect scheduling, because the granularity is coarsened and thereby the flexibility for the scheduler is reduced.

Simulated annealing, genetic algorithms and bin packing are well known algorithms often used for optimization problems. These algorithms have been used for problems similar to those described in this paper; bin packing, e.g., has been proposed in [22] for real-time scheduling. Here we briefly discuss how theses algorithms can be used with the described framework, to perform component to task allocations.

Bin Packing is a method well suited for our framework. In [23] a bin packing model that handles arbitrary conflicts (BPAC) is presented. The BPAC model constrains certain elements from being packed into the same bin, which directly can be used in our model as the isolation set I, and the bin-packing feasibility function is the schedulability.

Genetic algorithms can solve, roughly, any problem as long as there is some way of comparing two solutions. The framework proposed in this paper give the possibility to use the properties memory consumption, CPU-overhead and schedulability as grades for an allocation. In, e.g., [24] and [25], genetic algorithms are used for scheduling complex task sets and scheduling task sets in distributed systems.

Simulated annealing (SA) is a global optimization technique that is regularly used for solving NP-Hard problems. The energy function consists of a schedulability test, the memory consumption and CPU-overhead. In [6][26] simulated annealing is used to place tasks on nodes in distributed systems.

5   Evaluation

In order to evaluate the performance of the allocation approach the framework has been implemented. We have chosen to perform a set of allocations and compare the results to a corresponding one-to-one allocation where each component is allocated to a task. We compare the allocations with respect to if the allocation is feasible (real-time analysis), memory consumption and CPU overhead.

The implementation is based on genetic algorithms (GA) [27], and as Fig 6 shows, each gene represents a component and contains a reference to the task it is assigned. Each chromosome represents the entire system with all components assigned to tasks. Each allocation produced by the GA is evaluated by the framework, and is given a fitness value dependent on the validity of the allocation, the memory consumption and the CPU overhead.

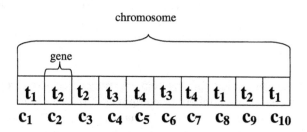

Fig. 6. The genetic algorithm view of the component to task allocation; a system with ten components, allocated to four tasks.

5.1   Fitness Function

The fitness function is based on the feasibility of the allocation together with the memory consumption and CPU overhead. The feasibility part of the fitness function is mandatory, i.e., the fitness value for a low memory and CPU overhead can never exceed the value for a feasible allocation. The feasibility function consists of: I which represents component isolation, IT representing intersecting transactions, Tr representing trigger types and period times, and finally Sc represent scheduling. Consider that each of these feasibility tests is assigned a value greater than 1 if they are true, and a value of 0 if they are false. The parameter n represents the total number of components. Then, the fitness function can be described as with equation (9).

$$Fitness = \left((I + IT + Tr + Sc)F + \left(\frac{n}{m_A} + \sum_{\forall i(t_i \in A)} \frac{\rho \cdot n}{T_i}\right)O\right) \cdot (I \cdot IT \cdot Tr \cdot Sc + 1) \quad (9)$$

Where the fitness is the sum of all feasibility values times a factor F, added with the inverted memory usage and performance overhead, times a factor O, and $F >> O$. The total fitness is multiplies with 1 if any feasibility test fail, and the products of all feasibility values plus 1 if all feasibility tests succeed.

5.2   Simulation Set Up

This section describes the simulation method and set up. For each simulation the genetic algorithm assigns components to tasks and evaluates the allocation, and incrementally finds new allocations.

The system data is produced by creating a random schedulable task set, on which all components are randomly allocated. The component properties are deduced from the task they are allocated. Transactions are deduced the same way from the task set. In this way it is always at least one solution for each system. However, it is not sure that all systems are solvable with a one-to-one allocation. The components and component transactions are used as input to the framework. Hereafter, systems that are referred to as generated systems are generated to form input to the framework. Systems that come out of the framework are referred to as allocated systems. The simulation parameters are set up as follows:

- The number of components of a system is randomly selected from a number of predefined sets. The numbers of components in the systems are ranging in twenty steps from 40 to 400, with a main point on 120 components.
- The period times for the components are randomly selected from a predefined set of different periods between 10 and 100 ms.
- The worst case execution time (WCET) is specified as a percentage of the period time and chosen from a predefined set. The WCETs together with the periods in the system constitutes the system load.
- The transaction size is the size of the generated transactions in percentage of the number of components in the system. The transaction size is randomly chosen from a predefined set. The longer the transactions, the more constraints, regarding schedulability, on how components may be allocated.
- The transaction deadline laxity is the percentage of the lowest possible transaction deadline for the generated system. The transaction deadline laxity is evenly distributed among all generated systems and is always greater or equal to one, to guarantee that the generated system is possible to map. The higher the laxity, the less constrained transaction deadlines.

One component can be involved in more than one transaction, resulting in more constraints in terms of timing. The probability that a component is participating in two transactions is set to 50% for all systems.

To get as realistic systems to simulate as possible, the values used to generate systems are gathered from some of our industrial partners. The industrial partners chosen are active within the vehicular embedded system segment. A complete table with all values and distributions, of the system generation values, can be found in [13]. The task switch time used for the system is 22 μs, and the tcb size is 300 bytes. The task switch time and tcb size are representative of commercial RTOS tcb sizes and context switch times for common CPUs.

The simulations are performed for four different utilization levels, 30%, 50%, 70% and 90%. For each level of utilization 1000 different systems are generated with the parameters presented above.

5.3   Results

A series of simulations have been carried out to evaluate the performance of the proposed framework. To evaluate the schedulability of the systems, FPS scheduling analysis is used. The priorities are randomly assigned by the genetic algorithm, and no two tasks have the same priority. We compare the allocation approach described in this paper to one-to-one allocations. Table 1 summarizes the results from the simulations. The columns entitled "stack" and "CPU" displays the average memory size (stack + tcb) and CPU overhead respectively, for all systems with a specific load and transaction deadline laxity. The column entitled "success" in the 1-1 allocation section displays the rate of systems that are solvable with the 1-1 allocation. The column entitled "success" in the GA allocation section displays the rate at which our framework finds allocations, since all systems has at least one solution. The stack and CPU values are only collected from systems where a solution was found.

The first graph for the simulations (Fig 7) shows the success ratio, i.e., the percentage of systems that were possible to map with the one-to-one allocation, and the GA allocation respectively. The success ratio is relative to the effort of the GA, and is expected to increase with a higher number of generations for each system. Something that might seem confusing is that the success ratio is lower for low utilization than for high utilizations, even though, intuitively, it should be the opposite. The explanation to this phenomenon is that the timing constraints become tighter as fewer tasks participate in each transaction (lower utilization often leads to fewer tasks). With fewer tasks the task phasing, due to different periods, will be lower, and the deadline can be set tighter.

The second graph (Fig 8) shows that the deadlines are relaxed with higher utilization, since the allocations with relaxed deadlines perform well, and the systems with a more constrained deadline show a clear improvement with higher utilization.

The third graph (Fig 9) shows for both approaches the average stack size for the systems at different utilization. The comparison is only amongst allocations that are have been successfully mapped by both strategies. The memory size

Load	Laxity	1-1 allocation			GA allocation		
		Stack	CPU	success	stack	CPU	success
30%	*All*	*28882*	*4,1%*	*74%*	*17380*	*2,0%*	*87%*
	1.1	25949	3,5%	39%	14970	1,6%	58%
	1.3	33077	4,4%	78%	21005	2,2%	97%
	1.5	26755	4,1%	95%	15503	2,0%	99%
50%	*All*	*37277*	*4,8%*	*82%*	*24297*	*2,4%*	*90%*
	1.1	35391	4,3%	49%	23146	2,3%	64%
	1.3	38251	4,8%	88%	25350	2,5%	96%
	1.5	37043	4,9%	98%	23740	2,3%	100%
70%	*All*	*44455*	*5,1%*	*85%*	*30694*	*2,7%*	*91%*
	1.1	44226	5,0%	58%	31638	2,7%	73%
	1.3	44267	5,1%	94%	30686	2,7%	98%
	1.5	44619	5,2%	98%	30232	2,6%	100%
90%	*All*	*46943*	*5,6%*	*87%*	*37733*	*3,1%*	*93%*
	1.1	54858	5,7%	65%	41207	3,4%	80%
	1.3	49607	5,5%	92%	35470	3,0%	98%
	1.5	53535	5,7%	98%	38260	3,1%	99%

Table 1. Memory, CPU overhead and success ratio for 1-1 and GA allocations

consists of the tcb and the stack size, and the tcb size is 300 bytes. As described earlier, each task allocates a stack that is equal to the size of the largest stack among its allocated components.

The fourth graph (Fig 10) shows the average task switch time in micro seconds for the entire system. The task switch overhead is only dependent on how many tasks there are in the system. The average improvement of GA allocation in comparison to the 1-1 allocation is, for the success ratio, 10%. The memory size is reduced by 32%, and the task switch overhead is reduced by 48%. Hence we can see a substantial improvement in using smart methods to map components to tasks. A better strategy for setting priorities would probably lead to an improvement in the success ratio. Further we observe that lower utilization admits larger improvements than higher laxity of the deadlines; and since lower utilization in the simulations often gives tighter deadlines, we can conclude that the allocation does not negatively impact schedulability. However, regarding the improvements, the more components the more constrains are put on each transaction, and thereby on the components, making it harder to perform *good* allocations.

6   Conclusions and Future Work

Resource efficiency is important for RTS, both regarding performance and memory. Schedulability, considering resource efficiency, has gained much focus, however the allocation between components to tasks has gained very little focus. Hence, in this paper we have described an allocation framework for allocating

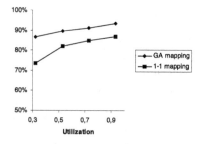

Fig. 7. Average success ratio

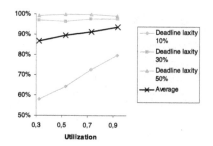

Fig. 8. Success rate for allocations

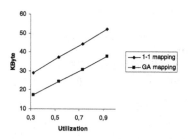

Fig. 9. Average memory size

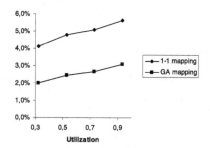

Fig. 10. Average task switch over-head

components to tasks, to facilitate existing scheduling and optimization algorithms such as genetic algorithms, bin packing and simulated annealing. The framework is designed to be used during compile-time to minimize resource usage and maximize timeliness. It can also be used iteratively in case of design changes; however with some obvious drawbacks on the results. The framework can easily be extended to support other optimizations, besides task switch overhead and memory consumption. Results from simulations show that the framework gives substantial improvements both in terms of memory consumption and task switch overhead. The described framework also has a high ratio in finding feasible allocations. Moreover, in comparison to allocations performed with a one-to-one allocation our framework performs very well, with 32% reduced memory size and 48% reduced task switch overhead. The simulations show that the proposed framework performs allocations on systems of a size that covers many embedded systems, and in a reasonable time for an off-line tool. We have also shown how CPU load and deadline laxity affects the allocation. Future work includes adding other allocation criteria, e.g., by looking at jitter requirements, and blocking. By adding jitter constraints and blocking, trade-offs arise between switch overhead and memory size versus deviation from nominal start and end times and blocking times. Furthermore, a more efficient scheduling policy and priority assignment will be applied. Due to the nature of GA it is easy to add new optimizations as the ones suggested above.

References

[1] Mills., K., Gomaa, H.: Knowledge-based automation of a design method for concurrent systems. IEEE Transactions on Software Engineering **28** (2002)

[2] Crnkovic, I.: Component-based approach for embedded systems. In: Ninth International Workshop on Component-Oriented Programming, Oslo. (2004)

[3] Bondarev, E., Muskens, J., de With, P., Chaudron, M., Lukkien, J.: Predicting real-time properties of component assemblies: a scenario-simulation approach. In: Proceedings of the 30th Euromicro conference, Rennes, France, IEEE (2004)

[4] Bondarev, E., Muskens, J., de With, P., Chaudron, M.: Towards predicting real-time properties of a component assembly. In: Proceedings of the 30th Euromicro conference, Rennes, France, IEEE (2004)

[5] Hou., C., Shin, K.G.: Allocation of periodic task modules with precedence and deadline constraints in distributed real-time system. IEEE Transactions on Computers **46** (1995)

[6] Tindell, K., Burns, A., Wellings, A.: Allocating hard real-time tasks (an np-hard problem made easy). Real-Time Systems **4** (1992)

[7] Douglas, B.P.: Doing Hard Time. 0201498375. Addison Wesely (1999)

[8] Gomaa, H.: Designing Concurrent Distributed, and Real-Time Applications with UML. 0-201-65793-7. Addison Wesely (2000)

[9] Kodase, S., Wang, S., Shin, K.G.: Transforming structural model to runtime model of embedded software with real-time constraints. In: In proceeding of Design, Automation and Test in Europe Conference and Exhibition, IEEE (1995) 170–175

[10] Shin, K.G., Wang, S.: An architecture for embedded software integration using reusable components. In: proceeding of the international conference on Compilers, architectures, and synthesis for embedded systems, San Jose, California, United States, IEEE (2000) 110–118

[11] Gai, P., Lippari, G., Natale, M.D.: Minimizing memory utilization of real-time task sets in single and multi-processor systems-on-a-chip. In: Proceedings of the Real-Time Systems Symposium, London (UK) Dec, IEEE (2001)

[12] Shin, K.G., Lee, I., Sang, M.: Embedded system design framework for minimizing code size and guaranteeing real-time requirements. In: Proceedings of the 23rd IEEE Real-Time Systems Symposium, RTSS 2002, Austin, TX, December 2-5, IEEE (2002)

[13] Fredriksson, J., Sandström, K., Åkerholm, M.: Optimizing resource usage in component-based real-time systems - appendix. Technical report, Technical Report, Mälardalen Real-Time Research Centre, Västerås, Sweden (2005) http://www.mrtc.mdh.se/publications/0836.pdf.

[14] Sandström, K., Fredriksson, J., Åkerholm, M.: Introducing a component technology for safety critical embedded real-time systems. In: Proceeding of CBSE7 International Symposium on Component-based Software Engi-neering, IEEE (2004)

[15] Hansson, H., M.Åkerholm, Crnkovic, I., Törngren, M.: Saveccm - a component model for safety-critical real-time systems. In: Euromicro Conference, Special Session Component Models for Dependable Systems Rennes, France, EEE (2004)

[16] Arcticus: Arcticus homepage: http://www.arcticus.se (2005)

[17] van Ommering, R., van der Linden, F., Kramer, J.: The koala component model for consumer electronics software. In: IEEE Computer, IEEE (2000) 78–85

[18] Stewart, D.B., Volpe, R.A., Khosla, P.K.: Design of dynamically reconfigurable real-time software using port-based objects. In: IEEE Transactions on Software Engineering, IEEE (1997) 759–776

[19] IEC: International standard IEC 1131: Programmable controllers (1992)
[20] Mathworks: Mathworks homepage : http://www.mathworks.com (2005)
[21] Bate, A., Burns, I.: An approach to task attribute assignment for uniprocessor systems. In: Proceedings of the 11th Euromicro Workshop on Real Time Systems, York, England, IEEE (1999)
[22] Oh, Y., Son, S.H.: On constrained bin-packing problem. Technical report, Technical Report, CS-95-14, Univeristy of Virginia (1995)
[23] Jansen, K., R, O.S.: Approximation algorithms for time constrained scheduling. In: proceeding of Workshop on Parallel Algorithms and Irregularly Structured Problems, IEEE (1995) 143–157
[24] Monnier, Y., Beauvis, J.P., Deplanche, J.M.: A genetic algorithm for scheduling tasks in a real-time distributed system. In: Proceeding of 24th Euromicro Conference, IEEE (1998) 708–714
[25] Montana, D., Brinn, M., Moore, S., Bidwell, G.: Genetic algorithms for complex, real-time scheduling. In: Proceeding of IEEE International Conference on Systems, Man, and Cybernetics, IEEE (1998) 2213–2218
[26] Cheng., S.T., K., A.A.: Allocation and scheduling of real-time periodic tasks with relative timing constraints. In: Second International Workshop on Real-Time Computing Systems and Applications (RTCSA), IEEE (1995)
[27] Fonseca., C.M., Flemming, P.J.: An overview of evolutionary algorithms in multiobjective optimization. Evolutionary computation **3** (1995)

Evaluating Performance Attributes of Layered Software Architecture

Vibhu Saujanya Sharma[1], Pankaj Jalote[1], Kishor S. Trivedi[2]

[1] Department of Computer Science and Engineering, Indian Institute of Technology Kanpur,
Kanpur, INDIA, 208016
{Vsharma, Jalote}@cse.iitk.ac.in
[2] Department of Electrical and Computer Engineering, Duke University,
Durham, NC 27708, USA
Kst@ee.duke.edu

Abstract. The architecture of a software system is the highest level of abstraction whereupon useful analysis of system properties is possible. Hence, performance analysis at this level can be useful for assessing whether a proposed architecture can meet the desired performance specifications and can help in making key architectural decisions. In this paper we propose an approach for performance evaluation of software systems following the layered architecture, which is a common architectural style for building software systems. Our approach initially models the system as a Discrete Time Markov Chain, and extracts parameters for constructing a closed Product Form Queueing Network model that is solved using the SHARPE software package. Our approach predicts the throughput and the average response time of the system under varying workloads and also identifies bottlenecks in the system, suggesting possibilities for their removal.

1 Introduction

Software architecture is an important phase in software lifecycle as it allows taking early design decisions about a system. Moreover it is also the earliest point in system development at which the system to be built could be analyzed [7], [9]. Analysis of a system at the architectural level enables the choice of the right architecture for the system under consideration, thus saving major potential modifications later in the development cycle or tuning the system after deployment.

Out of the various attributes that could be assessed, performance attributes are most sought after in any software system. Performance is an umbrella term describing various aspects, such as responsiveness, throughput, etc. of the system. Assessing and optimizing these aspects is essential for the smooth and efficient operation of the software system. There have been many approaches [2],[3],[4],[5],[12] for performance evaluation of software systems, the pioneering work being done by C.U. Smith, [2] which introduced the concept of Software Performance Engineering (SPE).

Layered software architecture is a very prevalent software architectural style that is followed by almost all client-server and web based systems. Layered architecture

G.T. Heineman et al. (Eds.): CBSE 2005, LNCS 3489, pp. 66–81, 2005.

helps to structure applications that can be decomposed into n groups of subtasks in which each group is at a particular level of abstraction with well-defined interfaces [8]. The ith layer could communicate with only the $(i-1)^{th}$ and the $(i+1)^{th}$ layer. Layered architecture is widely used in almost all web-based systems where performance is a critical factor. Hence, performance analysis of layered systems is of much importance to system architects. Moreover as a large number of layered systems already exist, performance predictions with varying number of clients or with the addition or scaling up of components in the system would be beneficial to system administrators, who manage such systems.

In this paper, we present an approach for performance evaluation of software systems following the layered architectural style. In the past SPE has been largely seen as an activity, which requires specialized skills and in-depth knowledge of both software architecture and performance modeling. Thus one of the motivating factors of our effort is to provide an approach that could be used by software engineers for designing new systems and system administrators for tweaking existing systems alike. The aim of the approach is to output the traditional performance parameters as well as suggest to the user bottleneck components that need to be scaled up. Our system thus removes the performance analyst from the loop in that the activities traditionally performed by him/her are automated.

Our approach consists of modeling the layered software system as a closed Product Form Queueing Network (PFQN) [1], and then solving it for finding performance attributes of the system. One of our aims is to ask for specifications that are easy to provide even for someone who is not an expert in this field. After getting the specifications we model the system initially as a Discrete Time Markov Chain (DTMC), with each layer in the system, corresponding to a state in the DTMC [13]. This DTMC is then analyzed to find the total service requirements of the software system over the different hardware nodes or machines. The closed PFQN model is then constructed using this information along with the specifications given by the user. Modeling machines having limited software resources such as threads is also performed at this stage using a hierarchical approach.

This closed PFQN model is then fed to SHARPE [11] which is a versatile software package for analyzing performance, reliability and performability models. The output from SHARPE is then further analyzed, and the results include the classical performance metrics such as the throughput and the average response time along with information about system bottlenecks and suggested scale-ups for them. Along with these, it predicts the improvement in system performance if the suggested scale-ups are done. This is done by reconstructing the model internally, accommodating the scaled-up components and solving it again, using our approach.

The tool, which we have developed as an implementation of this approach, requires minimal knowledge of queueing models or any other performance modeling techniques to use it. The specifications which are needed could be easily procured and hence the tool facilitates modeling new systems as well as helping in scaling existing systems.

2   Evaluating Performance of Software Architectures

System performance has become a major concern, as large, complex, mission critical and real time software systems proliferate in almost all domains. The inherent structural relationships among the components characterize the architecture that software system is following and usually could be classified into some well-known architectural styles [7], [8]. Since the performance attributes of a software system, such as number of jobs serviced per second (throughput), the average response time, etc. depend both on the time and resources spent in computation as well as in the communication between various components of the system, the architecture that a particular system follows has a lot of bearing on its performance. This forms the basis for the need of evaluating various software architectures for their performance attributes. In practice there are many questions that a performance assessment approach should answer. Some of the prominent ones are:

- What effect would varying the number of clients have on the throughput and the average response time of a particular system, if a particular architecture is followed?
- What would be the ideal number of clients the system would be able to handle before it saturates?
- Which software component should be allocated to which hardware node?
- What would be the bottlenecks in the system and how could they be removed?
- What would be the change in the performance attributes if a system component is enhanced or scaled up?

In the recent past there have been some efforts towards answering such questions and concerns regarding software architectures. A methodological approach for evaluation of software architectures for performance was first proposed by C.U. Smith in her pioneering work [2] and later with L.G. Williams [10] and is called Software Performance Engineering (SPE). Two models represent the system in SPE: the software execution model and the system execution model. The software execution model is specified using Execution Graphs (EGs), which have nodes representing the components and arcs representing transitions. The system execution model is basically a queueing network model, which relies on workload parameters derived from EGs.

Following the SPE approach, Petriu and Wang have used UML activity diagrams for the software execution model, and UML collaboration diagrams for the system execution model [3]. The latter is modeled as a Layered Queueing Network (LQN) which differs from Queueing Network (QN) models in that servers can become clients of other servers in the model. An LQN model is represented as an acyclic graph whose nodes are software entities and hardware devices and whose arcs denote software requests. Menasc´e and Gomaa proposed a proprietary language called CLISSPE (Client/Server Software Performance Evaluation) [5] for the performance assessment of client server systems. The specifications in CLISSPE are fed to a compiler which generates the QN model which is then solved using a performance model solver. Some authors have also followed a Stochastic Petri Net based approach [4] for modeling the systems.

Our approach follows the basic SPE methodology with a focus on layered software architecture. We represent the software model in terms of a DTMC which is then transformed into a closed PFQN model. However, the QN model we propose to use also models software resource constraints such as limited number of threads at a particular machine. This allows for a model which is closely related to the real system and its constraints. As the architecture to be analyzed has been fixed to layered, specifying the software system becomes relatively simple, unlike in other approaches that follow some proprietary languages. This was also one of the aims we set forth while developing this approach. We also allow analysis of the software model on different hardware architectures, by letting the user specify the rating factor of the hardware under consideration, as compared to the one in which the resource demands of the components were specified for the specific architecture.

The inherent simplicity of specification makes our model feasible to be used in practice more effortlessly and even by those with relatively little knowledge of performance analysis techniques. Moreover the close modeling of real systems by our QN model, and the results we provide to the user, including the suggested bottleneck scale-ups and predicted performance improvements for the same, make our approach well suited to be used for large layered systems with real world constraints. We present the details of our approach in the following sections.

3   System Model and Assumptions

Our approach assumes that the computer system under consideration is an interactive system, wherein the system gives responses to the inputs given by the users. Further this interactive system follows the layered software architecture, with each layer interacting only with the adjacent layers. The user interacts with the first layer, which passes the request, if needed, to the second layer, which may pass it to the next layer, and so on. The last layer sends its response back, which then traverses through the layers, till the user gets the output. In general a layered software system could be visualized as in Figure 1.

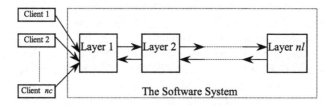

Fig. 1. The layered software architecture.

Note that different software components which constitute different layers, could be allocated to different (hardware) machines or some of them could be collocated on the same machine also. A layer acts as a functional unit providing some well defined services through appropriate interfaces and some computation and some I/O is done as the control passes through each software layer. The computation and I/O may be intermixed and done repeatedly till the layer has completed its task. It then either returns the result, or passes the request to the next layer either on the same machine or on a different machine as the case may be. There might also be limitations on how many concurrent pending requests can exist for computation on a machine (which frequently is the case when the software server or the operating system of the hardware node, limits the number of threads or available connections.) We assume that a software component runs on only one machine at a time, i.e., there is no concurrency within a software component. However, several layers could be allocated to run on a single machine.

To analyze the performance of this architecture, we need to specify the average CPU time for a request in each layer and the average I/O time, which we call the Disk time in our model. Note that even though in a layer, the CPU work and I/O may be intermixed, for modeling purposes, they can be assumed to occur in an aggregate fashion, i.e., first all the CPU processing and then all the I/O processing. This combination does not affect the performance analysis and is based on the known insensitivity result of the product form solution of closed networks [1]. The allocation or deployment of the layers on different hardware nodes is also very important and is taken as a part of the specifications. The tool could be used to aid in choosing different allocations by comparing them.

In addition, we need to model the impact of connectors between the layers that are allocated on different machines. We capture this by the size of the request, the capacity of the connector, and the probability with which a request is sent by one layer to another layer. To model the load on the system, we require the range of the number of clients that the system might be subjected to. In addition, an estimate of the number of requests generated per unit time by each client is also needed. Overall, the following properties about the architecture are needed:

- The range of the number of clients [$ncmin$, $ncmax$] accessing the system and the average think time of each client ttc.
- The total number of layers in the software system nl.
- The relationship between the machines and the software components, i.e., which software layer is located to which machine and the number of machines. Thus corresponding to each machine j, we have a set $L(j)$ containing indices of the layers residing on j, $0<j\leq nm$ and nm is the number of machines.
- The number of CPUs and disks on each of these machines and thread limitations if any, or $nCPU(i)$, $ndisk(i)$ and $tlim(i)$.
- The uplink and downlink capacities of the connectors connecting machines running adjacent layers of the system and the size of the packets going on these links or $capup(i)$, $capdn(i)$, $psizup(i)$ and $psizdn(i)$ where $0<i\leq nm$. Note that $capup(1)$ and $capdn(1)$ are the *total* uplink and downlink capacities respectively, of the connector(s) joining all the client to the machines.
- The service time required to service one request by a software layer given that it is using a standard CPU and a standard Disk for the purpose or $CPU(i)$ and $disk(i)$ where $0<i\leq nm$.
- Forward transition probabilities $p_{x(x+1)}$, i.e., the probability that a request being serviced by layer x would need the service of layer $(x + 1)$ next.

- The rating factors fcj and fdj of the CPU and Disks respectively of each machine, which are present in the system, with respect to a standard CPU and Disk as considered above in 6.

4 Analyzing Performance

For analyzing the performance of a layered software system, we follow these main steps, which are discussed in detail in the ensuing sections:
- Constructing the DTMC model.
- Determining the queuing network model parameters.
- Modeling thread limitations.
- Queuing model solution and outputs.

4.1 Constructing the DTMC Model

We model the software system following layered architecture using a DTMC [13]. The state of the application at any time is given by the component or layer in execution at that time. Moreover, transitions between states represent transfer of control from one layer to the other. Assume that the DTMC to be analyzed has k states. Then the DTMC is characterized by a k by k transition probability matrix $\mathbf{P} = [p_{ij}]$. All elements of a row in $\mathbf{P}$ add up to one and $0 \leq p_{ij} \leq 1$. We can calculate the expected total number of visits to a state j starting from state 1, V_j [1] by $V_j = \sum V_i p_{ij} + q_j$ where, q_j is the probability of starting in state j. Thus visit counts to a particular state could be obtained by solving a system of (n-1) linear equations. We can model a layered software system with nl layers as shown in the Figure 1 using a DTMC with $2nl+2$ states as shown in Figure 2.

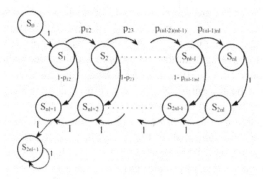

Fig. 2. The DTMC model for a layered software system.

The transition from state S_0 to S_1 represents a client sending request to the first layer with probability 1. The completion of a request's service by the layered system is denoted by a transition to state S_{2nl+1}, which is an absorbing state. Note that as the system is layered in nature, only transitions between adjacent layers are possible.

There is no incoming edge to S_0, which is the initial state, and no outgoing edge from S_{2nl+1}, which is the absorbing state. The states S_i and S_{nl+i} ($0 < i \le nl$) represent control flow arriving to layer i in the forward and return paths of the request respectively. In the forward path, upon receiving service at layer i, the request can proceed further to the next layer with probability $p_{i(i+1)}$, or may return with the probability $(1-p_{i(i+1)})$. Also note that we have:

$$0 \le p_{i(i+1)} \le 1 \qquad\qquad 0 \le i < nl$$

4.2 Determining Model Parameters

The layer to layer transition probabilities provided by the user and shown in Figure 2 can also be seen as a $(2nl+2)$ by $(2nl+2)$ transition probability matrix of a DTMC with $(2nl+2)$ states given by:

$$P = \begin{bmatrix}
0 & 1 & 0 & 0 & 0 & \cdots & 0 & 0 & 0 & \cdots & 0 \\
0 & 0 & p_{12} & 0 & 0 & \cdots & 1-p_{12} & 0 & 0 & \cdots & 0 \\
0 & 0 & 0 & p_{23} & 0 & \cdots & 0 & 1-p_{23} & 0 & \cdots & 0 \\
 & & \vdots & & & & & & & & \\
0 & 0 & 0 & 0 & 0 & \cdots & 0 & 0 & 0 & \cdots & 1 \\
0 & 0 & 0 & 0 & 0 & \cdots & 1 & 0 & 0 & \cdots & 0 \\
0 & 0 & 0 & 0 & 0 & \cdots & 0 & 1 & 0 & \cdots & 0 \\
 & & \vdots & & & & & & & & \\
0 & 0 & 0 & 0 & 0 & \cdots & 0 & 0 & 0 & \cdots & 1
\end{bmatrix}$$

As mentioned in Section 4.1, we could calculate the visit counts to each of the states $V(i)$, by solving the set of linear equations given in the previous section. If we assume that between each pair of layers an imaginary connector is present, then assuming the connectors to be bi-directional, the number of visits to this connector in the forward and the backward direction would be same as each request going forward will eventually return. For any layer i in the system, the fraction of all the arriving requests that proceed to the next layer is the same as $p_{i(i+1)}$ in the DTMC as shown in Figure 2. Hence, the average number of visits to a uplink connector i, joining layer i, to layer $(i+1)$, is given by $V(i)p_{i(i+1)}$. The backward or return visits to the (downlink) connector will also be the same. Hence, we could calculate the total visits to these imaginary connectors joining the layers.

However, note that not all of these imaginary connectors are present in the actual system. The chosen allocation of software layers on different machines determines the connectors that are present between layers, which lie on adjacent machines. Only these are the connectors that physically exist and need to be considered in the queueing model. Hence, we can get the visit count to the uplink and downlink connectors respectively between machines j-1 and j as $Vconup(j)$ and $Vcondn(j)$. Once the visit counts for the different layers and the connectors are calculated, the next step is to find the total service requirements on the actual CPUs and Disks on the machines as well as for the connectors that join these machines. For any machine j $(0 < j \le nm)$ we have the total CPU and Disk service requirements given by

$$tmcpu(j) = f_{cj} \sum_{i \in L(j)} V(i) \times cpu(i)$$

$$tmcdisk(j) = f_{dj} \sum_{i \in L(j)} V(i) \times disk(i)$$

The above equation simply states that the total CPU or Disk service requirement at a particular machine is given by the sum of individual CPU or Disk service requirements of all the layers present on that machine, multiplied by the rating factor of that hardware device. For the connector j with uplink and downlink capacities $capup(j)$ and $capdn(j)$ respectively, we can compute the average delays caused due to each request as:

$$delayup(j) = psizeup(j) \div capup(j)$$

$$delaydn(j) = psizedn(j) \div capdn(j)$$

where, $psizeup(j)$ and $psizedn(j)$ are the uplink and downlink average packet sizes on the connectors. Each time the connector is visited, the above delays occur depending upon whether the request is going from a lower indexed machine to a higher indexed machine or vice versa. So the total average service requirement at connector j would be given by:

$$tconup \ (j) = Vconup(j) \ \cdot delayup \ (j)$$

$$tcondn \ (j) = Vcondn(j) \ \cdot delaydn \ (j)$$

The performance model that we generate is a closed product form queueing network wherein queueing stations represent the connectors, CPUs and Disks. This is shown in Figure 3. The clients are modeled by an Infinite Server (IS) [11] which allows a new request to be generated after an average of ttc seconds of the completion of the previous request. The total number of jobs in the closed PFQN is kept same as the number of clients.

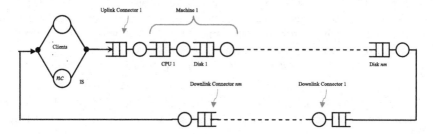

Fig. 3. The closed PFQN model of the system.

The connectors are modeled as FCFS stations [11] with rate as the reciprocal of the total average service requirements at that connector. The CPU for a machine is modeled by an FCFS station with CPU service rate for that machine. However, if there is more than one CPU present at a single machine, these are modeled as a multiple-server (MS) [11], with each server in MS having the rate as the CPU service rate for that machine. Thread limited systems are discussed in detail in the next section. The disk is modeled by an FCFS station with service rate same as the reciprocal of the total average disk service requirement at that machine. If there is more than one disk present at the machine, then all these disks are modeled as separate FCFS stations with equal probability of transition from the CPU to each of the disks. These are not modeled as a multi-server (unlike the case of CPUs), as a request would not go to just any free disk, but is targeted to some specific data, on a particular disk.

4.3 Modeling Thread Limited Systems

In real systems there exist machines that have some software resources such as number of available threads in limited quantity. So there is an upper limit on the number of jobs that a particular machine can handle. We can visualize this as in Figure 4.

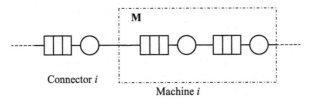

Fig. 4. Limited threads on a machine.

Here M is the upper limit on the number of jobs in that machine. We use a hierarchical combination of models so in the upper level model, the dotted box is represented a flow equivalent server. The lower level is modeled as a closed form PFQN. This is done by converting the subset of the model, which is shown inside the dotted region, to an equivalent closed PFQN. The rate of the flow equivalent server then equals the throughput $E[T(n)]$ of this inner PFQN, which is directly proportional to the utilization of the same[1]. The flow equivalent server should continue to serve jobs only until limit M and till this point its rate keeps on increasing. However, after this point the rate no longer increases with increase in the number of jobs, and the jobs have to wait before getting into this inner PFQN or equivalently this thread limited server. So the rate of the flow equivalent server is given by:

$$flrate(n) \quad = E[T(n)] \quad if \ n \leq M$$
$$= E[T(M)] \quad if \ n > M$$

Such hierarchical models are easily specified and solved by SHARPE. Note that the flow equivalent server is represented as a load dependent server (LDS) in SHARPE.

4.4 Model Solution and Outputs

The performance model would consist of an upper level PFQN and if flow equivalent servers are present, some lower level (inner) PFQNs along with output statements. This has to be fed to SHARPE for getting the throughput of the whole system for the range of clients specified by the user. Other measures such as the average response times, saturation number and bottlenecks would be found using the throughput along with the specifications provided by the user.

In case of thread limited servers present in the system, each of those will have a separate PFQN representing the flow equivalent server, and the corresponding LDS will be present in the top level PFQN. So in general the SHARPE input file will have the specifications of each of the inner PFQNs, if any, followed by the function that calculates their service rates, and the specification of the top level PFQN, followed by the output section. The model is fed to the SHARPE engine, which analyzes it and predicts the throughput of the whole system. The average throughput at each of the servers in the model for different number of clients is also calculated. This is required as unlike the FCFS or MS, the total service requirements per visit at the LDS change with varying number of clients in the system. This in turn affects the bottleneck analysis as is explained in the next section.

As part of the outputs, the approach provides for the throughput and the average response times of the whole system for the range of clients mentioned by the user. The approach also provides the saturation number of the system, which is the number of clients beyond which the system starts to saturate, i.e., the servers in the system start getting busy almost at all times and server utilization (the probability of finding a server busy) reaches unity. In practice the system should be running with the number of clients below the saturation number. Along with these it provides the bottleneck analysis as explained in section 5.

5   Bottleneck Analysis

One important part of our analysis is bottleneck analysis of the whole system. The bottleneck node of the system is defined as the one at which the total service requirement is the largest or the relative utilization (the probability of finding a server busy) is the highest. Hence in a closed PFQN, bottleneck nodes can be found out even before solving the queueing network model, by comparing the total service demands on the various nodes. However, if there is a thread limited server in the network, the total service requirements at this node is dependent upon the instantaneous number of jobs on that server (hence the name load dependent servers). Thus in such networks, we need the throughput values for the lower level closed PFQN for calculating the total service requirements at that node for varying number of clients from the SHARPE engine.

Bottleneck nodes are the ones, which are most busy (or have high relative utilizations), and most jobs will tend to queue up at these servers. They will cease to be the bottleneck if they are scaled up so that they no longer have the highest total service requirements (or the highest relative utilization). We provide information about the first as well as the second bottleneck(s) in the system. In general one can determine the minimum scaling up factor $Scale(k)$ of the kth bottleneck by the formula:

$$Scale(k) = \frac{\text{Avg. service requirements per job of } bottleneck(k)}{\text{Avg. service requirements per job of } bottleneck(k-1)}$$

One thing to be noted is that the bottleneck(s) of the system might change with the number of clients in the system. This is so, because the average service demands and hence the average service times per job of the thread limited servers are load dependent and would change with the number of clients in the system. Hence, we give the bottlenecks for the whole range of the clients as mentioned by the user.

Bottleneck information is then used to analyze the effect of scaling the bottleneck server up, on the average throughput and average response time of the whole system. This is done by iterating once again through the performance model generation phase with the bottleneck node's service rate scaled up by the suggested value, and then feeding the model to SHARPE and analyzing throughput again. Thus one can get the percentage change in system performance for the suggested scale up, and decide if the scale up is worthwhile for the system. Bottleneck analysis gives the user a good idea of the amount of improvement in system performance if he/she chooses to put in effort in scaling up / improving the bottleneck of the system.

6   An Example

We have implemented our approach as a web based tool, which automates our approach. The implementation of the tool was partially done as an undergraduate project [14], and was extended later on. The tool completely automates the task of performance analysis of layered software systems. This web tool is based on cgi scripting and renders html forms for the user to fill in the specifications of the layered system under consideration. The tool then uses the specifications and constructs a DTMC internally, representing the software system, calculates the service requirements and generates a SHARPE input file, which has the system model as a closed PFQN. This is then fed to SHARPE, which works as our model solver and backend. The results from SHARPE are further analyzed, for bottlenecks. The scale up for the primary bottleneck in the system is found and the QN model is reconstructed and again fed to SHARPE to get the new performance attribute values.

Consider an example of a 4-layered software architecture. Suppose that the current plan is to have these 4 layers run on 3 machines, with layer 1 running on machine 1, layer 2 on machine 2, and layers 3 and 4 on machine 3. Further assume that there is a limit of 25 threads on machine 2. In the baseline hardware configuration that we are planning for be that each machine has 2 CPUs and machines 1 and 2 have 1 Disk each, while machine 3 has 4 disks available. The data about the software architecture and the hardware that is being planned is summarized in Table 1.

Table 1. Example software and hardware specifications.

Number of Layers	4	Number of Machines	3
Layer 1 runs on Mc	1	Layer 2 runs on Mc	2
Layer 3 runs on Mc	3	Layer 3 runs on Mc	3
No. of CPUs on Mc 1	2	Thread Limit on Mc 1	No
No. of CPUs on Mc 2	2	Thread Limit on Mc 2	25
No. of CPUs on Mc 3	2	Thread Limit on Mc 3	No
No. of Disks on Mc 1	1	No. of Disks on Mc 2	1
No. of Disks on Mc 3	4		
Total capacity of connector joining Clients and Mc 1 Uplink/Downlink	56/512 Kbps	Capacity of connector joining Mc 1 and Mc 2 Uplink/Downlink	1/1 Mbps
Capacity of connector joining Mc 2 and Mc 1 Uplink/Downlink	1/1 Mbps	Capacity of connector joining Mc 2 and Mc 3 Uplink/Downlink	1/1 Mbps

Now we have to provide the system execution behavior estimates. We have taken the parameters resembling those, which might characterize a distributed transaction processing system following a 4 layered architecture. We take an example of an ADSL connection between the clients and the system as is evident from the asymmetry in the uplink and downlink capacities of the link joining clients to machine 1. Further, assume that the client request does much of its CPU processing in layers 2 and 3 and does most of its I/O operations in layer 4. Also, assume that 60% of all requests coming to layer 1 need to go to higher layers for service and similarly 90 % and 100 % of the requests which reach layer 2 and 3 respectively require service from higher layers. The values of the relevant parameters are as in Table 2.

Table 2. Example system execution behavior estimates.

Data packet sizes: (in bytes)			
From Client to Mc 1	250	from Mc 1 back to Clients	2000
From Mc 1 to Mc 2	250	From Mc 2 back to Mc 1	1000
From Mc 2 to Mc 3	250	From Mc 3 back to Mc 2	1000
Times per visit: (in secs)			
CPU time/visit of Layer 1	0.01	CPU time/visit of Layer 2	0.03
CPU time/visit of Layer 3	0.06	CPU time/visit of Layer 4	0.01
Disk time/visit of Layer 1	0.02	Disk time/visit of Layer 2	0.02
Disk time/visit of Layer 3	0.002	Disk time/visit of Layer 4	0.20
Probability of request flow from:			
Layer 1 to higher Layers	0.60	Layer 2 to higher Layers	0.90
Layer 3 to higher Layers	1.00		

Suppose we specify to the tool that we want to estimate the performance of this system for 1 to 75 clients, each client having an average think time of 1 sec and the rating factor for all the devices as unity. The tool does the analysis and gives the output as in Figure 5 and 6.

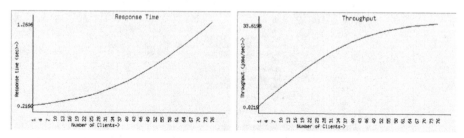

Fig. 5. Analysis output: The average response time and throughput graphs.

From Figure 5, we can see that the model suggests that the average response time is quite low initially, but then after around 8 clients the average response times starts to increase very fast. Similarly if we study the throughput graph, this shows the throughput constantly increasing with the number of clients initially, but then almost becoming constant if the number of clients is increased further, the maximum throughput of the system being about 34 jobs/sec. These two observations are due to the same phenomenon of the onset of saturation of the system - in this case occurring around 11 clients in the system. Below 11 clients, there are practically no queues at each of the machines, and so the average response time is fairly low, and the throughput of the system, increases almost linearly as new clients are added. But as the number of clients increase further, queues start to build up at different service centers, and jobs have to wait for other jobs to complete service, before they could be taken up. The servers in these conditions are busy almost all the time and server utilizations (the probability of finding the server busy) reaches unity. Thus congestion builds up in the system, and hence the average response time of the system keeps on increasing thereon as more and more clients are added. Because of the same reason, the throughput of the system reaches a limiting level, and does not increase after that (as most of the servers are already busy processing to their limit) and so we get the flat region in the throughput graph.

The graphs are very useful for a system architect as they show precisely how many clients would the system be able to handle efficiently. Practically a system should never be running in a saturated condition as then the system performance degrades very fast. These graphs could be used to ascertain the kind of the average response times and throughput the system would deliver for the specified range of clients and whether that meets the desired performance criteria or not. The system architect could also get an idea about the performance of the system, in conditions of excessive loads.

As shown in the bottleneck analysis in Figure 6, the tool predicts the primary and secondary bottlenecks in the system along with the minimum scale-up needed so that they no longer are the bottlenecks. As mentioned earlier, as the bottlenecks in the system may change upon changing the number of clients in the system, hence the tool provides the bottleneck analysis for the whole range of clients. In Figure 6, the same is shown for 43 clients. Moreover the tool iterates upon the analysis once more with the primary bottleneck scaled-up, and then shows the improvements in throughput, average response time, and saturation number of the system.

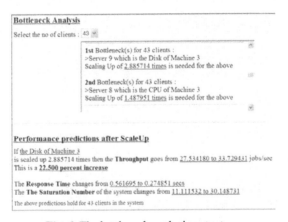

Fig. 6. The bottleneck analysis output.

In this example system, we can see the improvements - by scaling the disk of machine 3, we could get an improvement of more that 22.5% in the throughput of the system and about a 50% decrease in average response time. Figure 7 illustrates the comparative improvements using graphs, showing the system throughout and the average response time variation with load, before and after the suggested scale-up. We can see that if the suggested scale-up is done, then the system can sustain more number of clients, without degradation as compared to the initial configuration.

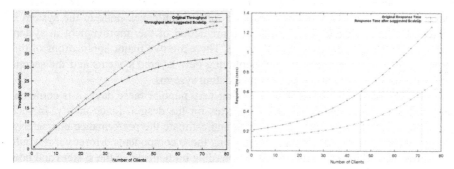

Fig. 7. The effect of system scaleup as suggested by our tool on average system throughput and response times.

From the capacity planning point of view, say if an average response time of upto 0.6 seconds is deemed acceptable for the system, one can observe from the average response time variation graph in Figure 7 that the capacity of the system increases from 46 to 72, if the suggested scaleup is done. One can also use to the tool to see the possible effects of any changes in the system hardware or software. We used the tool to evaluate the above example system but with the number of concurrent threads in Machine 3 limited to 25. The tool shows that this restriction causes the maximum throughput of the system to go down to 20 jobs/sec from 34 jobs/sec. In addition, the tool could be used for comparing the effect of different deployments of the layers on the available machines, on the overall system performance. One such comparison for the example system is shown in Table 3 which shows that the first deployment scheme is significantly better than the others in terms of maximum average through-put.

Table 3. Effect of different layer deployments on maximum average throughput.

Layer(s) deployed on			Maximum average throughput (jobs/s)
Machine 1	Machine 2	Machine 3	
1st	2nd	$3^{rd},4^{th}$	33.62
1st	$2^{nd},3^{rd}$	4th	19.84
$1^{st},2^{nd}$	3rd	4th	29.81

7 Discussion and Conclusion

In this paper we presented an approach of performance evaluation of systems follow-ing layered architecture. The approach deals with first constructing a DTMC model of the software system, using the specifications user has provided. This model is then solved to get the total visit counts to different layers of the system and calculate total service requirements of the system on the hardware over which the software system is deployed. These are then used to construct a closed PFQN model for the system. This model also takes care of limited software resources as threads on a particular machine. The PFQN model is solved using SHARPE as the backend, the outputs of which are analyzed, and various performance metrics such as throughput and the average response times, and saturation number are provided. Moreover bottleneck analysis is done and the minimum scale up for the bottleneck node in the system is suggested. The approach also allows for a prediction of the improvement in system performance if the scale up is actually done. There are two major applications of this approach: First is in architecting and deploying new layered systems and the second is in tweaking or upgrading or scaling up existing systems.

As COTS based development is becoming very popular these days, it is commonplace today to use components as black boxes for the desired functionality. In such cases the designer could use our approach and estimate the performance characteristics of the final system he wishes to build using those components. Moreover it would also allow the architect to know about the possible bottlenecks in the system and how much scaling up is needed for those components.

The second application as mentioned before is when an existing system has to be scaled up or some additional software or hardware component has to be added. The system administrator should have some idea of the change in the system performance due to the change in system hardware and/or software configuration. Our approach could be used to ascertain that. The system administrator need not have an in-depth knowledge of performance evaluation techniques for this and our tool could be employed for the same by providing some specifications, which are easy to get.

At the software architecture phase, the actual components, which would constitute the layers, would not be present (unless COTS approach is used) so, the service requirements of different components at different devices have to be estimated from previous experience with similar software components. If off the shelf components are being used, the CPU and I/O times taken by particular layers to execute once could be assessed by using built in tools provided by various operating systems like *iostat* or *sar*. Tests will have to be conducted for each layered component separately as the above mentioned tools do not provide application level break-up of the measurements. For testing purposes if a single layer is run on a single machine one can get the total CPU and I/O times for say n executions and then get the average CPU and I/O times per execution.

Each proposed component in a layer could be examined to find the components with which it interacts with a non-zero probability and known operational profiles of similar systems might be used to estimate the associated transition probabilities between the layers. For existing systems, techniques mentioned in [6] might be used to ascertain the transition probabilities. Specifications such as the capacity of connectors, the number of CPUs and disks or thread limitations are all system characteristics. Some measurements will be needed for the packet sizes on the connectors joining various machines and could be ascertained by using a suitable network analysis utility.

There are still lots of avenues in this approach for future work. Our approach is limited only to layered systems at present. We believe that this could be extended to general software architectural patterns also. However, the aim while doing so would be to keep the specifications needed as simple and practical as possible so that the approach is easily adoptable in practice. One other major extension could be to modify the approach so that it allows for optimizing the use of various system resources to provide the maximum possible performance. This would be beneficial to system architects as well as system administrators and will allow them to minimize investment and maximize performance of their systems. One of the many aims of this approach is to provide a thorough performance evaluation of the layered software system under concern. Moreover the approach is helpful both at the time of architecting new systems as well as scaling up or improving existing systems. The tool that we have built implements our approach and is very simple to use. We hope that our approach would help software engineers and performance experts to architect better layered systems, as well as allow those who are not specialists in this field to perform performance evaluation of their systems.

References

1. K. S. Trivedi, "Probability and Statistics with Reliability, Queuing, and Computer Science Applications", *John Wiley and Sons*, 2001.
2. C.U. Smith, "Performance Engineering of Software Systems", *Addison Wesley*, 1990
3. Dorina C. Petriu, X. Wang, "From UML descriptions of High-Level Software Architectures to LQN Performance Models", *Proceedings of AGTIVE'99*, Springer Verlag LNCS 1779, 1999.
4. P. King, R. Pooley, "Derivation of Petri Net Performance Models from UML Specifications of Communication Software", *Proceedings of XV UK Performance Engineering Workshop*, 1999.
5. D. A. Menasc´e, H. Gomaa, "A Method for design and Performance Modeling of Client/Server Systems", *IEEE Transactions on Software Engineering*, Vol. 26, No. 11, pp. 1066–1085, 2000.
6. K. Go˘seva–Popstojanova and K. Trivedi, "Architecture–based approach to reliability assessment of software systems", *Performance Evaluation*, 45:179-204, 2001.
7. L. Bass, P. Clements, R. Kazman, "Software Architecture in Practice". *SEI Series in Software Engineering*, Addison-Wesley, 1998.
8. F. Buschmann, R. Meunier, H. Rohnert, P. Sommerlad, M. Stal, "Pattern-Oriented Software Architecture, Volume 1: A System Of Patterns" , *John Wiley and Sons*, 2000.
9. M. Shaw, D. Garlan, "Software Architecture, Perspectives On An Emerging Discipline", *Prentice-Hall Inc.*, 1996.
10. C. U. Smith, L.G. Williams, "Software Performance Engineering: A Case Study Including Performance Comparison with Design Alternatives", *IEEE Transactions On Software Engineering, Vol 19, No7, Pages 720-741*, 1993.
11. R.A. Sahner, K.S. Trivedi, and A. Puliafito, "Performance and Reliability Analysis of Computer Systems: An Example-Based approach Using the SHARPE Software Package", *Kluwer Academic Publishers*, 1996.
12. Dorin Petriu, Murray Woodside, "Software Performance Models from System Scenarios in Use Case Maps", *Proc. Performance TOOLS 2002, London,* 2002.
13. Swapna S. Gokhale, W. Eric Wong. K. S. Trivedi, and J.R. Horgan, "An Analytical Approach to Architecture-Based Software Reliability Prediction", *IEEE Int. Comp. Perf. and Dependability Symposium*, Durham, NC, USA, Sept. 1998.
14. M. Vikram, P. Kant, "Evaluation of Layered Architecture Software Systems for Performance Attributes using Closed Product Form Queuing networks", *B.Tech Project Report, CSE, Indian Institute of Technology Kanpur*, India, 2003.

Component-Level Dataflow Analysis

Atanas Rountev

Ohio State University
rountev@cse.ohio-state.edu

Abstract. Interprocedural dataflow analysis has a wide range of uses in software maintenance, testing, verification, and optimization. Despite the large body of research on various analyses, the widespread adoption of these techniques faces serious challenges. In particular, when software is built with reusable components, the standard approaches for dataflow analysis cannot be applied. This paper proposes a model of *component-level* analysis which generalizes the traditional model of *whole-program* analysis. We outline the theoretical foundations of component-level analysis, discuss some of the key technical challenges for such analysis, and present initial results from our work on addressing these challenges.

1 Introduction

Interprocedural dataflow analysis is a form of static program analysis that has been investigated widely in the last two decades. For example, many analyses have been developed for use in tools for *software understanding and maintenance.* Other areas in which dataflow analysis is commonly used are *software testing* and *software verification,* both of which are essential for producing high-quality systems. Last but not least, dataflow analysis continues to play an important role in the area of *performance optimization,* by enabling compiler optimizations for numerous programming languages and hardware architectures.

Despite the continuing progress in dataflow analysis research, its widespread use in real-world tools is hindered by several serious challenges. One of the central problems is the underlying model of analysis assumed in most of the work in this area. The essence of this model is the assumption of a *whole-program analysis for a homogeneous program.* Interprocedural whole-program analysis takes as input an entire program and produces information about the possible run-time behavior of that program. A fundamental assumption of this analysis model is that the source code for the whole program in available for analysis. Furthermore, such analysis typically treats the entire program as a homogeneous entity, and does not take into account the program's modular structure.

Modern software systems have characteristics that present critical challenges for this traditional model of dataflow analysis. In particular, systems often incorporate *reusable components.* Whole-program analysis is based on the implicit assumption that it is appropriate and desirable to analyze the source code of the entire program as a single unit. However, this assumption is clearly violated for software systems that are built with reusable components:

G.T. Heineman et al. (Eds.): CBSE 2005, LNCS 3489, pp. 82–89, 2005.

- Some program components may be available only in binary form, without source code, which makes whole-program analysis impossible.
- Analysis results may be needed even when a whole program simply does not exist. For example, when the developer of a component wants to use a dataflow analysis for understanding, restructuring, or testing of her code, she often does this without having all other components that will eventually be combined to construct a complete application.
- From the point of view of analysis running time and memory usage, it is highly undesirable to reanalyze a component every time this component is used as part of a new system. For example, a popular library may be used in thousands of different applications, and whole-program analysis requires reanalysis of this library from scratch as part of each such application.
- Treating the program as a homogeneous entity means that code changes in one component typically require complete reanalysis of the entire application.
- The running time of whole-program analysis is often dominated by the analysis of the underlying large library components. Thus, to achieve practical running times, analyses often must employ approximations which typically reduce the precision and usefulness of the analysis solution.

The essence of the problem is the following: whole-program interprocedural dataflow analysis is often *impossible* or *inefficient* for software systems that employ reusable components. Thus, the real-world usefulness of hundreds of existing analyses remains questionable. In many case these analyses cannot be used at all. Even if they are possible, they have to be relatively approximate and imprecise in order to scale for industrial-sized software containing hundreds of thousands lines of code in multiple components. As a result of these approximations, the precision of the computed information usually suffers, which leads to problems such as spurious dependencies in program understanding tools, false warnings in verification tools, and infeasible test coverage requirements in testing tools. Such problems ultimately reduce the productivity of the software developers and testers that are clients of these tools.

Our work defines an alternative conceptual model of dataflow analysis which we refer to as *component-level analysis* (CLA). While a whole-program analysis takes as input the source code of a complete program, a component-level analysis processes the source code of a single program component, given some information about the environment of this component. This conceptual model presents a starting point for dataflow analyses that can be applied to software systems built with reusable components.

Given the CLA model, there are two major challenges that static analysis researchers need to address. First, what is the appropriate theoretical framework for designing CLA? Whole-program analyses can be defined in terms of a dataflow lattice, a set of dataflow functions, and algorithms that use the lattice and the functions to compute a dataflow solution [1]. How should this general framework be extended to handle CLA? Second, given the theoretical foundations for CLA, how should specific whole-program analyses be modified to fit the CLA model? For example, how should researchers and tool builders define

CLA versions of popular analyses such as pointer analysis, side-effect analysis, data dependence analysis, and constant propagation analysis?

The program analysis research community has been slow to respond to these challenges. For example, at present there does not exist a general theoretical framework for designing CLA. There have been several efforts to define CLA versions of specific kinds of analyses (due to space constraints, we do not discuss these efforts). However, this existing work has been somewhat sporadic and ad hoc in nature, and it has not addressed some of the key technical problems in this domain. The goal of this paper is to describe our initial work on defining the theoretical foundations of CLA. We consider these preliminary results to be a first step in a long-term research agenda aimed at dataflow analysis techniques that can be used for component-based software systems.

2   Component-Level Analysis

The limitations of whole-program dataflow analysis can be addressed by a conceptually different model for interprocedural dataflow analysis: *component-level analysis*. The differences between whole-program analysis and component-level analysis are illustrated in Fig. 1. Whole-program analysis takes as input the source code for all components in a complete program, and produces information about that entire program. Component-level analysis considers a particular component under analysis C_p that is built on top of existing components $C_j, \ldots, C_k$. The analysis input is the source code of C_p together with summary information about the rest of the components. The *summary information* is component metadata that encodes properties of $C_j, \ldots, C_k$ which are relevant for the analysis of C_p. This information can be enclosed with the binary code for the components, allowing analysis of C_p without having access to the source code of the other components. The analysis outputs a component-level solution for C_p and summary information for C_p.

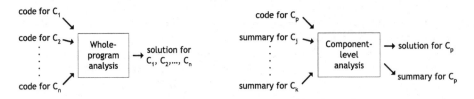

Fig. 1. Whole-program analysis vs. component-level analysis

The *component-level solution for C_p* represents properties of the possible behavior of C_p when it interacts with the existing components and with other unknown components. This solution should be computed with *conservative assumptions* about the behavior of components that have not been built yet, and about existing components for which summary information and source code are not available. Thus, the availability of summary information for other components determines the degree of conservativeness in the solution for C_p.

The *summary information for* C_p encodes properties that are relevant for subsequent analysis of components built on top of C_p. This information could be created either independently of the summaries for $C_j, \ldots, C_k$ (in which case it encodes properties of C_p that are independent of any other components), or it could be based on these summaries (and therefore describes properties of C_p in the context of $C_j, \ldots, C_k$). The summary information should be *precise* in the sense of allowing subsequent component-level analysis to be as precise as whole-program analysis would have been. For example, consider a complete program with two components: a library component *Lib* and a main component *Main*. If a summary for *Lib* is included together with the library binary, subsequent component-level analysis of *Main* should produce a solution which is equivalent to the solution for *Main* that would have been computed by a whole-program analysis which analyzed the source code of *Lib* and *Main* together.

Component-level analysis goes beyond the limitations of whole-program analysis because it allows: (1) analysis of a component without the source code of related components, by using the summary information for these components; (2) analysis in the absence of any summary information, by employing conservative assumptions; (3) reuse of the summary information in order to avoid repeated reanalysis of a component; and (4) reduced work to handle code changes, since components that are not affected by the changes do not need to be reanalyzed.

3   Theoretical Foundations

A key challenge for the widespread adoption of the analysis model described in the previous section is the lack of comprehensive theoretical foundations for such analysis. This motivates our ongoing work on defining a general theoretical framework for component-level analysis. This paper outlines initial work on defining a framework for one simple instantiation of the general CLA model. We consider analysis of a complete program that is built with two components: a library component *Lib* and a main component *Main*. The problem under consideration is to precompute summary information for *Lib* and to use it in a subsequent component-level analysis of *Main*. Even this simplified version of the model has important practical implications. For example, there are extensive standard libraries that are associated with languages such as C++, Java, and C#. A standard library could be considered as component *Lib*, while a program written on top of the library is component *Main*.

Our work makes some additional simplifying assumptions. First, the definition of a component is simply "a set of related procedures or classes". The interactions between components are exclusively through calls to methods and procedures and through accesses to shared variables. Clearly, our future work must consider more sophisticated component models; nevertheless, we believe that the simple model used in this paper is the appropriate starting point for this investigation. Another assumption is that the analysis takes into account only the source code and the summary information that is constructed from this source code. If, for example, a formal specification is available for a component C, it may be possible to utilize this information when analyzing other components that interact with C. Traditional whole-program analysis does not take into account information from formal specifications, but it is clear that future work on component-level analysis should investigate this possibility.

In the standard formulation [1], a whole-program interprocedural dataflow analysis constructs a tuple $\langle G, L, F, M, \eta \rangle$ where

- $G = (N, E)$ is an interprocedural control-flow graph in which each node represents a program statement and each edge represents potential flow of control. An edge (n_1, n_2) is *intraprocedural* when both n_1 and n_2 belong to the same procedure/method. *Interprocedural* edges connect a call node with the entry and exit nodes of the called procedure/method.
- L is a meet semi-lattice whose elements encode program properties. L is a partially ordered set with a partial order $\sqsubseteq$. Intuitively, if $l_1 \sqsubseteq l_2$, the property encoded by l_1 "subsumes" the property encoded by l_2. For each pair $l_1, l_2 \in L$, there exists a unique element $l \in L$ which is the "meet" of l_1 and l_2: $l = l_1 \sqcap l_2$. In essence, l represents a property which is the "merge" of the two properties encoded by l_1 and l_2.
- $F \subseteq \{f \mid f : L \to L\}$ is a monotone function space that is closed under functional composition and functional meet.
- $M : E \to F$ is an assignment of functions to graph edges. The dataflow function $f_e = M(e)$ encodes the effects of e's execution: if property $l \in L$ holds immediately before e, property $f_e(l)$ holds immediately after e.
- $\eta \in L$ is the dataflow solution at the start node of the program.

A path in G is a sequence of edges $p = (e_1, \ldots, e_k)$ such that the target of e_i is the same as the source of e_{i+1}. The dataflow function associated with p is the composition of the functions for the edges: $f_p = f_{e_1} \circ \ldots \circ f_{e_k}$. A *valid path* in G is a path on which calls and return are properly matched. That is, whenever a valid path contains an edge e from the exit node of a method/procedure m to some call node c, the last unmatched call-to-entry edge that precedes e in the path is an edge from c to the entry of m. A dataflow analysis algorithm defines an approach for computing a solution $S_n \in L$ at every node n such that $S_n \sqsubseteq f_p(\eta)$ for each path p from the start node of the program to n. This solution is guaranteed to represent all properties that may hold at n during run-time execution.

3.1   Restricted Component-Level Analysis

Consider again a complete program with two components *Lib* and *Main*. Suppose that this program does not use callbacks that allow the library to call back the main component. For example, in C and C++, the library does not make indirect calls through function pointers that point to functions defined in *Main*. Similarly, in C++ and Java, this means that the library does not make virtual calls that could be resolved through virtual dispatch to methods that are defined in *Main* and override existing methods from *Lib*.

Under this constraint, the classical theoretical framework for whole-program analysis can be adapted for component-level analysis. For each library method or procedure m that may be called by some main component, a *summary function* f_m can be precomputed in advance. This computation uses only the source code of *Lib* and is independent of *Main*. The set of summary functions constitutes the summary information for *Lib*. A subsequent component-level analysis of *Main* uses these f_m to model the effects of library calls being made by the main component. The resulting solution of the analysis of *Main* can be guaranteed to be as precise (with respect to *Main*) as the solution what would have been computed if a whole-program analysis of $Main \cup Lib$ were performed.

The summary function f_m for a library method/procedure m considers all valid paths that begin at the start node of m, end at the exit node of m, and contain an equal number of calls and returns. Each such path p represents a run-time execution from the moment when m is called to the moment m returns to its caller. Since there are no callbacks from *Lib* to *Main*, each such p stays entirely inside the library component. The summary function for m is $f_m = f_{p_1} \widehat{\sqcap} \ldots \widehat{\sqcap} f_{p_k}$ for all such paths p_i; this function captures all possible effects of calls to m. Here $\widehat{\sqcap}$ denotes the generalization of $\sqcap$ to functions: $(f_1 \widehat{\sqcap} f_2)(l) = f_1(l) \sqcap f_2(l)$ for any $l \in L$. When component-level analysis of some *Main* is performed, a call to m is modeled by applying f_m to the current lattice element at the call site.

For brevity, we do not discuss the numerous technical details related to this approach. The key observation is that this form of analysis is a natural generalization of a well-known traditional technique for whole-program analysis (the "functional approach" from [1]). Some existing work on specific analyses uses this approach, either explicitly or in spirit. The success of this technique depends primarily on having compact representations of dataflow functions and on inexpensive compositions and meets of such functions. This issue has been resolved for a broad range of popular analyses [2,3], but some open questions remain for certain classes of dataflow problems (e.g., non-distributive problems).

4   Generalized Component-Level Analysis

The approach described in Sect. 3.1 is based on a key assumption: the absence of callbacks from *Lib* to *Main*. However, callbacks are quite common in real-world software. Function pointers in C are often used for extending and customizing library functionality. For example, in order to allow a library function f to behave in a polymorphic manner, one of the formal parameters of f could be a function pointer g to a callback function defined in the main component. An indirect call (*g)(..) inside f invokes the callback function. The complete behavior of f is not known to a static analysis until after the library is combined with *Main*. Thus, it is impossible to construct a summary function for f using the approach described in Sect. 3.1. Existing work indicates that callbacks through function pointers are used extensively in real-world C libraries [4].

Callbacks occur naturally in object-oriented software. Consider a library method m(A *a) in C++ or m(A a) in Java, where A is a library class. Suppose some *Main* creates a subclass B of A that overrides some of A's methods. If *Main* calls m with an actual parameter that is a pointer to an instance of B, a virtual call through a inside m may invoke a method defined in B. In fact, this is the standard extensibility mechanism for object-oriented libraries. For example, a study from [5] shows that in several packages from the standard Java libraries, typically at least 5% of the virial call sites potentially invoke callback methods, and in some cases the percentage is higher than 30%. In the presence of overriding methods in the main component, it is impossible to use the approach from Sect. 3.1 to create summary information about an object-oriented library.

To address this problem, we propose a new approach for component-level analysis. The preanalysis of *Lib* constructs detailed information which is subsequently combined with the source code of *Main* to compute information that is as precise as the solution that would have been computed for *Main* by a whole-program analysis. For brevity, we present the approach through the example in Fig. 2 rather than describing the underlying formalism. The first part of the figure shows a library component with a set of methods/procedures $\mathcal{P} = \{m1, m2, m3\}$. The control-flow graph is shown together with the dataflow functions for graph edges. Assume that each element of $\mathcal{P}$ could be invoked by code in future main components. The second part of the figure shows the summary information constructed by our approach.

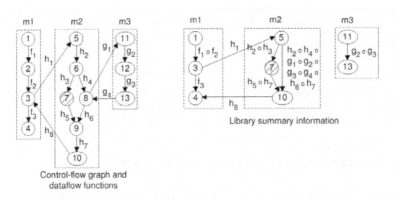

Control-flow graph and
dataflow functions

Library summary information

Fig. 2. Summary information in the presence of callbacks.

The generation of the summary information starts by identifying call nodes inside *Lib* that could call back some code in some future *Main*. Various techniques can be used to identify such call sites (e.g., conservative forms of pointer analysis); examples of such techniques are available in [6,5]. In Fig. 2, node 7 represents a callback site. A method or procedure $m \in \mathcal{P}$ is *incomplete* if m contains a callback site or if m invokes (directly or transitively) some other library method m' which contains a callback site. In Fig. 2, m1 and m2 are incomplete. If m is incomplete, it is impossible to represent the complete effects of calls to m during the preanalysis of the library.

The summary information for *Lib* contains a *reduced control-flow graph* $G' = (N', E')$. The node set N' is a subset of the node set in the "standard" control-flow graph G. Nodes in N' correspond to (1) start nodes and exit nodes of all incomplete $m \in \mathcal{P}$, (2) all call nodes that are potential callback sites, and (3) all call nodes that invoke incomplete $m \in \mathcal{P}$. Edges in E' represent *paths* in the standard graph G. Consider two nodes $n_1, n_2 \in N'$ such that both belong to the same $m \in \mathcal{P}$. The paths represented by an edge $(n_1, n_2) \in E'$ correspond to sequences of execution steps for which the preanalysis of the library has complete knowledge. For example, in Fig. 2, edge $(5, 10)$ represent the run-time behavior of a call to $m2$ during which the callback site 7 is *not* executed, and therefore all necessary information for the construction of a summary function is available. On the other hand, since the execution of 7 invokes unknown code, this node has to be preserved in the summary information. In essence, the summary functions capture the (incomplete) knowledge that can be inferred "locally" from the library source code. When the main component eventually becomes available, the standard dataflow-analysis techniques can be applied on the control-flow graph of *Main* combined with the reduced control-flow graph from the library.

5   Future Work

We are currently working on the detailed formulation of the proposed technique, and on applying it to specific analyses for Java software (e.g., pointer analysis and dependence analysis). In this context the standard Java libraries are component *Lib*, and the user program is component *Main*. Since the standard libraries contain thousands of classes, they present a challenging scalability problem for whole-program dataflow analyses. Our near-term goal is to demonstrate, both theoretically and experimentally, a set of techniques that allow practical and precise dataflow analysis of real-world Java software. A more general long-term goal is to consider various component models and the appropriate theoretical foundations for dataflow analyses in the context of these models.

References

1. Sharir, M., Pnueli, A.: Two approaches to interprocedural data flow analysis. In: Program Flow Analysis: Theory and Applications. Prentice Hall, 1981, 189–234
2. Reps, T., Horwitz, S., Sagiv, M.: Precise interprocedural dataflow analysis via graph reachability. ACM Symposium, Principles of Programming Languages,1995, 49–61
3. Sagiv, M., Reps, T., Horwitz, S.: Precise interprocedural dataflow analysis with applications to constant propagation. Theoretical Computer Science 167,1996, 131–170
4. Milanova, A., Rountev, A., Ryder, B.G.: Precise call graphs for C programs with function pointers. Journal of Automated Software Engineering **11**, 2004, 7–26
5. Kuck, F.C.: Class analysis for extensible Java software. Master's thesis, Ohio State University, 2004
6. Rountev, A., Ryder, B.G., Landi, W.: Data-flow analysis of program fragments. In: ACM SIGSOFT Symposium on the Foundations of Software Engineering. LNCS 1687, 1999, 235–252

Exogenous Connectors for Software Components

Kung-Kiu Lau*, Perla Velasco Elizondo, and Zheng Wang

School of Computer Science, The University of Manchester
Manchester M13 9PL, United Kingdom
{kung-kiu,pvelasco,zw}@cs.man.ac.uk

Abstract. In existing component models, control originates in components, and connectors are channels for passing on the control to other components. This provides a mechanism for message passing, which allows components to invoke one another's operations by method calls (or remote procedure calls) either directly or indirectly via a channel such as a bus. Thus components in these models mix computation with control, since in performing their computation they also initiate method calls and manage their returns, via connectors. Consequently, in terms of control, components are not loosely coupled. In this paper, we propose *exogenous* connectors, and demonstrate their use in a small example. In contrast to connectors in existing component models, exogenous connectors initiate calls and manage their returns, and are used to encapsulate control in a component model we are working on. In the example, we demonstrate the feasibility of exogenous connectors, and compare them with connectors in closely related architecture description languages.

1 Introduction

Components and connectors are the basis of many software component models. Architecture Description Languages (ADLs) [22] have always defined software systems in terms of components (boxes) and connectors (lines) that link components and thus define relationships between them. More recently, UML 2.0 [19] also uses connectors to compose components. Even component models that do not use connectors explicitly often have composition operators that can be interpreted as connectors at different levels of abstraction. Lower-level connectors act as wiring mechanisms, while higher-level connectors can correspond to sophisticated protocols or control structures. For example, direct method calls between components may be regarded as code-level connectors, and glue code or scripts [21] that combine components can be regarded as interface-level connectors. A large and detailed taxonomy of software connectors can be found in [16].

In existing component models, connectors are meant to encapsulate *interaction* or *communication* while components are meant to encapsulate *computation*. In these models, control originates in components, and connectors are channels for coordinating the control flow (as well as data flow) between components. This provides a mechanism for message passing, which allows components to invoke one another's operations by method calls (or remote procedure calls) either directly or indirectly via a channel such as a bus. Thus components in these models mix computation with control, since in

---

* Partially supported by CoLogNet, a European Network of Excellence funded by IST FET.

G.T. Heineman et al. (Eds.): CBSE 2005, LNCS 3489, pp. 90–106, 2005.

performing their computation they also initiate method calls and manage their returns, via connectors. Consequently, in terms of control, components are not loosely coupled. In particular, although they encapsulate communication, connectors do not encapsulate control: they only pass it on.

In this paper, we introduce *exogenous* connectors. These connectors are different in that they encapsulate control flow between components *totally*, i.e. they originate and coordinate *all* control. This means that components do not invoke methods or procedures in other components via these connectors; rather, this is done by the connectors.

Our main motivation for using exogenous connectors is to encapsulate control in a component model we are working on, in order to minimize coupling between components. In our model, components encapsulate data and functions, and are therefore loosely coupled in terms of these. Using exogenous connectors to encapsulate control completes the encapsulation that we wish to achieve, and thereby maximizes loose coupling, i.e. in terms of data, functions *and* control. A corollary of such complete encapsulation in our component model is that reasoning about components and their composition should become more tractable and hence practicable. This offers hope that our component model could have the capability for predictable assembly [23].

2   Exogenous Connectors

In this section, we introduce exogenous connectors as defined in our component model. By way of contrast, we first consider connectors in current component models, and briefly assess them for encapsulation and loose coupling.

Connectors in current component models fall into two main categories: (i) connectors that represent composition by *direct* message passing; and (ii) connectors that represent composition by *indirect* message passing. In these models, components are usually software units (typically classes or objects) with their own methods or functions which can be invoked by other components either directly by method calls or indirectly via code that links the components together.

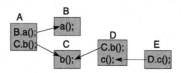

Fig. 1. Connecting components by direct message passing.

2.1   Connecting Components by Direct Message Passing

Connecting components by direct message passing is illustrated in Fig. 1. For convenience we borrow the dot notation from object-oriented languages for components and their methods. For example, in Fig. 1, if component A calls the method a of component

B, then it does so by passing a message directly to B. In a message passing scheme, there are two distinct roles: the *sender* and the *receiver* of a message. The identity of the receiver is either statically known to the sender or it is dynamically evaluated at execution time. Sometimes there can be more than one receiver, as for instance, the message may be multi-cast to several receivers or broadcast to all receivers in the system. From the sender's point of view, the identity of the intended receiver is known a priori, but the receiver does not have to know the sender at all. Thus the send operation is generally targeted by the sender at a specific set of receivers. Remote Procedure Calls (RPC), method and event delegation are well-known examples of message passing schemes. Software component models that adopt message passing schemes as composition operators are Enterprise JavaBeans [13], CORBA Component Model [20], COM [8], UML [19] and KobrA [6].

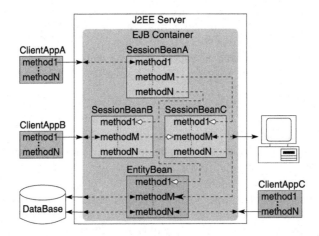

Fig. 2. Connecting beans by direct method calls in Enterprise JavaBeans.

For example, in Enterprise JavaBeans (EJB), the beans are Java classes in an EJB container that are connected by direct method calls, as illustrated by the example in Fig. 2. Even client applications are connected to the beans by method calls via the EJB container. In general, when components are connected by direct message passing, communication expressing control is mixed with computation, and sender components and their receivers are tightly coupled with each other. The worst problem in this regard is reentrant calls, when a method y called by a method x calls x itself. Also, there is no explicit code for connectors, since messages are 'hard-wired' into the components, and so these connectors are not separate entities and therefore cannot be reused. In particular, they cannot be pre-defined and deposited in a repository.

2.2   Connecting Components by Indirect Message Passing

Connecting components by *indirect* message passing is illustrated in Fig. 3. Here, connectors are separate entities that are defined explicitly. Typically they are glue code or scripts that pass messages between components indirectly. To connect a component to another component we use a connector that when notified by the former invokes a method in the latter. For example, in Fig. 3, component A is connected to component B by connector $Con1$, so whenever A sends a message to notify $Con1$, the latter passes a message to component B to invoke method a in B. In JavaBeans [9], for example, beans are connected precisely in this way, using adaptor classes as connectors. This kind of connector is at a slightly higher level of abstraction (and indirection) than direct method calls, but is nevertheless still rather low-level, since it essentially glues or wires components together.

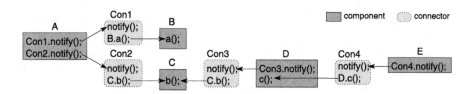

Fig. 3. Connecting components by indirect message passing.

More abstractly, when connected by indirect message passing, components can be viewed as computational units with *in* and *out* ports, and connectors connect matching ports to pass control as well as data between components. For example, in Fig. 3, component A has two out ports, B has one in port, and the connector $Con1$ connects one of A's out ports to B's in port. In ADLs, components are connected together by connectors via ports in precisely this way. For example, in Acme [12], Fig. 3 would be drawn as Fig. 4 (a), where ports are represented by triangles and connectors by two lines joined by a black dot.

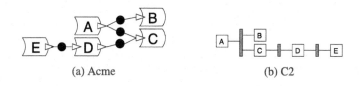

(a) Acme   (b) C2

Fig. 4. Connecting components in ADLs.

In ADLs, a component represents a primary computational element and data store of a system. The interface of a component is defined as a set of ports through which its functionalities are exposed. Components are connected by connectors that link their ports. The connectors mediate the communication and coordination activities among components. Typical connectors in ADLs are pipes used by components to pass information from one to another. Such information may be simple data values or messages for invoking methods.

In messaged-based ADLs, it is possible to have a still higher level of abstraction of indirect message passing. This is exemplified by C2 [25], where components are linked to a bus, and messages can be passed between components by broadcasting[1] them on the bus. For example, in C2, Fig. 3 would be drawn as Fig. 4 (b). The links are not directed, so it is not possible to say explicitly which component calls which. Instead, messages are placed on the bus and components linked to the bus must determine which messages are intended for them. Besides JavaBeans and ADLs, other software component models that adopt indirect message passing schemes are Koala [26], PIN [15] and PECOS [18].

In general, when components are connected by indirect message passing, communication (connectors) is separated from computation (components). However, this does not necessarily mean that control is separated from computation, since the information passed from and to a component may contain method calls. As a result, components are tightly coupled by connectors.

Although they are separate entities, connectors are usually not intended to be defined and deposited in a repository. Rather, they are pieces of code generated for specific sets of components. Therefore, these connectors are not reusable. For example in JavaBeans, only beans can be stored in a repository, but not connectors. The latter have to be generated (automatically by the builder tool) as adaptor classes for each specific pair of bean instances. In ADLs, both components and connectors are meant to represent design and not stored in a repository.

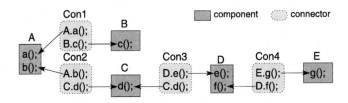

Fig. 5. Connecting components by exogenous connectors.

2.3   Connecting Components by Exogenous Connectors

Using connection by message passing, both direct and indirect, connected components invoke each other's methods, so their connection effects control, and possibly data, flow as well as computation. Connected components are thus tightly coupled, albeit to a varying degree depending on the level of indirection in the message passing; and control and computation are mixed up. In order to minimize coupling, and to maximize separation of control from computation, we propose exogenous connectors which encapsulate control and data flow between connected components. The idea is that in connected components, the connectors, rather than the components themselves, initiate method calls in the components, and handle any accompanying data flow, so that any

---

[1] Other modes of communication are possible in C2, but broadcasting is the most indirect.

control flow between the components is encapsulated by the connectors. This is illustrated in Fig. 5. In such a scheme, connected components react to their connector only, and not directly with each other. Components encapsulate computation, while the connectors encapsulate control. For example, in Fig. 5, the connector $Con1$ calls method a in component A and method c in B, but A and B do not directly interact with each other. Method calls may be accompanied by data flow between A and $Con1$ or between B and $Con1$, but again not between A and B directly.

Connection Scheme	Component Models	Control mixed with computation	Calls initiated from outside components
Direct message passing	EJB, CCM, COM, UML, KobrA	✓	✗
Indirect message passing	JavaBeans, ADLs, PECOS, Koala, PIN	✓	✗
Exogenous connection	Our proposed model	✗	✓

Fig. 6. Comparison of connection schemes.

Fig. 6 is a comparison of exogenous connectors with connectors used in existing component models. It shows clearly the contrast between exogenous connectors and non-exogenous ones: the former do not mix control and computation, whereas the latter do; using the former, method calls are initiated from outside components, whereas using the latter, they are initiated by components themselves. In the component model we are working on, we plan to use exogenous connectors for composition.

Although no existing component model uses it, exogenous connection has been defined as exogenous coordination in coordination languages for concurrent computation [3]. Also, in object-oriented programming, the courier pattern [11] uses the idea of exogenous connection whereby a courier object links a producer-consumer pair of objects by calling the *produce* method in the producer object and then calling the *consume* method in the consumer object with the result of the *produce* method.

3   Creating and Using Exogenous Connectors

In a component model we are working on, we want to use exogenous connectors as composition operators. In this section, we identify the types of exogenous connectors that we will need, and show how we create and use them in a preliminary implementation of our component model. First we outline the relevant aspects of our model.

In our component model, a component is a unit of software with (i) an *interface* that specifies the services it provides and the services it requires, and the dependencies between the two sets of services; and (ii) *code* that implements the provided services. In essence it is similar to Szyperski's definition [24]. However, components do not request services in other components. Rather, they perform their provided services only when invoked externally by connectors. Thus components encapsulate computation.

Connectors are composition operators that compose components into systems. They are in essence similar to connectors in ADLs, except of course that they are exogenous.

They initiate and coordinate method calls in components and handle their results. Thus they determine control flow and data flow, i.e. they encapsulate communication.

An important feature of our component model is the definition of the life cycle of components as consisting of two stages: (i) *repository*, or *design*, phase, and (ii) *deployment*, or *execution*, phase. In the repository phase, components as well as connectors have to be constructed, catalogued and stored in a repository in such a way that they can be retrieved later, as and when needed. Components in the repository are templates that are stateless. In the deployment phase, components are retrieved from the repository, and instantiated with initial data. Therefore components have *states* and are ready for execution. Similarly, connectors are retrieved and instantiated, and ready to execute.

In a preliminary implementation of our component model, for simplicity and for ease of implementation, components and connectors are defined as Java classes in the repository phase, so that instances can be created and deployed in the deployment phase. We do not yet address issues related to interfaces or repository management.

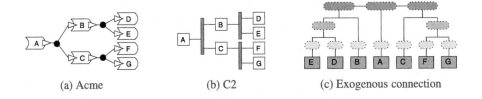

(a) Acme   (b) C2   (c) Exogenous connection

Fig. 7. Example architecture using exogenous connection, and equivalent ADL architectures.

3.1   Types of Exogenous Connectors

Since, in our component model, objects implementing components are not allowed to call methods in other components, we need an exogenous *method invocation connector*. This is a *unary* operator that takes a component, invokes one of its methods, and receives the result of the invocation. To structure the control and data flow in a set of components or a system, we need other connectors for sequencing exogenous method calls to different components. So we need *n-ary* connectors for connecting invocation connectors, and *n-ary* connectors for connecting these connectors, and so on. In other words, we need a hierarchy of connectors of different arities and types. This is illustrated by the example architecture in Fig. 7 (c), which represents a system that can be described in Acme and C2 by the respective architectures in Fig. 7 (a) and (b). In Fig. 7 (c), the lowest level of connectors are unary invocation connectors that connect to single components, the second-level connectors are binary and connect pairs of invocation connectors, and the third-level connectors are of variable arities and types.

In general, connectors at any level other than the first can be of variable arities; connectors at any level higher than two can be of variable arities *and* types; and we can define any number of levels of connectors. Connectors at level n for any $n > 1$ can be defined in terms of connectors at levels 1 to $(n-1)$, according to the following type hierarchy (omitting methods and their parameters):

$$
\begin{array}{ll}
\textit{Basic types} & \text{Component, Result;} \\
\textit{Connector types}\ L1 \equiv \text{Invocation} \equiv \text{Component} \longrightarrow \text{Result;} \\
\qquad\qquad L2 & \equiv L1 \times \ldots \times L1 \longrightarrow \text{Result;} \\
\qquad\qquad L3 & \equiv L \times \ldots \times L \longrightarrow \text{Result} \\
\qquad\qquad \ldots & \text{where } L \text{ is either } L1 \text{ or } L2;
\end{array}
$$

Thus level-one and level-two connectors are not polymorphic, but connectors at higher levels are. More formally, for an arbitrary number n of levels, the connector type hierarchy can be defined in terms of dependent types and polymorphism as follows:

$$
\begin{array}{c}
L1 \equiv \text{Component} \longrightarrow \text{Result;} \\
L2 \equiv L1 \times \ldots \times L1 \longrightarrow \text{Result;} \\
\text{For } 2 < i \leq n, \quad Li \equiv L(j_1) \times \ldots \times L(j_m) \longrightarrow \text{Result, for some } m \\
\text{where } j_k \in \{1, \ldots, (i-1)\} \text{ for } 1 \leq k \leq m, . \\
\text{and } L(i) = \left\{ \begin{array}{ll} L1, & i = 1 \\ \vdots & \\ Ln, & i = n. \end{array} \right.
\end{array}
$$

3.2   Implementing Exogenous Connectors

Having defined the types of the hierarchy of connectors for our component model, we need to find a way to implement connectors of these types in a generic way, such that: (i) in the repository phase, connector *templates* can be defined and stored in a repository (along with components); (ii) in the deployment phase, connector *instances* can be created (and deployed with component instances).

```
package connectors;
import java.lang.reflect.*;
public class Connector {
  public void execute (Method m, Object [] params) {}
  public void execute (Method[] ms, Object [] params) {}
}
```

Fig. 8. The *Connector* superclass.

We can do so by implementing the connectors as a hierarchy of Java classes, with a superclass *Connector* (Fig. 8). The *Connector* class has two *execute* methods for executing either a single given method (with its parameters) or a given set of methods (with their parameters). The Method class in the *execute* methods of *Connector* is provided by Java reflection. It provides the *invoke* method for calling method instances (see later). Using the *Connector* class, we can define a generic connector at any level of the hierarchy. Such a connector inherits from *Connector*, and implements the appropriate *execute* method(s). Any desired instances of this connector can then be created.

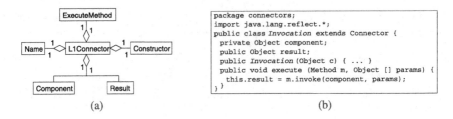

Fig. 9. Level-one (invocation) connectors: design and implementation.

A level-one connector is a *unary* invocation connector. The general design of level-one connectors is shown in Fig. 9 (a). Each connector *L1Connector* (with a unique *Name* and a *Constructor*) connects a single component. It executes a method *ExecuteMethod* that can invoke any method in that component, and yields a single *Result*. This design can be implemented in Java using reflection, as the invocation connector in Fig. 9 (b). The *execute* method of the invocation connector uses the *invoke* method provided by Java reflection to call the chosen method.

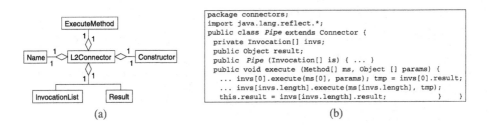

Fig. 10. Level-two connectors: design and implementation.

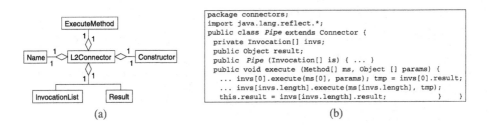

Fig. 11. Level-*m* connectors: design and implementation.

Level-two connectors are *n-ary* connectors that connect invocation connectors (Fig. 10 (a)). There are different kinds of connectors, with different implementations of their *ExecuteMethods*. For example, an *n-ary pipe* connector, used to pass values successively from the execution of a method of one component to the input of a method of the next component, can be implemented in the manner outlined in Fig. 10 (b). Another example of a level-two connector is a *n-ary selector* connector that selects one connector to execute. The *execute* method of a selector would first define how to choose the connector, before calling the *execute* method of the latter. Thus, for level-two connectors, the implementation of the *execute* method is connector-specific. However, the implementation technique is the same for all these connectors, since they are defined in terms of level-one connectors, which are implemented using Java reflection.

For an arbitrary level $m > 2$, connectors are *n-ary* and connect connectors of levels lower than m. Unlike level-one and level-two connectors, these connectors are polymorphic, so choices have to be made depending on the application in question. In general the design for level m connectors is shown in Fig. 11 (a), where a connector connects a list *ConnectorList* of connectors. Fig. 11 (b) shows the outline of the implementation of a level-m pipe.

4   An Example: The Bank System

Having defined and implemented the hierarchy of exogenous connectors that we need for our component model, we now demonstrate their use in a simple application, and use it to compare our approach with closely related work, viz. the Acme and C2 ADLs.

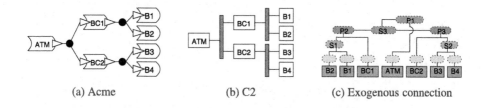

(a) Acme   (b) C2   (c) Exogenous connection

Fig. 12. Architectures of the bank example.

The example we have chosen is a simple bank system, whose architecture is described in ACME and C2 in Fig. 12 (a) and (b) respectively. The system has just one ATM that serves two bank consortia (BC1 and BC2), each with two bank branches (B1 and B2, B3 and B4 respectively). The ATM passes customer requests together with customer details to the customer's bank consortium, which in turn passes them on to the customer's bank branch. The bank branches provide the usual services of withdrawal, deposit, balance check, etc.

4.1   Implementation Using Exogenous Connectors

In our component model, using exogenous connectors, we implemented the architecture in Fig. 12 (c) for the bank system. The first step is to implement the components, and the second step is to construct a structure of connectors, i.e. a control structure, to sit on top of the components. The connector structure is constructed level by level. At level one, an invocation connector is connected to every component. This enables all the methods of a component to be invoked. Then at level two, invocation connectors are connected by level-two connectors which effect appropriate behavior among the components connected to the invocation connectors. At level three, level-two connectors are connected by level-three connectors, and so on. Execution of the system starts at the connector at the highest level; this connector is the one to initiate control flow.

In our implementation of the bank example (Fig. 12 (c)), components are Java objects with public methods (that can be invoked by the invocation connectors). These objects do not call methods in other components.

At level two, there is a selector connector $S1$ that is used to select the customer's bank branch from banks $B1$ and $B2$, prior to invoking that branch's methods requested by the customer. Similarly, there is a level-two selector connector $S2$ for choosing between $B3$ and $B4$, prior to invoking their methods requested by the customer. To pass values from one bank consortium to one of its banks we need a pipe connector; at level three, we have two pipe connectors $P2$ and $P3$, for $BC1$ and $BC2$ respectively. At level four, $S3$ is a selector connector that selects the customer's bank consortium from consortia $BC1$ and $BC2$. Finally, at level five, the pipe connector $P1$ initiates the banking system's operational cycle by passing customer requests and card information to the ATM, invoking the ATM's methods, and then passing resulting value to connector $S3$.

```
package system;
import java.lang.reflect.*;
import java.io.*;
import connectors.*;
public class BankSystem {
 public static void main (String[] args) {
  // create instances of components
  ATM atm = new ATM("1"); ... Bank bank4 = new Bank("4");
  // create level-one connectors
  Invocation invATM = new Invocation((Object) atm)); ... Invocation invB4 = new Invocation((Object) bank4));
  // create level-two connectors
  Invocation[] invsBank12 = new Invocation[2]; invsBank12[0] = invB1; invsBank12[1] = invB2;
  Selector s1 = new Selector(invsBank12);
  // create level-three connectors
  Connector[] consBC1 = new Connector[2];  consBC1[0] = invBC1;  consBC1[1] = s1;
  Pipem p2 = new Pipem(consBC1); ... Pipem p3 = new Pipem(consBC2);
  // create level-four connectors
  Connector[] consAB = new Connector[2]; consAB[0] = p2; consBC[1] = p3;
  Selectorm s3 = new Selectorm(consAB);
  // create level-five connectors
  Connector[] consm = new Connector[2]; consm[0] = invATM; consm[1] = s3;
  Pipem p1 = new Pipem(consm);
  // Display menu and initiate operations
  switch(Integer.parseInt(args[0]))) {
   case 1:
    System.out.println("Your balance is:");
    p1.execute(ms, params);
    break; ...                      } } }
```

Fig. 13. Outline of the code for the bank system.

Fig. 13 shows the outline of the code for the system. It reflects the hierarchical manner in which the bank system is built, by constructing the connectors level by level. We can illustrate the bank system's behavior by considering the example of a customer of $B3$ wishing to withdraw money from his account. First the customer inserts his card into the teller machine and keys in his PIN code. The $P1$ pipe connector initiates the system's operational cycle by passing the customer information and withdrawal request to the invocation connector of the *ATM* component to invoke the appropriate methods of the *ATM* for validating customer details and determining the customer's bank consortium. If the validation succeeds, $P1$ passes the bank consortium identity, $BC2$ (and the withdrawal request), to the selector $S3$. $S3$ selects the pipe $P3$, which is connected to $BC2$. $P3$ uses the invocation connector for $BC2$ to invoke a method for identifying the customer's bank branch, and passes the result, $B3$, to the selector $S2$ connector. $S2$ selects the invocation connector of $B3$ to invoke the *withdraw* method implemented by $B3$. The result is then the output of this operational cycle. It can be output by either the selector $S2$, or even the component $B3$.

4.2 Comparison with Acme and C2 Implementations

The implementation of the bank example demonstrates the feasibility of using exogenous connectors (and our component model) to build systems. In order to evaluate our approach against related work, we implemented the same example using Acme and C2, and compared these implementations with ours. We chose Acme because it is the most generic archetypal ADL. We chose C2 because, as a message-based ADL, it uses a higher level of abstraction of indirect message passing than non-message-based ADLs such as Acme, as explained in Section 2.2; thus connection in C2 is more indirect than Acme. These two provide a graded comparison with exogenous connection.

Another reason for choosing Acme and C2 is a practical one, namely that there are tools for generating implementations from architecture descriptions in these ADLs. The tools we chose are ArchJava [4,2] and ArchStudio 3 [5] for Acme and C2 respectively. Both these tools are based on Java, and generate Java code, so they allow easy and direct comparison with our example.

The main point of comparison is the separation of control and communication from computation. In our component model, components are supposed to encapsulate computation while exogenous connectors are supposed to encapsulate communication in general and control in particular. This distinguishes it from existing component models, in particular ADLs like Acme and C2, as shown in Fig. 6. Our experiment with the bank example bears this out very well.

At design time, as shown in Fig. 12, Acme and C2 architectures look 'as exogenous as' our approach. However, when the architectures are implemented, the resulting Acme/ArchJava and C2/ArchStudio systems show clearly the mixing of control and computation, and of computation and communication, whereas our system maintains their separation. Fig. 14 shows the structure of a BankConsortium (BC) component in Acme/ArchJava, C2/ArchStudio and our approach, distinguishing between code for computation, code that mixes computation and control, and code for communication.

In the case of Acme/ArchJava, Fig. 14 (a), components communicate through *ports* that must be defined in the component's class. Required operations are specified in *in*

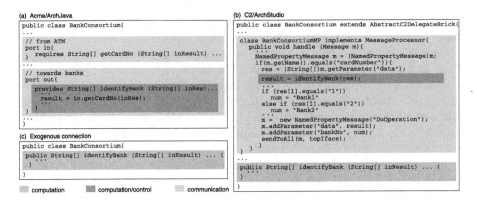

Fig. 14. Computation, control and communication in the BankConsortium component.

ports and provided operations are defined in *out* ports. Thus the provided operations are defined in the communication part of the component, i.e. mixing communication and computation. Moreover, by definition, the provided operations are defined in terms of the required operations, i.e. the former will call the latter, thus mixing computation with control. In the bank example, in the computation part (in the communication part) of the BankConsortium component, the provided operation *identifyBank* computes *result* by calling the required *getCardNo* operation named in an *in* port, and thus directs control flow to the (connector to the) ATM component, that provides this operation.

In the case of C2/ArchStudio (Fig. 14 (b)) to receive and send messages, a component must implement its own message processor. Message processors are objects that implement a *handle* method to deal with messages. In the bank example, the BankConsortium component uses the *BankConsortiumMP* inner class as its message processor. A message processor must identify messages intended for the component, and determine and execute appropriate actions upon receipt of such messages, which may include sending a message with the results of the actions. Here, communication is mixed up with computation that contains control. In the bank example, the message processor *BankConsortiumMP* computes *result* by calling the *identifyBank* method in the midst of its communication code, and thus directing control flow to this method.

By contrast, in our approach, Fig. 14 (c), the separation of computation from control and communication is maintained. A component has only code for computation. In the bank example, the BankConsortium component has only code for the *identifyBank* method. Communication, and control in particular, is embodied in connectors.

Another point of comparison is the supported patterns of communication, i.e. the set of connectors provided. Compared to Acme and C2, we have a potentially larger set of connectors, since our hierarchy of connector types is polymorphic and can be used to generate any number of kinds of connectors at any level. In contrast, Acme has just one level of connectors, viz. pipes, for indirect message passing such as remote procedure calls via components' ports; C2 uses a bus for connecting components at every level.

5   Evaluation and Discussion

The example in the previous section provides some useful initial feedback on exogenous connectors. In particular, the comparison of the implementation with those in Acme/ArchJava and C2/ArchStudio shows that exogenous connectors can offer some advantages. While it would be unwise to draw general conclusions from one small example, it is possible to make some general observations and discuss their import. In this section we evaluate exogenous connectors and discuss their potential usefulness, advantages and disadvantages, etc. with respect to CBSE.

The bank example demonstrates the feasibility of using exogenous connectors to encapsulate communication, in particular control flow. Separating computation from control means that control flow does not originate from components, but from connectors. So in a system, the components are decoupled from the structure of connectors which provides the control structure. For system maintenance and evolution, this decoupling should make it simpler to manage changes in the components and changes in the connectors separately. Another advantage should be separation of concerns in reasoning about system behaviors. The connectors encapsulate the computational paths, while the components encapsulate computation. In predictable assembly, this separation of concerns should make it more tractable and easier to reason about system behavior by reasoning about control and computation separately.

An important implication of this is that it should be possible to verify component properties, e.g. functional correctness, statically and store proven components in a repository. To this end, we plan to develop components with contracts [17], statically prove their contract compliance, and then place them in the repository. At deployment time, the developer can assume the components' contract compliance, and concentrate on developing the connector structure, and reasoning about its computational paths. Again, separating control from computation should make it more tractable and hence practicable to reason about components and their composition. Such an approach would make a fundamental contribution to CBSE, since it enables bottom-up assembly of components, starting with a component repository. The only existing component models that support this are Koala [26] and KobrA [6], which have repositories for productlines. Our approach is different in that the repository components form a flat tier at the bottom, and the control structure is built to sit on top, as clearly illustrated by Fig. 12 (c). By contrast, top-down design approaches, e.g. ADLs, do not use components from repositories, and do not allow composites to be constructed and stored in repositories for reuse in different applications. In fact, even our exogenous connectors can be stored in a repository, as we saw in the bank example.

Another practical advantage of exogenous connectors is their hierarchical nature. This provides a hierarchical way for developing systems, resulting in well-structured code for the final system, which is easy to understand, and therefore maintain. Adding, changing and replacing connectors is also made easier. It remains to be seen, however, whether these advantages pertain, or whether our approach is practical, when the application is very large, requiring a very sophisticated and involved control structure. It would be interesting to investigate the design and implementation of more complicated exogenous connectors than pipes and selectors, and whether their existence would make our approach practical for such applications.

The obvious potential disadvantage of exogenous connectors is a potential preponderance of connectors and connector levels, and hence inefficiency in communication. In the bank example, the number of levels of connectors is only five. Considering the architecture is a three-level architecture in Acme and C2, this is not bad. However, we have not studied how to predict the number of levels, nor the total number, of connectors. Also, to measure run-time performance sensibly, we need much larger examples.

6 Conclusion

In this paper we have presented exogenous connectors, their definition and implementation, and an example illustrating their use in building a simple system. The key distinguishing characteristic of these connectors is that they encapsulate control totally, i.e. control originates from them. This is in complete contrast to most software connectors, which encapsulate communication but not control. In ADLs, for example, control originates in components, and connectors pass it on to other components, and so on.

Our work on exogenous connectors is at a preliminary stage, however. We have considered only control flow, but not data flow, beyond passing results of method calls back to connectors. Data flow needs careful consideration, especially if components have private databases, or if some but not all components in a system share databases. In such systems, the precise ways in which global data and local data interact must be clearly defined and rigorously enforced.

We have not considered concurrency in the connectors either. In fact we have only used sequential composition. As a result, we cannot address the general issues of architectural reasoning, whereby typically connectors provide parallel or asynchronous communication between components. For example, one such issue is that of "correct architectures" in the sense of architectures with guaranteed temporal properties such as deadlock-freedom [14]; another issue concerns consistency between architecture and code, e.g. [1]. However, by using only sequential composition, we manage to avoid the problem of synchronization, which is present in even the simplest forms of message passing, such as direct method calls, when there are competing calls to the same callee.

The connectors we have presented in this paper belong to the deployment phase of our component model. We are in the process of investigating connectors for the other phase, the repository phase. In this phase, we want to store components as well as connectors. Our aim is to also allow the construction of composite components, and to store them in the repository, so as to make the task of composition in the deployment phase simpler. Top-down approaches such as software architectures do not use components from, or store them, in repositories. In ADLs, although they can be constructed and used at design time, composite components are not stored in repositories. By contrast, we want to do so. We believe that in the repository phase, it would be useful to have connectors that can be used to compose components into subsystems or even complete systems that can be stored in the repository. Such connectors would have to yield components from those they connect. The invocation connectors, pipes and selectors in this paper return results rather than components, and are therefore deployment phase connectors, and cannot be used to build composites in the repository phase.

In this paper, we have implemented components as Java classes. This is of course only for convenience. In our component model, components are not necessarily just classes. In particular, they have proper interfaces that may not be implementable using classes in object-oriented programming languages. For example, our interfaces contain contracts which specify the behavior of the components, apart from the signature of its operations. These contracts cannot be defined properly in Java using the *assert* statement, which is the only provision in Java for Design by Contract.

Apart from the issue of interfaces, Java is a good implementation language, or at least as good as any object-oriented language. Inheritance allows us to define our polymorphic connector hierarchy straightforwardly. However, the problems with inheritance are well-known, not least of which is any form of static analysis, which is important for reasoning purposes in the repository phase. In particular, inheritance works against our wish to statically verify component and connector contracts in the repository phase.

For predictable assembly, we believe the use of contracts in the repository phase is crucial, as is their static verification, and we have started investigating using ESC Java [10] for both components and connectors. We are also investigating other languages, in particular SPARK [7], which offer tool support for contracts and their static verification. Finally, in the longer term, it would be interesting to examine the taxonomy in [16] to see how widely the idea of exogenous connectors can be applied to that taxonomy.

Acknowledgements

We wish to thank David Garlan for helpful points of information about code generation from architecture descriptions.

References

1. J. Aldrich, C. Chambers, and D. Notkin. Architectural reasoning in ArchJava. In *Proc. 16th European Conference on Object-Oriented Programming*, pages 334–367. Springer-Verlag, 2002.
2. J. Aldrich, C. Chambers, and D. Notkin. ArchJava: Connecting software architecture to implimentation. In *Proc. 24th International Conference on Software Engineering*, pages 187–197. ACM Press, 2002.
3. F. Arbab. The IWIM model for coordination of concurrent activities. In P. Ciancarini and C. Hankin, editors, *Lecture Notes in Computer Science 1061*, pages 34–56. Springer-Verlag, 1996.
4. ArchJava web page. http://archjava.fluid.cs.cmu.edu/index.html.
5. ArchStudio 3 web page. http://www.isr.uci.edu/projects/archstudio/index.html.
6. C. Atkinson, J. Bayer, C. Bunse, E. Kamsties, O. Laitenberger, R. Laqua, D. Muthig, B. Paech, J. Wüst, and J. Zettel. *Component-based Product Line Engineering with UML*. Addison-Wesley, 2001.
7. J. Barnes. *High Integrity Software: The SPARK Approach to Safety and Security*. Addison-Wesley, 2003.
8. D. Box. *Essential COM*. Addison Wesley, 1998.
9. R. Englander. *Developing Java Beans*. O'Reilly & Associates, 1997.
10. Extended Static Checking for Java Home Page. http://research.compaq.com/SRC/esc/.

11. E. Gamma, R. Helm, R. Johnson, and J. Vlissides. The courier pattern. *Dr. Dobb's Journal*, Feburary 1996.
12. D. Garlan, R.T. Monroe, and D. Wile. ACME: Architectural description of component-based systems. In M. Sitaraman G.T. Leavens, editor, *Foundations of Component-Based Systems*, pages 47–68. Cambridge University Press, 2000.
13. R.M. Haefel. *Enterprise JavaBeans*. O'Reilly & Associates, 3rd edition, 2001.
14. P. Inverardi and M. Tivoli. Software architecture for correct components assembly. In *Formal Methods for the Design of Computer, Commmunication and Software Systems, Lecture Notes in Computer Science 2804*, pages 92–111. Springer, 2003.
15. J. Ivers, N. Sinha, and K.C Wallnau. A basis for composition language CL. Technical Report CMU/SEI-2002-TN-026, CMU SEI, 2002.
16. N.R. Mehta, N. Medvidovic, and S. Phadke. Towards a taxonomy of software connectors. In *Proc. 22nd International Conference on Software Engineering*, pages 178–187. ACM Press, 2000.
17. B. Meyer. Applying design by contract. *IEEE Computer*, 25(10):40–51, October 1992.
18. O. Nierstrasz, G. Arévalo, S. Ducasse, R. Wuyts, A. Black, P. Müller, C. Zeidler, T. Genssler, and R. van den Born. A component model for field devices. In *Proc. 1st International IFIP/ACM Working Conference on Component Deployment*, Berlin, Germany, 2002.
19. OMG, http://www.omg.org/cgi-bin/doc?ptc/2003-08-02. *UML 2.0 Superstructure Specification*.
20. OMG, http://www.omg.org/technology/documents/formal/components.htm. *CORBA Component Model, V3.0*, 2002.
21. J.G. Schneider and O. Nierstrasz. Components, scripts and glue. In L. Barroca, J. Hall, and P. Hall, editors, *Software Architectures – Advances and Applications*, pages 13–25. Springer-Verlag, 1999.
22. M. Shaw and D. Garlan. *Software Architecture: Perspectives on an Emerging Discipline*. Prentice Hall, 1996.
23. Software Engineering Institute, Carnegie-Mellon University. Predictable assembly from certifiable components. http://www.sei.cmu.edu/pacc/.
24. C. Szyperski, D. Gruntz, and S. Murer. *Component Software: Beyond Object-Oriented Programming*. Addison-Wesley, second edition, 2002.
25. R. N. Taylor, N. Medvidovic, K. M. Anderson, E. J. Whitehead Jr., J. E. Robbins, K. A. Nies, P. Oreizy, and D. L. Dubrow. A component- and message-based architectural style for GUI software. *Software Engineering*, 22(6):390–406, 1996.
26. R. van Ommering, F. van der Linden, J. Kramer, and J. Magee. The Koala component model for consumer electronics software. *IEEE Computer*, pages 78–85, March 2000.

Qinna, a Component-Based QoS Architecture

Jean-Charles Tournier[1], Jean-Philippe Babau[2], and Vincent Olive[1]

[1] France Télécom R&D Division,
28, Chemin du Vieux Chêne, BP98,
38243 Meylan, France
{jeancharles.tournier,vincent.olive}@francetelecom.com
[2] CITI/INSA Lyon
Bâtiment Léonard de Vinci,
69621 Villeurbanne Cedex, France
jean-philippe.babau@insa-lyon.fr

Abstract. Component-Based Software Engineering is quickly becoming a mainstream approach to software development. At the same time, there is a massive shift from desktop applications to embedded communicating systems (e.g. PDAs or smartphones): it is especially the case for multimedia applications such as video players, music players, etc. Moreover, embedded communicating systems have to deal with *open* aspect: applications may come or leave the system on the fly. A key point of these systems is its ability to rigorously manage Quality of Service due to resource constraints.

In this paper, we present a component-based QoS architecture well-suited for open systems, called Qinna. Qinna is defined using Fractal components and takes into consideration the main QoS concepts (specification, provision and management). An analysis and an experiment illustrate answers brought by Qinna to open system issues.

1 Introduction

Nowadays, handheld systems such as PDAs or smart-phones are everywhere in our life from office to home. These systems have to integrate more and more complex applications (video players, games, MP3 players, etc.) with a limited amount of resources (in terms of CPU power, memory, network or battery). Moreover, such systems have to be able to host or remove applications on the fly: they are called open systems. This property implies several non functional constraints that must be solved at run-time (QoS, security, fault tolerance, etc.)

Component-Based Software Engineering (CBSE) appears as a promising solution for the development of such kind of systems. Indeed, one of the claim of CBSE is to offer an easier way to build complex software by simply assembling components [4]. Moreover, CBSE may be one of the most efficient way to reduce time development due to the fact it is intrinsically oriented to reuse existing parts of a system [22]. As a system results from the assembly of components, CBSE increases re-usability, flexibility and maintainability of systems [7].

G.T. Heineman et al. (Eds.): CBSE 2005, LNCS 3489, pp. 107–122, 2005.

Several component models are available or developing. Industrial models include the Microsoft's® component family (COM, DCOM and more recently .NET [15]), the solution from SUN Microsystem® (JB, EJB [21]) or standardized model such as the proposal from OMG (CORBA Component Model [19] which is close to the EJB model). These models are designed for traditional workstation (such as PC) software and are mainly seen as *business models*. In the field of embedded systems, component models result mainly from the research domain. For instance, Think [14], COYOTE [17] or OSKit [3] allow to build an entire operating system as an assembly of components.

The main lack of these component models is that the functional point of view is well achieved, whereas the QoS one is not. Heterogeneity of the QoS in terms of specification, management or even hardware support tends to produce heavy and complex models with a huge cost.

In this paper, we present a component-based QoS architecture, called Qinna, well-suited for open systems. Qinna is based on the Fractal component model [10] and respects the main QoS concepts identified in [2]. As Qinna is defined through components, it brings component benefits to QoS (re-usability, flexibility and dynamicity) and allows an efficient QoS management in open systems.

The rest of this paper is organized as follows. The first section sets the context of our study: the Fractal component model is first introduced, followed by a survey of the main QoS concepts. We then enumerate and detail QoS requirements of open systems. The second section defines the Qinna architecture, while the third one validates and evaluates the architecture. We finally review some related works and conclude the paper.

2   Working Context

This work combines ideas from two clearly identified research areas. The first one is about CBSE and more precisely about the Fractal component model [10], while the second one is about QoS architectures. In the following two sub-sections, we present and define the main concepts of each research area. We finally highlight requirements of open systems from a QoS point of view.

2.1   Fractal

The Fractal component model is based on five key concepts: component, content, controller, interface and binding.

A component is formed out of two parts: a controller and a content.

The content of a component is composed of a finite number of other components, which are under the control of the controller of the enclosing component. For example a controller can control the life cycle of the content or its configuration.

A component can interact with its environment through service at identified access points, called interfaces. Services provide the basic interaction primitives in the Fractal component model. Interfaces are either client or server interfaces.

A server interface can receive service invocations, whereas a client interface emits service invocations.

A binding is a connection between two or several components. Fractal comprises primitive and composite bindings. A primitive binding is a directed connection between a client interface and a server interface. Primitive bindings are typically implemented as language level bindings. Composite bindings are realized through a combination of primitive bindings and ordinary components, i.e. composite bindings are themselves Fractal component.

Usually, a Fractal component type is defined by its required (client) and provided (server) interfaces, whereas a Fractal component class is defined by its type and its implementation.

Now, let us see the difference between a functional composition and a QoS one. For instance, from a functional point of view, a X component provides the x interface if, and only if, its y required interface is filled. From a QoS point of view, the QoS level provided on x interface depends on the QoS level seen on the interface y as well as the implementation of X. Generally, a *black box view* can be used for a functional composition, whereas *a grey box view* is needed for a QoS composition. Consequently, we can write:

$$QoS(Itf_{provided} = F(\overrightarrow{QoS(Itf_{required})}, Comp\_Implem)$$

A composition of two components is formalized by a contract. A contract is usually defined in four levels [1]: (a) the *syntactic* level which is provided by interface signature; (b) the *behavioral* level which defines the pre and post conditions of an interface; (c) the *synchronization* level which is a description of the sequence of messages, loops and alternative paths on an interface; and (d) the *QoS* level which specifies the QoS level required or provided by a component on its interface. This work focuses on the fourth level of the contract.

As Fractal is a model, there are several implementations depending on application domains. Think [14] is an implementation of the Fractal component model dedicated to operating systems for embedded platforms. Think allows to build a customized operating system as a composition of software components. It offers a homogeneous component view of all layers of the system. Think achieves speed-ups and decreases memory footprint over other general purpose operating systems. Moreover, performance measurements show no degradation due to kernel componentization. Two kinds of components are defined. The first ones reify the hardware layer of the platform. For example, these components include exceptions, interruptions, MMU or drivers (screen, keyboard, touch panel, etc.). They have been ported on several platforms such as Intel StrongARM (iPaq H3900 and H2200), Intel XScale (iPaq H3600 and H3800) or Portal Player (Apple iPod). The second kind of components provide classical operating system services: scheduler (round-robin, priority, etc.), memory management (flat, paged), network (ip, ethernet, bluetooth, GPRS), etc.

From a QoS point of view, one of the advantage of Think is that it allows a fine grain control over resources thanks to components.

2.2   QoS Concepts

Systems may manage QoS in different ways. At one end, QoS requirements can be met statically during design and implementation by proper design and configuration choices (such as scheduling rules, network bandwidth allocation, etc.). This will give a well-defined behavior, but without any flexibility. At the other end is the dynamic approach that lets systems negotiate at run-time the restrictions of the QoS characteristics they need for their activities. This approach often involves an adaptive aspect by having monitors and corrective steps to be taken when the QoS level drops below a certain threshold. This approach is very flexible as QoS policies can be changed at run-time, but the behavior is not well defined and performance may be degraded if costly adaptation schemes are used.

To be able to dynamically manage QoS, a QoS architecture should integrate at least the following abilities [2]:

- *QoS specification.* QoS specification is concerned with capturing the QoS level requirements and management policy. QoS specification is declarative in nature; users specify what is required rather than how this is to be achieved by underlying QoS mechanisms. A QoS specification is composed of several aspects [6] [11]:
  - *Performance* which characterizes performance requirements.
  - *Level of importance* which specifies the degree of importance required.
  - *QoS management policy* which allows to specify adaptation to the required performance.
- *QoS provision mechanism* is composed of the following aspects:
  - *QoS mapping* performs the function of automatic translation between representations of QoS at different system levels. Classically, four levels are considered: user level, application level, operating system level and resources level. For instance, a GOOD user QoS specification of a Video component is translated to 25 frames/sec at application level, 1 thread at operating system level and 60% CPU at resources level.
  - *Admission testing* is responsible for comparing resource requirements arising from the requested QoS against available resources in the system
  - *Resource reservation.*
- *QoS management.* To maintain agreed levels of QoS it is often not sufficient just to commit resources. QoS management is frequently required to ensure that the contracted QoS is still valid. Fundamentals of QoS management include:
  - *QoS observation* for allowing each level of the system to track the ongoing QoS levels achieved by the lower layer.
  - *QoS maintenance* for comparing the monitored quality of service against the expected performance and then exerts a tuning operation.
  - *QoS degradation* for indicating that the lower layers have failed to maintain the QoS level and nothing further can be done by the QoS maintenance mechanism.

2.3   Open System Requirements

In this paper, we define an open system as a system that can integrate new components at run time. Usually, these components are unforeseen: it means that the system and the component do not know each other before its arrival. From a QoS point of view, an open system raises several key issues that must be taken into consideration:

1. A new component may not know its own QoS requirements. For example, a Video component does not know how much resource it needs to be able to execute at 25 frames/sec.
2. A new component may have an estimation of its QoS requirements. This estimation may have been done by the programmer or determined from previous experiments. For example, in the case of the Video component, the programmer estimates that it needs 45% of the CPU and 150 kilobytes of memory to execute at 25 frames/sec.
3. Adding or leaving of a component must not destabilize the system. It means that the system must ensure the component will not consume a greater QoS level than the specified one.
4. As the system evolves dynamically, it must be able to manage its QoS dynamically too. For example, the QoS level of the Video component may be degraded to let enough resources to a more important component.
5. An open system must be generic enough to integrate various QoS management and QoS specifications. Every component has with its own QoS management mechanism and its own QoS specification. For example, a component which requires a non real-time thread must be satisfied even if the system is real-time.
6. Finally, an open system must be designed in order to improve re-usability of QoS management. For example, QoS management mechanisms for the Video component must be reusable for another platform.

In the following section, Qinna a QoS architecture suited for component-based open systems is presented. The architecture incorporates the main QoS concepts identified in section 2.2, in order to dynamically manage QoS, and is defined using Fractal components.

3   Qinna

3.1   Introduction

In this section we define a component-based QoS architecture for embedded open systems, called Qinna. The definition of Qinna is based on two hypotheses: (1) the system has a global knowledge of its available resources. It means that a request can not be delegated to another unknown system; (2) the system must be component-based itself in order to provide an homogeneous components' view at each layer (application, operating system, resources).

The philosophy of Qinna is to manage QoS using contracts (cf. figure 1). It means to each functional component that needs QoS management (called QoSComponent) a contract is set up. Contracts are managed (initialization, adaptation and maintenance) by a dedicated QoSComponentManager that delegates admission testing to a QoSComponentBroker. Moreover, contracts observation is performed by a QoSComponentObserver, while decision of contracts adaptation and maintenance is performed by the QoSDomain.

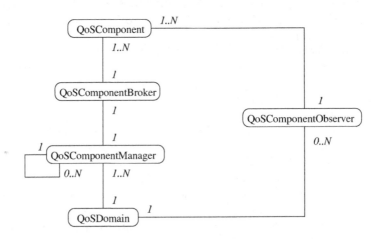

Fig. 1. Overview of the Qinna architecture.

More precisely, Qinna is defined through a set of component types, data types, APIs and its dynamic behavior.

3.2   Component Types

Qinna defines five different component types: QoSComponent, QoSComponent-Broker, QoSComponentManager, QoSComponentObserver and QoSDomain. Each service provided by Qinna interfaces are summarized in table 1.

A **QoSComponent** is a component which provides, at least, one functional interface and may require others. To provide a given QoS level on its provided interfaces, a QoSComponent needs a given QoS level on its required interfaces and must be configured via a local constraint (typed by T_LC).

In addition to its functional interfaces, a QoSComponent must provide the iLocalConstraint and iQoSObserver interfaces. The first interface allows to manage the local constraint, while the latter notifies the real provided QoS level.

A **QoSComponentBroker** relies on a global constraint (typed by T_GC) to accept, or not, to set the local constraint of a QoSComponent and give a reference to it. QoSComponentBroker is responsible for admission testing and reservation of QoSComponents. To each class of QoSComponent is associated a QoSComponentBroker.

Interfaces	Services
iLocalConstraint	int set(T_LC lc)
	T_LC get()
iQoSObserver	T_QoS get()
iQoSBroker	T_CID reserve(T_LC lc)
	int free(T_CID cid)
	int modify(T_CID cid, T_LC lc)
iQoSBrokerAdministration	int set(T_GC gc)
	T_GC get()
iQoSManager	T_CT_MANAGER reserve(T_QoS q)
	int free(T_CT_MANAGER ct)
	int modify(T_CT_MANAGER ct,T_QoS q)
iQoSAdapter	int degrade(T_CT_MANAGER ct)
	int upgrade(T_CT_MANAGER ct)
iQoSMaintener	int degrade(T_CT_MANAGER ct)
	int upgrade(T_CT_MANAGER ct)
iQoSManagerAdministration	int set(T_MT mt)
	T_MT get()
iQoSObserverLifeCycle	int start(T_CID, T_POL pol)
	int pause(T_CID)
	int stop(T_CID)
iQoSDomain	T_CID reserve(T_QoS qu, T_IMP imp)
	int free(T_CID cid)
	int modify(T_CID cid, T_QoS qu, T_IMP imp)
iQoSObserverException	int exception(T_CID cid, T_QoS observed_q)
iQoSDomainAdministration	int set(f_Order_Relation)
	bool f_Order_Relation(T_IMP imp1, T_IMP imp2)

T_LC: Local constraint type
T_GC: Global constraint type
T_QoS: QoS level type
T_CID: Component identifier type
T_CT_MANAGER: QoSComponentManager contract type
T_MT: Map table type
T_POL: Observation policy type
T_IMP: Importance type

Table 1. Qinna APIs.

QoSComponentBroker requires the iLocalConstraint interface. It provides the iQoSBroker interface in order to reserve, or modify, a QoSComponent with a given local constraint. Moreover, the iQoSBrokerAdministration interface is provided to be able to manage the global constraint.

A **QoSComponentManager** is responsible for the management of the QoS level provided by a QoSComponent. To each QoSComponentBroker is associated a QoSComponentManager. In order to manage QoS level, QoSComponentManager performs three tasks:

1. it initializes, from a QoS point of view, execution of a QoSComponent. From a given specification, which specifies the required QoS level, QoSComponentManager translates this information into specific QoS levels on required interfaces and a local constraint on its managed QoSComponent. The translation is performed using a map table (typed by T_MT). Subsequently, the QoSComponentManager establishes a contract (typed by T_CT_MANAGER) composed of:

   (a) an unique contract identifier, typed by T_CT_MANAGER.
   (b) the component identifier of the QoSComponent provided by QoSComponentBroker, typed by T_CID.
   (c) expected QoS level provided by the QoSComponent, typed by T_QoS.
   (d) a list of contract identifiers, it represents the established contracts to fill out the required interfaces of the QoSComponent.

   Moreover, QoSComponentManager integrates `T_QoS2 translate(T_QoS1 q)` operator. This operator translates a given QoS specification (T_QoS1) to an understandable one by the map table (T_QoS2).

2. it implements adaptation mechanisms
3. it implements maintenance mechanisms

QoSComponentManager requires the `iQoSBroker` interface and provides the `iQoSManager` one. This interface allows to do a reservation, or a modification, of a QoSComponent with a desired QoS level. It may also require several `iQoSManager` interfaces in order to get QoSComponents to fill out required interfaces of its managed QoSComponent. Moreover, QoSComponentManager provides `iQoSAdapter` and `iQoSMaintener` interfaces which implement adaptation and maintenance mechanisms. At last, it provides the interface `iQoSManagerAdministration` to set up the map table.

A **QoSComponentObserver** is responsible for the observation of the QoS level provided by a class of QoSComponents. It implements the observation policy.

QoSComponentObserver requires the interfaces `iQoSObserverException` and `iQoSObserver`. It provides the `iQoSObserverLifeCycle` interface in order to manage life cycle of observation (start, stop, pause). Observation policy is given to QoSComponentObserver when QoSComponentObserver is started.

A **QoSDomain** is the highest level of the architecture: all other Qinna components are encapsulated in a QoSDomain component. From a user point of view, it is the entry point for a QoSComponent request. QoSDomain defines adaptation and maintenance policies. These policies are based on a contract list (typed by T_CT_DOMAIN) which are linked to an importance level (typed by T_IMP) to a contract identifier provided by QoSComponentManager.

QoSDomain requires interfaces `iQoSManager`, `iQoSAdapter`, `iQoSMaintener` and `iQoSObserverLifeCycle`. It provides the `iQoSDomain` interface in order to reserve, or modify, a QoSComponent with a given QoS and importance level. It also provides the `iQoSObserverException` interface in order to be notified of a QoSComponentManager contract violation. At the end, the QoSDomain provides the `iQoSDomainAdministration` interface to set up the order relation of T_IMP type.

To summarize, a class of QoSComponents is bound to one QoSComponent-Broker which is itself bound to one QoSComponentManager. QoSComponent-Managers can be bound to each other and are bound to one QoSDomain. Finally, one QoSComponentObserver is bound to a class of QoSComponent and several QoSComponentObservers are bound to one QoSDomain.

3.3   Data Types

The Qinna architecture uses several different types. This section defines constraints on these types. First, there is a `default` element to initialize unknown data: T_GC, T_LC, T_QoS and T_IMP have a `default` element. Moreover, T_CID and T_CT_ID have a `NULL` element (no reference).

In order to work with QoS constraints, there are (1) some comparison operators: `compare(T_GC cg, T_LC lc)`, `compare(T_QoS q1, T_QoS q2)` and `compare (T_IMP i1, T_IMP i2)`; and (2) some calculus operators: `add(T_GC gc, T_LC lc)` and `sub(T_GC gc, T_LC lc)`. Moreover T_MT type has a mapping operator: `T_QoS map(T_QoS q)`.

3.4   Dynamic Behavior

The main operations of the dynamic behavior of Qinna are contract initialization, contract management and contract configuration. The first operation occurs when a QoSComponent is executed. The second operation is triggered in response to an exception or during activation of another QoSComponent. The third operation is done when a QoSComponent is configured or observed.

To activate a new QoSX component, a request is sent to the QoSDomain (service *reserve* of interface *iQoSDomain*). The request is then transmitted to the QoSXManager (service *reserve* of interface *iQoSManager*). According to the map table, requested components Y are reserved (thanks to the appropriate QoSComponentManagers) and QoSX is requested to QoSXBroker (service *reserve* of interface *iQoSBroker*) in order to configure it (service *set* of interface *iLocalConstraint*). If the desired QoS level can not be achieved, QoSDomain degrades the previous existing QoS levels according to importance level until an acceptable solution is found (service *degrade* of interface *iQoSAdapter*).

When a component is stopped (service *free* of interface *iQoSDomain*), the QoSDomain analyses its current contracts in order to upgrade the most important ones (service *upgrade* of interface *iQoSAdapter*). Likewise, an exception raised by a QoSComponentObserver (service *exception* of interface *iQoSObserverException*) or a QoSComponent modification (service *modify* of interface *iQoSDomain*) is followed by a global contracts analysis in order to determine optimal QoS levels.

Contract configuration is usually done when a component is activated according to the map table. Unknown data are set to *default* values and then dynamically evaluated using observations (services *get*, *exception* and *upgrade/degrade* of interfaces *iQoSObserver*, *iQoSObserverException* and *iQoSMaintener* respectively).

Finally, every operation executed by Qinna must be atomic in order to keep the global system coherent.

In the following section, we demonstrate how the Qinna architecture can manage QoS of open component-based systems.

4   Open Systems

This section details the way Qinna deals with specific issues of open component-based systems and presents an experiment in order to illustrate and evaluate the architecture.

4.1   Qinna for Open Systems

In section 2.3 we have identified six QoS issues that must be taken into consideration for open systems.

A new component may not know its QoS requirements on its required interfaces, it means that its map table is empty. To take this into account this first issue, Qinna sets up three mechanisms. Firstly, required QoS levels are set to *default*. Secondly, QoSComponentObserver are activated in order to observe the real provided QoS level. And thirdly, QoSComponentObserver sends exceptions to QoSDomain which runs the maintenance policy.

A component may have an estimation of its QoS requirements, i.e. its map table may be unreliable. This case is similar to the previous one, but instead of setting initial QoS requirement to *default*, they are set according to the map table. In comparison with a normal situation (reliable map table), QoSComponentObserver is activated and maintenance policy is triggered.

Adding or leaving of a component must not destabilize the system. Here, the answer is given by the implicit philosophy of Qinna. Indeed, Qinna prohibits a QoSComponent to consume a greater QoS level than the specified and allocated one: each time a functional service is requested a control is done. For example memory usage (e.g. *malloc(...)* service) is performed by memory components. Once an initial amount of memory, M, is requested, memory component controls each sub-request (e.g. *malloc(m)*) in order to enforce $\sum m_i < M$. In some cases, a QoSComponent can request all the available resources. Either the QoSComponent is the most important one of the system and Qinna is right to allow it, or the QoSComponent is malicious. In such instances security aspects, such as cryptography or authentication, must be integrated, but this is beyond the scope of our work.

In order to dynamically manage QoS, Qinna allows to integrate the main QoS concepts identified by [2]. Each QoS specification aspect is identified as a parameter of services of iQoSDomain interface. The mapping operation is done by QoSComponentManagers, whereas admission testing and reservation is done by QoSComponentBrokers. QoSComponentObserver is responsible for

QoS observation. Finally, QoS maintenance and QoS degradation are conjointly done by QoSComponentManagers and QoSDomain. Dynamic QoS management by Qinna is explained in detail in [13].

Qinna is generic enough to take into account heterogeneous aspects of QoS. It allows to implement various QoS management as real-time [12] or multimedia [13]. Moreover, to deal with heterogeneous QoS specifications, Qinna specifies the T_QoS translate(T_QoS q) operator. This operator translates an initial specification to an understandable one by the map table. To illustrate, if an initial specification is a function f and the map table only deals with fixed values, translate returns either $max(f)$ or default if f can not be analyzed. The operator necessarily accomplishes a semantic interpretation of the specification.

To improve re-usability, Qinna observes two principles. First, Qinna respects separation of concerns between the functional (QoSComponent) and the non functional ones (QoSComponentBroker, QoSComponentManager, QoSDomain and QoSComponentObserver). Second, Qinna decouple QoS policies and mechanisms. Indeed, policies are implemented by QoSDomain and QoSComponentObservers whereas mechanisms are implemented by QoSComponentManagers.

4.2   Experiment

The goal of this section is to illustrate how Qinna can be used in a open system. We then evaluate this specific Qinna implementation. The experiment involves the construction of a video player with QoS ability on a iPaq platform. For this experiment, we choose an H3800 iPaq with an intel StrongARM SA1100 processor at 206 MHz, 60 Mb of DRAM memory and 32 Mb of flash memory. From a software perspective, we choose the Think component-based framework. Think has been chosen for its properties: (1) it provides an homogeneous component view at each layer of the system; (2) it allows a fine grain control of the system; and (3) it is available for ARM processor.

Case Study The considered case study is composed of a GUI component which allows to control a Video component by specifying its QoS requirements. The Video component requires a Memory component and a Thread component. Finally, the Thread component requires a scheduler. We choose a simple round-robin scheduler which is able to ponderate thread execution. For example, if thread A and B have ponderation equals to 3 and 2, the resultant scheduling is: $ABABA|ABABA|AB....$ Moreover, the Video component has two QoS levels: GOOD and BAD, but the corresponding required QoS level are unknown (in terms of CPU and memory). This case study addresses two typical open system issues. Firstly, how can we determine the required QoS levels of the Video component? Secondly, how can we be sure that the Video component will not consume more CPU and memory than the ones allocated?

In order to take into account these issues, Qinna is integrated in the initial system. Each component which provides an interface with QoS management needs (Video, Thread, Memory, Scheduler) is renamed to QoSVideo, QoSThread,

QoSMem and QoSRRSched. A QoSComponentBroker and a QoSComponent-Manager are associated to every QoSComponent. Further, global constraints of QoSComponentBrokers are fixed. For QoSMemBroker, global constraint is set to 100 Kb. It represents the maximum amount of memory that can be allocated. For QoSThreadBroker, global constraint is set to 2, that allows to allocate only 2 Thread components. For QoSRRSchedBroker, global constraint is fixed to 50: it is the maximum number of available time slots. Finally, global constraint of QoSVideoBroker is set in order to allow only one GOOD or BAD Video component. Moreover, a QoSVideoObserver is added to QoSVideo because its QoS requirements are unknown. At last, a QoSDomain component encapsulates the previous Qinna components in order to bound the QoS management. Figure 2 represents an overview the system integrating Qinna.

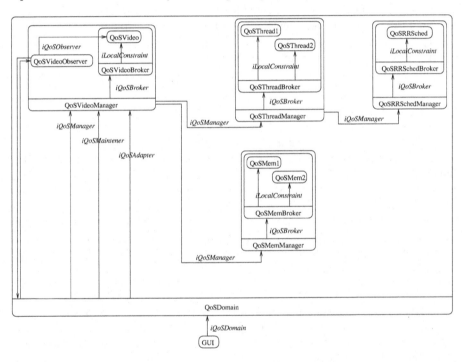

Fig. 2. Overview of the system integrating Qinna.

To illustrate the dynamic behavior of Qinna, we consider the scenario where an user requests a GOOD Video to the QoSDomain. The request is then transmitted to the QoSVideoManager. As the QoSVideoManager has an empty map table, it requests a QoSThread and a QoSMem components with a QoS level set to `default` to their respective QoSComponentManagers. Each QoSComponentManager returns a QoSComponent thanks to their QoSComponentBrokers. For instance, QoSMemManager returns a QoSMem with a QoS level fixed to 10 Kb. As a QoSThread requires a scheduler, QoSThreadManager requests a QoS-

RRSched to the QoSRRSchedManager with a QoS level equal to `default`. The latter returns a QoSRRSched with a QoS fixed to 1, that is to say the associated QoSThread will have a ponderation equal to 1. Then, QoSThreadManager binds a QoSThread and the QoSRRSched and returns it. QoSVideoManager binds a QoSVideo to the QoSThread and the QoSMem and returns the reference to the QoSDomain. Finally, the QoSDomain starts the QoSVideoObserver and specifies the observation policy: for instance, *periodic observation at 500 msec.*

While the QoSVideo is executed, the QoSVideoObserver notifies the QoSDomain of QoS violations. The QoSDomain runs maintenance policy and requests QoSVideoManager to upgrade the required QoS level of QoSVideo (thanks to iQoSMaintener interface). If the maintenance policy fails, that is to say no more QoS level can be allocated, the QoSVideo is degraded to BAD (thanks to iQoSAdapter interface).

Analysis We first analyze the way Qinna deals with the two specific open system issues and then evaluate the cost generated by Qinna. With regard to the two open system issues raised by the case study, Qinna implements:

1. a QoSVideoObserver in order to notify the QoSDomain of the real QoS level provided by the QoSVideo. In this experiment, to every notification the QoSDomain triggers the maintenance policy. The latter consists of the up-gradation of the QoS requirements step by step (for instance, memory requirements is increased by 10 Kb).
2. the QoSVideo can not consume a greater QoS level than the allocated one. For instance, after initialization the QoSMem controls that no more than 10 Kb is used by the QoSVideo. Moreover, the QoSThreadBroker has a global constraint constraint fixed to 2. it limits the effects of a malicious component that requires thread all the time. Finally, the use of a ponderated scheduler allows to know the current system load in order to accept, or not, a new thread.

Evaluations Qinna implies some overheads in terms of memory and time.

The maximum number of Qinna components if given by: $(Nb\_QoSComp \times 4) + 1$. In this experiment, the initial system size is 108 Kb, while the size is 112 Kb when Qinna is integrated. It represents a overhead about 5%. More precisely, the size of the whole Qinna components is 5528 bytes.

The overhead due to the QoS control is rather low. For example, the control made QoSMem is evaluated to $1,5\mu sec$.

The initial configuration of the QoSVideo is equal to 1,8 msec. It includes reservations and bindings of QoSThread, QoSMem, QoSRRSched and QoSVideo. We evaluated the delay needed by the QoSVideo to reach a QoS level equals to GOOD. This delay is about 2 seconds, but it depends on several parameters as the increasing QoS step (in this experiment the increasing step is set to 10 kB for memory and 1 slot for CPU). In this experiment, it needs 4 steps to get enough resources to provide a GOOD QoS level. It can be optimized thanks to ad-hoc mechanisms, but it is out of scope of our work.

From the QoSDomain point of view, a call to the maintenance mechanisms takes 1,9 msec. That is to say that it can be costly if the required is fluctuating (many calls to iQoSMaintener).

Finally, if the map tables are well known, the delay to degrade the QoSVideo from GOOD to BAD is 2,13 msec.

5   Related Works

Currently there are many works related to QoS for CBSE which can be classified in to three distinct kind of works. The first one focuses on embedded system. The second one deals with traditional work stations, while the last one is about QoS specifications.

SEESCOA [9] is a component-based approach for embedded real-time systems. In this approach, each binding between two components is formalized by a contract defined by [1]. As SEESCOA deals with real-time systems, it mainly focuses on the temporal aspect of QoS: to each interface, a timed MSC is associated in order to express their temporal constraints.

PECOS [18] is a component model for the same kind of systems with the same kind of constraints. Meanwhile, PECOS define some timed Petri networks to specify the relation between components. Moreover, it uses the CoCo language [5] in order to get a syntactic view of the whole system with its temporal constraints.

In comparison with our work, SEESCOA and PECOS handle the QoS aspects statically (before the execution of the system). It leads to a closed and unflexible system. Moreover, components are only available at design stage and not at runtime.

Moreover, works such as SATIN [23] or CARISMA [8] are typical from the mobile systems research area. The main characteristic of these works is their ability to deals with dynamic context evolution. Either these works define policies in order to manage context evolution (CARISMA), that could be integrated to Qinna. Or they provide some mechanisms to handle dynamic composition without taking care of QoS (SATIN).

[16] is a Java platform able to manage the resources needed by a component. This platform is made of two layers. A high layer, Jamus, is in charge of admission testing, contracts management and contracts monitoring. A low layer, Raje, is responsible for resources management. Several key points distinguish this work from ours. Firstly, the platform is not component-based that disables component benefits to QoS management (re-usability, adaptability, administration, etc.). Secondly, a component is not well defined: it is only seen as an application. This implies a coarse grain view of components. Thirdly, component view is not homogeneous: a component can require a QoS level from the platform (in terms of resources), but can not require a QoS level from another component. Fourthly, the resource control is difficult to implement because of the JVM.

The QuA project [20] aims to provide services to manage QoS for distributed applications. In QuA, an application is encapsulated in a QuA-component and the whole QoS mechanisms and policies are implemented by the global QuA platform. The latter is then viewed as a single component which leads to a complex administration and evolution of QoS management. Moreover, for this kind of systems it seems more significant that each application provides its own QoS mechanisms in order to be as autonomous as possible.

Finally, works on QoS specifications for components are complementary to ours. Indeed, Qinna does not define how specification must be achieved. In order to demonstrate this property we are actually working on the integration of CQML [11] to Qinna.

6   Conclusion

In this paper, we presented the Qinna architecture followed by an experiment for open systems. Qinna is a component-based QoS architecture suitable for specific open system issues. The experiment illustrated the way Qinna deals with these issues and allowed for a quantitative evaluation of the architecture.

In order to fully validate Qinna, we are working on several axis. First, CQML is integrated to demonstrate that Qinna is not specific to a QoS language. Second, we are integrating more complex QoS mechanisms and policies than the one presented here. Finally, we are taking into consideration the network resource in order to lead to an end to end QoS management for embedded distributed systems.

References

[1] A. Beugnard and J.M. Jézéquel and N. Plouzeau and D. Watkins. Making Components Contract Aware. *Computer*, 32(7):38–45, 1999.

[2] A. Campbell. A Quality of Service Architecture. *PhD Thesis, Lancaster University*, 1996.

[3] B. Ford and G. Back and G. Benson and J. Lepreau and A. Lin and O. Shivers. The Flux OSKit: a substrate for kernel and language research. In *Proceedings of the sixteenth ACM symposium on Operating systems principles*, pages 38–51, Saint Malo (France), 1997. ACM Press.

[4] B. Meyer and C. Mingins. Component-Based Development: from Buzz to Spark. *IEEE Computer*, 32(7):35–37, 1999.

[5] B. Schulz and T. Genssler and A. Christoph and M. Winter. Requirements for the Composition Environment. *Pecos Deliverable D3.1. http://www.pecos-project.org*, 1999.

[6] C. Aurrecoechea and A. Campbell and L. Hauw. A survey of QoS architectures. *Multimedia Systems*, 6(3):138–151, 1998.

[7] C. Szyperski. Component Software Beyond Object-Oriented Programming, 2nd Edition. *Addison-Wesley, ACM Press*, 1998.

[8] Licia Capra, Wolfgang Emmerich, and Cecilia Mascolo. CARISMA: Context-Aware Reflective mIddleware System for Mobile Applications. *IEEE Transactions of Software Engineering*, 29(10):929–945, 2003.

[9] D. Urting and S. Van Baelen and Y. Berbers. Embedded Software using Components and Contracts. In *European Conference on Object-Oriented Programming (ECOOP) 2001 Specification, Implementation and Validation of Object-oriented Embedded Systems (SIVOES) workshop*, pages 1–4, Budapest (Hungary), June 2001.

[10] E. Bruneton and T. Coupaye and J.B. Stefani. The Fractal Component Model. Specification v2. *http://fractal.objectweb.org*, 2003.

[11] J. Aagedal. *Quality of Service Support in Development of Distributed Systems*. PhD thesis, University of Oslo, 2001.

[12] J.C. Tournier and J.P. Babau and V. Olive. A Qinna Experiment: a Component-Based QoS Architecture for Real-Time Systems. In *Workshop Architectures for Cooperative Embedded Real-Time Systems (WACERTS) in conjunction with the 25th Real-Time System Symposium (RTSS'04)*, Lisbon (Portugal), December 2004.

[13] J.C. Tournier and J.P. Babau and V. Olive. An Evaluation of Qinna: a Component-Based QoS Architecture for Handheld Systems. In *Symposium on Applied Computing (SAC'05)*, Sante Fe (New Mexico - USA), March 2005.

[14] J.P. Fassino and J.B. Stefani and J.L. Lawall and G. Muller. Think: A Software Framework for Component-based Operating System Kernels. In *Proceedings of the General Track: 2002 USENIX Annual Technical Conference*, pages 73–86. USENIX Association, 2002.

[15] Microsoft Corporation. The .NET Framework. *http://www.microsoft.com/net*.

[16] N. Le Sommer. Contractualisation des ressources pour les composants logiciels: une approche réflexive. *Rapport de thèse. Université de Bretagne Sud*, 2003.

[17] N. T. Bhatti and M. A. Hiltunen and R. D. Schlichting and W. Chiu. Coyote: a system for constructing fine-grain configurable communication services. *ACM Transactions on Computer Systems*, 16(4):321–366, 1998.

[18] O. Nierstrasz and G. ArEvalo and S. Ducasse and R. Wuyts and A. P. Black and P. O. Mller and C. Zeidler and T. Genssler and R. van den Born. A Component Model for Field Devices. In *Proceedings of the IFIP/ACM Working Conference on Component Deployment*, pages 200–209. Springer-Verlag, 2002.

[19] Object Management Group. The Common Object Request Broker: Architecture and Specification. 2000.

[20] R. Staehli and F. Eliassen. QuA: A QoS-Aware Component Architecture. *Research report Simula Lab*, 2002.

[21] Sun Microsystems. The EJB 2.1 Specifications. *http://java.sun.com/products/ejb*.

[22] X. Cai and M. R. Lyu and K.-F. Wong Roy Ko. Component-Based Software Engineering: Technologies, Development Frameworks, and Quality Assurance Schemes. *International Journal of Software Engineering and Knowledge Engineering*, 2000.

[23] Stefanos Zachariadis, Cecilia Mascolo, and Wolfgang Emmerich. SATIN: A Component Model for Mobile Self-Organisation. *In. Proc. of Int. Symposium on Distributed Objects and Applications (DOA)*, 2004.

Architecture Based Deployment of Large-Scale Component Based Systems: The Tool and Principles

Ling Lan[1], Gang Huang[1]*, Liya Ma[1], Meng Wang[1], Hong Mei[1],
Long Zhang[2], Ying Chen[2]

[1]School of Electronics Engineering and Computer Science, Peking University,
Beijing, 100871, China
{lanling, huanggang, maly, wangmeng}@sei.pku.edu.cn,
meih@pku.edu.cn
[2]IBM China Research Lab,
No.7, St.5, ShangDi, HaiDian District, Beijing, 100085, China
{longzh, yingch}@cn.ibm.com

Abstract. After a component based system is developed, it has to be deployed into a target environment. As the system becomes much larger and more complex and the environment becomes open and dynamic, the deployment comes to be a difficult, tiring, error-prone and time-consuming task. This paper proposes an architecture based approach to deploying large-scale component based systems into open and dynamic environments in a systematic and semi-automatic manner. It does four contributions to facilitate the deployment: Firstly, a supporting tool is developed to visualize the software architecture of the system to be deployed to help deployers understand the structure, functions and desired qualities of the system. Secondly, the tool can automatically generate the deployment information from the architecture description produced in the phase of design and this will relieve deployers of inputting hundreds or thousands of deployment elements manually. Thirdly, the tool can monitor the up-to-date resource consumptions of the machines and support to partition one system into several subsystems and deploy the subsystems onto multiple machines simultaneously. Fourthly, a set of principles are proposed for guiding the deployment with the tool. The approach, especially the tool and principles are demonstrated on J2EE (Java 2 Platform Enterprise Edition).

1   Introduction

Component-Based Software Engineering (CBSE) focuses on the development of software intensive systems from pre-fabricated and reusable components, the development of components, and system maintenance and improvement by means of component replacement and customization [4][3]. As CBSE has become a prevalent approach to building the large-scale software systems, people always pay much attention to how to develop a component-based system (CBS) in a rapid, high-quality and cost-effective way but other stages of software lifecycle, especially software deployment are neglected.

---

* Corresponding author.

G.T. Heineman et al. (Eds.): CBSE 2005, LNCS 3489, pp. 123–138, 2005.

Before a CBS can operate with desired functions and qualities, it should have to be configured according to the runtime environments and installed correctly. This activity is called software deployment, which plays a key role in software lifecycle. Software deployment has been attached with more and more attentions over the past decade as rapid pervasiveness of the network and distributed systems. Kruchten [21] proposes the "4+1" view model to include logical view, process view, implementation view (previously called development view), and deployment view (previously called physical view). The deployment view describes the mapping(s) of the software to the distributed nodes. In OMG's UML (Unified Modeling Language) [20], four kinds of graphical diagrams are defined for modeling: use case diagram, class diagram, behavior diagram and implementation diagram. The last diagram includes component diagram and deployment diagram. The deployment diagrams show the configuration of runtime processing elements and the software components, processes, and objects that execute on them. In the specification of Java 2 Enterprise Edition (J2EE) [22], the development process of J2EE applications[1] is divided into three stages: component creation, assembly and deployment. During the deployment stage, the J2EE application is installed on the J2EE application servers with careful configuration and integration with the runtime environments.

Before the pervasiveness of Internet, a CBS usually ran in a closed and static environment with limited users. There were only a few simple factors to be considered in deployment. But recently, the exploding Internet makes CBS larger, more complex and the runtime environments extremely open and dynamic. On the one hand, in order to deploy the CBS into a distributed environment, the factors related to the deployment should be taken into account thoroughly and carefully. Therefore the deployers are required to understand the whole system to be deployed and sometimes even other systems already deployed in the same environment. For example, we should consider the amount of components, the profiles of every component and the dependencies among components, and so on. This will help to partition one system into several sub-systems and then distribute the sub-systems to the distributed nodes respectively. However, for the large-scale CBS, to understand the whole system to be deployed is too difficult without any high-level guidance. On the other hand, the CBS is always deployed in an open and dynamic environment. Different runtime environments have different features, such as various nodes, platforms, bandwidth and topology. These differences lead to a disastrous result that the deployment of a CBS in one environment cannot be reused in another environment. Furthermore, status varies even in a single environment, such as loads and resource consumptions. That is to say, the same system to be deployed in the same environment maybe need different deployment plans at different time. Without a comprehensive understanding of the whole system and the environment, the deployers could only accomplish the deployment according to their experiences. Such deployment may lead to serious problems: the system probably can't work correctly; the performance might descend significantly; and the newly deployed systems may impact the other systems in the same runtime environment, preventing them from operating with desired functionalities and qualities. To sum up, to deploy a CBS in modern networks, much more complex factors have to be taken into consideration and then the deployment becomes a hard, tiring, error-prone and time-consuming task.

---

[1] In this paper, we take the application and the system synonymous.

This paper presents an architecture based deployment approach to deploying the large-scale component based systems into open and dynamic environments correctly, rapidly and cost-effectively. This approach is preliminarily proposed in [9], which only discusses the motivation and benefits of introducing software architecture into the deployment. In this paper, we focus on the supporting tool and principles. The tool, specific to J2EE currently, can visualize the software architecture of the CBS to be deployed and the up-to-date resource consumption of the target machines. Moreover, the tool can parse the architecture description produced in the phase of design to retrieve deployment information which usually contains hundreds or thousands of description elements and is filled manually. To guide the architecture based deployment, we propose a set of principles that are illustrated in a detailed case study.

The rest of the paper is organized as follows: the next section illustrates a case and puts forward the challenges to deployment of J2EE applications; section 3 gives an overview of our approach; section 4 introduces the visual supporting tool and section 5 demonstrates the detailed steps of deployment of the case with a set of principles; section 6 provides the discussion and comparisons with some related work; the last section concludes this paper and identifies the future work.

2   Challenges to Deployment of J2EE Applications

J2EE architecture is designed to support 3-tier web-enabled distributed applications [22]. The components in J2EE can be classified into four categories: applets and normal Java applications at the client side, servlets/JSP (JavaServer Pages) and Enterprise JavaBean (EJB) at the server side [23]. Since the client side components can be downloaded from the server, the deployment of J2EE applications focuses on the server side components.

Java Pet Store (JPS) is one of the sample applications for J2EE Blueprints. It demonstrates how to use the capabilities of the J2EE platform to develop flexible, scalable, cross-platform e-business applications [25]. Assume we have a task to deploy JPS to its runtime environment. Table 1 shows the target environment in detail: two nodes are the independent servers, Server1 and Server2, and the third one is a cluster, which consists of two servers. The column Operating Environment shows the operating systems and J2EE application servers installed in the nodes. PKUAS is a J2EE-compliant, reflective application server which is the platform including J2SE, common services and one or both of Web Container and EJB Container [10]. The column Reliability shows the vendor-defined reliability of the nodes. Undoubtedly, how to accomplish the deployment is a touchy problem. There are also many challenges involved in deployment:

First, have a look of what the deployers do when deploying a J2EE application such as JPS. A mass of deployment descriptors, xml-format files for deployment in J2EE, are needed thus the deployers must write many description elements by hand even with some J2EE deployment tools. If just to write a simplest deployment descriptor file of the EJB, about 10 elements are needed, including the EJB name, EJB classes' names and EJB type, etc. However, most deployment descriptors in practice are much more complex than this. They always include tens of or even more than a hundred elements, which are provided to indicate the relationships of the EJBs, the configuration of security and transaction, etc. To write so many elements is troublesome of course. For instance, to deploy a J2EE application which is similar to JPS in this case, deployers need to write more than a thousand elements. In fact, almost all of the elements about deployment already exist from the phase of system design, and these elements can be refined or transformed into the final deployment descriptors. In this sense, a deployment tool is urgently needed to support the information transformation from design to deployment.

Table 1. The runtime environment of JPS

Node	Operating Environment	Has Database?	CPU	Memory	Reliability
Server 1	PKUAS +Windows NT	no	2.0G Hz ×2	1G	96.7%
Server 2	PKUAS + Linux	no	2.4G Hz	1G	94.5%
Cluster	PKUAS +Windows 2000 Server	yes	2.0G Hz ×2	2G	99.7%

Secondly, deployers have to partition the system into several parts and distribute these parts to the separate nodes. However, at present no deployment tool is available to support such operations. If deployers try to accomplish these operations with existing deployment tools, they have to decompose the system into individual components, rewrite the deployment descriptions, assemble the components that will be deployed on the same node to several sub-systems and then deploy every sub-system to the corresponding node. These operations are fallible, troublesome and as a matter of fact should be accomplished automatically by some tools.

Thirdly, when partitioning the systems, deployers had better have a high-level guidance. In this case, if deployers only have the codes or packages of JPS, what they know is the corresponding components to the system at first sight. Other information of this system such as dependencies of the components, interoperations between the components, and the security properties is sealed. But this information is very helpful for the deployment. It will take the deployers many days to understand the whole system by reading related documents or even the source codes, which is obviously challenging and inefficient. So a clear view of the whole system, including the components, the detailed structure and even the desired qualities, should be provided to the deployers in an understandable and precise way.

Last but not least, without knowing the up-to-date status of the runtime environment exactly, the deployers could only deploy the system with experiences. To deploy JPS in this case, how do the deployers decide which node they will deploy the appointed components on? Maybe the deployers can deploy some components, which will consume much memory, to the Cluster because this node provides the maximum memory 2G. But the value of 2G is just a static one. If there is another system already deployed on the Cluster and it consumes much memory, then the actual free memories of the Cluster maybe lower than that of the other two servers. In this condition deployers should deploy the former components onto the node which has the maximum free memory at that time. Anyway, the information of the runtime environment is crucial for the deployment and should be offered in an automated way.

3   Approach Overview

Since its first literal identification and discussion [7], software architecture becomes an important subfield of software engineering, receiving increasing attention from both academic and industrial community. It describes the gross structure of a software system with a collection of components, connectors and constraints [17]. In general, software architecture acts as a bridge between requirements and implementation and provides a blueprint for system construction and composition. It helps to understand large systems, support reuse at both components to be developed and their relationships and constraints, expose changeability of the system, verify and validate the target system at a high level and so on [6].

Due to the success of software architecture in the development, some researchers propose to maintain and evolve software systems with the help of software architecture [2]. Particularly, we propose a framework to make software architecture an entity at runtime, called Runtime Software Architecture (RSA) [8]. RSA can immediately capture changes of the runtime system so as to keep itself up-to-date, and ensure that changes made on RSA will immediately lead to corresponding changes of the runtime systems. In other words, the runtime system can be maintained and evolved online via RSA. This framework has already been implemented in PKUAS [10].

Recalling the challenges to deployment, it is a natural and feasible approach to introducing software architectures into the deployment. Both software architectures equipped with plentiful knowledge produced in the development and software architectures representing runtime information of operating environments are applied into the deployment. As a result, software architecture plays a centric role in the whole software lifecycle. When a deployed system does not work well, the functionalities or qualities of the software architecture will be damaged or decreased. Such case can be detected and repaired with the help of architecture based software maintenance. Then, once a system is deployed, it will keep operating until being undeployed.

All activities in this approach are done with software architectures, such as understanding the system to be deployed, evaluating the result of deployment of the system, monitoring the working status of the systems, and deploying, un-deploying or redeploying the systems. Fig.1 shows the process of architecture-based deployment. It is divided into the following phases and the tool facilitates the activities in all of the phases:

1) Building up the goals of the deployment: before the deployment, deployers need a clear view about the state which the system should achieve after being deployed. Deployers analyze the desired functions and qualities of the system based on the constraints from the software architecture, and then consider all the factors, whether the ones about technique or non-technique, and finally build up the goals of the deployment.

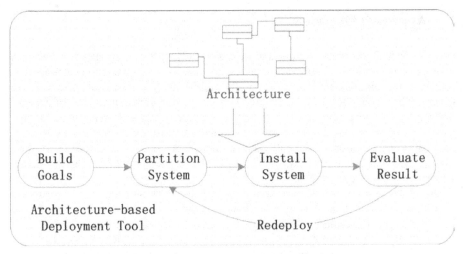

Fig. 1. The process of architecture-based deployment

2) Partitioning the system based on the software architecture and the runtime environment: in order to utilize the resources better and improve the performance further, the system should be partitioned into several parts and installed on distributed nodes respectively. On the one hand, as the description of software system's gross structure, the software architecture helps deployers to understand the components in the system and the relationships among them quickly, to further analyze the constraints of the components and the system. On the other hand, inspecting the runtime environment can help deployers to understand the environment and think over the factors of the environment totally that maybe affect the system. With the guidance of the two elements mentioned above, the software architecture and runtime environment, deployers can partition the system into several parts towards the goals of deployment and distribute the parts to the nodes.

3) Installing the system: before operating, some information should be added to the system for deployment. The information is called deployment information. It includes the binding names of the components in runtime, the announcements and entries of the resources, etc. During the design and implementation phases of CBS, the software architecture involves plenty of information. This information in the design and implementation can be transformed to the deployment information, and then in the phase of deployment, deployers just need to append a little of information to accomplish the installations.

4) Evaluating the result of the deployment: after the deployment, deployers should evaluate the result of the deployment based on the runtime information. The runtime information can be obtained with the help of the RSA. On the one hand, deployers should make a judgment whether the result meets the goals of deployment, and on the other hand, deployers should review other formerly deployed systems to ensure that they will not exert any negative impact on the newly deployed ones.

5) Redeployment: if the evaluating results can't meet the desires, then the systems should be redeployed. This phase consists of the foregoing phases from 2 to 4.

This phase will have to be repeated until all of the systems meet their goals of deployment.

4   CADTool: The Supporting Tool

CADTool is an assembly and deployment tool, which is based on software architecture, for J2EE applications deployed on PKUAS. It facilitates developers to visually pack as well as assemble components. More importantly, based on the software architecture, CADTool extracts most needed information in the deployment from the architecture models in the development.

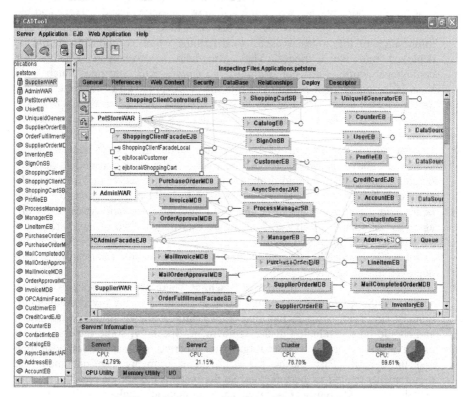

Fig. 2. Software architecture of deployed JPS

Fig. 2 shows the case of deploying JPS with CADTool. The "deploy" panel shows the software architecture of JPS, and the "Server's Information" panel shows real-time information of the runtime environment. CADTool can facilitate the deployment in the following functions:

■ Visualization of architecture models in the development: CADTool reuses the graphical elements of ABCTool, which supports architecture modeling with ABC/ADL in a visual way [11]. However, this visualization depends on the content of the deployable package. If the deployable package contains the architecture description in ABC/ADL, CADTool can display the syntax and semantics information produced in the development. If the deployable package also includes the layout description of the architecture, CADTool can display the architecture in the same layout as in the development, which helps to understand the intention of the designers. If the deployable package doesn't have the two descriptions, CADTool can automatically construct the architecture from the individual deployable components. However, the last case is not ideal, because the architecture lacks enough information derived from the development.

- Visualization of servers and their capabilities: Based on reflective mechanisms of PKUAS, CADTool can automatically collect and display the servers' information, such as CPU utilization, memory utilization, throughout. The four figures in the "Server's Information" panel show the three nodes in JPS's runtime environment, the two on the left show the Server1 and Server2 and the other two on the right show the two servers which compose the Cluster. The information of the nodes is useful to determine which components should be deployed into which nodes. They also help to investigate whether the deployment works well. For example, the *CatalogEJB* consumes much CPU time. If the component is deployed into the *Server1*, the CPU utilization of the *Server1* may exceed 90% and the *Server1* becomes unstable and easy to crash. Therefore, it is better to un-deploy the *CatalogEJB* in the *Server1* and re-deploy it into the cluster.

- Drag-and-drop deployment of components: With the two visual elements mentioned above, a component can be easily deployed into a node singly by dragging the component and dropping it on the target server or vice versa. In traditional deployment tools, deployers have to build a connection to a given node, load the components to be deployed into the node, and repeat the work again for another node. In Fig. 2, there are four nodes. Two of them are single servers and the other two form a cluster. The components *AsyncSenderJAR, UniqueidGeneratorEB, ShoppingClientFacadeEJB* and *CustomerEJB* are deployed into the *Server1*.

- Automatic calculation of deployment factors: There are many successful case studies on the quantitative and qualitative evaluations of the given architecture models. However, some factors may be wrongly predicted in the design phase and should be re-evaluated in the deployment. Specially, some factors may be only available after the services running for a period, such as the response time and throughput. This means the deployment probably can not meet the requirements related to these factors. So the systems have to be redeployed with actual factors. Currently, CADTool can automatically calculate the response time, throughput and reliability of a given use case.

5   Deployment Principles and the Case Study

5.1   Deployment Principles

To help deployers make decisions during deploying, we offer a set of principles to guide the deployment and at the same time build up a principle classification framework. The detailed principles will be presented in the next section step by step.

In the principle classification framework, all the principles are endued with priorities in terms of their effects on the goals of deployment. When the architecture-based approach is applied to deploy a system, the principles with higher PRI are considered prior to others. If deployers have to make a tradeoff between two or more principles, the priority is the warrant for the decision.

Table 2. The principle classfication framework

Priority	Goal	Serial Numbers of Principle
1	Ensure the system operate correctly	1,2,7
2	Meet the business requirements	6
3	Imporve QoS	3,4,5

Table 2 shows the principle classification framework. There are three types of priorities:

1)   At the phase of deployment, the chief goal is ensuring that the systems can operate properly. Consequently deployers must consider the necessary requirements at first. Those requirements refer to whether the operations of databases are required locally, some components must/mustn't run on the same node, some components have the security requirements for the nodes and some components maybe require the high reliability. In the meantime, the newly deployed system must never impair the desired functionalities and qualities in the same runtime environment of other deployed systems. If the newly deployed one does disturb the old ones, deployers must work out a new deploy plan for the system or redeploy other systems.

2)   Deployers should take the customers' business requirements into consideration besides the essential requirements. In order to achieve the maximum profit, deployers may reduce the QoS of the system if only the goals of deployment are met.

3)   For the systems to be deployed, it is possibly that more than one plan could meet the system's essential requirements. Each plan may have its advantages. For example, a system has two deployment plans, A and B. The system will achieve more throughputs if deployed as plan A and more reliability if deployed as B. Under such situation, deployers should make a tradeoff among numerous plans based on the goals of deployment and select the best one to optimize the QoS of the system.

5.2   The Case Study

In this section we will accomplish the deployment of JPS by the architecture-based approach step by step. We will apply a set of principles to guide the deployment with the help of CADTool.

5.2.1 Building Up the Goals of Deployment

After analyzing the software architecture of JPS in the CADTool, as shown in Fig.2, and the customers' requirements, the following goals of deployment are presented:

A)   The components *OPCAdminFacadeEJB*, *AdminWAR* and *SupplierWAR* should be deployed on the nodes which provide security service.

B)   The components *SignOnSB* and *PurchaseOrderEJB* should be deployed on the nodes whose reliability is no less than 98% and the reliability of the system should be no less than 95%;

C)   The response time of all of the business methods of *ShoppingCartSB* should be less than 0.1 second; The response time of the methods, *ProcessPending()* and *ProcessPO()* of the component *OrderFulfillmentFacadeSB* should be less than 0.15 seconds; The response time of the business methods of other components in JPS should be less than 0.2 seconds;

D)   The throughput of the system should reach 150 requests per second at least;

E)   The cost of operating should be agreed upon and as low as possible.

5.2.2 Partitioning the Systems Based on the Software Architecture and Runtime Environment

Principle1: partitioning the system with the help of software architecture.

Software architectures describe the components and the relationships among the components in detail. It provides deployers a clear and pellucid blueprint for system partitioning. With the guide of the blueprint, deployers can get the information of every component quickly, find out the dependency between components, the frequency of the communications of the components, etc. With so much information, deployers can understand the whole system sufficiently and have abundant clues to partition the system. For instance, in the software architecture of JPS, the components *ProfileEB, AddressEB, UserEB* all only provide the local interfaces but no remote ones. In J2EE specification, the local interface must be used in the same JVM. As a result, the components which will communicate with the former ones must be deployed to the same node. These components are *CustomerEB, CreditCardEB, SignOnSB*.

Principle2: considering the limits of resources and services of the nodes before distributing.

In a distributed environment, the nodes are different from one another and every node has its' own resource and service. So deployers must consider the limits of resources and services. In this case, there is just one node, the Cluster provides the security service and its reliability reaches 99.7%. According to the goal A and B, the components *OPCAdminFacadeEJB, AdminWAR, SupplierWAR, SignOnSB* and *PurchaseOrderEJB* must be deployed in the Cluster.

Principle3: considering the status of the network.

In a distributed environment, the bottleneck of a system sometimes is the network. The transmit delay, bandwidth and topology structure might affect the system's performance greatly. So deployers should try their best to avoid these effects. For example, the components which communicate frequently should be deployed on the same node; the components which communicate frequently but isn't allowed to be on a same node should be deployed on the nodes with high-quality network connection; the components which should access the resources frequently, such as databases, should be deployed on the node with the resources. In light of the relationships of the components, deployers can divide the whole system into three parts: part I is concentrated on the business processes of browse and purchase; part II is for orders management; part III is for the suppliers to offer.

Principle4: considering the condition of load in every node and try to keep the balance of the nodes' load.

Deployers should distribute the parts, which are partitioned from the system to the nodes, based on the resource requirement of every part. For example, the component which will be called frequently should be deployed on the node with low load. In JPS, the main business processes are concentrated on part I, business processes of browse and purchase, so this part should be deployed on the node with low load. From the resource consumption view of CADTool, deployers should find out that the Cluster meets the requirement first and then deploy the part I to the Cluster.

Principle5: when deploying the components which are involved in several composite components, deployers should deploy such components with the composite ones together.

In the software architecture, there are not only the simple components but also the composite components that are made up of several simple components. In general, interactions among the internal components of a composite component are very frequently. So these components should be deployed on the same node. The different composite components maybe involve the same simple components and as the result the same simple components might be deployed onto more than one node at the same time. In JPS, the composite components (*Customer, PurchaseOrder, Supplier, SupplierPO*) all involve with a set of simple components: *ContactInfoEB, CreditCardEJB, AddressEB*. The four composite components are deployed on the Cluster and the Server2. Then the deployers should deploy the three simple components on the two nodes also. Note that, without the software architecture rebuilt from the design artifact, it is impossible to make such decision, or the performance may be decreased significantly when deploying the three components onto only one node. In that sense, this principle partially proves the advantage of introducing software architecture into deployment and we hope to find more principles like that.

Principle6: Not only the factors of technique but the ones of non-technique should be considered in the deployment.

In fact, to deploy the system, deployers need to consider not only the technical factors but the ones of non-technique, such as the costs. Then deployers might have to make the tradeoff between the two kinds of factors to satisfy the customer. During the deployment of JPS, the components *AdminWAR* and *ShoppingClientControllEJB* are deployed on the Cluster. If deployers just consider the performance, the Component *AsyncSender.JAR*, which communicates with the former two components frequently, should be deployed on the Cluster also. But the cost of the Cluster is much higher than the costs of other two nodes. According to deployment goal E, deployers should make a tradeoff between principle 3 and 6. As the principle classification framework, the priority of principle 6 is higher than priority of principle 3. So the component *AsyncSender.JAR* should be deployed on the Server1, with lower performance but much lower cost.

With the principles mentioned above, deployers can work out the deployment plan. Table 3 shows the deployment plan. The column Principles shows which principles we consult to partition JPS.

Table 3. The deployment plan

Nodes	Components	Principles
Cluster	PetStoreWAR, ShoppingClientControllerEJB, ShoppingClientFacadeEJB, ShoppingCartSB CatalogEB, SignOnSB, UserEB, CustomerEB, ProfileEB, AccountEB, CreditCardEJB, ContactInfoEB, AddressEB, OPCAdminFacadeEJB, AdminWAR, PurchaseOrderMDB,InvoiceMDB, OrderApprovalMDB, PurchaseOrderEJB, ContactInfoEB, CreditCardEJB, AddressEB, LineItemEB, SupplierWAR	1,2,3,4,5
Server1	AsyncSenderJAR, ProcessManagerSB, ManagerEB, MailInvoiceMDB, MailOrderApprovalMDB, MailCompletedOrderMDB	1,3,4,6
Server2	SupplierOrderMDB, OrderFulfillmentFacadeEJB, InventoryEJB, SupplierOrderEJB, CreditCardEJB, ContactInfoEB, AddressEB,	1,3,4,5

5.2.3 Installing the Systems

Based on the deployment plan, deployers can use the CADTool to add essential information to every component, then partition the systems into three parts and distribute every part to the corresponding node. In fact, in terms of the drag-and-drop deployment of CADTool, after deployers analyzing the system with the principles, the system has already been partitioned and which nodes the components should be deployed onto is also specified.

5.2.4 Evaluating the Results of the Deployment and Redeployment when Necessary

Principle7: the newly deployed system should work well and not affect the deployed ones too badly. Otherwise deployers have to revise the deployment plan.

From the feedback of the runtime systems, deployers can get the result of deployment and judge whether the deployed systems meet all of their deployment goals. If not, a redeployment is needed. In this case, supposed that the deployed JPS meets the goals, but it consumes vast CPU and memory in the Server1. As a result, another J2EE application JST (Java Smart Tickets) [26], which is deployed on the Server1 previously, doesn't have the desired throughput and response time. At the same time, the Server2's load is comparatively light. Considering the software architecture and runtime environment of JPS and JST, deployers can make the decision to redeploy the JST to the Server2.

6   Discussion and Related Work

The greatest contribution of this approach is to introduce software architecture into deployment. Though we utilize ABCTool for architecture modeling with ABC/ADL in the case study, the approach is general and doesn't rely on ABCTool and ABC/ADL. When a new modeling language is introduced to describe the architecture, we just need to work out a new parser for the CADTool to parse the new language. The CADTool is built to help deployers to deal with the challenges of the deployment, which are mentioned in section 2. It visualizes the architecture models in the development and some essential factors of the runtime environment also, transforms the information from the development to the deployment, and provides the operations to partition and distribute the systems visually. In practice, some work such as building the goals or determining the tradeoffs, must be performed by deployers themselves. The CADTool only shows the factors to be considered in the deployment and the principles simply play a guider's role. The deployment is just semi-automatic in the approach at present.

We would like to consider some related work about the deployment and correlative tools. Traditional deployment tools in J2EE support to deploy an application into any local or remote application servers [24]. Some tools claim to be built for the Model Driven Architecture (MDA) [19], supporting to generate the source code and deployment information automatically from the design artifacts. However, to the best of our knowledge, none of them helps deployers to understand and analyze the desired functions and qualities of the systems to be deployed, provides the runtime states of the distributed environment, and allows partitioning and deploying the system onto more than one node simultaneously.

Rutherford et al. discussed an approach to J2EE deployment [16]. In this approach, a prototype tool, called BARK (the Bean Automatic Reconfiguration framework), is designed to facilitate the management and automation of all the activities in the deployment life cycle for EJBs. SmartFrog (Smart Framework for Object Groups) is a framework for describing, deploying, igniting and managing distributed applications [12]. This framework has a deployment infrastructure that interprets system descriptions, realizes the systems' subcomponents in the correct order and binds them together. BARK and SmartFrog concentrate on the aspect that how to perform the activities in the deployment correctly and efficiently according to the configuration that deployers provide, while our approach emphasize supporting deployers to work out a better configuration of the deployment.

Dearle et al. proposed a framework for constraint-based deployment and automatic management of distributed systems [1]. In this framework, a purely declarative and descriptive architectural description language, named Deladas, is used to describe a deployment goal. To satisfy the goal, an automatic deployment and management engine (ADME) tries to generate a configuration, which describes which components are deployed in which nodes. After the initial deployment, the ADME will monitor the deployed system to check whether the deployment satisfies the original goal and re-deploy the application if necessary. This approach has the similar philosophy to our approach on the role of software architecture in the deployment. However, this approach ignores the plentiful knowledge derived from the development and the runtime states of nodes. Without such knowledge, it is very difficult to generate the proper configuration in a manual or automatic way.

Rakic et al. propose the DeSi environment to support flexible and tailorable specification, manipulation, visualization, and (re)estimation of deployment architectures for large-scale, highly distributed systems [18]. DeSi studies deeply on how to take the availability into account in the deployment, including defining a formal foundation and investigating six algorithms to automatically generate the deployment plan. However, in DeSi, the formal specification of the deployed system has to be written by hand and some values in the specification are difficult to retrieve without the support of runtime environments. On the other hand, the formal specification can be automatically generated in CADTool with the plentiful knowledge derived from the development and runtime states of nodes. In our opinion, the work of DeSi can improve the reliability calculation of CADTool, which is under development. Moreover, DeSi only takes the availability into account while CADTool tries to facilitate the tradeoff between multiple qualities.

Clarke et al. provide an object confinement discipline for static verification of components' integrity when the components are deployed into a J2EE application server [5]. The confinement rules are simple for developers to understand, require no annotation to the code of EJB components. In our approach, the deployment information is transformed from the design artifacts automatically, which in nature ensures the components' integrity. However, if the design artifacts are not available, deployers have to fill the numerous deployment description elements by hand. At that time the object confinement discipline is helpful to accomplish the verification.

In some sense, the deployment can be considered as a means to allocate resources for the best-of-the-breed resource utilizations. Resource management is a hot topic in some emerging new paradigms of distributed computing, especially the grid computing [14][13] and autonomic computing [15]. They try to automatically allocate the resources for a given application without human intervention. It is ideal but as they claim it is very far away from implementation and practice. Moreover, in this paper, we can conclude that the resource allocation is so challenging for an expert. In our opinion, only after people know how to allocate resources and conclude a set of sophisticated principles, the degree of automation can be improved more or less but the full automation still has a long way to go. In other words, it is feasible, practical and urgent to study how to facilitate instead of substitute people in deployment nowadays.

7   Conclusion and Future Work

In this paper an architecture-based approach is proposed for deploying large-scale component-based systems into open and dynamic runtime environments. With the help of the software architecture, deployers can understand the whole system precisely and quickly, build up the goals of the deployment, partition the system, evaluate the result of the deployment plan and re-deploy when necessary. We demonstrate this approach in J2EE. A graphical assembly and deployment tool, called CADTool, is built to assist the deployment. Furthermore, a set of principles are provided to help deployers make decisions when deploying. A case, which shows how to deploy a J2EE blueprint application in a distributed environment, is illustrated.

As we discussed previously, there are many open issue to be addressed. Our future work will focus on the following aspects: carry out more tests or benchmarks and try to apply the approach for industrial software systems; establish quantitative models to describe the goals and the result of the deployment; formulize the principles; based on the models and formulations, devise the algorithms to deploy/redeploy systems more automatically.

Acknowledgements

This effort is partially sponsored by the National Key Basic Research and Development Program of China (973) under Grant No. 2002CB31200003; the National High-Tech Research and Development Plan of China (863) under Grant No. 2004AA112070; the National Natural Science Foundation of China under Grant No. 60125206, 60233010, 60403030, 90412011; and the IBM University Joint Study Program.

References

1. A. Dearle, G.N.C Kirby, A.J. McCarthy: A Framework for Constraint-Based Deployment and Autonomic Management of Distributed Applications. International Conference on Autonomic Computing (ICAC'04), New York, USA (2004)
2. A. van Deursen: Software Architecture Recovery and Modeling: [WCRE 2001 discussion forum report]. ACM SIGAPP Applied Computing Review, Vol. 10, No. 1 (2002) 4–7
3. Brown, A.W., Wallnau, K.C.: The Current State of CBSE. IEEE Software. Vol. 15, No. 5 (1998) 37–46
4. C. Szyperski: Component Software: Beyond Object-Oriented Programming, Addison-Wesley (1997)
5. D. Clarke, M. Richmond, J. Nobel: Saving the World from Bad Beans: Deployment-time Confinement Checking. Object-Oriented Programming, Systems, Languages & Applications (2003) 374–387
6. D. Garlan: Software Architecture: A Roadmap, The Future of Software Engineering 2000, Proceedings of 22nd International Conference on Software Engineering, ACM Press, (2000) 91–101
7. D. Perry, A. Wolf: Foundations for the Study of Software Architecture, ACM SIGSOFT Software Engineering Notes, Vol. 17, No. 4, (1992) 40–52

8. G. Huang, H. Mei, Q.X. Wang: Towards Software Architecture at Runtime. ACM SIGSOFT Software Engineering Notes, Vol. 28, No. 2, March (2003)
9. G. Huang, M. Wang, L. Ma, L. Lan, T. Liu, H. Mei: Towards Architecture Model based Deployment for Dynamic Grid Services. In Proceedings of IEEE International Conference on E-Commerce Technology for Dynamic E-Business (CEC-EAST) (2004) 14–21
10. H. Mei, G. Huang: PKUAS: An Architecture-based Reflective Component Operating Platform, invited paper, 10th IEEE International Workshop on Future Trends of Distributed Computing Systems, Suzhou, China, May (2004) 26–28
11. H. Mei, J.C. Chang, F.Q. Yang: Software Component Composition based on ADL and Middleware, Science in China(F), Vol. 44, No. 2, (2001) 136–151
12. HP Labs: SmartFrog, http://www.hpl.hp.com/research/smartfrog
13. I. Foster, C. Kesselman, J. M. Nick, S. Tuecke: The Physiology of the Grid: An Open Grid Services Architecture for Distributed Systems Integration. June (2002)
14. I. Foster, C. Kesselman, S. Tuecke: The Anatomy of the Grid: Enabling Scalable Virtual Organizations. International Journal of High Performance Computing Applications, Vol. 15, No. 3 (2001) 200–222
15. J.O. Kephart, D.M. Chess: The Vision of Autonomic Computing. IEEE Computer, January (2003) 41–50
16. M. Rutherford, K. Anderson, A. Carzaniga, D. Heimbigner, A. Wolf: Reconfiguration in the Enterprise JavaBean Component Model. 1st International Working Conference on Component Deployment, Berlin (2002) 67–81
17. M. Shaw, D. Garlan: Software Architecture: Perspectives on an Emerging Discipline, Prentice Hall (1996)
18. M.M. Rakic, S. Malek, N. Beckman, N. Medvidovic: A Tailorable Environment for Assessing the Quality of Deployment Architectures in Highly Distributed Settings, 2nd International Working Conference on Component Deployment, Edinburgh, UK (2004) 1-17
19. OMG: Model Driven Architecture, http://www.omg.org/mda
20. OMG: OMG Unified Modeling Language Specification, Version 1.5, formal, http://www.omg.org/uml (2001)
21. P. Kruchten: The 4+1 view model of architecture. IEEE Software, Vol. 12, No. 6 (1995) 42–50
22. Sun Microsystems. Java 2 Platform Enterprise Edition Specification, Version 1.3, Proposed Final Draft 4, http://java.sun.com/j2ee (2001)
23. Sun Microsystems: Enterprise JavaBeans Spec. Version 2.1 (2002)
24. Sun Microsystems: Java 2 Platform Enterprise Edition Management Specification, v1.0 (2002)
25. Sun Microsystems: Java Pet Store Sample Application. http://java.sun.com/developer/releases/petstore
26. Sun Microsystems: Java Smart Ticket Sample Application. http://java.sun.com/developer/releases/smarticket

Component-Based Open Middleware Supporting Aspect-Oriented Software Composition

Bert Lagaisse and Wouter Joosen

Dept. of Computer Science, K.U.Leuven, Belgium,
{Bert.Lagaisse, Wouter.Joosen}@cs.kuleuven.ac.be

Abstract. State-of-the-art middleware for component-based distributed applications requires openness to support a broad and varying range of services. It also requires powerful and maintainable composition between application logic and middleware services. In this paper we describe DyMAC (Dynamic Middleware with Aspect-Components), a component and aspect-based middleware framework that supports component-based development of middleware services and offers the power of aspect-oriented composition to connect the application logic to the middleware services. We discuss the issue of a lack of expressive power in the contracts of components and aspects when combining component-based and state-of-the-art aspect-oriented development. We describe how the DyMAC framework offers a component model that solves this problem with aspect integration contracts.

1 Introduction

Software systems nowadays often have a complex distributed architecture. Non-functional requirements like availability or security therefore involve complex support based on distributed algorithms. A typical example is a large-scale distributed application with distributed transactional behavior and a centralized authentication server. The goal of a middleware layer is to isolate this complex support from the functional application logic. We focus in this paper on component-based systems that offer support for designing the application logic of distributed applications. An example of such a component framework is Enterprise Java Beans [11]. The middleware layer we envisage for such a component framework is a set of services that supports the implementation of the non-functional concerns. Our DyMAC framework offers support for two important challenges that state-of-the-art commercial middleware layers still are troubled with.

1. First, the services offered by current middleware layers and platforms are often a closed, limited set. They are not, or only in a limited way adaptable or extensible. Such middleware can be seen as a kind of black box [3]. But the different requirements of software developers towards the middleware layer are often application specific or beyond the provided services of the middleware. This requires that the middleware is extensible with application specific middleware services. But also the different requirements of the

G.T. Heineman et al. (Eds.): CBSE 2005, LNCS 3489, pp. 139–154, 2005.

simultaneous end-users of the application require new and potentially concurrent versions of certain middleware services [16]. Also updates of existing services of the middleware layer occur frequently. All these new requirements involve adaptability and extensibility of the middleware layer. It has to evolve from a black box to an open framework where middleware services can be adapted and added.

2. The second problem is situated in the composition of the application logic with the middleware services. The composition logic for services like transactions and security is strongly intermixed with the application logic. The composition problem with such concerns is often referred to as the crosscutting concern problem [4].

Both component-based as well as aspect-based software engineering techniques can contribute to a solution. The first problem can be addressed by integrating properties of component-based software development (CBSD)[1]. The second problem can be tackled by applying concepts from aspect-oriented software development (AOSD)[4]. AOSD is a promising technology for the problem of crosscutting concerns. Middleware and non-functional development concerns are part of the key application domain of AOSD research [9] [10]. In this paper we discuss the DyMAC middleware framework that offers a solution for the challenges mentioned above by combining the advantages of CBSD and AOSD.

The paper is organized as follows: in the second section we summarize how aspect-oriented software design and component-based software design can contribute to a solution for the challenges we mentioned above. In the third section we discuss the problems that are introduced by combining the two software development paradigms. The fourth section illustrates these problems with an example. In the fifth section we describe our DyMAC framework. In the sixth section we compare our solution with the related work in the research domain. Finally, we conclude.

2   The Promise of Integrating Advantages from CBSD and AOSD

In this section we summarize how CBSD and AOSD can contribute to a solution for the challenges we mentioned above. First we explain how component-based techniques can offer extensibility and adaptability of the middleware layer. In the second subsection we explain how aspect-based software composition can contribute to the problem of crosscutting composition logic.

2.1   Component-Based Open Middleware

Our first goal is to define a modularly adaptable and extensible architecture for middleware platforms. This includes a definition of the best unit of modularity for a middleware service. It should be possible to make a middleware service deployable and reusable as one software unit. Component-based software development brings a unit of modularity that can achieve our first goal. In [1] a software component is defined as a unit of composition with contractually specified interfaces and explicit context dependencies only. A software component can be deployed independently and is subject to composition by third parties. A component-based approach to a middleware platform, where middleware services are modularized as software components, meets the requirements of extensibility and adaptability. Middleware services can be developed by third parties as components and can be deployed into a middleware framework. Composition of application logic with the middleware services (which are components) can be realized using the connectors of the provided interface.

However, the connectors of the provided interfaces of components are often methods. This is a consequence of the object-oriented design on which a lot of component frameworks are based. The calls to the provided methods of the middleware service are scattered throughout the application logic, and this causes the problem of crosscutting composition logic.

2.2   Aspect-Based Middleware

Aspect-oriented software design is about modularizing crosscutting concerns. Aspects are first class entities that encapsulate a certain behavior (often called advice) and also the instructions on where, when and how to invoke this behavior [4]. Aspect-oriented programming languages offer special programming constructs to specify well localized places in the structure or execution flow of an application. These places are called join points and depend on the main decomposition paradigm of the application. In an object-oriented application, join points can be method definitions, method calls, access to private class members, constructor calls ... The programming constructs that can define a set of those join points are called pointcut designators. These pointcut designators are the key for enabling the modularization of crosscutting concerns. They provide a way to talk about doing something at many places in a program with a single statement (also called quantification [6]).

An aspect-based approach for the composition of application logic and middleware services offers a solution for the problem of crosscutting composition. It is even possible to manipulate internal application logic and application state, e.g. by accessing and modifying internal class members. From one point of view this could be interesting, because middleware services sometimes need access to the internal state of the application logic, e.g. for persistence, state synchronization in load balancing systems or state transferal in fail-over systems. But from another point of view, access to the whole internal structure of an application breaks encapsulation and can cause a lot of unforeseen problems, which are discussed in the next section.

3   Technical Challenges when CBSD Meets AOSD

A lot of recent research in aspect-oriented software development is situated in the domain of the integration of AOSD and CBSD (Caesar [14], JasCo [13], JAC [12], JBoss/AOP [15]). This integration of AOSD and CBSD is twofold.

1. A first facet of the integration is integrating AOSD into CBSD. This includes offering support for aspect-oriented composition in a component-based system.
2. A second facet of the integration is applying the principles of CBSD onto AOSD software modules. Aspects itself should be handled as components.

In this twofold integration, aspects evolve into a concept of software modules combining the advantages of components and aspects. We shall call these new software modules aspect-components. A typical form of aspect-components is that they encapsulate the advice of an aspect. The interface of an aspect-component provides connectors that make it possible to superimpose the advice on join points in the base components, which are often object-oriented. The kind of advice that the aspect-components can provide is before-advice, after-advice and around-advice [5]. The actual composition of the base components with the aspect-components is specified separately in the composition logic that composes the different components into an application. In this composition logic the base components and aspect-components are connected using pointcut designators that define the set of join points where the aspect-component is superimposed. In the remainder of this section we first discuss the problems that occur when combining the advantages of components and aspects into this new software module.

When composing multiple software components, one of the important issues is managing interference. This means one needs to express and control which modules may use and affect each other. In an object-oriented or component-based software design, each artifact can be equipped with a contract that specifies the provided functionality and the needed (required) functionality that describes the dependencies of a component on other components. In principle, correct behavior can be guaranteed if a component has been designed defensively and if it strictly implements its contract. When aspect-oriented composition is applied, this is no longer guaranteed. The composition of a component with an aspect can cause a component to no longer meet its contractual obligations.

We observe that the state-of-the-art notion of a contract is no longer sufficient in an aspect-oriented programming environment. When a component is composed with an aspect by means of superimposition, there is no expressive power to specify the following:

1. The component must specify what the component provides towards the aspect, i.e. which interference is permitted from certain (types of) aspects. Aspects are often services that are orthogonal with the components functionality, and therefore, the component's contract and provided interfaces are not always suitable for composition with an aspect. Therefore the contract of the component needs to be extended with the required expressive power about composition with aspects.
2. An aspect must specify what the aspect requires from the components it is applied to and which behavior it provides. This also includes in which way it affects those components.

These two facets of the lack of expressive power are explained hereafter. The most important consequences of these shortcomings are also shortly discussed.

The first lack of expressive power : the component contract. The first lack of expressive power is problematic in combination with certain join point models of aspect-oriented technologies. The join point model is the set of possible places in the structure or execution flow of an application that can be localized by the aspect language to apply certain behavior. In current state-of-the-art aspect-component technologies, we can distinguish two approaches to join point models:

1. Some aspect technologies allow complete, uncontrolled access to the whole internal implementation of the (component-based) application logic, overriding all scope modifiers and breaking encapsulation. This approach neglects the provided interfaces of the component because of the orthogonality of the component and the aspect. This can lead to uncontrolled semantic interference. This uncontrolled semantic interference of an aspect with the base component can cause undesirable exposure and modification of data and undesirable exposure and modification of behavior. A more detailed illustration of these problems is elaborated in [17].
   A second problem with providing the whole implementation structure of the component as an interface towards aspects is that it also makes an aspect too strongly tied to the component and therefore reusability of the aspect is compromised. It is clear that the notion of provided interface towards aspects must respect a certain form of encapsulation to achieve reusable aspects and adaptable application components.
2. Other aspect technologies limit the join point model to the interface of a functional component that is provided towards other functional components (e.g. in JasCo [13] only public methods of a Java Bean are a possible join point for aspects). From our point of view, where aspect technology is used for composition with middleware services, this approach is not powerful enough. Because, as mentioned above, middleware services sometimes need access to the internal state of the application. An example of this need is illustrated in the next section.

The second lack of expressive power: the aspect contract. State-of-the-art aspect technologies do not offer the possibility to contractually specify an aspect. There is also no clear notion of what really defines the interface of an aspect. This lack of expressive power is problematic in order to obtain a notion of aspect-component. An aspect should be able to include in its specification what it requires from other components, other aspect-components and the underlying platform. The specification should also include what functionality the aspect provides and in which way it affects the components it is composed with.

The scope of this paper is the composition of a component with an aspect-component and hence we focus on the specification of aspect-components concerning their requirements towards the base components and how they affect those components. In the example in the next section we illustrate these two needs of expressive power.

4   Illustration

To explain the problems above we illustrate them with a rather pedagogical example. Suppose that an entity *person* is the key abstraction in a software system. A person is uniquely defined by his social security number and has a name and a birth date. The software entity *person* also provides an inspector isAdult to check if the person is an adult. Because of privacy reasons a person object should never expose its age or birth date. But it is a necessary property to know whether a person is an adult. The birth date also needs to be stored in a database. If the persistence service is delivered as an aspect, then the persistence aspect needs access to the birth date property, while other software entities should not be able to access this property. The code of the person and the persistence example is shortly illustrated below in Java and pseudo-Aspect/J [5]:

```
public class Person{
  private Date birthDate;
  private String name, ssn;
  public Person(String ssn, String name, Date birthDate){
  //initialization}
  private void setBirthDate(Date bd){}
  private Date getBirthDate{...}
  public void setName(String name){}
  public String getName(){...}
  public String getSsn(){...}
  public boolean isAdult(){
  // derived from birthDate}}
```

```
Aspect PersonPersistence{
//on constructor execution insert into database
after(Person p): execution (Person.new(..)) && this(p){
    DataBase.insert(p.ssn, p.name, p.birthDate); }
//after mutator execution update database
after(Person p): execution(* set *(..)) && this(p){
    DataBase.update(p.ssn, p.name, p.birthDate);}}
```

The contract of the person class certainly specifies that it provides the *isAdult* functionality. Towards other modules the birth date property remains hidden. However, this property has to be exposed towards the persistence aspect, because that aspect requires *person* to expose encapsulated state that needs to be persistent. Therefore the contract of the persistence aspect must specify that it requires access to the encapsulated (i.e. private) state of a person object. The aspect also needs to specify how it affects the state: will it inspect and/or modify the state.

This section described an example that illustrated the lack of expressive power in the specification of the functional components as well as in the specification of the aspect. In the next section we describe how the component model of DyMAC offers the kind of component types to support aspect-oriented composition. We also describe how the component model offers the expressive power in the specification of components and aspect-components to tackle the problems we discussed.

5   DyMAC: Dynamic Middleware with Aspect-Components

DyMAC is an initial step in our search for a component-based open middleware framework with support for aspect-oriented composition. In this section we first describe the structure of DyMAC applications and the different abstractions into which a DyMAC application can be decomposed. In the second subsection we explain how we applied the principles of component-based software development to those abstractions mentioned in the previous subsection. In this way we achieve component-based building blocks for applications. We also discuss the specification of the components that relates to aspect-oriented composition with other components. Next, we explain how applications can be composed out of those component-based building blocks and how aspect-oriented composition is supported.

5.1   Structure and Overview

The top-level architecture of a DyMAC application can be described as a distributed and layered architecture. As mentioned in the introduction and motivation, the domain of our research is middleware for complex distributed applications. A DyMAC application consists of different subsystems that are running on different nodes in a network. A second property of the top level architecture is its subdivision into two layers: A functional layer on top and a middleware layer underneath. The functional layer contains the core application (or business) logic. The middleware layer offers non-functional services. In [2] a layer is defined as a coherent set of related functionality. In a strictly layered structure, layer n may only use the services of layer n-1. In practice this structural restriction is often lessened; Layers are often designed as abstractions that hide implementation specifics below. This latter approach is also what applies to the middleware layer in DyMAC. Sometimes application specific information is needed from the functional layer towards the middleware layer (recall the person persistence aspect). This can cause up-calls from the middleware layer to the application logic, which breaks the restriction of strictly layered structures.

Each layer in the architecture of a DyMAC application further decomposes into abstractions that are the basic building blocks for the applications. In the remainder of this subsection we describe these abstractions and their main function. In the next subsection we elaborate on how these abstractions can be specified as components to achieve a component-based decomposition.

Functional Layer Decomposition. The functional layer contains two kinds of components: functional components (abbreviated to *funcos*) and client components (shortly called *clients*).

A funco abstracts a key concept of the functional domain. It provides a constructor to instantiate objects that can have a certain state and that provide certain operations. An object of a functional component can send a message to

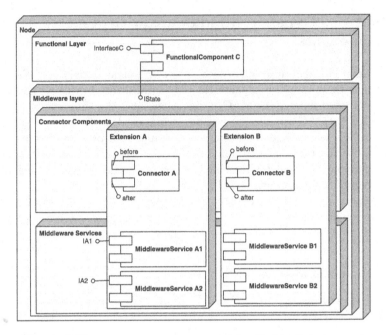

Fig. 1. Different component types in the DyMAC framework

another object of any functional component to invoke an operation. That other object sends a return message with the result of that operation.

Client components are a special kind of funcos. They only provide one operation: an entry point for starting the execution of an application.

Middleware Layer Decomposition. The middleware layer consists of a collection of middleware extensions that offer non-functional services to the functional layer of the application. The middleware layer has a 2-layer architecture. On the lowest layer it has a service layer, providing the different middleware services, on the highest layer it contains connectors, which are used to connect the functional components to the middleware services. Thus, a middleware extension typically consists of a collection of connectors and middleware services.

The service layer is decomposed into *middleware service components*. These components are abstractions of the different non-functional services in the service layer. Alike functional components, middleware services can be instantiated and can have state and behavior. Possible examples of middleware services are an encryption service or an authentication service.

The connector layer is decomposed into *connector components*. A connector component encapsulates the (otherwise crosscutted) calls to the middleware services. The state of the funcos and the runtime arguments of invoked behavior on funcos are possible arguments of the connector's invocations to the middleware services. Therefore a connector component has to be able to inspect and modify the state of a component in the functional layer, but it also has to be able to inspect and modify the messages that are sent between the components in the functional layer. The connectors use the middleware service components to apply the non-functional services to the functional components. The connectors can intercept any message that is sent and add behavior before and after they forward the message to its destination. They can also alter the message or even block it. The technique of interception is a widely used mechanism to achieve aspect-oriented composition. Further is illustrated how these connectors provide a mechanism for quantification.

Decomposition into extensions. The middleware layer is decomposed into middleware extensions. These middleware extensions contain a set of caller-extensions and callee-extensions. Caller and callee refer to the sender and receiver when a message is sent between two functional components.

- Caller extensions itself consist of a collection of connectors that can intercept outgoing messages of funcos and a collection of middleware service components needed at the caller-side.
- Callee extensions itself consist of a collection of connectors that can intercept incoming messages and a collection of middleware service components needed at the callee side.

5.2   Component Types

Each abstraction in the framework has to be modularized in the form of a component, i.e. a unit of composition with contractually specified interfaces and explicit context dependencies only. Each abstraction should be deployable independently and can be subject to composition by third parties. We believe only strict compliance with Szyperski's definition, which contains the basic principles to achieve a true component-based architecture, can eliminate today's problems that are involved with aspect-oriented composition. In the description of the component model we will focus on the specification of the functional components and middleware extensions as units of composition with contractually specified interfaces and explicit context dependencies. Especially we will elaborate on the provided interface of a functional component towards a middleware extension and the dependencies of a middleware extension towards a functional component.

Functional Components. A funco abstracts a key concept of the functional domain. We discuss the interfaces and the contracts of a functional component and especially focus on the interfaces and contracts towards the middleware extensions. Because the description of client components is analogue we will not elaborate on them.

Requirements and provisions towards other functional components. As a component a funco has to specify its provided and required interfaces. The provided interface specifies the operations that it provides towards other components in the functional layer. This provided interface consists first of a specification how to instantiate the component, and secondly it contains the provided methods on instantiations of the component. The required interfaces are the dependencies of the component. They specify the operations that are required of other functional components in the system.

Requirements and provisions towards middleware extensions. The aspect integration contract of the functional component specifies what its requirements and provisions are towards middleware extensions. This specification contains where the functional component requires, allows or denies interference of middleware extensions.

First a functional component specifies which middleware extensions it requires: e.g. a transaction around some of its method-implementations. So this part of the contract specifies which middleware extensions the component needs to function properly. These required extensions are typically needed by the implementation of the component. To avoid intermixing non-functional development concerns in the implementation of the functional component, these concerns are specified in the requirements part of the aspect integration contract. In other aspect technologies, the concept obliviousness [6] is often used to argument that non-functional development concerns should be completely separated of the functional components. In case of required services to function properly, keeping the whole functional component oblivious to this need would mean an essential deficit in the specification of the component. We believe that the concept of obliviousness of non-functional middleware services only applies to the implementation of the component, and not the specification of it. Of course, non-functional services that are not required to function properly should be kept oblivious of the whole functional component: implementation and specification.

The interface that a functional component provides towards the middleware layer underneath is a little more complex. It contains the incoming and outgoing messages that can be inspected and modified, and also the different members of the state that can be inspected or modified. These two parts of the provided interface need some explanation:

1. The provided interface towards the functional components mentioned above defines the collection of incoming messages. The required interfaces define the collection of outgoing messages.
2. The state of a funco is defined by the properties of the component. These properties are defined by a get and set operation that access the internal representation, which is one or more private class variables. Using properties to decouple the state of a funco from the actual representation allows changes to the representation without affecting the provided state members. These state properties are not directly accessible by the middleware extensions, but all funcos provide an interface towards the middleware layer underneath to inspect or manipulate the state of a funco. This interface is a reflective backdoor/callback interface for the connectors in the middleware layer. It defines operations for inspecting the state and to modify the state. This enables decoupling of the middleware extension from a specific functional component

and makes it reusable for other applications. Providing this generic interface to access the state also restricts the access of the (aspectual) middleware extensions to the internal part of the functional component that the middleware extensions actually need to access. This is a strongly restricted interface in comparison with some aspect technologies that provide the whole implementation structure of the functional component (E.g. The implementation of the operations). When comparing it to the more restrictive aspect technologies, that do not provide a way to access the internal state of a component, this approach certainly offers advantages.

The allowed interference (state inspection and modification and behavior inspection and modification) can be specified in two ways.

1. For each middleware extensions and for each of the funco's members (behavior or state) it can specify if inspection or modification is allowed. This first approach was explained in detail in [17]. It offers the most detailed possibility to control the interference by middleware extensions but it does limit the extensibility of the application. It also makes it impossible to keep certain middleware services oblivious from the functional component. Therefore a more generic way of specifying interference is also possible.
2. The funco specifies a subset of its behavior and its state that is considered *sensitive*. Only middleware extensions that are marked privileged by the deployer can interfere with this sensitive behavior and state.

An example in DyMAC.NET. Recall the example with the person component. We shortly list the code of the functional interface and the implementation of the person component in the .NET implementation of the DyMAC framework. The functional interface of the component consists of a C# interface specifying how to instantiate a person, a second C# interface specifying the methods it provides and a third C# class that implements the specified interfaces. This implementation also specifies the state properties and the internal representation.

This implementation has to provide a constructor with the same arguments as specified in the specification of the instantiation (IPersonCreate). The DyMAC framework uses this constructor to instantiate the component when the DyMAC instantiator is called. The DyMAC instantiator is a static method with a variable numbers of arguments. In this way it can easily be used to instantiate any functional component.

```
public interface IPersonCreate{
  IPerson create(string ssn, string name, Date birthDate);}
public interface IPerson{
  string getSsn();
  void setName(string name);
  string getName();
public class Person : FunCo, IPerson{
  public Person(string ssn, string name, Date birthDate){...}
  private Date BirthDate{
    get{...}
    set(Date value){...}
  }
...}
```

For the specification of components in DyMAC.NET we use XML-files. It contains the name of the component, the provided interfaces, the required interfaces, the implementation, and the *aspect integration contract*. The current form of an aspect integration contract in DyMAC specifies the members of the component that are provided to normal middleware extensions and the sensitive members that are only provided towards privileged middleware extensions. The members of a component can be constructors, methods and state members. Specifying required middleware extensions is still part of our ongoing work.

The following example illustrates the structure of the specification and focuses on the aspect integration contract. All members of the component that are related with the birth date are marked sensitive for inspection and modification.

```
<funco><name>Person</name>
 <provided>...</provided>
 <implementation>...</implementation>
 <required>...<required>
 <aspect-integration>
  <provided> <!-- towards all aspect-components -->
   <method>string getSsn()</method>
   <method>void setName(string name)</method>
   <method>string getName()</method>
   <method>string askName(IPerson p2)</method>
   <method>IPerson clone()</method>
   <state>string name</state>
  <provided>
  <sensitive><inspect/><modify/>
   <constructor>create(string ssn, string name, Date bd)</constructor>
   <method>void setBirthDate(Date bd)</method>
   <method>Date getBirthDate()</method>
   <state>Date birthDate</state>
  </sensitive>
 </aspect-integration>
</funco>
```

The Service Layer Components. Middleware service components are specified in quite the same way as functional components. They specify their provided interfaces towards the connectors and other middleware services. They also specify the interfaces they require from other middleware services they use.

The main difference is they don't have to specify an aspect integration contract. Aspect-oriented composition is only supported between the functional layer and the middleware layer. A hierarchic aspect-oriented composition strategy, where messages between service layer components can be intercepted is out of the scope of this paper, but certainly not out of the scope of our ongoing work.

When we return to the example, the interfaces and implementation of the person persistence service are straightforward.

```
public interface IPersonPersistence { ...
 void insert(string ssn, string name, Date bd);}
public interface IPersonPersistenceCreate{
 IPersonPersistence create();}
public class PersonPersistence{...
 public void insert(...){
 //insert into persistent storage (database, XML-file ...)
}}
```

```
<service><name>personpersistence</name>
 <provided>
  <method-interface>IPersonPersistence</method-interface>
  <create-interface>IPersonPersistenceCreate</create-interface>
 </provided>
 <implementation><class>PersonPersistence</class></implementation>
</service>
```

Connector Components. All connector components have the same provided interface: a before and after method that contains the calls to the middleware services before and after a message is sent or received.

The connector has to specify the set of middleware services it uses as required interfaces. As a second part of what is required for the connector, the specification contains explicit dependencies towards the functional components. This part of the connector's requirements contains the different members of the functional components that the connector depends on. Next to that, the connector also specifies how it interferes with those members: i.e. inspecting and/or modifying them. This interference can be specified on a per member basis or for all members at once (as in the example below).

In its XML-file the connector also specifies if it applies to the caller or callee side of the message it is superimposed on. Depending on the side that the message is superimposed on, a reference to the functional object is provided. So the connector can inspect or modify the state of that object.

In the example we have to define two kinds of connectors: one for the construction call to insert the person into the persistent storage and one for a mutator call to update the persistent storage. We have illustrated the code of the mutator connector and its specification file.

```
public class MutatorConnector : IConnector{
 public void before(MessageCall mc, FunCo object){}
 public void after(MessageCall mc, ReturnMessage rm, FunCo object){
  IPersonPersistence ipp = DyMAC.createService("service/persistence");
  string ssn = (string)object.getState("Ssn");
  string name = (string)object.getState("Name");
  Date bd = (Date)object.getState("BirthDate");
  ipp.update(ssn, name, bd);}}
```

```
<connector><name>mutator connector</name><callee/>
 <class>MutatorConnector</class>
 <required>
  <service>...</service>
  <funco></inspection></modification>
   <state>String Ssn</state>
   <state>String Name</state>
   <state>Date BirthDate</state>
  </funco>
 </required>
</connector>
```

Middleware Extensions as Components. Middleware extensions consist of a collection of connectors and middleware services. The provided interface of the middleware extension is first defined by the provided interfaces of the middleware services it encapsulates and secondly by the connectors that it contains. The provided interfaces of the middleware services can also be used by the connectors of other middleware extensions. These interfaces define the part of the provided interface of the middleware extension that supports object-oriented composition. The connectors define the part of the provided interface of the middleware extension that supports aspect-oriented composition. As illustrated below, the specification of a middleware extension is a simple list of the components it contains.

```
<extension><name>person persistence extension</name>
 <connector>constructorconnector.xml</connector>
 <connector>mutatorconnector.xml</connector>
 <service>personpersistence.xml</service>
</extension>
```

5.3   Application Assembly

The different components of the application are assembled and composed by means of a declarative specification. First, all components of the application are enumerated by linking to the file with their specification. Secondly, the concrete connections are specified between the functional components and the middleware extensions of the application. In this connection, quantification is realized by using pointcut designators to compose one or more messages of one or more components with one or more connectors. In case multiple connectors are superimposed on a join point, they are invoked with the following precedence rules: first the before advices from connector 1 to n are executed, and then the after advices from connector n to 1.

In the example below, all extensions of the application are marked *privileged*. But it is also possible to specify it more fine grained on a per extension, per connection or per connector basis. The connections in the example are defined in the scope of the persistence extension, therefore the used connectors in a connection should be defined in the persistence extension. But in DyMAC, it is also possible to define connections that are out of the scope of one extension and that superimpose connectors of different extensions.

```
<application><name>PersonApplication</name>
 ... <!-- components in the application -->
 <superimposition><privileged/>
  <extension>persistence extension
  <connection>
   <component>Person</component>
   <constructor>create(string ssn, string name, Date date)</constructor>
   <connector>constructor connector</connector>
  </connection>
  <connection>
   <component>Person</component>
   <method>* set*(..)</method>
   <connector>mutator connector</connector>
  </connection>
  </extension>
 </superimposition>
</application>
```

In the initial problem statement, we defined middleware extensions as application specific. Therefore extensions can only be connected to components within the same application. It is our intention to extend the connections so it is also possible to define system wide middleware extensions that can be connected to funcos of other applications in the system.

How the deployment of the application is specified is beyond the scope of this paper. In this deployment specification, the dependencies of all components are bound to actual components in the system. The deployment specification also allocates the different components of an application on the different nodes in the network.

6 Related Work

Open ORB [3] starts from the same problem: the need for adaptable middleware due to application specific needs. Their solution takes the form of reflective middleware. It uses a reflective API to modify the middleware platform and introspect its implementation.

JBOSS/AOP, JAsCO and JAC offer support for aspect-oriented composition in a Java component-based system. They introduce the concept of aspects that can be used to implement middleware services. But they do not support a true component-based approach to the aspects itself. The base components in the functional layer are not aware of possible interfering aspects, and cannot specify in which way they want to control interference of aspects, e.g. by means of an aspect integration contract as in the DyMAC framework. In these systems any possible join point of each Java component can be superimposed with any aspect.

The join point model of JBOSS/AOP exposes a lot of the internal implementation of components. Possible join points are reads and writes to fields of the class, but also calls of methods and constructors within the implementation of a method or constructor. This exposes details about the implementation of the latter method or constructor. JAsCo limits its join point model to the public methods and events of Java Beans. As mentioned earlier this limits the possibilities for middleware extensions when they need access to the state of the component.

In JAC, the pointcuts that specify where to superimpose an aspect are strings in the code of the aspect, which limits runtime adaptability of the composition logic. Externalizing and modularizing this composition logic in a declarative specification offers better support to change the composition logic without re-compiling the application.

Lasagne is a runtime architecture that enables dynamic customization of systems. Based on client-specific needs and context properties it can select and activate the different extensions in the system. These extensions have the form of wrappers that implement the same interface as the components they are superimposed on. Just like in the DyMAC framework, wrappers can add behavior before and after the invocation of a method. Lasagne also lacks the expressive power to specify which kind of extensions a base component allows. The composition logic of Lasagne is also specified in the meta data of the applications, and not hard coded.

7   Conclusion

In this paper we discussed DyMAC (Dynamic Middleware with Aspect-Components), a component and aspect-based middleware framework that offers adaptability and extensibility. It supports component-based development of middleware services and offers the power of aspect-oriented composition to connect the application logic to the middleware services.

DyMAC solves the issue of the lack of expressive power in the contracts of components and aspects and introduces a kind of aspect-component. It also solves the too strong or too weak composition model of existing aspect-component technologies with a more balanced composition model.

References

1. Clemens Szyperski, Component software: beyond object-oriented programming. Second Edition. ACM Press/Addison-Wesley Publishing Co., New York, NY, 2002.
2. Len Bass, Paul Clements, and Rick Kazman. Software Architecture in Practice, Second Edition. Addison-Wesley, 2003.
3. G. S. Blair, et al. The design and implementation of OpenORB version 2. IEEE Distributed Systems Online Journal, 2(6), 2001
4. Kiczales, G. et al. Aspect-Oriented Programming. In Proc. of ECOOP 1997.
5. Kiczales, G. et al. An Overview of AspectJ. In Proc. of ECOOP 2001.
6. R. Filman et al. Aspect-oriented programming is quantification and obliviousness. In OOPSLA Workshop on Advanced Separation of Concerns, 2000.
7. Bertrand Meyer. Design by contract: building bug-free O-O software. In Hotline on Object-Oriented Technology, volume 4, Number 2, December 1992, pages 4-8.
8. Andreas Rausch, Design by Contract + Componentware = Design by Signed Contract. Journal of Object Technology, In Proc. of Tools Usa, 2002.
9. R. Bodkin et al. Applying AOP for Middleware Platform Independence. Practitioner Reports, AOSD 2003.
10. Adrian Colyer et al, Large-scale AOSD for middleware. In Proc. of AOSD 2004.
11. Sun Microsystems, Inc. Enterprise Java-Beans (EJB) Specification v2.0, 2001.
12. R. Pawlak et al. JAC: A Flexible Solution for Aspect-oriented Programming in Java. In 3rd International Conference on Meta-level Architectures and Separation of Concerns (Reflection), volume 2192 of Lecture Notes in Computer Science, pages 1-25. Springer-Verlag, 2001.
13. D. Suvée et al. JAsCo: An aspect-oriented approach tailored for component-based software development. In Proc. of AOSD 2003.
14. Mira Mezini et al, Conquering aspects with Caesar. In proc. of AOSD 2003.
15. JBoss AOP homepage, http://www.jboss.org/developers/projects/jboss/aop.jsp
16. E. Truyen, et al. Dynamic and Selective Combination of Extensions in Component-Based Applications. In Proc. of ICSE'01.
17. B. Lagaisse et al. Managing Semantic Interference with Aspect Integration Contracts. In workshop SPLAT'04, http://www.daimi.au.dk/ eernst/splat04/

An Empirical Study on the Specification and Selection of Components Using Fuzzy Logic

Kendra Cooper, João W. Cangussu, Rong Lin, Ganesan Sankaranarayanan,
Ragouramane Soundararadjane, and Eric Wong

[1] The University of Texas at Dallas
Mail Station EC 31, 2601 N. Floyd Rd.
Richardson, Texas, USA
{kcooper, cangussu, rxl029000, sxg013900, rxs011610, ewong}@utdallas.edu

Abstract. The rigorous specification of components is necessary to support their selection, adaptation, and integration in component-based software engineering techniques. The specification needs to include the functional and non-functional attributes. The non-functional part of the specification is particularly challenging, as these attributes are often described subjectively, such as *Fast Performance* or *Low Memory*. Here, we propose the use of infinite value logic, fuzzy logic, to formally specify components. A significant advantage of fuzzy logic is that it supports linguistic variables, or hedges (e.g., terms such as slow, fast, very fast, etc.), which are convenient for describing non-functional attributes. In this paper, a new systematic approach for the specification of components using fuzzy logic is presented. First, an empirical study is conducted to gather data on five components that provide data compression capabilities; each uses a different algorithm (Arithmetic Encoding, Huffman, Wavelet, Fractal, and Burrows-Wheeler Transform). Data on the response time performance, memory use, compression ratio, and root mean square error are collected by executing the components on a collection of 75 images with different file formats and sizes. The data are fuzzified and represented as membership functions. The fuzzy component specifications are ranked using a set of test queries. Fuzzy multi-criteria decision making algorithms are going to be investigated for the selection of components in the next phase of the work.

1 Introduction

Component-based software engineering (CBSE) techniques are of keen interest to researchers and practitioners as they hold promise to support the timely, cost effective development of large-scale, complex systems. Such techniques are crucial to effectively meet the needs of rapidly changing business environments.

Effective CBSE techniques need to address a complex set of problems, as the issues are inter-related and span business, legal, and technical areas [1][2][3][4][5]. The prediction of short and long term costs and benefits of using components needs to be supported, as project managers consider the cost of the components, quality of the

G.T. Heineman et al. (Eds.): CBSE 2005, LNCS 3489, pp. 155–170, 2005.

vendor, lack of control over the support and evolution of the COTS components, licensing issues, and the associated risks. Technical issues include the specification, certification, selection, and composition of sets of components, and the impact on the concurrent, iterative modeling of various software engineering artifacts.

The term *component* has a wide variety of definitions in the literature [6]. Here, a software component is an independent, reusable blackbox that, ideally, has a comprehensive interface description including:

- A specification of the functional and non-functional capabilities of the component. The non-functional description includes quality of service attributes (response time performance, memory, etc.)

- A programmer interface description, which defines how to use the component (e.g., an API definition with method names, parameter lists, return types, etc.)

The specification of components has been considered using a variety of notations and approaches. Formal notations offer a means to specify components concisely and unambiguously. XML [7][8], fuzzy logic [8], first-order logic [9], the RESOLVE notation [10], as well as architectural description languages and coordination languages [11] have been proposed for formally representing component specifications. The well known Unified Modeling Language (UML), a semi-formal notation, has also been used to specify components [12]. Alternative approaches including interface definitions [13] and templates [14] have also been investigated, which are based on informal, English descriptions.

A key issue in the specification of components is the problem of how to represent and reason about the non-functional attributes, such as performance, adaptability, security, etc. These attributes are often described subjectively, using terms like "extremely fast," "very fast," "quite fast," and "moderately fast" rather than simply "fast" and "not fast." Fuzzy logic, developed as a solution to this kind of problem, provides an effective way to represent and reason with such vague and ambiguous terms. It provides a theoretical foundation for approximate reasoning using imprecise propositions, which is based on fuzzy set theory.

This paper presents an approach that utilizes fuzzy logic in the specification of software components. Fuzzy logic has been applied to a number of interesting problems in a wide variety of domains such as medicine, manufacturing, software engineering, etc. [15][16]. Currently, it has received very limited attention from the CBSE community. The approach described in Section 0 uses fuzzy logic to select components but does not present a well defined process to create fuzzy specifications for the non-functional attributes of the components [8].

The process to define the fuzzy specification of the components is accomplished in steps. The software components that provide specific functional capabilities are executed in order to collect data about their non-functional behavior. Data are collected for their response time performance, memory use, and quality attributes that are of particular interest for the component. For example, quality attributes for components that provide compression capabilities include the root mean square error (RMSE) and compression ratios. The data are fuzzified (i.e., the data are represented as a collection of fuzzy membership functions) and the components are ranked using a set of test queries.

The approach is illustrated using a study involving a collection of components that provide data compression capabilities. Each component implements a different algorithm: Arithmetic Encoding, Huffman coding, Burrows-Wheeler Transform (BWT), Fractal Image Encoding, and Embedded zero-tree wavelet encoder. The image compression components are executed on a single platform with over 75 images (of various formats like jpg, pgm, raw, and bmp). Execution time (system time + user time) and memory usage for compression and decompression components, the compression ratio, and the RMSE are collected. Once gathered, the data are fuzzified (i.e., represented as fuzzy membership functions). Each fuzzy specification is composed of the requirements interface (functional and non-functional capabilities) and the programmer interface (e.g., API definition) represented as fuzzy membership functions. In addition, design and implementation constraints such as programming language, code form (e.g., source code, executable, byte code), as well as the execution environment (e.g., machine hardware = sun4u, OS version = 5.9, Processor type = sparc, Hardware = SUNW, Sun-Fire-280R) are captured in the specification. The fuzzy representations of the components are ranked using a set of test queries.

This paper is structured as follows. An overview of fuzzy logic is presented in Section 2 as background material. The approach to build and rank a collection of fuzzy components is presented in Section 3. The example study is illustrated in Section 4. Section 5 presents some related work while conclusions and future work are in Section 6.

2 Fuzzy Logic

When one admits that nothing is certain one must, I think also add that some things are more nearly certain than others.

- Bertrand Russell

Numerous approaches are available to represent and reason about uncertainty including probabilistic reasoning, neural network theory, and fuzzy logic [17]. Fuzzy logic was proposed by Zadeh in the 1960's [18] while working on the problem of natural language processing. Natural language, like many activities in the real world, is not easily translated into the absolute terms of 0 and 1 provided by classical logic. Fuzzy logic is well suited for representing and reasoning with vague and ambiguous conditions, where an exact true or false value cannot always be determined. Instead, degrees of truth and falsity are needed. Fuzzy logic offers infinite set of values [0.0..1.0].

Suppose, for example, you ask the following question to a group of people: *Is the component very fast?* The variety of responses reflects the individuals' experiences and knowledge. For example, the component vendor may reply 1 (true); an engineer in a high performance domain may reply 0.6 (somewhat true); an engineer in an information system domain may reply 0.8 (quite true), etc. People can achieve this high level of abstraction when considering such questions; fuzzy logic has been compared to the human decision making process. The ultimate goal of fuzzy logic is to provide a theoretical foundation for approximate reasoning using imprecise proposi-

a theoretical foundation for approximate reasoning using imprecise propositions based on fuzzy set theory.

Fuzzy Sets. A classical (crisp) set is defined as a collection of elements; each element either belongs or does not belong to a set. These classical sets can be described by enumerating the elements of the list, using conditions for membership (e.g., set A only contains elements less than 5), or by using a characteristic function to define the member elements, where 1 indicates membership and 0 indicates non-membership.

The definition of set membership is modified for fuzzy sets, in which a characteristic function gives a degree of membership for each element of a given set. Membership functions can be formed using piecewise lines (e.g., triangular or trapezoidal), Gaussian distribution, Bell, Sigmoid, quadratic and cubic polynomial curves, etc. In this paper, the generalized bell membership function is used, because it generated the least error in the fuzzification of the data collected for the components. The generalized bell function depends on three parameters a, b, and c as given by Equation (1). These parameters determine the shape of the curve. The parameter a determines the width of the curve, b is related to the slope at the point $c+a$, and c locates the center of the curve.

$$F(x; a, b, c) = \frac{1}{1 + \left| \dfrac{x - c}{a} \right|^{2b}} \tag{1}$$

Fuzzy Definitions. Basic definitions for fuzzy logic are presented below, followed by an example that clarifies the semantic distinction between fuzzy logic and probability theory.

Definition 1: Let X be some set of objects, with elements noted as x. Thus, $X = \{x\}$.

Definition 2: A fuzzy set A in X is characterized by a membership function mA(x) mA: $x \to y$, $y \in R \mid 0.0 \le y \le 1.0$ In other words, the membership function maps each element in X onto the real interval [0.0, 1.0]. As mA(x) approaches 1.0, the degree of membership of x in A increases.

Definition 3: Empty fuzzy set. A is EMPTY $\Leftrightarrow \forall x\ mA(x) = 0.0$.

Definition 4: Fuzzy set equality. $A = B \Leftrightarrow \forall x\ mA(x) = mB(x)$

Definition 5: Fuzzy subset. A is CONTAINED in B $\Leftrightarrow \forall x\ mA(x) \le mB(x)$.

Definition 6: NOT operator (Complement of the fuzzy set). NOT (mA (x)) = 1 - mA(x).

Definition 7: OR operator (Union of fuzzy sets). C = A OR B, where: mC(x) = MAX(mA(x), mB(x)).

Definition 8: AND operator (Intersection of fuzzy sets). C = A AND B where: mC(x) = MIN(mA(x), mB(x)).

Definition 9: IMPLICATION operator. A → B = (NOT A) OR B = MAX{1-A, MIN{A,B}}

In a fuzzy system, the rules have the form: IF (x1 AND x2 AND ... AND *xn*) THEN *y*.

Fuzzy Logic Vs. Probabilistic Theory. The last two fuzzy set operations, AND and OR, clearly illustrate the semantic differences from their counterparts in probabilistic theory. Suppose, for example, x = Fred, P is the fuzzy set of pleasant people, and A is the fuzzy set of athletic people. Let's use P(x) = 0.90 and A(x) = 0.90 to describe the probability that Fred is very pleasant and Fred is very athletic and mP(x) = 0.90 and mA(x) = 0.90 to describe the memberships functions that Fred is very pleasant and Fred is very athletic. The probabilistic calculation is P(x) * A(x) = 0.81, whereas the fuzzy result is MIN(mP(x), mA(x)) = 0.90. Therefore, the probabilistic calculation yields the statement:

If Fred is very pleasant and Fred is very athletic, then Fred is a quite pleasant, athletic person, using 0.81 to describe "quite".

The fuzzy calculation, however, yields:
If Fred is very pleasant and Fred is very athletic, then Fred is a very pleasant, athletic person, once again using 0.90 to describe "very".

As more factors are included into the equations (the fuzzy set of intelligent people, tall people, wealthy people, etc.), the result of a series of AND's approaches 0.0 in the probabilistic calculation, even if all factors are initially high. Our intuition for the problem better matches the fuzzy set calculation in which, for example, five factors of the value 0.90 ("very") ANDed together gives the answer 0.90 ("very"), not anything lower.

The probabilistic version of A OR B is (A+B - A*B), which approaches 1.0 as additional factors are considered. Again, the fuzzy set calculation uses the maximum of the membership values to limit the resulting membership degree.

It is important to note that the assignment of values to linguistic meanings (such as 0.90 to "very") and vice versa is subjective. Fuzzy systems do not claim to establish formal procedure for assignments at this level. What fuzzy logic does propose is to establish a formal method of operating on these values, once the primitives have been established.

3 Fuzzy Component Specification Process: A Case Study on Compression Components

A series of steps are defined to create a fuzzy specification that can be used to facilitate the analysis and ranking of components according to some specific criteria. Each step in our approach is described next along with a case study based on image compression algorithms.

Step 1 - Component collection: Before actually starting specifying components using fuzzy logic, a set of functionally equivalent components must be selected. Assume we are interested in a certain set of functionality $F=\{f_1, f_2, ..., f_n\}$. Then, a collection of components $C=\{c_1, c_2, ..., c_m\}$ that implements F is formed. In addition to F the components may present any other extra functionality.

The problem of compressing images is an interesting one. Some algorithms take less time but use more memory, while others behave the other way around. Quality issues, such as the compression ratio or RMSE, also have trade-offs in different algorithms. For example, an algorithm may be acceptable in terms of time and memory, but have a poor compression ratio. In some cases image restoration is compromised to achieve a good compression ratio. In short, Image Compression components have clear trade-offs, in terms of execution time, memory, compression ratio, and RMSE. Also since there are many well-established algorithms and their implementations are available over the Internet, image compression components have been chosen for this study and $F=\{$image compression$\}$.

A survey of image compression algorithms has been performed; the components have been chosen in such a way that there is a clear trade-off in terms of execution time, compression ratio, and the root mean square error (RMSE) between the original image and the uncompressed image. Available components have been selected, their non-functional features analyzed, and the results used to derive a fuzzy specification of these features. Five image compression algorithms have been chosen for this study: Arithmetic Encoding (AREC), Huffman coding (HUFF), Burrows-Wheeler Transform (BWT), Fractal Image Encoding (FRAC), and Embedded Zero-Tree Wavelet Encoder (WAVE). Therefore $C=\{$AREC,HUFF,BWT,FRAC,WAVE$\}$. Source code for these components is available over the Internet. As a first step, the credibility of the source code for both compression and un-compression has been assured based on available reviews and references given by various web sites, a thorough code walk through, and testing the components. In some cases the source code has been modified so that it could compile in the lab environment using the g++ compiler (with default settings) on Sun Solaris. It should be clear that the availability of source code is not required for the fuzzy specification of the components.

Step 2 - Input fuzzification: Based on the functionality set F, the input attributes $A=\{a_1, a_2, ..., a_q\}$ affecting F are determined. Then, a body of distinct test inputs $T=\{t_1, t_2, ..., t_j\}$ is created to exercise all the components in C; data are collected. Neuro-adaptive learning techniques [170] are then used to create K_i membership functions for each attribute a_i in A. The value of K_i depends on the characteristics of a_i and the desired granularity. For example, if a_i represents the size of the input, one could select K_i =3 for {small, medium, large}, K_i =5 for {small, medium, large, very large, extremely large}, or any other representative set of the linguistic characteristics of a_i.

The inputs affecting the functional and non-functional behavior of the distinct components are identified in this step. In the case of compression algorithms, two features are of interest. The first is the type of images a compression algorithm can handle (i.e., the file format). The second refers to how the size of an image affects the component's non-functional behavior. When searching for a compression component, one could think of the following query: "Search for a component that has low memory usage for large images". What is the size of a large image is the immediate question that comes from this query. As expected, the definition of a large (very small, small, medium, very large, etc.) image is not crisp but rather fuzzy, therefore justifying the fuzzy specification approach proposed here. This results in a single element set for A={image size}.

In order to fuzzify the input size, images of various sizes and types were downloaded from the Internet, where the size ranged from 11 KB to 4096 KB. Also, components depend on the image formats like raw or pgm. Due to the difficulty of finding images in raw or pgm formats, ReaConverter Pro v3.4 has been used to convert some images to the desired format. In effect, the study was conducted on 75 images of type jpg, raw, and pgm leading to $T=\{t_1,t_2,...,t_{74},t_{75}\}$. With these images three (K=3) membership functions have been generated (using MatLab Fuzzy Logic Toolbox) based on the size of the images. The choice of three membership functions (small, medium, and large) is arbitrary and done here to simplify the results of the case study. There is no restriction in selecting a different number of functions. Neuro-adaptive learning techniques [170] have been used to generate the size based membership function depicted in Figure 1. Also a generalized bell format has been selected for the membership functions due to its concise and powerful representation features. We are aware that a much larger set of images would be required to fully capture the fuzzy features of image size. However, the selected set appears to be large enough to demonstrate the applicability of the proposed approach.

Step 3 - Non-functional attributes selection: A set of non-functional attributes $NF=\{nf_1,nf_2,...,nf_p\}$ for the components is selected. This set must express important attributes related to the components. Also, some attributes in NF may not be applicable/identifiable to all the components

Based on the characteristics of compression algorithms, four attributes are analyzed here: NF={total execution time, compression ratio, maximum memory usage, RMSE}, where total execution time is the combination of compression plus decompression time and RMSE is a quality measure. Other features can be easily included according to users' needs.

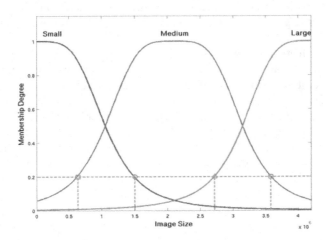

Figure 1: Fuzzification of input based on image size: three membership functions for small, medium, and large images.

Step 4 - Component independent fuzzification of non-functional attributes: In this step all the components in C are executed for all test inputs in T, and measurements of all attributes in NF are collected. As for the input fuzzification (Step 2), neuro-adaptive learning techniques are used to create K_i membership functions for each of the nf_i attributes in NF. Notice that the measurements for the NF attributes are collected for the set of components; the membership functions are created based on all combined results and not on individual components.

Once the features to be analyzed are selected in Step 3, the components are executed for all small images, and data for the four features are collected. The same is done for medium and large images. The selection of images (that is, the creation of the subsets TS) is done according to the membership functions in Figure 1. Notice that if any degree of membership is selected for the three functions, then the three sets of small, medium, and large images would be the same. Therefore, a cutoff for the membership degree has to be determined to decrease the overlap. In the case of Figure 1, a cutoff of 0.5 reduces the overlap to zero; due to the fuzzy characteristics of the problem, some overlap is desired. In general, the smaller the cutoff, the larger the overlap and consequently, the less distinct the results of the fuzzification. Experiments with distinct cutoffs have been conducted. We limit our description here to a specified cutoff of 0.2 for the degree of membership.

Using a 0.2 cutoff results in small images with size less than 1.5 MB, medium images with size ranging from 0.7 MB to 3.6 MB, and large images with size greater than 2.8 MB. Now, each component is executed for the three sets of images, and the collected data are used to generate membership functions for each set of images and features. Again, a generalized bell curve is used to create the membership functions. However, no learning technique needs to be applied in this case since the image sets already have the information we need. After the execution of a component for all small images, the average and standard deviation for a specific feature is computed and used to create the membership function. The same procedure is followed for medium and large size images. Figure 2 shows the results for the Wavelet component. As expected, the execution time increases as the size of the images increases. In this case, we note a large overlap between the three curves. Compression ratio follows the same scheme as execution time (the larger the image, the better the compression ratio) but with more distinct membership functions, i.e., less overlap. As seen in Figure 2, the quality of the image measured by the RMSE is better for large images than for medium or small size images. Again, there is less overlap in this case than the membership functions for execution time. The memory usage for the Wavelet component presents very distinct results with almost no overlap between the curves.

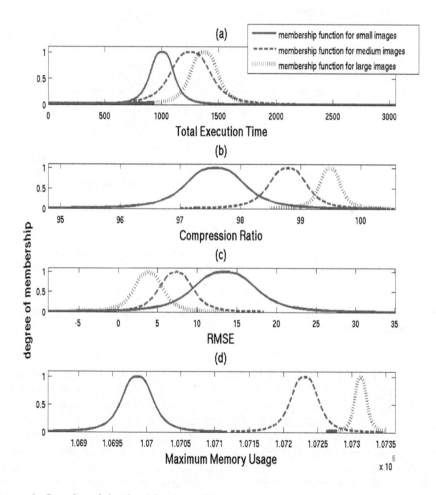

Figure 2: Results of the fuzzification of the Wavelet compression component: four selected non-functional attributes.

The results for the BWT component are presented in Figure 3. As can be observed there is no plot for the RMSE feature since BWT is a lossless approach. Also, the maximum memory usage is the same for all images and therefore constitutes a crisp value with no need for fuzzification. The results for total execution time and compression ratio are similar and show a better execution time (compression ratio) for small images with decreasing performance as the size of the images increase.

The results for the other three components (Huffman, Arithmetic Encoding, and Fractal) are quite similar and are not presented here.

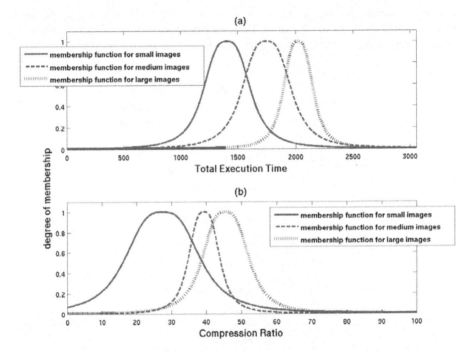

Figure 3: Results of the fuzzification of the BWT compression component: four selected non-functional attributes.

Step 5 - Input dependent fuzzification of non-functional attributes: The test inputs T are divided into K subsets $TS=\{Ts_1, Ts_2, ..., Ts_k\}$, where K is the number of membership functions used in the input fuzzification (Step 2). Overlap is expected among the subsets, and the amount of overlap can be determined by a cutoff value for the degree of membership. That is, an input t_i is added to a subset Ts_j only if the membership degree is greater than the cutoff. In general, the larger the value of the cutoff, the smaller the overlap. Each component c_l is executed for the inputs in the subset Ts_l. Measurements of all the non-functional attributes in NF are collected, and one membership function is created based on the values of the measurements. For example, mean and standard deviation values may be used to create generalized bell membership functions. The process is repeated for each subset TS_i in TS and for each component c_j in C.

Similar to image size, the non-functional attributes are also fuzzy by nature. That is, there is no crisp definition of what is a fast compression algorithm or an approach with moderate use of memory. Therefore, as it has been done for the input, neural-adaptive techniques are used to generate three membership functions for the four specified non-functional attributes, as can be seen in Figure 4.

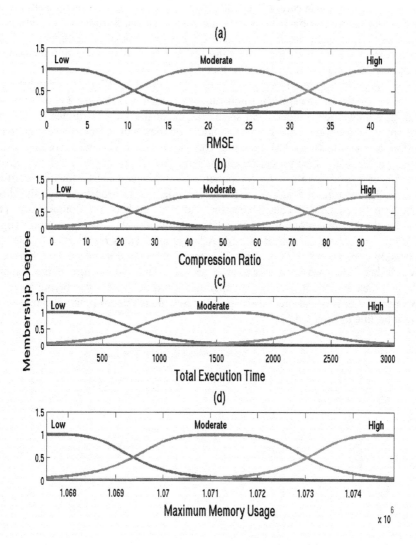

Figure 4: Component independent fuzzification of the four non-functional attributes selected.

Step 6 - Components ranking: Once the components are specified in fuzzy logic (Steps 1-5), we can search for components using linguistic rather than numeric variables/values. Any search with respect to the input attributes A and the non-functional attributes *NF* can be conducted. Since the focus of this paper is on the fuzzy specification, the ranking is restricted to individual non-functional attributes; multi-criteria techniques are the subject of future work. In order to rank the components, specified membership functions for a non-functional attribute are combined (using an OR fuzzy operator) and then merged (using an AND fuzzy operator) with the membership function associated with the specified input attribute. The resulting new membership functions (one for each component) represent the query results. Sorting the maximum or the mean value for each function produces the desired rank of components. The use of maximum or mean values may affect the ranking, but a discussion of which one is more appropriate is beyond the scope of this paper.

Up to this point we have fuzzy specifications for the input (Figure 1) and for each of the components and the specified non-functional attributes (Figure 2 and Figure 3), as well as a component independent specification for the same attributes (Figure 4). These specifications are now used to conduct queries and select/rank components according to some features. For example, consider a search is done according to the following criteria: a fast compression component. The size of the images is not specified in this case, and therefore the components should be considered for images of all sizes (small, medium, and large). A fuzzy OR operator is used to merge the three membership functions for Total Execution Time for each of the components. The results for the OR operator for the wavelet component are shown in Figure 5 (light dashed line - referred to hereafter as mf_1). A fast component is represented by the low membership function of Figure 4(c). The same curve is also plotted in Figure 5 (heavy dashed line - referred to hereafter as mf_2). The comparison of the wavelet results and the component independent specification is achieved by applying an AND fuzzy operator for mf_1 and mf_2 resulting in the new membership function represented by the solid line in Figure 5.

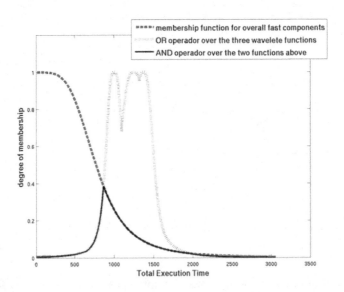

Figure 5: Membership function of the Wavelet component: searching for a fast component.

The same process is conducted for each of the components. The ranking of the components can be achieved by sorting the resulting membership functions by the largest value or by the mean value. The ranking results when searching for a fast component are shown in Table 1.

Table 1: Results of ranking the components according to two queries.

Query: fast component			Query: high compression ratio for large images		
Rank	Largest Value	Mean Value	Rank	Largest Value	Mean Value
1	HUFF - 0.82	HUFF – 0.11	1	WAVE – 0.99	BWT – 0.026
2	AREC – 0.56	AREC – 0.08	2	BWT – 0.12	WAVE – 0.023
3	WAVE – 0.38	WAVE – 0.05	3	AREC – 0.05	AREC – 0.014
4	BWT – 0.21	BWT – 0.03	4	HUFF – 0.04	HUFF – 0.012
5	FRAC – 0.18	FRAC – 0.01			

Now, consider we are searching for components with high compression ratio for large images. The process above is repeated, but there is no need to apply the OR operator to merge the membership functions for each of the components. In this case mf_1 is represented only by the Compression Ratio membership function for large images. The result for this new query is also shown in Table 1. Fractal is not displayed in the table due to lack of sufficient large images to collect meaningful results.

Additional test queries have been executed for memory usage and RMSE to rank the components. The results from these tests indicate the applicability of our approach to specify and rank components using fuzzy logic; they have not been included in the paper due to space constraints.

4 Related Work

A substantial body of work exists on the specification of components. Here, due to space constraints, we restrict the discussion of related material to the work done on IP-Based Design [18]. This technique is closer to our approach as it uses fuzzy logic in the selection of components.

Zhang, Benini, and Micheli [18] have identified the fuzzy characteristics of component selection and have proposed a technique based on IP (Intellectual Property) Design. Assuming an IP repository is available where specifications are represented using XML, the XML document is parsed into a Document Object Model tree (DOM tree). This tree is based on a grammar named Document Type Definition (DTD) and therefore represents the syntax structure of the specification. Further, semantic information is added to the tree.

Once the semantic trees for the components are available, the proximity of the trees to the query specification (also done in XML) is ordered using fuzzy logic. First, leaf nodes are scored using any specified fuzzy membership function. Then, the nodes are aggregated using an un-weighted or a weighted function. The second case is applicable when the user wants to emphasize some features of the desired components. As pointed out by the authors, the use of a specific fuzzy membership function does not need to be based on strong mathematical arguments, but mainly on the characteristics of the domain it represents. The ordered results from the query provide the user a ranked list of components with a higher probability of fulfilling the design requirements.

An interesting approach is used for the fuzzy representation of non-numeric values. For example, to represent functionality as a fuzzy object, the number of occurrences and the probability of one occurrence of some keyword in the specification is used:

$(1-p^n)$, where p is the probability and n is the number of occurrences.

The IP-Based approach and the approach proposed here are based on the same assumptions that component specification and behavior cannot be completely determined by a crisp function and fuzzy logic appears to properly address this problem. Both approaches have as the ultimate goal the selection of components that better match some specification. However, while the IP-Based approach relies on the existence of a XML specification, our approach includes steps to systematically select components, identify the inputs that affect the functional and non-functional behavior of the components, create input to exercise the components, collect and fuzzify data, and rank components [18].

5 Conclusions and Future Work

The rigorous specification of software components is necessary so that we can reason about them in useful ways, such as selecting individual components or collections of interacting components. Part of the complexity of this problem stems from the challenges in representing the uncertainty of the non-functional attributes in a meaningful way. Here, we present a systematic approach for the specification of components using fuzzy logic. A significant advantage of fuzzy logic is that it supports linguistic variables, or hedges (e.g., terms such as slow, fast, very fast, etc.), which are very convenient for describing non-functional attributes. Our process involves conducting an empirical study to gather data on five components that provide data compression capabilities; each uses a different algorithm (Arithmetic Encoding, Huffman, Wavelet, Fractal, and BWT). Data on non-functional attributes, response time performance, memory use, compression ratio, and root mean square error are collected by executing the components on a collection of images with different file formats and sizes. The data are fuzzified and represented as membership functions. The fuzzy component specifications are successfully ranked with respect to a set of test queries.

Limitations of the study include the fact that the components only provide one functional capability (data compression), and one execution environment has been used to collect data. In addition, the ability to select components based on multiple attributes is not addressed in this work.

There are a number of interesting directions for our future work. First, the problem of selecting components based on multiple attributes is going to be investigated using fuzzy multi-criteria decision making algorithms (FMCDM). In multi-criteria decision problems, relevant alternatives are evaluated according to a set of criteria, and the best alternative can be picked depending on the evaluation results. A study comparing a collection of FMCDM algorithms, including the Fuzzy Weighted Sum Method, Fuzzy Weighted Product Method, and Fuzzy Analytic Hierarchy Process, is going to be conducted. Our proposed study will replicate the work presented by Triantaphyllou [20] and extend it with additional FMCDM algorithms. In addition, a study can be conducted to compare alternatives to the fuzzy logic evaluation of the components. This study would clarify the advantages and disadvantages of our approach. Second, the component specification can be refined with the addition of attributes, both functional and non-functional; the repository of components will be extended to include components with different functional capabilities. Component data will be collected on a more comprehensive collection of platforms (i.e., hardware/operating system); the behavior of the platforms can also be represented as fuzzy membership functions. Third, the process definition will also be extended to include entry and exit conditions, while refining the descriptions of the inputs, outputs, and purpose of each activity.

References

1. Crnkovic, I., Component-Based Software Engineering — New Challenges in Software Development: Journal of Computing & Information Technology; Sep2003, Vol. 11 Issue 3, p. 151-162.
2. Haddad, H.M. and Biberoglu, E., Component-based software engineering: issues and concerns, In Proceedings, International Conference on Software Engineering Research and Practice SERP'03, Las Vegas, USA, 2003, p. 391-397.
3. Heineman, G. T., Councill, W.T., *Component-Based Software Engineering – Putting the Pieces Together*, Addison Wesley, 2001.
4. Szyperski, C., *Component Software*, Addison-Wesley, 2 edition, 2002.
5. Voas, J., "The Challenges of Using COTS Software in Component-Based Development", *IEEE Computer*, June 1998, Vol. 31 Issue 6, pp. 44-45.
6. Carney, D. and Long, F. What Do You Mean by COTS? Finally a Useful Answer, *IEEE Software*, 17(2), 2000, 83-86.
7. Seacord, R., Mundie, D., & Boonsiri, S. "K-BACEE: Knowledge-Based Automated Component Ensemble Evaluation," in Proceedings, Workshop on Component-Based Software Engineering, Warsaw, Poland, 2001, p. 56-62.
8. Zhang, T., Benini, L., and de Micheli, G., "Component Selection and Matching for IP-Based Design", in Proceedings, Conference on Design, automation and test in Europe, Munich, Germany, 2001, p. 40 - 46.
9. Lau K. and Ornaghi M., "A Formal Approach to Software Component Specification", in Proceedings, Specification and Verification of Component-Based Systems Workshop, OOPSLA 2001, Tampa Bay, Florida, p. 88-96.
10. Addy, E. and Sitaraman, M., "Formal specification of COTS-based software: a case study", in Proceedings, *5th Symposium on Software Reusability*, 1999, pp. 83-91.
11. Poizat, P., Royer, J-C., and Salaün, G., "Formal Methods for Component Description, Coordination and Adaptation", in Proceedings, 1st International Workshop on Coordination and Adaptation Techniques for Software Entities, June 14, 2004, Oslo, Norway.
12. Cheesman, J. and Daniels, J., *UML Components A Simple Process for Specifying Component-Based Software*, Addison Wesley, 2000.

13. Han, J., "A Comprehensive interface definition framework for software components", in Proceedings, 1998 Asia-Pacific Software Engineering Conference, Taipei, Taiwan, pp. 110-117.

14. Kallio, P. and Niemela, E., "Documented Quality of COTS and OCM Components", in Proceedings, 4th ICSE Workshop on Component-Based Software Engineering, May 14-15, 2001, Toronto, Canada, available at http://www.sei.cmu.edu/pacc/CBSE4-Proceedings.html.

15. Carlsson, C. and Fuller, R., *Fuzzy Reasoning in Decision Making and Optimization.* Physica-Verlag, 2001.

16. Klir, G. and Yuan, B., *Fuzzy sets and fuzzy logic: theory and applications*, Prentice Hall 1995.

17. J. Halpern, *Reasoning about Uncertainty*, The MIT Press, 2003.

18. Zadeh, L.A., Fuzzy sets, in Information and Control, Vol. 8, 1965, pp. 338-353.

19. Jang, J.-S. R., ANFIS: Adaptive-Network-based Fuzzy Inference Systems, *IEEE Transactions on Systems, Man, and Cybernetics*, vol. 23, no. 3, pp. 665-685, May 1993.

20. E. Triantaphyllou, http://www.directtextbook.com/title/prices/0792366077*Multi-Criteria Decision Making Methods: A comparative Study*, Kluwer Academic Publishers, 2000.

Finding a Needle in the Haystack: A Technique for Ranking Matches Between Components

Naiyana Tansalarak and Kajal Claypool

Department of Computer Science,
University of Massachusetts - Lowell
{ntansala,kajal}@cs.uml.edu
http://www.cs.uml.edu/dsl/index.html

Abstract. Searching and subsequently selecting reusable components from component repositories has become a key impediment for not only component-based development but also for achieving the overall usability of component development environments and the ultimate re-usability of the components themselves. Component matching, a fundamental aspect of the component search problem, has been a well-studied problem, resulting in many different matching techniques such as keyword, facet, signature and specification matching techniques. However, each matching technique individually applied for component search often yields a small or large number of (sometimes irrelevant) hits. In this paper, we propose a disciplined combination of the different matching techniques to provide a ranked set of highly qualified components from component repositories. Our work is based on a unique *Quality of Match* (QoM) metric that measures the overall "goodness" of the match between two given components. In particular, we provide *qualitative* and *quantitative* analysis to evaluate the QoM of two given components based on component information. Moreover, we present *QoMym*, a QoM-based hybrid match algorithm, that combines the strengths of different matching techniques and provides higher accuracy than existing matching techniques.

1 Introduction

Component-based software engineering has gained popularity over the past few years as the preferred mode for software construction, spurring the development of both commercial and freeware off-the-shelf components. However, while the wide availability of components is essential for the success of component-based software engineering, retrieving the *qualified* components[1] from the large number of available off-the-shelf components has rapidly become a key challenge for software developers. Today, developers are faced with a lack of search tools that can effectively aid the procurement of qualified components from one or more heterogeneous repositories, based on a given query component or a given set of requirements.

---

[1] The *qualified* component is a component that is determined to be fit for use in the context of (i) meeting the core application requirements; and (ii) inter-operating with respect to *component model*, *syntactic*, *semantic*, *design* and *platform* requirements [5, 20] of previously developed components that are deployed as part of the new system(the system under consideration).

G.T. Heineman et al. (Eds.): CBSE 2005, LNCS 3489, pp. 171–186, 2005.

Many techniques ranging from *keyword-based* to full-fledged *specification-based* heuristics have been proposed in the literature [7, 12, 8, 21, 22, 6, 4] to provide effective retrieval of qualified components during the discovery process. The keyword-based approach [7] is simple and flexible as users simply specify the query as a set of keywords representing the component requirements in which they are interested. This approach while simple is also prone to low accuracy resulting in either too many or too few hits, or in some cases even completely unrelated hits [15]. The faceted approach [12] classifies components based on predefined taxonomies. While this approach provides a better description of components than a pure keyword-based approach, users must be familiar with the classification scheme to effectively retrieve a needed component. Moreover, it is often hard to manage classification schemes when domain knowledge evolves and as a result the component falls into two or more categories [15]. Signature matching approaches [21] decide the match between two given components, the query and library components, based on the signatures of the methods in the two components. While signature matching uses intrinsic built-in information about the component, that is its *type information*, it often still returns irrelevant hits [22, 4]. For example, consider the methods `strcpy` and `strcat` in the standard C library. These methods have the same signature but encode different behaviors. The specification matching approach [22, 6], introduced to overcome the problem of signature matching, uses the method's pre- and post-conditions that capture the functionality of the method. While specification matching provides more accurate hits, it is too time-consuming to be practical as its implementation, often based on theorem proving techniques, is expensive [4]. Another drawback of the specification approach is the practical lack of pre- and post-conditions in component code. An approach using test cases [4] that captures the partial semantics of the required functionality via method interactions attempts to address these drawbacks. While this approach tends to improve the performance of the discovery process, defining precise test cases that represent the required functionality is often too hard to describe.

While these techniques take steps in the right direction, each approach individually is limited in the *quality* of the matches produced, resulting often in too many (sometimes irrelevant) matches or in some cases even no matches. In this paper, we now propose a novel matching technique – a disciplined application of different matching algorithms to all aspects of a component thereby exploiting the diversity of semantic and syntactic information inherent in a component. The goal of our matching technique is to provide a ranked set of highly qualified matches from component repositories based on a given query component. Our work is based on a unique *Quality of Match* (QoM) metric that measures the "goodness" of a match. We define a *match taxonomy* and a weight-based *match model* that qualitatively and quantitatively classify the match between a query and a library component. These are based on information ranging from the type hierarchy to the labels of properties and methods of the two components. The match taxonomy and the match model together form the basis of the QoM-based *hybrid match* algorithm, *QoMym*. The *QoMym* algorithm uses the match taxonomy as a guide for the algorithm execution, and also utilizes the weight-based match model to calculate the QoM for each element of the two components. We present a set of preliminary experiments that show the benefits of *QoMym* over using individual matching techniques and other combination techniques, and provide an empirical measure of the quality of *QoMym*.

Roadmap: The rest of paper is organized as follows. Section 2 describes XCM, our unifying component description model, that provides a descriptive superset of information for components conforming to various component models in the market. XCM is the abstract component description model for QoMym. Section 3 presents the QoM-based match taxonomy, while Section 4 defines the weight-based match model, a quantitative measure of QoM. Section 5 introduces the QoMym algorithm. Experimental evaluation of the QoMym algorithm is given in Section 6. We conclude in Section 7.

2 The XML-based Unifying Component Description Model

In the context of component matching, the diversity in component models [10, 13, 14, 11, 2] imposes a restriction that often limits component searching to the features specified for a single component model. To extend component matching to encompass a heterogeneous set of components, we now present an XML-based unifying component description model, **XCM**, that crosscuts the information of components conforming to these diverse component models [18].

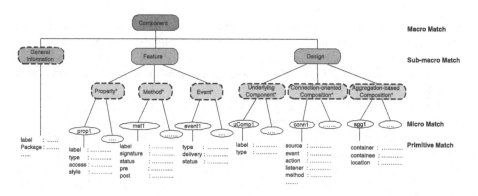

Fig. 1. The XCM Hierarchical Component Structure.

Figure 1 represents the XCM hierarchical component structure. Here, a component is defined via (i) `general information` that encapsulates the *label*, *version*, *package*, *language*, *component model*, *domain*, *operating system* and *publisher* of a component; (ii) `feature` that encapsulates the component's set of properties, methods and events; and (iii) finally `design`[2] that encapsulates the connection-oriented and

---

[2] The design is the description of the layout that describes how a composite component is constructed using a set of pre-existing components. A primitive component is a stand-alone component that does not rely on any other component for its functionality, while a composite component is constructed by either connecting (*connection-oriented*) or aggregating (*aggregation-based*) [1] a set of pre-existing components.

aggregation-based compositions of a set of pre-existing components. The hierarchical component structure in Figure 1 can be represented as an XML document, while the general structure of the description model – the XCM concepts – can be described as an XML Schema. Full details of the XCM component ontology can be found in [18].

3   The Qualitative Analysis – Match Taxonomy

In this section, we define a *match taxonomy* that qualitatively provides the quality of match (QoM) between two given components. The match taxonomy classifies the matches at the leaf, internal and root nodes of the XCM hierarchical structure (Figure 1) as (i) *primitive* match - match at the leaf level; (ii) *micro* match - match at the level of properties (or methods, events, underlying components, and connection-oriented as well as aggregation-based compositions of underlying components); (iii) *sub-macro* match - match at the level of features and design; and finally (iv) *macro* match - match at the level of the component. Each level of these matches is tightly coupled and hence heavily dependent on its lower level.

3.1   Primitive Match

A *primitive* match is the match between two corresponding leaf elements, that is the primitive information captured in the XCM structure, such as the label or the type (Figure 1). Each primitive element is classified as either *syntactic* or *semantic* based on the type of information encapsulated in the element. For example, a label imparts semantic information and hence is classified as a semantic element, while the domain type is regarded as a syntactic element.

The match between two given primitive elements is categorized as *exact* ($=$), *relaxed* ($\approx$) or *no match* ($\neq$). Dependent on the type of primitive elements, different matching techniques can be employed to determine the actual match and hence the classification between the two values of a given primitive element. For example, the label and the description of a property are best matched via a *linguistic* algorithm. A match is said to be *exact* in this case if the values are identical, *relaxed* if the values are synonyms, hypernyms, or come from the same stem, and a *no match* otherwise. Domain types, on the other hand, are best compared based on their relationships in the overall type hierarchy, requiring specialized type hierarchy comparison algorithms. Two domain types are said to be an *exact* match if their values are identical, *relaxed* if they are in the same path in the type hierarchy or *convertible* if there exists a known function to convert the source type to the target type, and a *no match* otherwise.

3.2   Micro Match

A *micro* match is the match between two given properties, methods, events, underlying components, connection-oriented or aggregation-based compositions of underlying components [3]. It is defined as a match of all its primitive elements.

---

[3] For the rest of the section, we describe the matches based on the properties. The match for the other features and design elements are similar.

The QoM of a micro match between two given properties is said to be (i) *exact* ($=$) - if all primitive elements of the source property match exactly to those of the target property; (ii) *relaxed* ($\approx$) - if either (a) all primitive elements of the source property have a combination of exact and relaxed matches in the target property, or (b) some (but not all) primitive elements of the source property have matches in the target property; or (iii) *no match* ($\neq$) - otherwise. Consider for example the two properties String day and int day. The micro match between these properties is *relaxed* as the labels are an exact match but the domain types are convertible.

3.3 Sub-macro Match

Moving up the XCM hierarchy, we define a *sub-macro* match as the match between two sets of *component features* or two sets of *component design*. The match of each set is the collection of matches of its individual elements. The match of the component feature is thus defined on the basis of the matches of all properties, methods and events, while the match of the design is defined based on the matches of all underlying components and their compositions.

The QoM for a sub-macro match is classified based on (1) the number of micro matches; and (2) the quality of the micro matches. Based on the number of micro matches, the QoM of a sub-macro match is classified as either a *total* or a *partial* match. In a total match, all elements (properties, methods and events) of the source feature match some or all elements of the target feature, while in a partial match some (but not all) elements of the source feature match those in the target feature. Combining the two criteria, number of matches and the quality of micro matches, we now define four classifications for the QoM at the sub-macro level: *total exact, total relaxed, partial exact* and *partial relaxed*.

3.4 Macro Match

A match at the highest level, between two components, is termed a *macro* match. A *macro* match is defined as a match of the primitive elements of the two components, that is a match of their labels and descriptions, as well as a match of their non-primitive elements at the sub-macro level, that is their component features and design.

The QoM for a macro match is categorized on the basis of (1) the number and quality of the primitive element matches for labels, description and invariants; and (2) the number and quality of the sub-macro matches for the component features and design. Similar to the sub-macro match, the QoM at the macro level is classified as *total exact, total relaxed, partial exact* or *partial relaxed*.

4 The Quantitative Analysis – Weight-Based Match Model

Based on the qualitative analysis, it is often easy to evaluate when one match is better than the other. For example, an exact match is always better than a relaxed match. However, in some cases such a distinction between the QoM for two or more matches cannot be established as easily. For example, based on qualitative analysis alone we cannot accurately determine whether a total relaxed match is better than a partial exact match, or one partial exact match is better than another partial exact or even a partial relaxed match. To address this deficiency, in this section, we now present a *weight-based match model* that quantitatively determines and ranks the QoM. We define this quantitative model at each level of the match taxonomy.

4.1   Primitive Element Match Model

Match between two primitive elements is classified as exact ($=$), relaxed ($\approx$) or no match ($\neq$). We term $=$, $\approx$ and $\neq$ the core *match operators* and assign a numeric weight to each of these match operators. The operator $=$ is assigned a weight of 1.0 to indicate an exact match, $\approx$ a weight ranging from 0.1 to 0.9 to denote a relaxed match, and $\neq$ a weight of 0.0 to represent a no match. These weights form the basis of the match model, and represent the *match weight* of two given primitive elements, denoted as $\mathcal{W}(\epsilon_s, \epsilon_t)$ where ϵ_s and ϵ_t are source and target primitive elements, respectively.

4.2   Micro Match Model

Based on the weight of the primitive matches, we now define the quantitative value for the micro match of two properties[4] as the normalized sum of the match weights of all its primitive matches. Formally, the QoM of a micro match, denoted as $QoM(\alpha_s, \alpha_t)$, is given as:

$$QoM(\alpha_s, \alpha_t) = \sum \mathcal{V}_\epsilon \, \mathcal{W}(\epsilon_s, \epsilon_t) \tag{1}$$

Here, (i) α_s and α_t are the source and target property; and (ii) $\epsilon_s \in \alpha_s$ and $\epsilon_t \in \alpha_t$ are the source and target primitive elements. Intuitively, it can be observed that not all primitive elements have an equal significance in determining the QoM between a source and a target properties. For example, for a property, the domain type typically has more significance than the property style. We thus specify $\mathcal{V}_\epsilon$ as the *significance value* of the specified primitive element ϵ. In keeping with this intuition, we assign significance values as *absolute numeric numbers* to all primitive elements of a property where the total significance value of all primitive elements for a property is 1.0.

4.3   Sub-macro Match Model

To provide a quantitative value for the sub-macro QoM, we define two measures, *micro match weight* and *cardinality ratio*. The micro match weight, denoted as $\mathcal{R}_W(\beta_s, \beta_t)$, is the normalized sum of QoM of all micro matches of the component feature (or design) and is given as:

$$\mathcal{R}_W(\beta_s, \beta_t) = \sum_{i=1}^{n} \mathcal{V}_i \frac{\sum QoM(\alpha_{si}, \alpha_{ti})}{|\beta_{si}|} \tag{2}$$

---

[4] The quantitative value for the micro match of two methods, events, underlying components or compositions of underlying components is defined in a similar manner.

Here (i) $\beta_s \in C_s$ and $\beta_t \in C_t$ are the source and target component feature; (ii) i is the element type that is the property, method or event type; (iii) n is the number of element types defined in the source component feature; (iv) $\alpha_{si} \in \beta_s$ and $\alpha_{ti} \in \beta_t$ are the source and target elements for the specified type i; (v) $|\beta_{si}|$ is the number of source elements for the specified type; (vi) $\mathcal{V}_i$ is the significance value of the specified element type i. For example, in the component feature, the method denoting the behavior of the component would typically have more significance than the property.

The cardinality ratio, denoted as $\mathcal{R}_S(\beta_s, \beta_t)$, is the ratio of the number of micro matches and the cardinality of the source component feature (or design) and is given as:

$$\mathcal{R}_S(\beta_s, \beta_t) = \sum_{i=1}^{n} \mathcal{V}_i \frac{|(\beta_{si})^m|}{|\beta_{si}|} \tag{3}$$

where $|(\beta_{si})^m|$ is the number of micro matches for the specified element type i.

The QoM of a sub-macro match, denoted as $QoM(\beta_s, \beta_t)$, is now defined as the normalized sum of the micro match weight and its cardinality ratio.

$$QoM(\beta_s, \beta_t) = \frac{\mathcal{R}_W(\beta_s, \beta_t) + \mathcal{R}_S(\beta_s, \beta_t)}{2} \tag{4}$$

4.4   Macro Match Model

The macro QoM, denoted as $QoM(C_s, C_t)$, is defined as the normalized sum of primitive element matches for label and description as well as the QoM of sub-macro matches. Formally, $QoM(C_s, C_t)$ is given as:

$$QoM(C_s, C_t) = \sum \mathcal{V}_\epsilon \mathcal{W}(\epsilon_s, \epsilon_t) + \sum \mathcal{V}_\beta QoM(\beta_s, \beta_t) \tag{5}$$

where (i) C_s and C_t present the source and target component; (ii) $\epsilon_s \in C_s$ and $\epsilon_t \in C_t$ are the source and target primitive element; (iii) $\mathcal{V}_\epsilon$ and $\mathcal{V}_\beta$ are the significance values of the specified primitive elements, and the component feature and design; and (iv) $\beta_s \in C_s$ and $\beta_t \in C_t$ represent the source and target component feature (or design).

5   The QoMym Algorithm

The *QoMym* algorithm is a depth-first match algorithm that is guided by the match taxonomy presented in Section 3 and is directly based on the match model given in Section 4. The overall execution of *QoMym* is depicted in Figure 2 and its pseudo-code is given in Figures 3 - 6. The *QoMym* algorithm first evaluates the match values for all primitive elements, that is all leaf nodes including the label, the description, the type etc. of the component itself. The primitive element matches are evaluated based on their type. For example, a linguistic algorithm is employed to determine the level of match between two labels (or descriptions). Our linguistic algorithm uses a combination of WordNet [9] and a domain-specific dictionary that includes commonly used abbreviations. A full description of the linguistic algorithm is beyond the scope of this paper. For more details please refer to [17]. Similarly, to match two domain types we have developed an algorithm to compare the types along the specified type hierarchy. For better performance, the type hierarchies were converted using a dewey-based numbering scheme [19] that captured the relationship and the hierarchy of the given types. In particular, each primitive domain type of a component is automatically mapped into its dewey-based number before a match is determined.

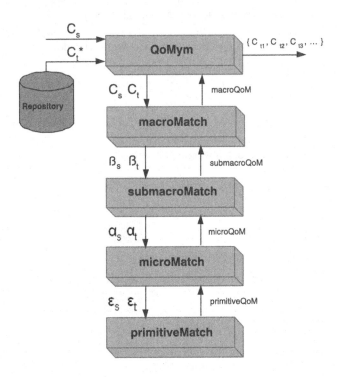

Fig. 2. The Overall Execuation of QoMym.

Each source primitive element is compared with every target primitive element, and all match values above the threshold are saved. This threshold was determined empirically after running a set of controlled experiments (see details in Section 6). Once all primitive matches are computed, the micro matches are evaluated using the *micro-Match* module given in Figure 4. All match values above a certain threshold are saved. The *submacroMatch* module given in Figure 5 determines the match value for the feature and the design. The submacro match values are used to determine a single macro match value - the match value of the source and target components - using the *macroMatch* module given in Figure 6. The QoMym module (Figure 3) finally returns a set of qualified components that have macro match values above threshold.

The running time for the algorithm lies in $\theta(|R||C_t||C_s|)$ where $|R|$ represents the number of components in the repository, and $|C_t|$ as well as $|C_s|$ the cardinality of a target and a source component.

```
Set QoMym (Component Cₛ) {

    result ← ∅;
    for each Component Cₜ ∈ Repository R {
        macroQoM = macroMatch(Cₛ, Cₜ);
        if macroQoM ≥ macroThreshold
            result ← result ∪ < Cₜ, macroQoM>;
    }

    return result;
}
```

Fig. 3. The QoMymAlgorithm.

```
double microMatch (Micro αₛ, Micro αₜ) {

    microQoM ← ∅;

    // εₛ ∈ αₛ and εₜ ∈ αₜ
    for each corresponding primitive pair (εₛ, εₜ) {
        primitiveQoM ← primitiveMatch (εₛ, εₜ);
        sig ← DB.getSignificance (εₛ.getType());
        microQoM ← microQoM + (sig * primitiveQoM);
    }

    if microQoM ≥ microThreshold
        return microQoM;
    else
        return 0;
}
```

Fig. 4. The microMatch Algorithm.

6   Preliminary Experimental Results

The goal of the *QoMym* algorithm is to improve the overall match quality of the qualified components retrieved in response to a specified query component. We conducted several experiments to evaluate the potential benefits of the *QoMym* algorithm over other existing algorithms. In this section, we describe our experimental setup and methodology together with our results.

6.1   Experimental Setup and Methodology

Figure 7 illustrates the overall architecture of the QoM system. The QoM system together with *QoMym* algorithm is implemented in Java (SDK 2.0) and deployed on a standalone PC Pentium IV 2.8 GHz with 512 Mb RAM running Microsoft Windows XP. The QoM system takes a query component as input, matches the query component against a set of library components using the *QoMym* algorithm, and returns the

```
double submacroMatch (Component Cs, Component Ct,
               String submacroType) {

    // get source and target micro elements
    source ← Cs.getMicroElements (submacroType) ;
    target ← Ct.getMicroElements (submacroType) ;

    initialize microQoM[|Cs|][|Ct|];

    // calculate QoM for all (αs,αt);
    for each micro αs ∈ source {
        for each micro αt ∈ target {
            if αs.getType() == αt.getType()
                microQoM[αs][αt] ← microMatch (αs, αt);
    }

    // calculate the submacro QoM
    RW ← getMicroMatchWeight (microQoM);
    RS ← getCardinality (microQoM);
    submacroQoM ← (RW + RS) / 2;

    return submacroQoM;
}
```

Fig. 5. The submacroMatch Algorithm.

match results to the user. The repository used for the experiments contained JavaBean components across four domains: 24 GUI components, 12 data collection components, 8 calendar components, and 16 components for testing. These components were automatically introspected, transformed into XCM documents and subsequently loaded into the repository.

Measure Of Match Quality. To evaluate our approach, we compared the manually determined real matches (R) for a given match task[5] with the matches P returned by the match algorithm. We determined the true positives, i.e., the correctly identified matches, I; the false positives, i.e., the incorrectly identified matches, $F = P \setminus I$, and the false negatives, i.e., the missed matches, $M = R \setminus I$. Based on the cardinalities of these sets, the *Precision* and *Recall*[6] of the match algorithm were computed.

- $Precision = \frac{|I|}{|P|} = \frac{|I|}{|I|+|F|}$ estimates the reliability of the match predictions.
- $Recall = \frac{|I|}{|R|}$ specifies the share of real matches that is discovered by the algorithm.
- $Overall = 1 - \frac{|F|+|M|}{|R|} = \frac{|I|-|F|}{|R|} = Recall*(2-\frac{1}{Precision})$ represents a combined measure of match quality, taking into account the post-match effort needed for both removing false matches and adding missed matches.

[5] Here a match task denotes the matching of a query component with the components in the repository to determine the qualified components.
[6] Precision and Recall are taken from Information Retrieval literature

```
double macroMatch (Component Cₛ, Component Cₜ) {

    // get the primitive QoM
    Wₗ ← linguisticMatch (Cₛ.getLabel(), Cₜ.getLabel());
    Wₐ ← lingusiticMatch (Cₛ.getDescription(), Cₜ.getDescription());

    // get the submacro QoM
    subQoMf ← submacroMatch (Cₛ, Cₜ, "feature");
    subQoMₐ ← submacroMatch (Cₛ, Cₜ, "design");

    // get the significant values
    Vf ← DB.getSignificance ("feature");
    Vₐ ← DB.getSignificance ("design");
    Vₗ ← DB.getSignificance ("label");
    Vₐ ← DB.getSignificance ("desc");

    // calculate the macro QoM
    macroQoM = (Vₗ * Wₗ) + (Vₐ * Wₐ) +
               (Vf * subQoMf) + (Vₐ * subQoMₐ);

    return macroQoM;
}
```

Fig. 6. The macroMatch Algorithm.

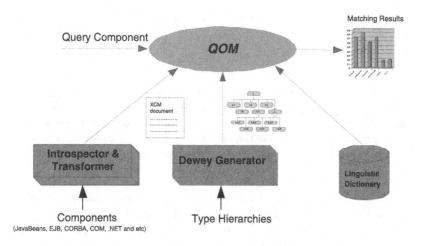

Fig. 7. The Overall Architecture of the QoM System.

6.2   Determining Threshold and Significance Values

The accuracy of the *QoMym* algorithm is dependent on the *threshold* and *significance values* that are an integral part of the weight-based match model defined in Section 4.

To determine optimal values for these parameters (threshold and significance), we conducted a set of experiments that randomly compared a set of query components against a small number of library components for different threshold and significance values. The overall match values obtained via the *QoMym* algorithm for the different threshold and significance values were compared against a manual benchmark that we had setup prior to running the experiments. We then gradually added more library components from different domains to determine if the selected threshold and significance values would hold or would need to be adjusted.

There are four major threshold parameters: *label* and *signature* thresholds at the primitive level, as well as *micro* and *macro* thresholds at the micro and macro levels respectively. Figure 8 - 9 depicts the average precision and recall for different label and signature thresholds. Here, the results were obtained by comparing the labels and signatures of a set of query components against those of the components in repository. High precision and recall values are good indicators of the quality of the match. Thus, based on these results, we determined the optimal label threshold to be in the range $\{0.7 \; -- \; 0.9\}$, and the optimal signature threshold to be in $\{0.6 \; -- \; 0.8\}$.

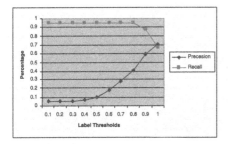 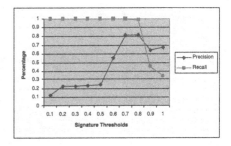

Fig. 8. Variance in the precision and recall obtained for different label threshold values. The label threshold value is represented on the X-Axis, and the percentage of precision and recall is depicted on the Y-Axis.

Fig. 9. Variance in the precision and recall obtained for different signature threshold values. The label threshold value is represented on the X-Axis, and the percentage of precision and recall is depicted on the Y-Axis.

Next, to determine the optimal values for the significance parameters of label and signature, we fixed the label and signature threshold values, and compared the precision and recall obtained by varying the significance values and micro thresholds. Figure 10 shows the precision and recall obtained by the algorithm for different significance values [7] and micro thresholds. We found that for obtaining optimal precision and recall, the significance of the signature should be in the range $\{0.1 \; -- \; 0.2\}$, while the micro thresholds should be in the range $\{0.6 \; -- \; 0.8\}$.

Finally, to determine the optimal macro thresholds, we fixed the significance value and the micro threshold, and compared the precision and recall obtained by varying the

---

[7] We show signature significance, but the results can be interpreted for label significance value (label = 1 - signature).

macro thresholds as shown in Figure 11. We found the optimal macro threshold to be in the range {0.8 -- 0.9}.

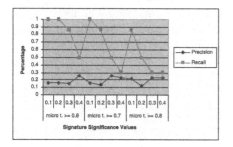
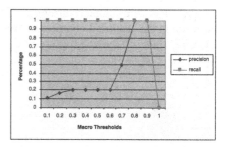

Fig. 10. Variance in the precision and recall obtained for different signature significance values as well as the micro thresholds. Label and signature thresholds were kept constance at 0.8 and 0.7 respectively.

Fig. 11. Variance in the precision and recall obtained for different macro values. Signature significance values and micro thresholds were kept constant at 0.2 and 0.7 respectively.

In the subsequent experiments, we fix the label threshold for the QoMym algorithm at 0.8, the signature threshold at 0.7, the micro threshold at 0.7, the macro threshold at 0.8, and the significance values of label and signature at 0.2 and 0.8 respectively.

6.3   QoMym Match Quality

Based on the threshold and significance values determined in Section 6.2, we ran a set of experiments to evaluate the accuracy of the *QoMym* algorithm. We did this by comparing *QoMym* with our manual benchmark as well as with other state-of-the art algorithms found in literature, namely a signature, linguistic, and a filtering algorithm that uses signature matching as a filter prior to applying a linguistic match algorithm. For these experiments, we selected the Calendar component shown in Figure 12 as the query component, and compared it to the components in the repository. Figure 13 shows the results in terms of the number of qualified components returned from the library by the different algorithms for the query component Calendar.

```
Component Calendar {
        void setDay (int)                    int getDay ();
        void setMonth (int);                 int getMonth ();
        void setYear (int);                  int getYear ();
        void setStyle (int);                 int getStyle ();
        void setLocale (java.util.Locale);   java.util.Local getLocale ();
}
```

Fig. 12. The Query Component - Calendar.

Here the expected number of hits for the `Calendar` component were 4. The *QoMym* algorithm performed the best returning exactly 4 components, while the signature-based algorithm performed the worst and returned 43 qualified components. It was interesting to note that the filtering algorithm also did better than linguistic and signature algorithms alone returning 6 qualified components. We found there was no difference in the qualified components returned (in this case) if the order of filtering was varied (that is linguistic followed by signature and vice versa).

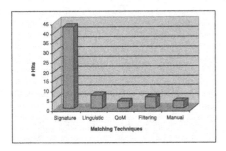
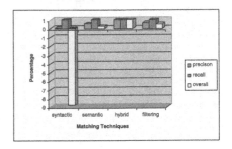

Fig. 13. The Number of Qualified Components Returned For the Different Matching Techniques.

Fig. 14. The Match Quality of the Different Matching Techniques.

Figure 14 depicts the precision and recall of the the different algorithms together with their overall quality. In general, high precision and recall are indicators of high overall quality of the match algorithms. We found that all algorithms had high recall (1.0), that is all algorithms were able to find the expected qualified components. The algorithms however varied in their precision with signature based algorithm having low precision to the *QoMym* algorithm having the best precision. The filtering algorithm shows that the combination of linguistic and signature algorithms can result in higher precision than if the algorithms were used individually. This is in step with the intuitive argument that has been made before [22, 6, 4].

While filtering is a good first step toward combining different algorithms, the preliminary experimental results presented here indicate that a disciplined hybrid combination of the two (and in the future more) algorithms can result in higher overall quality of the retrieved qualified components. It is mainly due to the fact that the significance values are employed to weigh the importance of these algorithms. This allows QoMym to not only discover matches that may have been missed but to also reject matches that are discovered by the filtering technique as different algorithms work independently.

7   Conclusions

The QoMym algorithm offers many advantages over the previously developed component matching approaches. For example, while previous approaches take into account the *method signature* they often discount the importance of labels[8] and the semantic information imparted by the same. In our work we now exploit not only the semantic information in labels, but also the syntactic and semantic information contained in properties, event, and the design that are intrinsic parts of a component. In fact we find that with the combined use of the semantic and syntactic information we are able to achieve higher precision and recall without the performance overhead associated with approaches like specification matching. Moreover, our preliminary results suggest that a disciplined combination of different algorithms (linguistic and signature) can provide better overall quality than a naive filter-based approach.

References

[1] Dietrich Birngruber. CoML: Yet Another, But Simple Component Composition Language. In *Workshop on Composition Language*, 2001.

[2] Don Box. *Essential COM*. Addison-Wesley Publishing Company, 1998.

[3] Kajal T. Claypool, Vaishali Hegde, and Naiyana Tansalarak. QMatch: A Hybrid Match Algorithm for XML Schemas. In *Proceedings of the 2nd International Workshop on XML Schema and Data Management (to appear)*, April 2005.

[4] Joseph Goguen, Doan Nguyen, Jose Meseguer, Luqi, Du Zhang, and Valdis Berzins. Software Component Search. *Journal of Systems Integration*, 6(1/2):93–134, March 1996.

[5] Thomas Gschwind, Johann Oberleitner, and Mehdi Jazayeri. Dynamic Component Extension to Support Cross-Platform Development. Technical Report TUV-1841-2002-19, Technische Universitt Wien, 2002.

[6] Jun-Jang Jeng and Betty H. C. Cheng. Specification Matching for Software Reuse: A Foundation*. In *Proceedings of the 1995 Symposium on Software reusability*. ACM Press, 1995.

[7] Y. Matsumoto. A Software Factory: An Overall Approach to Software Production. In P. Freeman, editor, *Tutorial: Software Reusability*. IEEE Computer Society Press, 1987.

[8] A. Mili, R. Mili, and R. Mittermeir. Storing and retrieving software components: a refinement based system. In *Proceedings of the 16th international conference on Software engineering*, pages 91–100, 1994.

[9] G.A. Miller. Wordnet: A Lexical Database for English Language. cogsci.princeton.edu/ wn/, 2002.

[10] Hans Muller and Mark Davidson. JavaBeans Specification: Getting Listeners from JavaBeans. http://java.sun.com/products/javabeans, 1996.

[11] Frank Pilhofer. Writing and Using CORBA Components. http://www.cs.indiana.edu/ srikrish/orals/mico-ccm.pdf, 2002.

[12] R. Prieto-Diaz and P. Freeman. Classifying Software for Reusability. *IEEE Software*, 4(1):6–16, 1987.

[13] Bill Roth. An Introduction to Enterprise JavaBeans Technology. http://java.sun.com/products/ejb, 1998.

[14] J. Siegel. *CORBA: Fundamentals and Programming for the 21st century*. John Wiley, New York, 1996.

[15] Vijayan Sugumaran and Veda C. Storey. A semantic-based approach to component retrieval. *ACM SIGMIS Database*, 34(3):8–24, 2003.

---

[8] The method label should in general provide semantic information to partially characterize the methods if component developers implement components by following the software development guide.

[16] Naiyana Tansalarak and Kajal T. Claypool. QoM: Qualitative and Quantitative Schema Match Measure. In *Proceedings of the 22nd International Conference on Conceptual Modeling (ER 2003)*, October 2003.

[17] Naiyana Tansalarak and Kajal T. Claypool. QoMym: The QoM-based Hybrid Match Algorithm. Technical Report 2004-009, Department of Computer Science, University of Massachusetts - Lowell, August 2004. Available at http://www.cs.uml.edu/techrpts/reports.jsp.

[18] Naiyana Tansalarak and Kajal T. Claypool. XCM: A Component Ontology. In *Workshop on Ontologies as Software Engineering Artifacts joint with the 19th Annual ACM Conference on Object-Oriented Programming, Systems, Languages, and Applications*, 2004.

[19] Igor Tatarinov and Stratis D. Viglas. Storing and Querying Ordered XML Using a Relational Database System. In *Proceedings of the 2002 ACM SIGMOD international conference on Management of data*, pages 204 – 215. ACM, June 2002.

[20] A. Vallecillo, J. Hernandez, and J. Troya. Component Interoperability. Technical Report ITI-2000-37, Departmento de Lenguajes y Ciencias de la Computacion, University of Malaga, July 2000. Available at http://www.lcc.uma.es/~av/Publicaciones/00/Interoperability.pdf.

[21] Amy Moormann Zaremski and Jeannette M. Wing. Signature Matching: a Tool for Using Software Libraries. In *ACM Transactions on Software Engineering and Methodology (TOSEM)*. ACM Press, 1995.

[22] Amy Moormann Zaremski and Jeannette M. Wing. Specification Matching of Software Components. In *ACM Transactions on Software Engineering and Methodology (TOSEM)*. ACM Press, 1997.

A Contracting System
for Hierarchical Components

Philippe Collet[1], Roger Rousseau[1], Thierry Coupaye[2], and Nicolas Rivierre[2]

[1] University of Nice - Sophia Antipolis, I3S Laboratory, France,
Philippe.Collet@unice.fr
[2] France Telecom R&D Division,
MAPS/AMS Laboratory, Grenoble & Issy les Moulineaux, France

Abstract. This article presents the contracting system *ConFract* for the open and hierarchical component model *Fractal*. Contracts are dynamically built from specifications, currently executable assertions, at assembly times, and are updated according to dynamic reconfigurations. These contracts are not restricted to the scope of interfaces, taken separately. On the contrary, new kinds of *composition contracts* can be built in order to associate several external interfaces of a component, providing an "usage contract", or several interfaces inside the component, providing an "assembly and implementation contract". All these contracts identify fine-grained responsibilities and developers can thus easily organize the handling of contract violations and the resulting reconfigurations.

1 Introduction

Since McIlroy's appeal in 1968, component-based software engineering (CBSE) has gone through an important evolution. Components were at first units of compilation, then modules fitting together with an explicit interface (*Modula2, Ada* ...), then classes associated by use or inheritance links (*Eiffel, C++* ...), and finally, black boxes, organized in a (re-)configurable architecture and capable of communicating on a network through several interfaces (*CCM, EJB, .NET* ...). Nowadays one would like to reconcile the advantages of all these notions of software components, while having the means to manage the resulting architecture, separate concerns and choose the right level of abstraction. A "modern" software component can be thus considered as a runtime entity which communicates through (possibly remote) interfaces which can be dynamically bound, as well as a hierarchy of subcomponents, with possible sharings. This supposes elaborated component models such as *Fractal* [1], which makes possible to extend technical services with its openness capabilities, while separating concerns.

Such models drastically change the processes of traditional software engineering, by mixing static, dynamic, functional and extra-functional properties. To ensure the reliability of the resulting applications, it is necessary to integrate verifications into adapted but complex development processes. As a component is usually defined as "an unit of composition with contractually specified interfaces" [2], the notion of contract appears as a natural solution to express and

G.T. Heineman et al. (Eds.): CBSE 2005, LNCS 3489, pp. 187–202, 2005.

organize specifications and verifications [3]. But when components are organized hierarchically, these contracts must not be only associated to interfaces, taken separately, they also have to take into account this hierarchy by being defined on components themselves. With the possibility of dynamic reconfigurations, contracts must also be built and updated dynamically, according to any dependent change in the architecture. Moreover, if contracts are updated, they can be used to check the consistency of the dynamic reconfigurations. Finally, in order to handle at best contract violations, the contracting system must determine fine-grained responsibilities on each element of a contract.

This article presents *ConFract*, a contracting system for hierarchical components that meets these requirements and is targeted to the *Fractal* component model[1]. In its integration, *ConFract* also uses the reflexive capababilities and the control features of extra-functional concerns provided by the *Fractal* platform. Section 2 describes the rationale for a contracting system on components such as the *Fractal* ones. Examples of specifications with executable assertions are given in section 3. Section 4 presents the *ConFract* system by describing its types of contract and their responsibilities. Contract checking and some examples of dynamic reconfigurations are also presented. The implementation is described in the section 5 and section 6 discusses related work. Finally, section 7 concludes this article.

2   Rationale for Contracting Components

2.1   Context

The *Fractal* component model [1][3] is a general component model with the following main features: composite components (to have a uniform view of applications at various levels of abstraction), shared components (to model resources and resource sharing while maintaining component encapsulation), reflective capabilities (introspection capabilities to monitor a running system and re-configuration capabilities to deploy and dynamically configure a system) and openness (in the model, almost everything is optional and can be extended). The *Fractal* component model basically enables developers to hierarchically organize an application, with components being built from other subcomponents. Components can be connected through server (provided) and client (required) interfaces. Throughout this paper, we illustrate our approach with the example of a simplified simulator of a black and white copier (see Figure 1).

From an external point of view, the copier component <cp> provides two server interfaces, a control panel (pp) and an output tray for copies (ot). The client interfaces manage everything the environment has to supply to make a copy: some black ink (bi), an input tray (it), a glass pane with the original (gs) and AC power (ap). At assembly times, the surrounding root component <topLevel> connects all these interfaces with interfaces of compatible type,

---

[3] The reader can find a more detailed description of the model in [4] and at http://fractal.objectweb.org

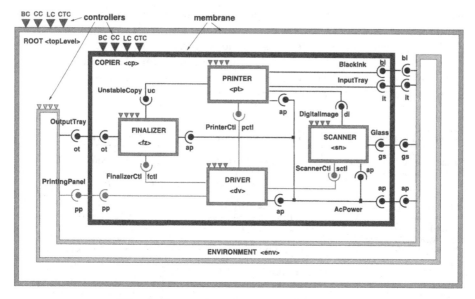

Fig. 1. Internal architecture of the copier.

but inverse role (client becomes server and conversely), which come from an `<environment>` component simulating the user behavior.

Internally, a *Fractal* component is formed out of two parts: a membrane and a content. The content of a composite component is composed of other components, called subcomponents, which are under the control of the enclosing component. The *Fractal* model is thus recursive and allows components to be nested. The membrane embodies the control behavior associated with a particular component. In particular, it can *i)* intercept oncoming and outgoing operation invocations targeting or originating from the component's subcomponents, *ii)* superpose a control behavior to the behavior of the component's subcomponents or *iii)* provide an explicit and causally connected representation of the component's subcomponents.

From an internal point of view, the copier `<cp>` is thus the assembly of four subcomponents: `<dv>`, which distributes the internal control flow, `<sn>`, which scans the original document, `<pt>`, which prints the required copies and `<fz>`, which dries the ink or cooks the toner. The assembly is under the control of the copier membrane, which is made of interceptors (not shown on figure) and controller objects, provided by the *Fractal* platform. To connect the external interfaces of a composite component with its subcomponents, the *Fractal* model provides the concept of internal interface. Every internal interface is connected with an external interface, of the same name, but with a inverse role. For example, the component `<fz>` provides the server interface `ot`, which implements the server interface `ot` of the component `<cp>`, via the internal interface `ot` of `<cp>`. The internal connections bind the interfaces `ap` of power supply, distribute the control flow from `<dv>` through the interfaces `sctl`, `pctl` and `fctl`. The data flow is shown by the path of the paper via it, uc, ot, of the digital image via gs, di, uc, ot and of the ink via bi, uc and ot.

The signatures of the interfaces are defined using the underlying language of the implementation *Julia* [1] of *Fractal*, currently *Java* [4], as shown on Figure 2. These signatures can refer to library interfaces or classes, such as Sheet, SheetImage, InkCartridge or Stack in this example.

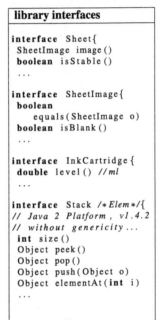

Fig. 2. Partial signatures of the copier interfaces.

2.2 Motivations

It is now well accepted that interface signatures, even with comments, are insufficient to capture and control the salient properties of an application [3]. More complete specifications are needed on the functional and extra-functional aspects (architecture, performances, quality of services, etc.).

Some properties can be checked early, using static analyses or proofs. Other properties, often extra-functional, which refer to runtime values, can only be dynamically verified. In the case of hierarchical components where the assemblies are dynamic, we liken the word *static* to *"before the component is started"*. For example, in the case of the copier, one should be able to verify statically that all the subcomponents are connected to a power supply or to prove the functional properties of very stable library interfaces (Sheet, Stack, etc.).

---

[4] For space's sake, the keyword public and ";" are omitted.

Either static or dynamic, many different properties can be expressed, using different specification formalisms [5,6,7,8]. For example, interface automata [6] enables a specification to capture input assumptions about the order in which the methods of a component are called and output guarantees about the order of called external methods. Checking compatibility and refinement between interface models is then possible. Behavior protocols [7] express traces on interface method calls with a form of regular expressions and takes into account hierarchical components. These protocols can be defined on interfaces, frames (aka component types) and architectures (aka component internal assembly). Refinement of specifications are verified at design time, while adherence of a component's implementation to its specification is checked at run time.

We decide to first focus on the contracting mechanisms, rather than on the expressiveness of the specification formalism. We use executable assertions, the formalism first used with contracts [9], to reason about component contracts using both functional and extra-functional specifications. Nevertheless, to obtain a high confidence degree, it will be necessary, at long term, to take into account, in the same platform, different specification formalisms, formal or semi-formal, for proofs, static or dynamic checking.

To our knowledge, the proposals to explicitly support contracts for components all focus on interfaces or connectors, taken separetely. They aim at specifying behavior [8], architectural constraints [10] or quality of services [11]. As such they lack several important features to be well suited to our definition of components: they do not take into account a hierarchical assembly of components; contracts are not built incrementally and not updated if any dynamic reconfiguration occurs; the responsabilities of contracts are not precisely determined to handle violation in the most efficient way.

Facing all the problems stated above, we define the requirements of the ConFract system to the following.

- Specifications can be either functional or extra-functional. They can be verified either statically (at assembly time) or dynamically (at runtime). They state properties that are related to interfaces, but also to the components themselves, while respecting visibility rules of the *Fractal* model.
- *Specifications*, which play the role of provisions, are distinguished from *Contracts*, which are reified and incrementally built following configuration actions. Contracts are also updated when dynamic reconfigurations occur, so that they can be used to check the modified architecture.
- Responsibilities among the contract participants must also be clearly defined to enable the developers to precisely handle contract violations (log, renegotiation of contracts, dynamic reconfigurations, organized panic, etc.).

Consequently, contracts in the *ConFract* system will take their usual sense of *"document negotiated between several parties, the responsibilities of which are clearly established for each provision"*.

3   Examples of Specification

3.1   Informal Descriptions

As in current proposals for contracting components [11,8], it must be possible
to use the connection point between two interfaces, client and server, to define
some specifications. In the case of the method copy, on the control panel of the
copier, one can express the precondition:

*"the parameter **n** must be positive"*   **s1**

or the postcondition:

"the copier is no more in the state isCopying."   **s2**

These properties are certainly useful, but with a rather poor semantics.

To express more relevant properties, it is necessary **to compose** external or
internal properties by widening the scope, while respecting encapsulation, which
is controlled by the membranes. As for the method copy of the control panel,
one could express, as precondition:

*"enough ink is available on interface **bi**, enough paper on **it**, an
original is placed on **gs** and the power is supplied on **ap**"*   **s3**

as functional postcondition:

*"the copies in the tray **ot** are the sheets that were in the inverse
order in the tray **it** before the copy, all printed with the image of the
original on **gs** and stabilized"*   **s4**

and as extra-functional postcondition:

*"the duration of a copy conforms to the printing speed of the copier,
in number of pages per minute."*   **s5**

Moreover, in the case of a composite component, it is also necessary to compose its internal properties, visible through its internal interfaces[5] or through
the external interfaces of its subcomponents. So, for the component <cp>, one
could express, as functional postcondition of <dv>.pp.copy():

*"the copies of the tray **ot** are printed with the image scanned from
<sn>.**di** on a blank paper sheet <pt>.**it** and stabilized"*   **s6**

or as extra-functional postcondition of <dv>.pp.copy():

*"the duration of n copies is the sum of the duration of the scan plus
the duration of n printings and stabilizations."*   **s7**

With such possibilities of expression, one could then reason in a compositional
way [3], for example by verifying that the external behavior of the copier is
properly obtained by the organization and the internal behavior that implement
it.

3.2   Executable Assertions

In the *ConFract* system, specifications are currently written in the language
CCL-J (*Component Constraint Language for Java*), which is inspired by *OCL*

---

[5] In *Fractal*, internal interfaces are systematically and complementarilly associated to
external interfaces, in order to go through the membrane of composite components,
as on Figure 1.

[12] and enhanced to be adapted to *Fractal*. Currently, the categories of specifications are classic [13], **pre**, **post**, **inv**, **rely** and **guarantee**[6]. Each category consists of one or more clauses, identified by a number or a label and bound by a logical conjunction.

The scope of specifications is adapted using variants of the **context** construct. It can refer to a method of a *Java* interface: **context** *method-signature* (Fig. 3); a component type: **on COPIER context** (Fig. 4); or a particular component (instance or template of *Fractal* components [1]): **on <cp> context** (Fig. 5).

on Fractal interfaces
context void PrintingPanel.copy(int n)
pre   0 < n   //cf spec [1]
rely   isPowerOn()
guarantee isCopying()
post   !isCopying()   //cf spec [2]
context InputTray
inv   tray().size() <= capacity()

on Java interfaces
context void Stack.push(Object o)
post:
peek() == o
size() == size()@pre + 1
forEach (int i in 1 .. size()−1
elementAt(i) = elementAt(i)@pre
...

Fig. 3. Examples of interface specifications with *CCL-J*.

CCL-J also enables one to specify classic assertions on interfaces (without reference to other interfaces) or classes. The left part of Figure 3 then shows the specifications **s1** and **s2** in *CCL-J*; the right part gives a partial specification of the class **Stack**.

```
on COPIER context void pp.copy(int n)
pre // cf spec [3]
  bi.cartridge().level() >= bi.minLevel()
  n <= it.tray().size() && ! it.isPaperJam()
  gs.originalOnGlass()
  ap.isPluggedIn()
post // cf spec [4]
  forEach i in 1..n : ot.sheets().elementAt(i).
              equals(gs.original().image())
  bi.cartridge.level() <= bi.cartridge.level()@pre
  it.tray().size() == it.tray().size()@pre − n
post // cf spec [5]
  speed: duration() <= n*60/attributes.CPM
              // CPM = copies /minute
end on
```

```
on SCANNER context void sctl.scan()
pre
  gs.originalOnGlass()
post
  di.image().equals(gs.original().image()
end on

on SCANNER context void sctl.scan()
post
  let(double md = time() − time()@pre)
  md−0.01 <= sctl.duration() <= md+0.01
end on

on COPIER context * pp.*(*)
  pre // cf spec [8]
    ap.isPluggedIn();
end on
```

Fig. 4. Examples of external component specifications with *CCL-J*.

But as previously stated, it is more relevant to specify compositional properties, refering to several interfaces or several components. This is the main

---

[6] rely, resp. **guarantee**, states conditions that a method can rely, resp. must guarantee, during its entire execution.

contribution of the *CCL-J* language. Figure 4 shows some examples of specifications of external compositions with *CCL-J*. All the properties are located on *component types*, as they are valid whatever is the internal assembly. On the left part, the behavior of a COPIER component type is expressed, (equivalent of the specifications **s3**, **s4** and **s5**) with one construct **on** to define the component scope, and with references to all interfaces in the logical formulas. On the right part, the behavior of a SCANNER component type is also defined, but the functional and extra-functional aspects are differentiated, illustrating the flexibility of the language. *CCL-J* also provides an operator * to denote any list of arguments or to factorize a property that is common to several specifications. The example at the lower right part of Figure 4 expresses:

> *"that the preconditions of all methods of the interface pp require that the interface ap has a connected power supply."* s8

```
on <cp> context <dv>.pp.copy(int n)
  post // cf spec [6]
   (let Stack /*Sheet*/ r = <fz>.ot.sheets() ;  // output sheets
        int o = <fz>.ot.sheets().size()@pre ;   // sheets nb before copy in ot
        int p = <pt>.it.tray().size()@pre ;     // sheets nb before copy in it
   )
   forEach(i in 1 .. n:
     r.elementAt(o+i).image().equals(<sn>.di.image()) &&
     r.elementAt(o+i).image().isStable() &&
     r.elementAt(o+i) == <pt>.it.tray().elementAt(p−i+1)@pre)
end on
```

```
on <cp> context <dv>.pp.copy(int n)
  post // cf spec [7]
   let(double thd = <sn>.sctl.duration() +
       n*(<pt>.pctl.duration() + <fz>.fctl.duration()))
   thd −1 <= duration() <= thd+1
end on
```

```
on <cp>
  inv // cf spec [9]
   let(Component[] subc=Fractal.getContentController(this).getFcSubComponents())
   forEach i in 1.. subc.length :
     Arrays.asList(subc[i].getFcInterfaces()).exists(Interface ir :
        Class.forName(ir.getFcItfSignature()).conformsTo(ACPower.class)
     && ir.isFcClientItf());
end on
```

Fig. 5. Examples of internal component specifications with *CCL-J*.

In the same way, Figure 5 shows some examples of internal composition specifications. All the properties are located on component instances, as they are dependent from a specific assembly. The top example is the equivalent of the functional property **s6**, and of the extra-functional property **s7**. The bottom example of the figure illustrates an architectural constraint, using the introspection capabilities of *Fractal*:

> *"that all the subcomponents of <cp> have at least a client interface of type ACPower."* s9

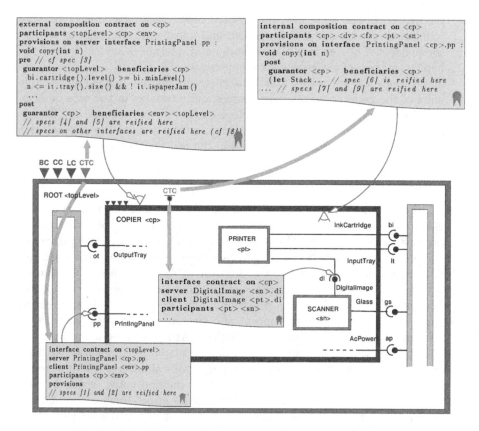

Fig. 6. The contracts built from the copier's specifications.

4   The *ConFract* System

4.1   Types of Contract

The *ConFract* system distinguishes several types of contracts according to the specifications given by the designers (see Figure 6).

- *interface contracts* are established on the connection point between a pair of client and server interfaces (for example `pp` between `<cp>` and its environment `<env>` or `di` between `<pt>` and `<sn>`). The retained specifications only refer to methods and entities in the interface scope.
- *external composition contracts* are located on the external side of each component membrane (for example the one of `<cp>`, at the top left of the figure). They consist of specifications which refer only to external interfaces of the component. They thus express the usage and external behavior rules of the component.
- *internal composition contracts* are located on the internal side of a composite component membrane (for example the one of `<cp>` at the top right of

the figure). In the same way, they consist of specifications which refer only to internal interfaces of the component and to external interfaces of its sub-components. They express the assembly and internal behavior rules of the implementation of the composite component.

- *library contracts* are mostly functional contracts that are defined on reusable units of the underlying language, classes and interfaces in the case of *Java*. They are relevant only for the implementation of components and do not participate in the assembly negotiations. As they are not the original part of our work, we will not refer to them in the rest of this paper.

4.2 Responsibilities

During the reification of a contract, the *ConFract* system determines the responsibilities associated to each specification, among the list of participating components in the contract. These responsibilities can be either *i) guarantor*, the component that must be notified in case of violation of the provision, and which has the capacity to react to the problem, or *ii) beneficiaries*, the components which can rely on the provision, or *iii)* possible *contributors*, which are components needed to check the provision. Contrary to most object-oriented contracting systems, there is no concept of blame or guilty party in our model, as it is more dynamic and open to negotiations. As a result, on a contract violation, the focus is more on how to dynamically adapt the application at best, preserving robustness, rather that on assigning blame about a correctness issue. In the copier example, if the precondition of the method `copy`, which states n `<= it.tray().size()` is false, a negotiation could either limit n through the control panel, or change the interface `InputTray` to have a tray of paper with a larger capacity. For this provision, the guarantor is `<topLevel>`, which leads the negotiation, `<cp>` the beneficiary and, `<env>` and `<cp>` are contributors, through the interfaces `it` and `pp`.

For brevity's sake we only describe here the responsibilities of pre and post-conditions on composition contracts. Considering Figure 1, the responsibilities of the external composition contract of the printer `<pt>` are given by the following table:

interface role	construct	guarantor	beneficiaries
server: *pctl, uc*	pre	`<cp>`	`<pt>`
server: *pctl, uc*	post	`<pt>`	`<cp>`, `<dv>` *(pctl)*, `<fz>` *(uc)*
client: *ap, di, bi, it*	pre	`<pt>`	`<cp>` *(ap, it, bi)*, `<sn>` *(di)*
client: *ap, di, bi, it*	post	`<cp>`	`<pt>`

For example, on the component `<pt>`, for the postcondition of a method on its server interface uc, the guarantor is the component itself— as it implements the method and provides the interface — and the beneficiaries are `<cp>`, which contains `<pt>`, and `<fz>`, which is connected to the interface uc. As the external composition contract represents the usage rules of the component `<pt>`, it is logical to attribute the responsibility of this provision to the component `<cp>`, which contains `<pt>`, as it is `<cp>` that has to handle its internal assembly. As for the responsibilities associated to the internal composition contract of `<cp>`, they are straightforward, as `<cp>` is at the same time the guarantor and the beneficiary in all cases, being entirely responsible of its own implementation.

4.3   Progressive Closure of Contracts

When a component is inserted into an assembly, *ConFract* creates its internal composition contract if it is composite, and its external composition contract if it has some specifications bound to several of its interfaces. For every specification bound to some composition contracts, a provision *template* is created and attached to the composition contract. Every template is waiting for all its contributors to *close up*. When a new subcomponent is added into a composite, all the templates that participate in the concerned composition contract have their responsibilities completed. When all the contributors of a template are known, it is closed and becomes a provision. When all the provision templates of an internal composition contract are closed, the contract is *closed* as well, as all the responsibilities are identified, and the component can be finally started.

For an interface contract, the life cycle is very simple, as there are only two participants in the contract. It is thus created during the connection between the interfaces and is automatically closed.

4.4   Contract Checking

When building the contract, the *ConFract* system includes in each provision of a contract, the specification predicate (currently a *CCL-J* assertion), an interception context (the times and locations where the provision is supposed to be satisfied) and the necessary references to the context (component, interfaces, etc.). The contracts are then evaluated when the appropriate event occurs (see section 5.2).

At configuration time, the provisions of composition contracts that define invariant properties on components (*cf.* spec. **s9**) are checked. As for preconditions, postconditions and method invariants of all contracts, they are checked at runtime. When a method is called on a *Fractal* interface, the provisions of the different contracts that refer to this method are checked in the following way. Preconditions from the interface contract are first checked. As they are created from the client and server specifications, they also check hierarchy errors to ensure behavioral subtyping [14]. Preconditions from the external composition contract of the component receiving the call, are then checked, ensuring the environment of the component is as expected. Preconditions from the internal composition contract are then checked. It should be noted that preconditions from the three different kinds of contract are simply checked sequentially. No specific rule is needed to ensure substituability as the interface contract already defined it, and that the other preconditions are not sharing the same scope and responsibilities. A similar checking is done with postconditions and method invariants after the call.

4.5   Examples of Dynamic Reconfiguration

We now illustrate two cases that can occur when a dynamic reconfiguration takes place and we show how the contracts follow the reconfiguration, help in checking their consistency and facilitate precise violation handling.

Let us suppose that one dynamically changes the scanner component <sn> with a new one, <newsn>. When <sn> is removed from the copier, its internal composition contract opens and the concerned provisions become provision templates again (interface contracts on the bindings of <sn> are also removed). When <newsn> is inserted in the copier, its internal composition contract closes again. Let us now suppose the <newsn> has no required interfaces ap of type AcPower. The internal composition contract of the copier will be evaluated before its starting and the provision s9 will be violated. For this kind of provision, the responsibility is on the component carrying the contract, that is the copier <cp>. It is indeed the only component that has the appropriate scope to handle the violation, for example by changing the scanner component again.

Let us now suppose that <newsn> has the appropriate interface, but that its scanning process is too slow. As the external composition contract on <cp> will be also updated in this case, the runtime checking of the postcondition of the method copy (on the pp interface of the copier, Figure 3) will fail, on the provision related to the printing speed (cf. spec. s5). Following the table page 196, the copier is also the responsible component, and is thus notified of the failure. Obviously, as the assertion on printing speed refers to the speed of several components, the reconfiguration could be optimized according to different criteria, but this is a combinatorial optimization problem, which can be handled by a negotiation[7].

5   Implementation

The *ConFract* system is currently integrated into *Fractal* using its reference implementation in *Java*, named *Julia* [1]. Julia is a software framework dedicated to components membrane programming. It is a small run-time library together with bytecode generators that relies on an AOP-like mechanism based on *mixins* and *interceptors*. A component membrane in Julia is basically a set of *controllers* and *interceptors* objects. A *mixin* mechanism based on lexicographical conventions is used to compose controller classes. Julia comes with a library of mixins and interceptors classes the programmer can compose and extend.

5.1   The Contract Controller

The various contracts are managed by *contract controllers* (CTC on Figure 6), located on the membrane of every component. As subcomponents are under the control of the enclosing component, every contract controller of a composite component manages the life cycle and the evaluation of the contracts that refer to its subcomponents and their bindings:

---

[7] The study of negotiation mechanisms in *ConFract* is in progress[15].

- the internal composition contract of the composite on which it is placed,
- the external composition contract of each of the subcomponents,
- the interface contract of every connection in its content.

During the creation of a composite component, the initialization of its contract controller creates its internal composition contract. The other contracts are built and updated by mixins.

5.2   Mixins and Interceptors

According to the configuration actions made on components, the contract controller reacts as different *mixins* are placed on the other *Fractal* controllers (*cf.* Figure 6):

- *Binding Controller* (BC). As this controller manages the creation and destruction of the connections between component interfaces, a mixin notifies the surrounding contract controller of connections (resp. disconnections) to instantiate (resp. to suppress) the corresponding interface contract.
- *Content Controller* (CC). This controller manages the insertion of subcomponents inside a composite. A mixin notifies the contract controller of each insertion, so that it builds the external composition contract of the new subcomponent C. The contract controller also closes the provisions that refers to C in the internal composition contract. The inverse actions are realized during the removal of a subcomponent.
- *Life-cycle Controller* (LC). As the *Fractal* model is very open, the only moment when one can be sure that a component is completely configured is just before it is started, using the `start` method of the life-cycle controller. As a result, a mixin is added to perform "static" checks (*cf.* section 2.2). The contract controller of the component (resp. of the surrounding component) verifies that its internal composition contract (resp. external) is closed. Finally, the contract provisions that are statically verifiable, such as component invariants, are checked.

As for the evaluation of dynamic contract provisions, *Julia* interceptors are used. Every *Fractal* interface related to a contract receives an interceptor on its methods entry and/or exit. In the case of *CCL-J*, when a method is called on an interface, the contract controller is then notified and it applies the checking rules described in section 4.4.

6   Related Work

Since the *Eiffel* language, numerous works focused on executable assertions in object-oriented languages, notably for *Java* [5,16]. *JML* [5] combines executable assertions with some features of abstract programs. It allows the developer to build executable models which use abstraction functions on the specified classes. *CCL-J* is much simpler than *JML* in terms of available constructs, but we only use *CCL-J* to validate the contracting mechanisms of *ConFract*. The composition contract provided by *ConFract* can be compared to collaboration contracts on objects proposed by Helm and Holland [17]. The notion of views in the collaboration is similar to the roles of the participants in our contracts. However, in the *ConFract* system, the composition contracts are carried by components — which allows one to distribute them in the hierarchy — and are automatically generated and updated according to the actions of assembly and connection.

Works on contracting components focus on using adapted formalisms to specify component interfaces. For example, contracts on *.NET* assemblies have been proposed [8], using *AsmL* as a specification language. Abstract programs are then interpreted in parallel with the code, but the contracts are only associated with interfaces. Numerous works rely on the formalism *QML* (*QoS Modeling Language*) [18], for example to contract QoS related properties on components [19]. *QML* allows the designer to describe such contracts by specifying the expected levels of the qualities on interfaces, but does not allow one, unlike *CCL-J*, to combine functional and extra-functional aspects in the same specification (for example, it is not possible to link a extra-functional constraint to some input parameter of a method). Several works have also proposed contracts for *UML* components. In [10], contracts between service providers and service users are formulated based on abstractions of action and operation behaviour using the pre and postcondition technique. A refinement relation is provided among contracts but they only concerns peer to peer composition in this approach. In the same way, a graphical notation for contracting *UML* components is proposed in [11], focusing on expressing both functional (with *OCL* [12]) and extra-functional (with *QML* [18]) contracts on component ports. Here again, only the connection of components is considered and checking means are not discussed. More recently Defour et. al. [20] proposed a variant of the contracts of [11] with *QML*, which can be used for constraints solving at design time. The version 2 of the *UML* notation supports a form of hierarchical components but contrary to *Fractal*, it focuses more on component connectors than on a composite structures. Moreover, version 2 of OCL [21] does not provide any extension to express compositional constraints. Consequently, it is likely to become quite cumbersome to express *CCL-J*-like composition constraints with *OCL*.

ADLs have been proposed for modelling software architectures in terms of components and their overall interconnection structure. Many of these languages support formal notations to specify components and connectors behaviors. For example, Wright [22] and Darwin [23] use CSP-based notations, Rapide [24] uses partially ordered sets of events and supports simulation of reactive architectures. These formalisms allow to verify correctness of component assemblies, checking properties such as deadlock freedom. Some ADLs support implementation issues, typically by generating code to connect component implementation, however most of the work on applying formal verifications to component interactions has focused on design time. A notable exception is the SOFA component model and its behavior protocol formalism [7], based on regular-like expressions, that permit the designer to verify the adherence of a component's implementation to its specification at runtime.

7   Conclusion

Recent component platforms, such as *Fractal*, combine the advantages of various approaches for CBSE: dynamic and distributed assemblies from middlewares, hierarchical architecture from the modular approaches and the possibilities of factorization and adaptation from object-oriented systems. Still correction and robustness of both functional and extra-functional properties must be ensured. In this paper, we have described the *ConFract* system, which proposes a contractual approach for hierarchical component models. Contracts are dynamically built from specifications, at assembly time, and are updated according to dynamic reconfigurations. These contracts are not restricted to the scope of interfaces, taken separately. On the contrary, new kinds of contracts can be associated to the scope of a whole component. These *composition contracts* constrain either several external interfaces of a component, providing some kind of "usage contract", or several interfaces inside the component, providing a sort of "assembly and implementation contract". In *ConFract*, the responsibilities are identified in a fine-grained way, at the level of each provision of a contract. As a result, developers can easily organize violation handling and adaptations with possible negotiations. The current implementation of *ConFract* follows the principle of separation of concerns by using *Fractal* controllers, which manage extra-functional services at the component level.

Currently, *ConFract* uses the executable assertions language *CCL-J* to express specifications at interface and component levels. This language allows the developer to express interesting properties at the component level, but it must be enhanced to improve its expressiveness on extra-functional constraints and provide efficient evaluation techniques such as the ones we have previously proposed [25]. Other specification formalisms are going to be integrated, using the metamodel of the *ConFract* system. In order to better handle contract violations, the integration of negotiation mechanisms is also in progress [15]. They will enable the system to relax constraints by negotiating with beneficiary components, or to request the guarantor component to make an effort.

Acknowledgements. This work was supported by France Telecom under the collaboration contract number 422721832-I3S. The authors thank Alain Ozanne for its contribution to the implementation.

References

1. Bruneton, E., Coupaye, T., Leclercq, M., Quéma, V., Stefani, J.B.: An Open Component Model and Its Support in Java. In: ICSE 2004 - CBSE7. Volume 3054 of LNCS., Springer Verlag (2004)
2. Szyperski, C.: Component Software: Beyond Object-Oriented Programming. 2nd edition edn. Addison-Wesley (2002)
3. Bachman, F., Bass, L., Buhman, C., Comella-Dorda, S., Long, F., Robert, J., Seacord, R., Wallnau, K.: Technical Concepts of Component-Based Software Engineering. CMU/SEI-2000-TR-008, Software Engineering Institute (2000) vol. 2.

4. Bruneton, E., Coupaye, T., Stefani, J.B.: The Fractal Component Model. Specification v1, v2, The ObjectWeb Consortium (2002,2003) http://fractal.objectweb.org.
5. Leavens, G.T., Baker, A.L., Ruby, C.: JML: A notation for detailed design. In Kilov, H., Rumpe, B., Simmonds, I., eds.: Behavioral Specifications of Businesses and Systems, Kluwer (1999) 175–188
6. de Alfaro, L., Henzinger, T.A.: Interface Automata. In: Ninth Annual Symposium on Foundations of Software Engineering (FSE), ACM Press (2001) 109–120
7. Plasil, F., Visnovsky, S.: Behavior Protocols for Software Components. IEEE Trans. on Soft. Eng. **28** (2002)
8. Barnett, M., Schulte, W.: Runtime Verification of .NET Contracts. Journal of Systems and Software **65** (2003) 199–208
9. Meyer, B.: Applying "Design by contract". IEEE Computer **25** (1992) 40–51
10. Pahl, C.: Components, Contracts and Connectors for the Unified Modelling Language UML. In Verlag, S., ed.: FME2001 - Formal Methods Europe. Volume 2021 of LNCS. (2001) 259–277
11. Weis, T., Becker, C., Geihs, K., Plouzeau, N.: A UML Meta-model for Contract Aware Components. In: UML 2001 - The Unified Modeling Language. Volume 2185 of Lecture Notes in Computer Science., Springer Verlag (2001) 442–456
12. Object Management Group, I.: Object Constraint Language Specification. Technical Report version 1.1, ad/97-08-08, IBM www.software.ibm.com/ad/ocl (1997)
13. D'Souza, D.F., Wills, A.C.: Object, Components and Frameworks with UML: The Catalysis Approach. Addison-Wesley Publishing Co. (Reading, MA) (1998)
14. Findler, R.B., Felleisen, M.: Contract Soundness for Object-Oriented Languages. In: Proceedings of OOPSLA'2001. (2001)
15. Chang, H., Collet, P.: Towards Contracts Negotiation in Software Components (in french). In: LMO'2005 (Object Models and Languages), Lavoisier (2005)
16. Plösch, R.: Evaluation of Assertion Support for the Java Programming Language. In: Journal of Object Technology, Volume 1,3. (2002) 5–17
17. Helm, R., Holland, I.M., Gangopadhyay, D.: Contracts: Specifying Behavioral compositions in Object-Oriented Systems. In Meyrowitz, N., ed.: OOPSLA/E-COOP'90, Ottawa, Canada (1990) 169–180
18. Frølund, S., Koistinen, J.: Quality of Service in Distributed Object Systems Design. In: 4th USENIX Conference on Object-Oriented Technologies and Systems (COOTS), Santa Fe (New Mexico), USENIX (1998)
19. Loques, O., Sztajnberg, A.: Customizing Component-Based Architectures by Contract. In: Proceedings of Component Deployment 2004, Edinburgh, UK. (2004)
20. Defour, O., Jézéquel, J.M., Plouzeau, N.: Extra-Functional Contract Support in Components. In Crnkovic, I., Stafford, J., Schmidt, H., Wallnau, K., eds.: ICSE 2004 - CBSE7. Volume 3054 of LNCS., Springer Verlag (2004) 217–232
21. OMG: UML 2 OCL Final Adopted Specification. Technical Report ptc/03-10-14, Object Management Group (2003)
22. Allen, R.J., Garlan, D.: A Formal Basis for Architectural Connection. ACM Trans. on Soft. Eng. and Methodology **6** (1997)
23. Magee, J., Kramer, J., Giannakopoulou, D.: Behaviour Analysis of Software Architectures. In: 1st Working IFIP Conference on Software Architecture (WICSA1), San Antonio, USA (1999)
24. Luckham, D.C., all: Specification and Analysis of System Architecture using Rapide. IEEE Trans. on Soft. Eng. **24** (1995) 336–355
25. Collet, P., Rousseau, R.: Efficient Implementation Techniques for Advanced Assertion Languages. L'objet **5** (1999) 417–442

Tailored Responsibility Within Component-Based Systems

Elke Franz and Ute Wappler

Department of Computer Science
Dresden University of Technology, Dresden, Germany
{Elke.Franz|Ute.Wappler}@inf.tu-dresden.de

Abstract. The concept of responsibility aims at making a computing system trustworthy for its users despite the fact that failures of IT systems cannot be completely excluded. The presented concept comprises the following issues: In case of failures, the responsible stakeholder can be identified and it is ensured that this stakeholder is willing to compensate arisen loss. This enables users to claim damages. Until now, responsibility in this sense is not considered in practical systems. We especially investigate possibilities for integration of responsibility into component-based systems whereas the interests of all involved stakeholders should be considered. The newly introduced concept of tailored responsibility enables users to pose flexible demands for responsibility.

1 Introduction

IT systems are increasingly used in all fields of daily life, e.g. for governmental tasks, banking, for health care or for controlling airplanes. Consequently, the dependability of IT systems is of increasing importance. Failures of IT systems cannot only cause annoying loss of time for users, but also big economic damage. In the worst case, they even endanger health and life of people.

Quality assurance measurements and special design methodologies obviously reduce fault rates. However, it is not possible to design and implement absolutely faultless software. Furthermore, one has to consider that even if software would be functional correct, failures during runtime could still occur: Software is just passive program code which needs to be executed by an infrastructure in order to deliver any service. This infrastructure mostly consists of a computer with an operating system. In case of component-based software, it additionally comprises a runtime environment for the software components, the container. The needed infrastructure may contain faults, too. A faulty infrastructure can also cause failures due to erroneous execution of the possibly correct software components. To conclude, failures of IT systems cannot be prevented completely.

The concept of responsibility aims at giving users a basis for trusting an IT system despite these facts.

Responsibility: In case of failures, it is guaranteed that the responsible stakeholder can be identified and that he is willing to compensate arisen loss.

G.T. Heineman et al. (Eds.): CBSE 2005, LNCS 3489, pp. 203–218, 2005.

That means, we do not exclude failures in spite of the fact, that their probability should be quite small due to careful design, implementation and operation of IT systems. The assignment of responsibility makes it possible to compensate arisen loss. However, compensation has to be done outside of IT systems and requires additional legal arrangements which are beyond the scope of this paper.

A general concept for realizing responsibility was already presented in 1991 in [2]. An implementation is still missing. We focus at mapping this general concept onto component-based systems. Thereby, we especially aim at considering the interests of all involved stakeholders. Note, that stakeholders shall only be held responsible for failures which they have caused.

Since Component-Based Software Engineering (CBSE) is an ongoing research field it seems to be interesting and important to discuss responsibility in this context. Software components are used for developing component-based applications. These components are black boxes which means that only the interface of the component is known but nothing about the internal realization of the provided functionality. Components are mostly developed without knowledge about their future deployment. Component developers only implement business logic. Other required services such as resource management or persistence are provided by the used container. Because of this clear role concept component-based systems are especially suited to support responsibility. Second, services required for supporting responsibility can be integrated into the used container. Third, the structure of component based applications allows us to realize fine grained responsibility demands and offers. This enables us to restrict the effort required for realizing responsibility.

An IT system providing responsibility is more trustworthy for its users. We also expect an increased software quality, if developers are held responsible for failures caused by their products. A developer who has to bear the risk of claims for indemnification will put more effort in the development of his software. However, this in return increases the costs. Therefore, users should be enabled to flexibly demand responsibility for an application according to their actual needs. Tailored demands should be possible despite the fact, that users mostly do not know anything about the component-based structure of the used application.

We have introduced a first discussion about responsibility within CBSE in [4]. Now we newly introduce the concept of *tailored responsibility*. Moreover, we discuss possibilities for optimization as well as problems implied by persistent data. The concept of tailored responsibility supports the flexible demand for responsibility required above.

In the following, we first introduce the general concept of responsibility and give an outlook on realization issues (Sec. 2). Afterwards, we discuss responsibilities within component-based systems (Sec. 3). We especially focus on the used role concept, since it is important for responsibility assignment. Sec. 4 introduces possible concepts for the realization of responsibility. We discuss implementation issues of the selected concept in Sec. 5. Finally, Sec. 6 concludes and points out open issues.

2 Responsibility

2.1 General Approach

As mentioned above, either faulty software or its faulty execution by the used infrastructure can cause a failure of an IT system. Basically, we must be able to decide whether erroneous software or erroneous execution has caused the failure in order to assign responsibility for the failure.

The authors of [2] consider the executed software and the infrastructure needed to execute the software as service providing unit. Since we need a possibility to reconstruct execution ex post, all inputs to and outputs from these units are logged by the executing machine. In case of a failure, the logged data is used to localize the error causing unit. Within the localized unit, it has to be clarified whether the software or the executing infrastructure has caused the failure. Therefor, the software is executed again within a correct execution environment using the same input data. If further circumstances, such as internal states, influence execution, they must be logged, too. Particularly, if random events determine execution, the exact values of the random variables have to be logged. Generally, the executing machine must log all events that cannot be reconstructed.

However, a correct execution environment does not exist in practice. Therefore, the authors suggest to approximate it by using a number of diverse execution environments and to subsequently acquire the result of the repetition by majority voting. Another possibility is to simulate execution using diverse simulation environments.

Based on the results of this repeated execution, responsibility is assigned as follows:

- If the repeated execution did not cause a failure, it is assumed that the failure at runtime was caused by an erroneous executing system. The stakeholder who is responsible for the executing infrastructure is made responsible for the damages.
- If the same failure occurred, it is apparently caused by the software. Consequently, the software provider has to compensate arisen loss.
- If another failure occurred, both software and executing infrastructure apparently are erroneous. Responsibility is assigned to both software and infrastructure provider.

To the best of our knowledge, there are currently no realizations of this concept in practical systems. Of course, providers will not volunteer for responsibility. Legal restraints or appropriate purchasing patterns are necessary to establish responsibility. In fact, in software license agreements providers usually state that they are not willing to take any responsibility for damages caused by their product (disclaimer of warranty). However, we assume that responsibility is a desirable feature from the user's point of view since it will increase trustworthiness of IT systems.

2.2   Requirements on a Realization

Integrating this concept into component-based systems requires to extend the software development process as well as the runtime environment of components — the container. In the following, we sketch necessary requirements on the integration and the general process of service delivery considering responsibility. The different participating roles and their responsibilities are discussed in more detail in the next section.

We cannot expect that all software providers will take responsibility for their software components since it is not common nowadays. Therefore, providers must be enabled to specify whether they are willing to take responsibility and under which conditions [4]. Users must be enabled to demand responsibility before they start an application. The container has to be enabled to prove whether the user's demands can be fulfilled. If this is not the case, further negotiation steps must be initiated. If the negotiation phase could be finished successfully, users get a signed affirmation stating the demanded and granted service including responsibility requirements. In case of a failure, the user shows this affirmation to prove the acceptance of his demands by the service provider. The service provider, on the other hand, also gets a signed contract in order to be able to prove the requirements of the user.

If responsibility should be provided, the container has to enforce that only products are used which their providers have assured responsibility for. Furthermore, the container has to check whether conditions of these providers are fulfilled. During execution, the container has to log all relevant events. If the user recognizes a failure, he claims damages from the service provider. He shows the data he has received and the signed affirmation. The service provider uses the data logged during execution for localizing the error and to assign responsibility. As already mentioned, compensation of arisen loss is out of scope of the computing system. Figure 1 summarizes this procedure.

The flexibility of the solution is important due to a number of reasons:

- Execution of software components without responsibility assurances must still be possible. A container that executes only software components with responsibility assurances is too restrictive and, therefore, not of practical relevance. We assume that component implementations are chosen at instantiation time when the user requirements are known. A fix selection of component implementations at development or deploy time is too inflexible, not only w.r.t. responsibility requirements (Section 3.2).
- Furthermore, there are different users with very different needs. The computing system should be able to adapt to these different needs.
- Finally, the question of cost crucially influences the decision of the user whether responsibility should be considered or not. Development of software components for which responsibility is assured surely requires more costs. Consequently, these components will be more expensive which influences the user's demands. But also cost in terms of required computing power or delivered performance are important. Particularly, the necessary logging has an impact on these features.

System of service provider   **System of user**

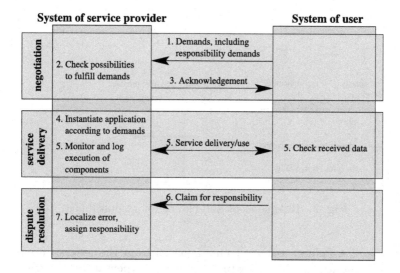

Fig. 1. Service delivery considering responsibility.

To conclude, we need a solution that enables users to demand responsibility in a fine grained manner in order to realize a balanced trade-off between responsibility on the one side and costs, performance and needed computing power on the other side.

3 Responsibilities Within Component Based Systems

3.1 Role Concept

Component-Based Software Engineering (CBSE) is a software paradigm of growing importance. The use of prefabricated software components with well-defined interfaces and well-defined functionality aims at developing component-based applications faster and reasonably priced.

Different stakeholders are involved in the development and execution of component-based applications. Faults in their products can cause failures of the computing systems. A clear definition of the stakeholders' tasks — a role concept — is necessary in order to enable assignment of responsibility. Figure 2 shows a part of the role concepts which is relevant for responsibility and depicts claims for responsibility between roles.

The *service provider* provides a component-based application to the *users*. An *application designer* is responsible for developing this application. He specifies used components provided by *component developers*. The application designer selects suitable components and integrates them into the application which is assembled into an archive. The archive is delivered to the service providers. The service provider commissions the *system provider* to install the application onto the target machine in order to make it available to users.

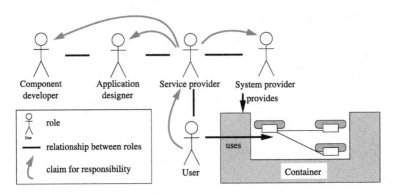

Fig. 2. Role concept and claims for responsibility.

In case of a failure, a user claims damages from the service provider. Of course, the service provider does not want to compensate losses which were caused by others. Therefore, he must be able to find the actual responsible stakeholder:

- The corresponding *component developer* is responsible if his component implementation was erroneous or if he has not sufficiently specified requirements on the infrastructure.
- The *application designer* is responsible if the assembly of components was erroneous.
- The *system provider* is responsible if the execution of the component-based application has caused the failure.

In the first case, we can only recognize a deviation from the specified behavior of the component. It is not possible to determine the actual cause of the error. Despite this fact, the component developer should be responsible for the erroneous behavior of his component implementation. Since he knows the internal realization of the component implementation, he is the only one who could determine dependencies from the environment. Consequently, it is important to enable component developers to define requirements on the executing environment. Particularly, they will require specific versions of specific containers which correspond to their working and testing environment.

In the second case, all software components behaved as specified, but the whole system has not met its specification and the failure occurs again in the repeated execution. In this case, the components were used or connected wrongly. In the third case, the failure could not be reconstructed during the repeated execution on a different infrastructure.

Concurrent execution surely complicates error diagnostic. As mentioned above, we have to log all events required for reconstruction.

The last case simplifies the fact that different stakeholders are responsible for the executing infrastructure and, therefore, could have been responsible for the failure. We assume that the system provider uses an infrastructure that he trusts. In case of a failure, he takes responsibility for erroneous execution. A more detailed responsibility assignment would require a more detailed logging as well as a quite complex reconstruction: One would have to inspect every part of the infrastructure. If cases of erroneous execution increase, the system provider would try to localize the error and possibly modify his infrastructure.

The stakeholders only take responsibility if their conditions are fulfilled. They only take responsibility

- if really their products were used (digital signatures ensure execution of authentic, unmodified software),
- if the software was executed according to their specifications (e.g., requirements on the input data, on existing services such as databases, or on specific versions of the container), and
- if the software was executed within an environment they trust (e.g., based on certificates confirming the existence of expertises by independent third parties [10]).

A more detailed discussion of these conditions is given in [4].

3.2   Context of Our Work

Our work is based on the component model developed within the project COMQUAD (*COMponents with QUantitative properties and ADaptivity*) at Dresden University of Technology. COMQUAD aimed at a system architecture and matching design methodology that support the composition of adaptive software from software components with consideration of agreed non-functional properties. Non-functional properties, e.g. response times and throughput, describe how a computing system delivers its service. Considering non-functional properties and enforcing users demands on them requires extensions of the usual component model.

The component architecture developed in the project COMQUAD is based on the component model by Cheesman and Daniels [1]: Component specifications describe the functionality of a component by means of interfaces. Component implementations realize this functionality. Implementations are installed into the container and instantiated if the application is started.

The model developed in the project COMQUAD utilizes the fact that different implementations differ in their non-functional properties. These differences are caused by the use of different algorithms or resources. In order to enable adaptation to different user requirements, diverse component implementations for one specification can be included in an application archive. The non-functional properties of these component implementations are explicitly described using the description language CQML$^+$ which was developed within the project [8].

The application designer defines the application structure as assembly of component specifications. If a user wants to use an application's service, he specifies the desired non-functional properties. The COMQUAD container selects suitable component implementations from the archive and instantiates them in order to provide the service in the required quality. If the user's demands cannot be met, for example due to the current system load, the container informs the user who can reduce his requirements or try to get the service at a later point in time.

We aim at treating responsibility also as non-functional property. This approach allows us to reuse mechanisms developed within the project COMQUAD, since our solution has also to support selection of suitable component implementations at application start up.

4   Possible Concepts

4.1   Absolute Responsibility

The direct application of the approach introduced in [2] yields the concept of absolute responsibility. This concept enables a user to demand either responsibility for the whole application, or no responsibility at all. In the former case, all involved stakeholders have to offer responsibility for their products. Involved stakeholders are the developers of instantiated components and the application designer (Fig. 3). Furthermore, the conditions posed by this stakeholders have to be fulfilled. Only if this is the case they are willing to assure the offered responsibility and to compensate arisen loss in case of failure caused by their products. The evaluation of conditions can be integrated as service into the used container. The `client` depicted in Fig. 3 is a special component which acts in behalf of the user.

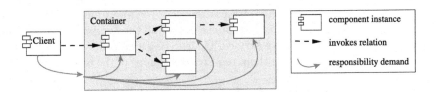

Fig. 3. Absolute responsibility.

The concept of absolute responsibility does not fulfill our requirement for flexibility. First, a user cannot demand responsibility according to his actual needs. Second, as soon as only one responsibility assurance is missing, it is not possible to assure responsibility for the whole application. This is very likely in case of complex applications. In that case, the user has to pass on his demand for responsibility or to use another adequate application for which his demand can be fulfilled.

4.2   Partial Responsibility

A first naive approach to improve this situation leads to the concept of partial responsibility. That concept enables a user to restrict his demands on responsibility. For example, he can demand that for 90% of the used component implementations responsibility is assured. The probability to fulfill user demands increases.

But this concept has to be dismissed, because a user cannot assess the risk he bears. He does not know if the 10% of the component implementations for which no responsibility is assured provide functionality which is especially important for him. Thus, a failure of the message board of an application might be less critical. Whereas, a failure of an important control mechanism of a plane can have disastrous consequences.

Consequently, users should be enabled to pose fine grained responsibility demands depending on the used functionality. Only in that case they can assess the risk they have to bear.

4.3   Tailored Responsibility

Tailored responsibility enables users to demand responsibility for certain functionalities of an application. Users can adapt their responsibility demands to their actual needs and assess the remaining risk. While instantiating an application, responsibility only has to be assured for component implementations which take part in the realization of a functionality for which the user has demanded responsibility.

The application shown in Fig. 4 provides two functionalities F1 and F2. The user demands responsibility for F2. Accordingly, it is required that responsibility is assured for the two component implementations which participate in the realization of functionality F2: First, their developers must offer responsibility for their products and, second, the conditions posed by these developers must be fulfilled.

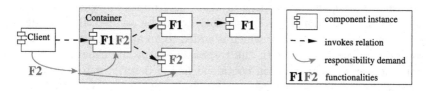

Fig. 4. Tailored responsibility.

The concept of tailored responsibility supports the required flexibility. Therefore, we have chosen it for further development.

5   Realization of Tailored Responsibility

5.1   Level of Detail for Responsibility Demands and Offers

Responsibility demands of users and responsibility offers of developers can be specified on the level of methods, interfaces or components. These three levels are different with respect to flexibility and effort necessary for realization. Demands and offers on the *level of methods* map user requirements in a very detailed manner, but require a higher specification effort than the other solutions. The same conclusions can be drawn for the comparison of interface level and component level. But the last two possibilities appear more appropriate since interfaces as well as components have the purpose to encapsulate functionalities which meets our requirement to enable users to demand responsibility w.r.t. different functionalities.

The complexity of components influences the decision between interface level and component level. Specification at *component level* is sufficient for simple components which contain solely one functionality. However, specification at *interface level* is better suited for complex components which provide more than one functionality encapsulated through different interfaces.

We realize specification at interface level in order to leave open both possibilities. Furthermore, responsibility demands/offers at component level can be emulated through a demand/offer on all interfaces of a component.

5.2   Mapping Demands to Offers

A user can pose demands for responsibility only w.r.t. his client, because he does not have any knowledge about the application structure. To instantiate an appropriate application instance, these responsibility demands of a user must be mapped onto responsibility offers of involved developers. In the following, we discuss possible approaches for mapping.

Mapping by application designer.   The application designer defines different responsibility profiles which are provided by the client to the user. At instantiation time, the user selects one of these profiles.

For each profile, the application designer determines for which of the interfaces of the used components responsibility has to be assured. He provides this information within a descriptor which is added to an application. The container instantiates an application with the responsibility profile chosen by the user. Thereby, it uses the information contained in the descriptor to examine if all required responsibility assurances are fulfilled. Therefor, it also needs the responsibility offers and conditions which have to be provided by the component developers. Fig. 5 shows an example for this mapping. The figure depicts for which interfaces responsibility has to be assured, if the user requires responsibility for one of the client's interfaces.

This mapping is problematic, since the application designer does not have any knowledge about the internal realization of a component implementation. He is not able to definitely assess which interfaces depend on each other and are involved in the implementation of a special functionality. He can only guess these dependencies using interface and method names and descriptions of component implementations. Nevertheless, he is responsible for wrong decisions caused by this procedure. For example, he could not recognize that an interface participates in the realization of a functionality. Later on, a user requires responsibility

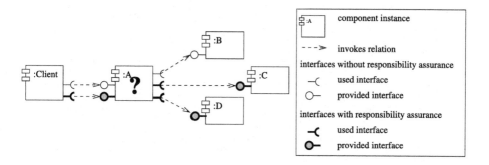

Fig. 5. Requirements mapping made by the application designer.

for that functionality and the implementation of the overlooked interface causes a failure. But due to the erroneous specification delivered by the application designer, the container has not mapped responsibility demands on the error causing component. Consequently, its developer cannot be held responsible. Since this situation was caused by the application designer, he would be held responsible. Obviously, no application designer would like to bear that risk.

Automatic mapping. Such a mapping requires to know *intra functional dependencies*. These are dependencies within a component implementation in contrast to inter functional dependencies between the interfaces of different components. Fig. 6 depicts how intra functional dependencies can be used to map responsibility demands onto offers. Responsibility demands on interfaces of component implementations are calculated with the help of responsibility demands on client interfaces and intra functional dependencies. We simply have to follow the dependencies starting from the client component. This is done before instantiating and executing an application. Since only the component developer knows the internal realization of his component implementation, only he is able to specify its intra functional dependencies. The specification is based on the general procedure described in [4].

Intra functional dependencies are caused by data flows between the interfaces of a component instance. Data could be input into a component as parameter, if a method of a component instance is called. Strictly speaking, the method call itself is a data input. Furthermore, data can be input as return value of a method which was called by the component instance. There are two kinds of intra functional dependencies:

– *Direct intra functional dependency*: Component instances can forward (possibly processed) input data to other component instances as parameter or return value.
– *Indirect intra functional dependencies*: Stateful component instances maintain a state between method calls. Input data surely influences this state. Later on, the state influences the output of these component instances.

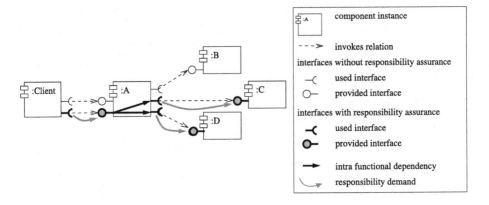

Fig. 6. Utilizing intra functional dependencies for mapping responsibility demands.

The specification of intra functional dependencies requires some effort from the component developer. Particularly, indirect intra functional dependencies are difficult to recognize. If a developer is not willing to specify the dependencies, we have to assume that all interfaces of a component implementation affect each other. This results in overstated responsibility demands. For example, the mapping shown in Fig. 6 would contain an additional responsibility demand on component B in that case. Obviously, overstated demands decrease the probability that users' demands on responsibility can be fulfilled.

5.3   Optimized Monitoring and Logging

To assign responsibility in case of a failure it is required to monitor and log the execution of an application (Sec. 2.1). Such an all-embracing monitoring and logging is quite expensive. However, the concept of tailored responsibility reduces monitoring and logging effort. The *knowledge of intra functional dependencies* allows us to restrict monitoring to component interfaces for which a responsibility demand exists. The remaining interfaces contained in an application need not to be monitored, since they have no influence on interfaces with a responsibility demand. The application execution should be reconstructable without logged data from interfaces without responsibility demand. For the repeated execution, different input values for the interfaces not monitored can be used in order to detect overlooked dependencies.

Problems may occur, if a developer has forgotten to specify some intra functional dependencies for an interface, and responsibility is demanded for that interface. If a failure is caused by one of these unknown dependent interfaces, the actual originator of this failure cannot be found. Finally, the component developer who forgot the dependency is made responsible for the failure. This decision is acceptable, since he is responsible for the insufficient specification.

Another reduction of monitoring and logging effort can be achieved if *responsibility realms are merged*. For example, one developer delivered three component implementations which depend on each other and provide well defined interfaces to the outer world. If responsibility demands exist for some of the outer interfaces, it is only necessary to monitor these interfaces and depending other outer interfaces. But it is not necessary to monitor communication between components provided by the same developer. For assigning responsibility, the responsibility realm is repeatedly executed as a whole.

In case of data streams such as in video or audio transmission another reduction of monitoring and logging overhead is required, since logging video or audio streams on the whole would be too complex. Instead of this, we consider logging of relevant data such as start and end of transmission, transmission rates or other statistical data.

5.4   Problems with Persistent Data

Until now we assumed that the stage of mapping demands onto assurances and the following application execution (see fig. 1) form a unity which is secluded. If a user instantiates the same application for another time he can pose new responsibility demands which are completely independent from all application instances he used before.

But if application data is made persistent — e.g., in a data base — consecutively created application instances are not independent from each other. They are connected through the stored data, and that affects the realization of responsibility. We have to consider two kinds of dependencies which are discussed in the following.

Dependency between application instances of one user. The following example shall illustrate the problem. A user demands no responsibility for a functionality which stores data to a data base. The stored data is faulty or is falsified during saving. At a later point in time, the same user starts another instance of that application. But this time, he demands responsibility for a functionality which processes the previously stored data. The application fails and the user wants compensation for a damage which was caused by the storing component implementation.

With the help of logged data it is only possible to determine that the failure was not caused by the current application instance. But for the previous application instance no logging was done, because no responsibility demand was made. This prevents a determination of the actual cause of the failure. But even if it would be possible to determine the cause, nobody assured responsibility for the faulty application part. The responsibility which was assured to the user for the second application instance is not satisfiable. Multiple solutions to this problem exist.

First solution: As soon as data is made persistent, responsibility is demanded implicitly. Consequently, responsibility assurances are checked and monitoring and logging are done. However, this solution increases user demands.

Second solution: The data to be stored has to be tested for correctness. Especially in the context of data base systems, concepts and implementations for such consistency checks already exist. But the required description of semantical correctness of data is very difficult and only possible to a very limited degree.

Third solution: The user is restricted in his possible responsibility demands. He is not allowed to increase his responsibility demands between two dependent application instances. For succeeding dependent application instances he is only allowed to use the same responsibility demands as for the previous instance or to reduce his demands. The concept of responsibility exhibits a monotony behavior as confidentiality or anonymity do [7]. We suggest this third solution.

Dependency between application instances of different users. An application is usually used by more than one user. Data of these users is mostly stored at the same place, e.g., a data base. Therefore, it is possible that not only the data of the current user is falsified but possibly also the data of other users. A conflict arises if the current user has not demanded responsibility for the concerned functionality, but the user whose data was falsified has done so. By means of a digital signature or a hash value we can detect that the data was modified. However, it is not possible to identify who is responsible. Furthermore, the responsible stakeholder has also not assured responsibility. Thus, no responsibility assignment is possible.

The simplest solution would be to determine **one** responsibility demand for all users — the union of all user demands. However, this approach implies overstated responsibility demands. Furthermore, the achieved flexibility is lost.

Another solution is that the container enforces authentication and authorization before access to persistent data is granted. Therefor, it is necessary to execute the application with the access rights of the current user. Thus, a user can only access his own data. If it is detected that a data set was modified and no error within the application execution can be found, the container which implements authentication and authorization must have been faulty. In this case the system provider is responsible.

If we assume that integrity assurance measurements for persistent data and logging work correctly, authentication and authorization before data access are a suitable solution of the described problem. The enforcement of access authorization by the container is done already in some component models (e.g. Access Control Lists in the Corba Component Model).

6   Conclusion and Outlook

Despite the fact that it is not possible to exclude failures completely, users need to trust IT systems, because they influence all aspects of their life. Therefore, the realization of responsibility in IT systems is an important step for increasing the trustworthiness of these systems for users. The concept of responsibility assures that a responsible stakeholder can be found who is willing to compensate arisen loss.

Realizing responsibility assignments is quite complex and comprises the following tasks:

- Component developers have to specify their responsibility offers and conditions which have to be fulfilled for turning their offers into assurances. Therefor, the development process has to be extended.
- Component developers have to be identifiable. This can be realized with the help of digital signatures.
- The evaluation of responsibility demands of the user has to be implemented. The container needs to be extended. First, it has to map users' demands onto responsibility offers which is done via following specified intra functional dependencies. Second, it has to automatically test the fulfillment of conditions posed by developers.
- The application execution has to be reconstructable which is achieved by the implementation of monitoring and logging.
- The responsibility assignment must be possible. Therefor, the evaluation of logging data and repeated execution of application parts in a reference environment are required (Sec. 2.1).
- Apart from the extension of the used IT system, legal arrangements for responsibility assignments have to be made.

More details for specification issues, the required container extensions and an implementation of these extensions are discussed in [4]. The required container extensions where implemented within the prototypic container which was developed within COMQUAD. The reuse of the existing architecture reduced the needed effort. The evaluation of responsibility demands is done while instantiating the application. Therefore, it does not influence the application execution.

Within this paper, we discussed concepts for realizing fine grained responsibility demands within the context of component-based systems. We have shown that the concept of *tailored responsibility* is the most suitable one, since it provides the users with the biggest flexibility. *Intra functional dependencies* enable us not only to map user demands to offers, but make it also possible to reduce monitoring and logging. We addressed problems which arise due to such reductions. Furthermore, we also pointed out possible problems resulting from dependencies between different application instances due to persistent data and introduced solutions for these problems.

There are a lot of tasks that still need to be investigated. Currently, we are testing the performance overhead introduced by logging. Error localization, repeated execution, and actual responsibility assignment are subject of future work. Error localization is a problem which is studied in the field of fault tolerance. Approaches are already described in [6]. For repeated execution, we consider to execute localized components (or groups of components, if we consider responsibility realms as discussed in Sec. 5.3). This execution should be done by a trusted third party using exactly the runtime environment which was required by the software developers. If personal data are required as input, we additionally have to consider privacy aspects.

Until now, the discussed approaches facilitate application structure dependent responsibility demands. Future investigations are necessary in order to decide whether a service oriented solution is more suitable. Such an approach would enable a user to demand responsibility only for exactly one activity without other connected activities. The following example shows the difference: A user uses an application which enables him to subscribe to a video stream for which he has to pay. The subscription consists of two activities: payment and stream delivery. These activities are dependent because data is exchanged between them. Because of this dependence it is not possible to demand responsibility for the payment activity only if the approach presented in this paper is used. We expect that a specification of responsibility demands and offers for services such as defined in [9, 3, 5] would solve this problem.

Another goal of future research is to analyze whether the presented concepts are applicable to other component models than the COMQUAD component model. We expect that such an application will require much more effort, since our current solution can reuse existing functionality to a great deal.

References

[1] John Cheesman and John Daniels. *UML Components: A Simple Process for Specifying Component-Based Software*. Addison-Wesley Longman Publishing Co., Inc., 2000.

[2] Wolfgang Clesle and Andreas Pfitzmann. Rechnerkonzept mit digital signierten Schnittstellenprotokollen erlaubt individuelle Verantwortungszuweisung. English title: Computing Concept with digitally signed Interface Protocols supporting Individual Responsibility Assignment. *Datenschutz-Berater*, 14(8/9):8–38, 1991.

[3] Martin Deubler, Johannes Grünbauer, Gerhard Popp, Guido Wimmel, and Christian Salzmann. Towards a Model-Based and Incremental Development Process for Service-Based Systems. *IASTED International Conference on Software Engineering (IASTED SE 2004)*, 2004.

[4] Henrik Eichenhardt, Elke Franz, Simone Röttger, and Ute Wappler. Adapting Component Models to Support Responsibility. 2004. Presented at ISOLA 2004, 1st Int. Symposium on Leveraging Applications of Formal Methods.

[5] Ingolf Krüger. Service Specification with MSCs and Roles. *IASTED International Conference on Software Engineering (IASTED SE 2004)*, 2004.

[6] P. A. Lee and T. Anderson. *Fault tolerance — principles and practice*. Springer, Wien; New York, second, revised edition, 1990.

[7] Andreas Pfitzmann and Gritta Wolf. Properties of Protection Goals and their Integration into a User Interface. *Computer Networks*, 32:685–699, 2000.

[8] Simone Röttger and Steffen Zschaler. CQML$^+$: Enhancements to CQML. In Jean-Michel Bruel, editor, *1st Intl. Workshop on Quality of Service in Component-Based Software Engineering*, pages 43–56, Toulouse, France, June 2003. Cépaduès-Éditions.

[9] Christian Salzmann and Bernhard Schätz. Service Based Software Specification. *Proceedings of Intl. International Workshop on Test and Analysis of Component Based Systems (TACOS)*, 2003.

[10] Jeffrey Voas. Developing a Usage-Based Software Certification Process. *IEEE Computer*, pages 32–37, August 2000.

Efficient Upgrading in a Purely Functional Component Deployment Model

Eelco Dolstra

Utrecht University, P.O. Box 80089,
3508 TB Utrecht, The Netherlands
eelco@cs.uu.nl

Abstract. Safe and efficient deployment of software components is an important aspect of CBSE. The Nix deployment system enables side-by-side deployment of different versions and variants of components, complete installation, safe upgrades, and safe uninstalls through garbage collection. It accomplishes this through a purely functional deployment model, meaning that the file system content of a component only depends on the inputs used to build it, and never changes afterwards. An apparent downside to this model is that upgrading "fundamental" components used as build inputs by many other components becomes expensive, since all of these must be rebuilt and redeployed. In this paper we show that binary patching between sets of components enables efficient deployment of upgrades in the purely functional model, transparently to users. Sequences of patches can be combined automatically to enable upgrading between arbitrary versions. The approach was empirically validated.

1   Introduction

An important aspect of Component-Based Software Engineering (CBSE) is the correct and efficient deployment of components after they have been developed [1]. This is often surprisingly hard. The main issues are dealing with side-by-side deployment of different versions or variants, isolation between components, ensuring complete component dependencies, and so on [2].

The Nix deployment system addresses these problems [3, 4]. The central idea is that each binary component is stored in isolation in the file system under a path name that contains a cryptographic hash of *all* inputs used to build the component, e.g., /nix/store/920e492a10af...-firefox-1.0. These inputs include (recursively) the component's build-time dependencies, build scripts, build parameters, platform, and so on.

The advantage is that we get variability support "for free": if two components are different in any way, they are stored in different locations in the file system. This isolation prevents undeclared build-time component dependencies. The hashes enable determination of run-time dependencies through a conservative pointer scanning approach [3]. This enables Nix to support side-by-side deployment of different versions and variants of components, complete installation, safe upgrades, and safe uninstalls through garbage collection.

G.T. Heineman et al. (Eds.): CBSE 2005, LNCS 3489, pp. 219–234, 2005.
© Springer-Verlag Berlin Heidelberg 2005

However, there is a downside: *upgrading* becomes a much more resource-intensive operation. If we change any build-time input to a component, the hash of the component changes, and so it will need to be rebuilt and redeployed. This is the right thing to do, since the change to the input might actually matter in an observable way, i.e., we have obtained a new variant. However, for upgrades to "fundamental" components that are used directly or indirectly by many others, the cost of redeployment may be substantial. For instance, in the dependency graph of a typical Linux system, virtually all components depend on the GNU C Library (Glibc). An update to Glibc would therefore trigger a rebuild of all components in the system, similar to how a change to a common header file will cause massive recompilation in Make [5]. This is not a major issue since it takes place on the distributor's systems. Worse, however, is that in order to re-deploy the Glibc upgrade to end-users, each of them would need to download all rebuilt dependent components in addition to the new Glibc. This requires very substantial network resources; e.g., a small bug fix to Glibc might induce hundreds of megabytes worth of downloads.

In more conventional deployment models, upgrades are delivered as "destructive updates" that overwrite the older version of the component. This is more efficient but it short-circuits the dependency graph, inhibits rollbacks, and may break other installed components.

However, the inefficiency of deploying upgrades in Nix would suggest that the Nix system is not practical. *In this paper we show that it is.* By deploying *binary patches*, we can efficiently distribute new versions or variants of components to the end-user systems. For instance, a Glibc update typically causes a download of just a few hundred kilobytes in patches for around 150 components, a modest amount even on slow network connections.

Contributions The contributions of this paper are as follows.

- We show that the Nix deployment model can support efficient deployment of upgrades through the use of automatically generated binary patches that are transparently used by client machines.
- We introduce the technique of automatic *patch chaining* to relief the burden of having to generate patches between arbitrary releases.
- We show that patches between components can easily be produced, even in the presence of file or directory renames and moves, by producing deltas between *archives* of the components.

The techniques discussed in this paper have been implemented, and we discuss their effectiveness.

Outline The remainder of this paper is structured as follows. Section 2 gives a brief overview of the Nix system and motivates why we need binary patch deployment in Nix. Section 3 describes binary patch deployment in Nix, including the concept of patch chaining. The problem of selecting the right base components for patches is addressed in Section 4. We describe our experiences in Section 5. Related work is discussed in Section 6, and we conclude in Section 7.

Fig. 1. The Nix store

2 Motivation

2.1 The Nix Deployment System

Nix is a system for software deployment [3, 4]. Its job is to build components, support their deployment to client machines, and manage the components on those clients. It has several important features:

- It supports component variability, allowing arbitrary side-by-side existence of multiple versions and variants (preventing the "DLL Hell"). Users or processes can have different "views" on the set of installed components.
- It helps ensure complete dependency specifications. Typical Unix package management systems such as RPM [6] require developers to specify their component's dependencies on other components. However, there is no assurance that such a specification is complete. This leads to incomplete deployment, i.e., references to missing components at run-time.
- It ensures consistency between components; e.g., that they are not removed from the system if they are required by other installed components.
- Components are built from a flexible component specification language — *Nix expressions* — supporting the concise specification of variability in components, such as domain features and dependencies.
- It supports binary deployment of components as an essentially transparent optimisation of source deployment, as explained below.

The central idea in the Nix system is that every component is stored in isolation in the *Nix store*. The store is a designated part of the file system (typically /nix/store), each subdirectory of which contains a component. An example of a

```
{ stdenv, fetchurl, pkgconfig, gtk  # function arguments
, perl, zip, libIDL, libXi }:

assert libIDL.glib == gtk.glib;  # consistency requirement

stdenv.mkDerivation {  # the function result: a build action
  name = "firefox-1.0";

  builder = ./builder.sh;  # the build script
  src = fetchurl {  # the sources
    url = ftp://.../firefox/1.0/source/firefox-1.0-source.tar.bz2;
    md5 = "49c16a71f4de014ea471be81e46b1da8";
  };

  buildInputs = [pkgconfig gtk perl zip libIDL libXi];
}
```

Fig. 2. Nix expression for Firefox

number of Nix components on a Linux system is shown in Figure 1. The name of each component directory contains, apart from a symbolic identifier of the component such as firefox-1.0, a unique hexadecimal number which is a *cryptographic hash* of *all* inputs involved in building the component.

For instance, for the Firefox component, the inputs include the operating system and platform for which we are building (e.g., i686-linux), the C++ compiler, the GNU C library, the GTK widget library, the X11 windowing system client libraries, the script that builds the component, the full sources of the component, and so on.

The arrows in Figure 1 denote file system references between components (note that it shows only a subset of Firefox's run-time dependencies; in reality Firefox has many more). For instance, the Firefox binary contains in its executable image the full path of the C and GTK libraries to be used at run-time (these are specified in the "RPATH" of Unix ELF executables [7]). That is, while those libraries are dynamically loaded at run-time, their locations are hard-coded into the components at build-time.

Nix components are built from *Nix expressions*, which is a simple functional language, a model well-suited for specifying components. Figure 2 shows the Nix expression for the Firefox component. This is actually a *function*[1] that accepts a number of arguments (e.g., gtk) and returns a *derivation*, which is Nix-speak for a component build action[2]. Likewise, there are Nix expressions specifying how to build the GNU C library (glibc), GTK, etc., when called with the appropriate

---

[1] I.e., it specifies *requires* interfaces of the component [2].
[2] A more complete description of the Nix expression language is given in [4] and in the Nix manual [8].

```
rec {

  firefox = (import ../applications/firefox) {  # function call
    inherit fetchurl stdenv pkgconfig gtk ...;  # arguments
  };

  gtk = (import ../development/libraries/gtk) {
    inherit fetchurl stdenv;
  };

  fetchurl = ...;
  stdenv = ...;
}
```

Fig. 3. Nix expression composing Firefox, GTK, etc.

arguments. Since these are all functions, to instantiate actual components, they must be called (i.e., *composed*). This is done in the Nix expression in Figure 3. When we evaluate the firefox attribute thus defined, Nix will recursively build all components insofar as they are not already present on the system.

As stated above, for each component Nix computes its path name in the Nix store by hashing all inputs used to build it. This is a recursive process: if the hash of any direct or indirect dependency of a component changes, the hash of the component itself will also change (since the hashes are 128-bit MD5 hashes, the chances of a hash collision are very slight indeed). For instance, if in the specification of the GTK component we change the source file from which it is built from release 2.2.4 to 2.4.13, the hash of Firefox will also change (Figure 4). Hence, both GTK and Firefox will be rebuilt.

Note that as we do so, any previous versions of GTK and Firefox are left untouched since they reside in a different location in the file system. This has important advantages. First, the previous installation of Firefox is unaffected. For instance, if the new GTK is not quite backwards compatible, it will not break the installed Firefox. Nix never relies on any notion of component interface compatibility, since those in practice cannot be trusted to completely specify the behaviour of the component. Only the implementation constitutes a full specification. Second, different users or processes can easily have different "activated" components (essentially, by having, for instance, different versions of Firefox in their PATH environment variables). Third, it enables efficient roll-back to previous versions if necessary, since the old version is still available until it is removed by running the Nix *garbage collector*.

Nix, as described above, implements a source deployment model (as do, e.g., FreeBSD [9] and Gentoo Linux [10]). That is, to deploy a component, we deploy to the clients the Nix expressions that describe how to build from source the component and its dependencies. While this is convenient for the developer, it is generally not appropriate for end-users since builds can consume substantial

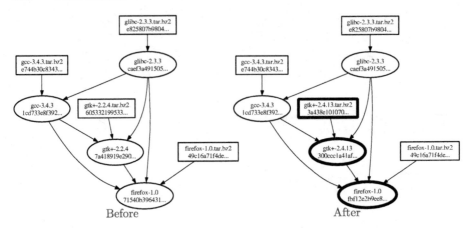

Fig. 4. Hash change propagation in the build-time dependency graph of the Firefox component after a GTK upgrade. Square nodes denote sources, with cryptographic hashes of the contents. Round nodes denote components, with store path hashes. Arrows indicate build-time dependencies.

CPU, disk, and network resources. Also, it is inappropriate for closed source products. However, Nix can almost *transparently* support binary deployment thanks to the hashing scheme through its *substitute* mechanism, which works as follows. The component developer or distributor builds the Nix expression and uploads the resulting components to a repository accessible by the clients, typically a web server. A *manifest* on the server describes the available pre-built components, e.g,

```
{ StorePath: /nix/store/075931820cae...-firefox-1.0
  NarURL: http://server/075931820cae...-firefox-1.0.nar.bz2
  Size: 11480169 }
```

Then, when the client attempts to build the Nix expression, Nix will see that the path /nix/store/075931820cae...-firefox-1.0 that it wants to build is already present on the server. It will download the component from the URL given in the manifest and unpack it. On the other hand, if the path that it wants to build is not present on the server, if will fall back to building it from source, if possible.

2.2 Installing Upgrades

This paper is concerned with the efficient distribution of upgrades to components. Examples include the deployment of a security or other fix for Firefox or Glibc, or an ordinary version upgrade, such as Firefox 0.9 being updated to 1.0.

In conventional deployment models, upgrades are deployed "destructively". For instance, in RPM [6], we would just install a new Glibc RPM package that overwrites the old one. This however prevents side-by-side deployment of variants (what if some component *needs* the old Glibc because it is incompatible with the new one?), makes roll-backs much harder (essential in server environments), and is generally bad from a SCM perspective (since it becomes much harder to identify the current configuration). Also, such destructive upgrades only work with dynamic linking and other late-binding techniques; if the component has been statically linked into other components at build time, we must identify all affected components and upgrade them as well. This was for instance a major problem when a security bug was discovered in the ubiquitous Zlib compression library [11].

In Nix, on the other hand, as shown in Figure 4, the change to a component affects the hashes of all components that depend on it. That is, Nix has a *purely functional deployment model*: the "value" (i.e., file system contents) of a component only depends on the inputs used to build it, and never changes afterwards. This has two effects. First, all affected components must be rebuilt. This is exactly right, since the change to the dependencies may of course affect the derivates. This is the case even if interfaces haven't changed, e.g., in the case of statically linked libraries, smart cross-module inlining, changes to the compiler affecting the binary interface, and so on.

The second effect is that *all affected components must be re-deployed to the clients*, i.e., the clients must download and install each affected component. This is the scalability issue that this paper addresses. For instance, if we want to deploy a 100-byte bug fix to Glibc, almost all components in the system must be downloaded again, since at the very least the RPATHs of dependent binaries will have changed to point at the new Glibc. Depending on network characteristics, this can take many hours even on fast connections. Note that this is much worse than the first effect (having to rebuild the components), since that can be done centralised and only needs to be done once. The re-deployment, on the other hand, must be done for each client.

So why don't we just destructively update components in place, as is done in other deployment systems, e.g., by overwriting the old Glibc with the new one? The reason is that this violates the crucial deployment invariant that the hash of a path uniquely describes the component. (This is similar to allowing assignments in purely functional programming languages such as Haskell [12].) From a configuration management perspective, the hashes identify the configuration of the components, and destructive updates remove the ability to identify what we have on our system. Also, it destroys the component isolation property, i.e., that an upgrade to one component cannot cause the failure to another component. If an upgrade is not entirely backwards compatible, this no longer holds.

One might ask whether the relative difficulty (in terms of hardware resources, not developer or user effort) of deploying upgrades doesn't show that Nix is unsuitable for large-scale software deployment. However, Nix's advantages in supporting side-by-side variability, correct dependency, atomic rollbacks, and so on, in the face of a quasi-component model (i.e., the huge base of existing Unix packages) not designed to support those features, makes it compelling to seek a solution to the upgrade deployment problem within the Nix framework. The remainder of this paper shows such a solution.

3   Binary Patch Deployment

The previous section showed the explosion in the number of components to be re-deployed in case of an update to a fundamental component such as Glibc. In this section we solve this problem by transparently deploying *binary patches* between component releases. For instance, if a bug fix to Glibc induces a switch from /nix/store/219a...-glibc-2.3.3 to /nix/store/ff9c...-glibc-2.3.3p1, then we compute the delta (the *binary patch*) between the contents of those paths and make the patch available to clients. We also do this for all components depending on it. Subsequently the clients can apply those patches to the old version to produce the new version. As we shall see in Section 5, patches for components affected by a change to a dependency are generally very small.

A binary patch describes a set of edit operations that transforms a *base* component stored at path X in the Nix store into a *target* component stored at path Y. Thus, if a client needs path Y *and* it has path X already installed, then it can speed up the installation of Y by downloading the patch from X to Y, copy X to Y in the Nix store, and finally apply the patch to Y.

This fits nicely into Nix's substitute mechanism used to implement trans-parent binary deployment. We just extend its download capabilities: rather than doing a full download, if a patch is available, we download that instead. Manifests can specify the availability of patches. For instance,

```
patch {
    StorePath: /nix/store/5bfd71c253db...-firefox-1.0
    NarURL: http://server/52c036147222...-firefox-1.0-to-1.0.nar-bsdiff
    Size: 357
    BasePath: /nix/store/075931820cae...-firefox-1.0
}
```

describes a 357-byte patch from the Firefox component shown in the previous section (stored at BasePath) to a new one (stored at StorePath) induced by a Glibc upgrade. If a patch is not available, or if the base component is not installed, we fall back to a full download of the new component; or even a local build if no download is available.

3.1   Binary Patch Creation

There are many off-the-shelf algorithms and implementations to compute binary deltas between two arbitrary files. We used the bsdiff utility [13] because it produced the smallest patches compared to others (see Section 6).

However, the components in the Nix store are arbitrary directory trees. How do we produce deltas between directories trees? A "simple" solution would be to compute deltas between corresponding regular files (i.e., with the same relative path in the components) and distribute all deltas together. The full contents of all new files in the target should also be added, as well as a list describing file deletions, changes to symlink contents, etc. Files not listed would be assumed to be unchanged.

This method is both complex and has the severe problem of not following renames. For instance, the Firefox component stores most of its files in a subdirectory lib/firefox-*version*. The method described above would fail to patch, e.g., lib/firefox-0.9/libmozjs.so into lib/firefox-1.0/libmozjs.so since the path names do not correspond; rather, the latter file would be stored in full in the patch. Hence, patching would not be very effective in the presence of renames.

There is however a much simpler and more effective solution: we take the patch between *archive files* of the components. For instance, we can produce an uncompressed Zip or Tar file[3] containing the full contents of the directory trees of the two components, and compute the binary delta between those files. This automatically takes renames, deletions, file type changes, etc. into account, since these are just simple changes within the archive files. To apply a patch, a client must also create an archive of the base component, apply the binary patch to it, and unpack the resulting archive into the target path.

For instance, for the example above, the base archive will at some point contain a filename lib/firefox-0.9/libmozjs.so followed by the contents of that file, while the target archive will contain a filename lib/firefox-1.0/libmozjs.so followed by its contents, which may or may not be the same as the original file. The binary delta algorithm will just emit an edit operation that changes the first file name into the second, followed by the appropriate edit operations for the file contents. It does not matter whether the position of the file in the archive has changed: contrary to delta algorithms like the standard diff tool, bsdiff can handle re-ordering of the data.

3.2   Patch Chaining

It is generally infeasible to produce patches between every pair of releases of a set of components. The number of patches would be $O(n^2m)$, where n is the number of releases and m is the number of components. As an example, consider the *Nix Packages collection* (Nixpkgs). It is a set of existing Unix components ranging from GCC to Firefox. Pre-releases of Nixpkgs are made on every commit to its version management repository, which typically is several times a day. Developers and users can stay up-to-date by subscribing to a *channel*, which is just a convenience mechanism for updating Nix expressions on client machines.

Since pre-releases appear so often, we cannot feasibly produce patches between each pair of pre-releases. So as a general policy we only produce patches between immediately succeeding pre-releases. For instance, given releases 0.7pre1899, 0.7pre1928 and 0.7pre1931, we produce patches between 0.7pre1899 and 0.7pre1928, and between 0.7pre1928 and 0.7pre1931. This creates a problem, however: suppose that a user has Firefox from 0.7pre1899 installed, and Firefox

---

[3] In actuality, we produce a "Nar file", which is Nix's archive file format. Nar files, unlike Tar or Zip files, have a *canonical form*: there is a single, uniquely defined archive for the contents of a directory. For instance, directory entries are always stored in the same order. This minimises the chances of a patch failing to apply due to version differences in the archiving tool.

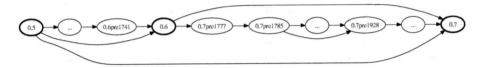

Fig. 5. Patch set created between Nixpkgs releases. Arrows indicate the existence of a patch set.

changed in both succeeding releases, then there would be no patch that brings the user up-to-date.

The solution is to automatically *chain* patches, i.e., using a *series* of available patches $X_1 \to \ldots \to X_n \to Y$ to produce path Y. In the example above, we have a Firefox component installed that can be used as the base path to a patch in the 0.7pre1928 release, to produce a component that can in turn serve as a base path to a patch in the 0.7pre1931 release.

However, such patch sequences can eventually become so large that they approach, or become larger than, full downloads. In that case we can "short-circuit" the sequence by adding patches between additional releases. Figure 5 shows an example sequence of patches between releases thus formed. Here, patch sets are produced by directly succeeding pre-releases, and between any successive stable releases. An additional "short-circuit" patch set between 0.7pre1785 and 0.7pre1928 was also made.

In the presence of patch sets between arbitrary releases, it is not directly obvious which sequence of patches or full downloads is optimal. To be fully general, the Nix substitute downloader runs a shortest path algorithm on a directed acyclic graph that, intuitively, represents components already installed, available patches between components, and available full downloads of components. Formally, the graph is defined as follows:

- The nodes are the store paths for which pre-built binaries are available on the server, either as full downloads or as patches, plus any store paths that serve as bases to patches. There is also a special **start** node.
- There are three types of edges:
  - *Patch edges* between store paths that represent available patches. The edge weight is the size of the patch (in bytes).
  - *Full download edges* from **start** to a store path for which we have a full download available. The edge weight is the size of full download.
  - *Free edges* from **start** to a store path representing that a store path is already available on the system. The edge weight is 0.

We then find the shortest path between **start** and the path of the requested component using Dijkstra's shortest path algorithm. This method can find any of the following:

- A sequence of patches transforming an already installed component into the requested component.
- A full download of the requested component.

- A full download of some component X which is then transformed using a sequence of patches into the requested component. Generally, this will be longer than immediately doing a full download of the requested component, but this allows one to make *only* patches available for upgrades.

Above, edge weight was defined as the size in bytes of downloads. We could take other factors into account, such as protocol/network overhead per download, the CPU resources necessary to apply patches, and so on. For instance, on a reasonably fast connection, a full download might be preferable over a long sequence of patches even if the combined byte count of those patches is less than the full download.

4 Base Selection

To deploy an upgrade, we have to produce patches between "corresponding" components. This is intuitively simple: for instance, to deploy a Glibc upgrade, we have to produce patches between the old Glibc and the new one, but also between the components depending on it, e.g., between the old Firefox and the new one. However, a complication is that the dependency graphs might not be isomorphic. For instance, components may have been removed or added, dependencies moved, component names changed (e.g., Phoenix to Firebird to Firefox), and so on. Also, even disregarding component renames, simply matching by name is insufficient because there may be multiple component instances with the same name (e.g., builds for different platforms).

The *base selection problem* is the problem, when deploying a set of target components $\mathbb{Y}$, of selecting from a set of base components $\mathbb{X}$ a set of patches $(X, Y) \in (\mathbb{X} \times \mathbb{Y})$ such that the probability of the Xs being present on the clients is maximised *within* certain resource constraints.

Clearly, we could produce patches between all Xs and Ys. This policy is "optimal" in the sense that the client would always be able to select the absolutely shortest sequence of patches. However, it is infeasible in terms of time and space since producing a patch takes a non-negligible amount of time, and most such patches will be large since they will be between unrelated components (for instance, patching Acrobat Reader into Firefox is obviously inefficient).

Therefore, we need to select some subset of $(\mathbb{X} \times \mathbb{Y})$. The solution currently implemented is heuristical: we use a number of properties of the components to guess whether they "match" (i.e., are conceptually the "same" component). Indeed, the selection problem seems inherently heuristical for two reasons. First, there can be arbitrary changes between releases. Second, we cannot feasibly produce all patches to select the "best" according to some objective criterion.

Possible heuristics include the following:

- *Same component name.* This is clearly one of the simplest and most effective criteria. However, there is a complication: there can be multiple components with the same name. For instance, Nixpkgs contains the GNU C Compiler gcc at several levels in the dependency graph (due to bootstrapping). Also, it contains two components called firefox — one is the "real thing", the other is a shell script wrapper around the first to enable some plugins. Finally, Nixpkgs contains the same components for multiple platforms.

– The *weighted number of uses* can be used to disambiguate between components at different bootstrapping levels such as GCC mentioned above, or disambiguate between certain variants of a component. It is defined for a component at path p as follows:

$$w(p) = \sum_{q \in \text{users}(p)} \frac{1}{r^{d(q,p)}}$$

where users(p) is the set of components from which p is reachable in the build-time dependency graph, i.e., the components that are directly or indirectly dependent on p; where $d(q,p)$ is the unweighted distance from component q to p in the build-time dependency graph; and where $r \geq 1$ is an empirically determined value that causes less weight to be given to "distant" dependencies than to "nearby" dependencies.

For instance, in the Nixpkgs dependency graph, there is a "bootstrap" GCC and a "final" GCC, the former being used to compile the latter, and the latter being used to compile almost all other packages. If we were to take the unweighted number of uses ($r = 1$), then the bootstrap GCC would have a slightly higher number of uses than the final GCC (since any component using the latter is indirectly dependent on the former), but the difference is too small for disambiguation — such a difference could also be caused by the addition or removal of dependent components. However, if we take, e.g., $r = 2$, then the weighted number of uses for the final GCC will be almost twice as large. This is because the bootstrap GCC is at least one step further away in the dependency graph from the majority of components, thus halving their contribution to its $w(p)$.

Thus, if the ratio between $w(p)$ and $w(q)$ is greater than some empirically determined value k, then components p and q are considered unrelated, and no patch between them is produced. A good value for k would be around 2, e.g., $k = 1.9$.

– *Size* of the component. If the ratio between the sizes of two components differs more than some value l, then the components are considered unrelated. A typical value would be $l = 3$; even if components differing in size by a factor of 3 *are* related, then patching is unlikely to be effectual. This trivial heuristic can disambiguate between the two Firefox components mentioned above, since the wrapper script component is much smaller than the real Firefox component.

– *Platform.* In general, it is pointless to create a patch between components for different platforms (e.g., Linux and Mac OS X), since it is unlikely that a client has components for a different platform installed.

5   Experience

We have implemented the binary patch deployment scheme described above in the Nix system, and used it to produce patches between 50 subsequent (pre-) releases of the Nix Packages collection[4]. Base components were selected on the basis of matching names, using the size and weighted number of uses heuristics described in the previous section to disambiguate between a number of components with equal names. The use of patches is automatic and completely transparent to users; an upgrade action in Nix uses (a sequence of) patches if available and applicable, and falls back to full downloads otherwise. In this section we provide some data to show that the patching scheme succeeds in its main goal, i.e., reducing network bandwidth consumption in the face of updates to fundamental components such as Glibc or GCC to an "acceptable" level.

We computed for each pair of subsequent releases how large an upgrade using *full downloads* of changed components would be, versus downloading *patches* to changed components. Also, the average and median sizes of each patch for the changed components (or full download, if no patch was possible) were computed. New top-level components (e.g., applications introduced in the new release) were disregarded. Table 1 summarises the results for a number of selected releases, representing various types of upgrades. File sizes are in bytes unless specified otherwise. Omitted releases were typically upgrades of single leaf components such as applications. An example is the Firefox upgrade in revision 0.6pre1702.

Release	Comps. changed	Full size	Total patch size	Savings	Avg. patch size	Median patch size	Remarks
0.6pre1069	27	31.6M	162K	99.5%	6172	898	X11 client libraries update
0.6pre1489	147	180M	71M	**60.5%**	495K	81K	Glibc 2.3.2 → 2.3.3, GCC 3.3.3 → 3.4.2, many other changes[5]
0.6pre1538	147	176.7M	364K	99.8%	2536	509	Standard build environment changes
0.6pre1542	1	9.3M	67K	99.3%	67K	67K	Firefox extensions/profiles bug fix
0.6pre1672	26	38.0M	562K	98.6%	22155	6475	GTK updates
0.6pre1702	3	11.0M	190K	98.3%	63K	234K	Firefox 1.0rc1 → 1.0rc2
0.7pre1820	154	188.6M	598K	99.7%	3981	446	Glibc loadlocale bug fix
0.7pre1931	1	1164K	45K	96.1%	45K	45K	Subversion 1.1.1 → 1.1.2
0.7pre1977	153	196.3M	743K	99.6%	4977	440	Glibc UTF-8 locales patch
0.7pre1980	154	197.2M	3748K	98.1%	24924	974	GCC 3.4.2 → 3.4.3

Table 1. Statistics for patch sets between selected Nixpkgs releases and their immediate predecessors

---

[4] The releases are available at http://catamaran.labs.cs.uu.nl/dist/nix, and the Nix expressions from which they were generated at
https://svn.cs.uu.nl:12443/viewcvs/trace/nixpkgs/trunk/.

Efficient upgrades or patches to fundamental components are the main goal of this paper. For instance, release 0.7pre1980 upgraded the GNU C Compiler used to build all other components, while releases 0.7pre1820 and 0.7pre1977 provided bug fixes to the GNU C Library, also used at build-time and run-time by all other components. The patches resulting from the Glibc changes in particular are tiny: the median patch size is around 440 bytes. This is because such patches generally only need to modify the RPATH in executable and shared libraries. The average is higher (around 4K) because a handful of applications and libraries statically link against Glibc components. Still, the *total* size of the patches for all components is only 598K and 743K, respectively — a fairly trivial size even on slow modem connections.

On the other hand, release 0.6pre1489 is not small at all — the patch savings are only 60.5%. However, this release contained many significant changes. In particular, there was a major upgrade to GCC, with important changes to the generated code in all components. In general, compilers should not be switched lightly. (If *individual* components need an upgraded version, e.g., to fix a code generation bug, that is no problem: Nix expressions, being a functional language, can easily express that different components must be built with different compilers.) Minor compiler upgrades need not be a problem; release 0.7pre1980, which featured a minor upgrade to GCC, has a 98.1% patch effectiveness.

Patch generation is a relatively slow process. For example, the generation of the patch set for release 0.7pre1820 took 49 minutes on a 3.2 GHz Pentium 4 machine with 1 GB of RAM running Linux 2.4.26. The bsdiff program also needs a large amount of memory; its documentation recommends a working set of at least 8 times the base file. For a large component such as Glibc, which takes 46M of disk space, this works out to 368M of RAM.

A final point not addressed previously is the disk space consumption of upgrades. A change to a component such as Glibc will still cause every component to be duplicated on disk, even if they do no longer have to be downloaded in full. However, after an upgrade, a user can run the Nix garbage collector that safely and automatically removes unused components. Nonetheless, as an optimisation, we observe that many files in those components will be exactly the same (e.g., header files, scripts, documentation, JAR files). Therefore, we implemented a tool that "optimises" the Nix store by finding all identical regular files in the store, and replacing them with hard links [14] to a single copy. On typical Nix stores (i.e., subject to normal evolution over a period of time) this saved between 15–30% of disk space. While this is useful, it is not an order of complexity change as is the case with the amount of bandwidth saved using patches.

6   Related Work

Binary patching has a long history, going back to manual patching of binaries on mainframes in the 1960s, where it was often a more efficient method of fixing bugs than recompiling from source. Binary patching has been available in

---

[5] First release since 0.6pre1398.

commercial patch tools such as .RTPatch, and interactive installer tools such as InstallShield. Most Unix binary package managers only support upgrades through full downloads (SuSE's "Patch RPMs" include full copies of all changed files). Microsoft recently introduced binary patching in Windows XP Service Pack 2 as a method to speed up bug fix deployment [15].

A method for automatically computing and distributing binary patches between FreeBSD releases is described in [16]. It addresses the additional complication that FreeBSD systems are often built from source, and the resulting binaries can differ even if the sources are the same, for instance, due to timestamps being stored in files. In the Nix patching scheme we guard against this possibility by providing the MD5 hash of the archive to which the patch applies. If it does not apply, we fall back to a full download. In general, however, this situation does not occur because patches are obtained from the same source as the original binaries.

In Nix, the use of patches is completely hidden from users, who only observe it as a speed increase. In general, deployment methods often require users to figure out what files to download to install an upgrade (e.g., hotfixes in Windows). Also, if sequences of patches are required, these must be applied manually by the user, unless the distributor has consolidated them into a single patch. The creation of patches is often a manual and error-prone process, e.g., figuring out what components to redeploy as a result of a security bug like [11]. In our approach, this determination is automatic.

The bsdiff program [13] that Nix uses to generate patches is based on the *qsufsort* algorithm [17]. In our experience bsdiff outperformed methods such as ZDelta [18] and VDelta [19, 20], but a comparison of delta algorithms is beyond the scope of this paper. An overview of some delta algorithms is given in [19].

The problem of keeping derivates consistent with sources and dependency graph specifications occurs in all build systems, e.g., Make [5]. To ensure correctness, such systems must rebuild all dependent objects if some source changes. If a source is fundamental, then a large number of build actions may be necessary. So this problem is not unique in any way to Nix. However, the problems of build systems affect developers, not end users, while Nix is a *deployment* system first and foremost. This is why it is important to ensure that end users are not affected by the use of a strict update propagation semantics.

7 Conclusion

In a previous ICSE paper [3] we introduced the purely functional deployment model underlying Nix, where components are stored in isolation in paths in the file system that contain a hash of all build-time inputs used to construct the component, and argued that this has substantial advantages for the safe deployment of software. However, as we noted then, the downside to such a model is that updates to fundamental components require all components depending on them to be updated also. In this paper we have shown that using binary patch deployment, Nix's functional deployment model can in fact efficiently and transparently support such operations.

Acknowledgements This research was supported by CIBIT | SERC and the NWO Jacquard program. The author would like to thank Martin Bravenboer and Eelco Visser for commenting on drafts of this paper.

References

[1] Carzaniga, A., Fuggetta, A., Hall, R.S., Heimbigner, D., van der Hoek, A., Wolf, A.L.: A characterization framework for software deployment technologies. Technical Report CU-CS-857-98, Dept. of Computer Science, University of Colorado (1998)

[2] Szyperski, C.: Component technology—what, where, and how? In: Proceedings of the 25th International Conference on Software Engineering (ICSE 2003). (2003) 684–693

[3] Dolstra, E., Visser, E., de Jonge, M.: Imposing a memory management discipline on software deployment. In: Proceedings of the 26th International Conference on Software Engineering (ICSE 2004), IEEE Computer Society (2004) 583–592

[4] Dolstra, E., de Jonge, M., Visser, E.: Nix: A safe and policy-free system for software deployment. In Damon, L., ed.: 18th Large Installation System Administration Conference (LISA '04), Atlanta, Georgia, USA, USENIX (2004) 79–92

[5] Feldman, S.I.: Make—a program for maintaining computer programs. Software—Practice and Experience **9** (1979) 255–65

[6] Foster-Johnson, E.: Red Hat RPM Guide. John Wiley and Sons (2003)

[7] TIS Committee: Tool Interface Specification (TIS) Executable and Linking Format (ELF) Specification, Version 1.2. http://www.x86.org/ftp/manuals/tools/elf.pdf (1995)

[8] TraCE Project: Nix deployment system. http://www.cs.uu.nl/groups/ST/Trace/Nix (2005)

[9] FreeBSD Project: FreeBSD Ports Collection. http://www.freebsd.org/ports/ (2005)

[10] Gentoo Project: Gentoo Linux. http://www.gentoo.org/ (2005)

[11] Adler, M., Gailly, J.: Zlib advisory 2002-03-11. http://www.gzip.org/zlib/advisory-2002-03-11.txt (2002)

[12] Peyton Jones, S., ed.: Haskell 98 Language and Libraries: The Revised Report. Cambridge University Press (2004)

[13] Percival, C.: Binary diff/patch utility. http://www.daemonology.net/bsdiff/ (2003)

[14] Stevens, W.R.: Advanced Programming in the UNIX Environment. Addison-Wesley (1993)

[15] Microsoft Corporation: Binary delta compression. Whitepaper (2002)

[16] Percival, C.: An automated binary security update system for FreeBSD. In: Proceedings of BSDCON '03, USENIX (2003)

[17] Larsson, N.J., Sadakane, K.: Faster suffix sorting. Technical Report LU-CS-TR-99-214, Lund University (1999)

[18] Trendafilov, D., Memon, N., Suel, T.: zdelta: An efficient delta compression tool. Technical Report TR-CIS-2002-02, Polytechnic University (2002)

[19] Hunt, J.J., Vo, K.P., Tichy, W.F.: Delta algorithms: An empirical analysis. ACM Transactions on Software Engineering and Methodology **7** (1998) 192–214

[20] Korn, D., Vo, K.: vdelta: Differencing and compression. In Krishnamurthy, B., ed.: Practical Reusable UNIX Software. John Wiley & Sons (1995)

Real-Time Scheduling Techniques for Implementation Synthesis from Component-Based Software Models

Zonghua Gu and Zhimin He

Dept. of Computer Science
University of Virginia
Charlottesville, VA 22903, USA
{zg4v, zh5f}@cs.virginia.edu

Abstract. We consider a class of component-based software models with interaction style of buffered asynchronous message passing between components with ports, represented by UML-RT. After building a logical software model, it is necessary to synthesize a multi-threaded implementation that runs on a given target hardware platform and satisfies timing constraints. Commercial code generators generate functional code, but ignore concurrency and timing issues. In this paper, we compare alternative multi-threading strategies for implementation synthesis from this class of software models, and describe real-time scheduling analysis techniques that are useful during design space exploration for implementation synthesis. We use the elevator control application to illustrate our analysis techniques.

1 Introduction

We consider a class of component-based software models with interaction style of buffered asynchronous message passing between components with ports. This programming style is prevalent in development of event-driven real-time software. One representative example is UML-RT, a UML Profile for an architecture description language based on Real-Time Object-Oriented Modeling (ROOM) [1], supported by CASE Tools from IBM Rational [2]. Another example is the Quantum Framework [3], which advocates this programming style without the need for expensive CASE tools. It has a number of benefits from a software engineering perspective, such as modularity, encapsulation, decoupling of interactions, etc. This programming style is ideally combined with event-driven middleware like CORBA Event Service [4] as the application's communication substrate. One real-world application example is the Avionics Mission Computing software [5].

After building a logical software model, it is necessary to synthesize a multi-threaded implementation that runs on a given target hardware platform and satisfies timing constraints. Commercial code generators, e.g., the code generator for UML-RT, generate functional code, but ignore concurrency and timing

G.T. Heineman et al. (Eds.): CBSE 2005, LNCS 3489, pp. 235–250, 2005.

issues. It is up to the designer to choose a multi-threading strategy to ensure satisfaction of system timing constraints. In this paper, we compare alternative multi-threading strategies for implementation synthesis from this class of software models, and describe real-time scheduling techniques that are useful during design space exploration for implementation synthesis.

We use UML-RT as a representative example in the following discussions, but note that the analysis techniques discussed in this paper have much wider applicability to the general class of component-based software models with interaction style of buffered asynchronous message passing between components with ports.

This paper is structured as follows: section 2 discusses different implementation alternatives for UML-RT models. Section 3 discusses real-time scheduling analysis for the native runtime model of UML-RT. Section 4 uses the elevator control application to illustrate our analysis technique. Section 5 discusses pros and cons of different multi-threading strategies; Section 6 discusses related work, and section 7 draws conclusions.

2   Multi-threading Strategies for UML-RT Models

We provide a brief introduction to the basic concepts of UML-RT. A *capsule* is an active object with its own logical thread of control. *In the context of this paper, capsules are synonymous with components.* Capsules communicate with each other through sending and receiving messages asynchronously through *ports. Connectors* represent message passing connections between ports. The explicit representation of port and connectors enable construction of architectural models from a collection of capsules.

The runtime model of UML-RT follows the *Run-To-Completion* (RTC) semantics for each capsule, that is, once triggered by a message at its input port, the capsule must execute the triggered action to completion before processing the next message. RTC is useful for reducing the number of concurrency bugs when a capsule can take part in multiple end-to-end scenarios. Messages can be assigned priorities and queued in priority order instead of FIFO order. Each OS thread processes incoming messages for the capsules assigned to it in a *priority-based, non-preemptive* manner, consistent with the RTC semantics. However, there can be preemptions between different threads in a multi-threaded system, that is, a capsule executing in the context of a higher-priority thread can preempt another capsule executing in a lower-priority thread.

It is important to distinguish between the concepts of design-level concurrency and implementation-level concurrency [6]. At the design level, each capsule conceptually contains its own logical thread of execution, but each logical thread is not necessarily mapped into an OS thread at the implementation level. Although it is possible for each capsule to have its own OS thread, it may incur too much context-switching overhead if there are a large number of capsules. There are a number of possible multi-threading strategies for implementation synthesis, as discussed below.

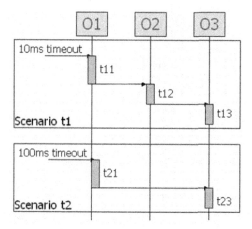

Fig. 1. An example application scenario.

Suppose we have a logical UML-RT model as shown in Figure 1, consisting of three capsules O_1, O_2, O_3 and two end-to-end scenarios t_1, t_2. Each scenario consists of multiple subtasks, which are triggered actions executed by the capsules. Scenario t_1 is initially triggered by a periodic timeout message with period 10 ms that triggers an action t_{11} in capsule O_1, which in turn sends a message to capsule O_2 and triggers action t_{12} in O_2. Finally, O_2 sends a message to O_3 and triggers action t_{13}. We can view this scenario as a logical end-to-end thread t_1 consisting of three precedence-constrained subtasks t_{11}, t_{12} and t_{13}. Similarly, scenario t_2 is an end-to-end thread consisting of two subtasks t_{21} and t_{23}, triggered by a 100ms periodic timeout message. Given this logical model, how to implement it on a multi-threaded real-time operating system?

Despite the word *Real-Time* in its name, the designers of the UML-RT have not put much emphasis on real-time issues when implementing a logical model on the target platform. The default runtime model is single-threaded, that is, all capsules are mapped into the same thread of execution. It is desirable to introduce more parallelism and concurrency into the system to improve predictability, by adopting a multi-threaded execution architecture. Commercial code generators for UML-RT, e.g., that from IBM Rational, provide options for creating multiple threads, each containing one or more capsules. Each thread is assigned a fixed priority. We call this the *native runtime model* of UML-RT. Some authors have proposed alternative runtime models, as discussed below.

1. **Capsule-Based Multi-threading, Scenario-Based Priority-Assignment (CMSP)** This is proposed by Saksena in [6]. As shown in Figure 2, one or more capsules are grouped into the same thread. Priorities are associated with the end-to-end scenarios, and the thread priorities are adjusted dynamically to maintain a uniform priority across each application scenario.
2. **Scenario-Based Multi-Threading, Scenario-Based Priority-Assignment (SMSP)** This is proposed by Saehwa Kim in [7]. As shown in Figure 3,

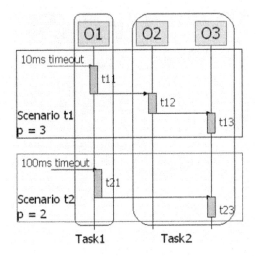

Fig. 2. *Capsule-Based Multi-threading, Scenario-Based Priority-Assignment* (CMSP). Note that we use the words *thread* and *task* interchangeably in this paper.

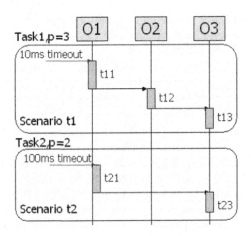

Fig. 3. *Capsule-Based Multi-Threading, Scenario-Based Priority-Assignment* (SMSP).

each application scenario is mapped into a separate thread with uniform priority.

3. **Capsule-Based Multi-threading, Capsule-Based Priority-Assignment (CMCP)** As shown in Figure 4, one or more capsules are grouped into a thread with uniform priority. This is the native runtime model of UML-RT. The figure only shows one of many possibilities for grouping cap-

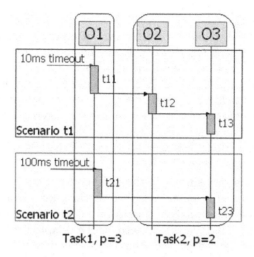

Fig. 4. *Capsule-Based Multi-threading, Capsule-Based Priority-Assignment* (CMCP).

sules into threads. Two extreme cases are mapping all capsules into a single thread, or mapping each capsule into its own thread.

4. **Scenario-Based Multi-Threading, Capsule-Based Priority-Assignment (SMCP)** Even though this combination is conceptually possible, we do not know of any real applications that adopt it, so we will not consider it further.

Rate Monotonic Analysis (RMA) [8] is a well-known analysis technique for determining schedulability of a set of real-time tasks/threads, which must satisfy the following set of assumptions: each task must

1. be preemptively scheduled.
2. be independent.
3. be periodic.
4. have bounded *Worst-Case Execution Time* (WCET).
5. have uniform, static priority.

For scenario-based priority assignment, RMA assumptions are satisfied since each end-to-end scenario can be viewed as a task with uniform, static priority. But for capsule-based priority assignment, RMA assumptions are not satisfied, since each end-to-end task consists of multiple subtasks of varying priority. We describe real-time scheduling analysis techniques for this situation in the next section.

3   Real-Time Scheduling Techniques for CMCP

Consider a UML-RT model consisting of m capsules $O_1, O_2, \ldots, O_m$, and n end-to-end scenarios, where each scenario is mapped into an *end-to-end virtual thread*, forming the taskset $\tau_1, \tau_2, \ldots, \tau_n$. Here we use the word *virtual* to denote the fact that each end-to-end thread consists of multiple segments of subtasks distributed over different OS threads. Each end-to-end thread $\tau_i, i = 1, \ldots, n$ cuts through one or more capsules, and triggers an action within each capsule, forming a chain of subtasks $\tau_{i1}, \ldots, \tau_{im(i)}$. We use $O(\tau_{ij})$ to denote the capsule that the subtask τ_{ij} belongs to, and $PO(\tau_{ij})$ to denote the passive objects that τ_{ij} accesses. Each subtask τ_{ij} is actually an event-triggered action within a capsule $O(\tau_{ij})$. Each subtask τ_{ij} is characterized by parameters (C_{ij}, P_{ij}), where C_{ij} is its worst-case execution time, and P_{ij} is its priority. Each end-to-end thread τ_i has an end-to-end deadline D_i.

The task model is very similar to the task model of end-to-end threads with subtasks with varying priority, as described by Harbour, Klein, Lehoczky in [9]. We call the schedulability analysis algorithm introduced in [9] the *HKL algorithm*. However, the HKL algorithm needs to be adapted to take into account extra blocking time caused by the Run-To-Completion (RTC) semantics and shared data objects, in order to be applicable to UML-RT. A capsule may be involved in multiple sub-tasks within one end-to-end thread, or in multiple end-to-end threads. Due to RTC semantics, a subtask may suffer a blocking time equal to the largest execution time of other subtasks sharing the same capsule. Blocking time can also be caused by sharing of passive objects by multiple end-to-end threads. We do not model method invocations to passive objects as separate subtasks, since the passive object can be viewed as an extension of the invoking capsule, and inherits the thread and priority from it. But we do need to take into account blocking time caused by sharing of passive objects.

We first briefly describe the HKL algorithm. The *canonical form* of a task τ_i is a new task τ_i' with the same sequence of subtasks as τ_i, but with strictly increasing priorities. One example transformation is a task-chain consisting of subtasks with priority sequence (8, 2, 5, 4, 3). The canonical form of this task-chain consists of priority sequence (2, 2, 3, 3, 3). It was proven in [9] that transforming a task into its canonical form does not affect its schedulability. This result allows one to check whether the canonical form of τ_i is schedulable instead of τ_i itself, which simplifies the analysis considerably.

Now define $P_{min}(i)$ to be the minimum priority of all subtasks of τ_i. The next step is to classify all tasks $\tau_j, j \neq i$ according to their relative priority levels with respect to $P_{min}(i)$. For example, if the canonical form of τ_i consists of a single segment of priority 18, and τ_j consists of priority sequence (19, 10, 19, 10, 25, 10), or, (H, L, H, L, H, L), where H stands for "higher", and L stands for "lower". There are five types of tasks [10]:

- Type 1, or H^+, tasks, with all subtask priorities higher or equal to τ_i. These tasks can preempt task τ_i multiple times.
- Type 2, or $(H^+L^+)^+$, tasks. The first subtask has higher priority than τ_i, but it can only preempt τ_i once, since it is followed by subtasks of lower priority. Multiple tasks of this type may preempt τ_i, but only for the first segment. The non-first high-priority segments cause a *blocking* effect.

- Type 3, or $((HL)^+H)$, tasks. They differ from type 2 since they end with a high priority segment. We omit the discussion of type 3 tasks, since they do not appear in the example we consider here.
- Type 4, or $(L^+H^+)^+L^+$, tasks. The first subtask has lower priority than τ_i. Any one of the following subtask segments can have a *blocking* effect on τ_i, but only one such segment among all tasks of type 4 can have such a blocking effect.
- Type 5, or L^+, tasks. They have no effect on completion time of τ_i, and can be ignored.

Suppose we are calculating response time of task t_i. To simplify discussions, let's assume the canonical form of t_i consists of subtasks of uniform priority P_i. Define $H_1(i), H_2(i), H_4(i)$ to be the indices of all tasks of type 1, 2, 4, respectively.

For each $j \in H_2(i)$, let $B_2(i,j)$ be the execution time of the *first* H^+ segment of task τ_j. $B_2(i,j)$ denotes the *preemption* time caused by τ_j to τ_i. Then the total preemption time suffered by τ_i is:

$$B_2(i) = \sum_{j \in H_2(i)} B_2(i,j)$$

For each $j \in H_2(i) \cup H_4(i)$, let $B_4(i,j)$ be the *blocking* time suffered by τ_i, caused by all H^+ segments of task τ_j of type 4, and all *non-first* H^+ segments of task τ_j of type 2. Then the total blocking time suffered by τ_i is:

$$B_4(i) = \max(B_4(i,j) | j \in H_4(i) \cup H_2(i))$$

For a Type 2 task, only the first higher priority segment should be counted in $B_2(i)$, while the remaining segments should be counted in $B_4(i)$. Since multiple tasks of Type 2 can use their *first* segments to preempt t_i, therefore $B_2(i)$ is a *sum* of them; while only one task of Type 2 or 3 can use its *non-first* segment to preempt t_i, therefore $B_4(i)$ is a *max* of them.

In order to adapt the HKL algorithm to the UML-RT model, we need to take into account additional blocking time $B(i)$:

$$B(i) = \max(C_{kl} | \forall k, l, j, k! = i, O(\tau_{kl}) = O(\tau_{ij})) + \max(C_{mn} | \forall m, n, j, m! = i, P_{mn} < P_{ij}, PO(\tau_{mn}) \cap PO(\tau_{ij}) \neq \phi)$$

where the first term denotes blocking time caused by other subtasks sharing the same capsule with some subtask of thread i due to the RTC semantics, and the second term denotes blocking time caused by other lower-priority subtasks accessing shared passive objects.

The equation for calculating the *Worst-Case Response Time* (WCRT) of task τ_i is:

$$\text{WCRT}(i) = \text{WCET}(i) + B_2(i) + B_4(i) + B(i) + \sum_{j \in H_1(i)} \lceil \frac{\text{WCRT}(i)}{\text{Period}(j)} \rceil \cdot \text{WCET}(j)$$

$$(1)$$

where $\text{WCET}(i)$ is the worst-case execution time of τ_i, and $\text{Period}(j)$ is the execution period of τ_j if it is a periodic task, or the minimum inter-arrival time of execution triggers for τ_j if it is a sporadic task. The last term is preemption time caused by Type 1 tasks. τ_i is schedulable if the calculated $WCRT(i)$ is less than its deadline. This is a recursive equation that can be solved iteratively.

One limitation of our approach is that it can only handle linear task-chains, but not more general trees or graphs. It is an open research issue as to how to extend the HKL algorithm to deal with task-trees or graphs.

4   The Elevator Control Application Example

We use the elevator control system as an application example, taken from [11], assuming that it is implemented with UML-RT. (Note that the original example in [11] is not based on UML-RT.) Figure 5 shows the 8 capsules and 1 passive data object involved in a single-processor implementation. There are three end-to-end threads consisting of subtasks of varying priorities:

1. **Stop Elevator at Floor.** The elevator is equipped with arrival sensors that trigger an interrupt to the capsule *arrival sensors interface* when the elevator approaches a floor, which in turn sends a message *approaching floor* to the capsule *elevator controller*. The *elevator controller* invokes a synchronous method call on the passive data object *elevator status and plan* to determine whether the elevator should stop or not.
2. **Select Destination.** The user presses a button in the elevator to choose his/her destination, which triggers an interrupt to the capsule *elevator buttons interface*, which in turn sends a message *elevator request* to the capsule *elevator manager*. The *elevator manager* receives the message and records destination in the passive object *elevator status and plan*.
3. **Request Elevator.** The user presses the up or down button at a floor, which triggers an interrupt to the capsule *floor buttons interface*, which in turn sends a message *service request* to the capsule *scheduler*. The *scheduler* receives message and interrogates the passive object *elevator status and plan* to determine if an elevator is on its way to this floor. If not, the *scheduler* selects an elevator and sends a message *elevator request* to the capsule *elevator manager*. The *elevator manager* receives the message and records destination in the passive object *elevator status and plan*.

Consider a building with 10 floors and 3 elevators. All end-to-end threads are interrupt driven, not periodic. In order to perform schedulability analysis, we estimate the worst-case arrival rate of the interrupts and use them as approximations for periods assigned to each task. For example, the **Request Elevator** scenario is assigned a period of 200 ms by assuming that all 18 floor buttons (up and down buttons for each floor, except the top and bottom floors) are pressed within 3.6 seconds, which is likely to be the worst-case arrival rate.

We can use classic RMA to analyze system schedulability if we adopt scenario-based priority assignment. Instead, we adopt CMCP (Capsule-based Multi-threading, Capsule-based Priority-assignment), where each capsule is assigned a fixed priority, and apply the schedulability analysis technique discussed in Section 3.

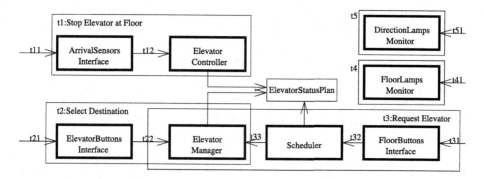

Fig. 5. The collaboration diagram for the single-processor elevator control system. Capsules are drawn with thick borders, and passive objects are drawn with thin borders.

Task	Period	WCET	Priority	WCRT
t_1: **Stop elevator at floor**				
t_{11}: Arrival Sensors Interface	50	2	9	-
t_{12}: Elevator Controller	50	5	6	20
t_2: **Select Destination**				
t_{21}: Elevator Buttons Interface	100	3	8	-
t_{22}: Elevator Manager	100	6	5	31
t_3: **Request Elevator**				
t_{31}: Floor Buttons Interface	200	4	7	-
t_{32}: Scheduler	200	2	4	-
t_{33}: Elevator Manager	200	6	5	33
t_4, t_5: **Other Tasks**				
t_{41}: Floor Lamps Monitor	500	5	3	33
t_{51}: Direction Lamps Monitor	500	5	2	38

Table 1. The taskset of the single-processor elevator control system. Higher number denotes higher priority.

Table 1 shows the taskset of the elevator control system running on a single processor. The priorities are assigned in a rate monotonic fashion, that is, tasks with shorter periods are assigned a higher priority. In addition, the interrupt handler tasks [8], that is, the *Interface* subtasks, are assigned higher priorities than the other tasks in order to avoid losing any interrupts. Other priority assignment schemes are also possible. We do not address the priority assignment problem here, but only address scheduling analysis given existing priority assignments to subtasks.

As an example, let's consider the end-to-end task t_2 **Select Destination**, which consists of two subtasks with execution time 3 and 6, priorities 8 and 5, respectively. Its canonical form is a single task with execution time 9 and priority 5. Other tasks can be classified as follows:

– t_1 is a type 1 task, with a single higher-priority segment with WCET 7.
– t_3 is a type 2 task, with a higher-priority segment t_{31} followed by lower-priority segments t_{32} and t_{33}.
– t_4 and t_5 are type 5 tasks, with all segments having priorities lower than 5.

Blocking time $B_2(2)$ caused by type 2 tasks is WCET(t_{31}) = 4. There are no Type 4 tasks. Blocking time due to RTC semantics is WCET(t_{33}) = 6; blocking time due to shared passive objects is max(WCET(t_{12}), WCET(t_{32})) = max(5, 2). We use Equation 1 to get:

$$\text{WCRT}(2) = \text{WCET}(2) + B_2(2) + B_4(2) + B(2) + \sum_{j \in H_1(2)} \lceil \frac{\text{WCRT}(2)}{\text{Period}(j)} \rceil \cdot \text{WCET}(j)$$

$$= 9 + 4 + 6 + \max(5, 2) + \lceil \frac{\text{WCRT}(2)}{50} \rceil \cdot 7 = 31$$

We can calculate WCRT for the end-to-end threads based on Equation 1, as shown in the WCRT column of Table 1. We associate the WCRT of the end-to-end thread with the last segment of the task in the table. No deadlines are missed, and the system is schedulable. Note t_4 and t_5 have relatively small WCRTs despite the fact that they have the lowest priority, since they do not suffer from blocking time caused by RTC semantics or shared passive objects.

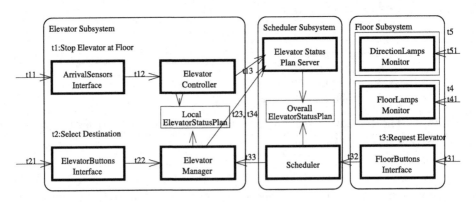

Fig. 6. The collaboration diagram for the distributed elevator control system.

The single-processor system may become overloaded when more floors and elevators are involved. In order to be scalable to a large number of floors and elevators, the system needs to be redesigned to take advantage of multiple processors connected via a network, for example, the Controller Area Network (CAN). Figure 6 shows the system architecture. There is one *ElevatorCPU* for each elevator, and one *FloorCPU* for each floor. There is only one *SchedulerCPU* that is a central decision point for scheduling elevator requests, consisting of the capsule *scheduler* as well as another capsule *elevator status and plan server* for handling updates and queries from the capsules from the *ElevatorCPU* and *FloorCPU*. Each scenario spans multiple processors, and we need to take into account delays caused by scheduling of network packets. For a multi-processor elevator control system consisting of 12 elevators and 40 floors, we use the holistic schedulability analysis technique [12] to calculate the end-to-end WCRT of distributed tasks, with Equation 1 as a subroutine for calculation of local WCRT on a single processor. We omit the details of this calculation due to space limitations, but the analysis results show that all tasks meet their deadlines.

From the above analysis, we conclude that the CMCP approach is adequate in terms of meeting system timing constraints, and we do not need to customize the UML-RT runtime to be either CMSP or SMSP. In this case, all three approaches result in meeting system deadlines, but it may not always be true. In general, we need to perform design space exploration, including choice of multithreading strategies and priority assignment, in order to determine the optimal implementation approach.

5   Discussions

Depending on application characteristics, it may be appropriate to adopt different multi-threading strategies. If there is very little interaction between different application scenarios, then Scenario-Based Multi-Threading is appropriate. This is the case for Avionics Mission Computing software [5], for example. However, if there is intensive interaction among different scenarios, then Capsule-Based Multi-Threading is more appropriate in order to avoid excessive locking and unlocking of shared capsules.

CMSP requires the programmer to stick to a programming discipline of dynamically adjusting capsule priorities to reflect the priority of the currently executing end-to-end scenario. This approach hurts the encapsulation of capsules by mixing system-level concerns (scenarios) with component-level concerns (capsules). It also involves runtime system-call overheads that may or may not be acceptable to certain resource-constrained embedded systems. Certain small RTOSes may not even provide APIs to dynamically change thread priorities. SMSP eliminates the need for dynamic priority adjustments, but creates shared data and necessitates error-prone concurrency control mechanisms, such as mutexes, semaphores and monitors. This breaks a key advantage of UML-RT, which is to use buffered asynchronous message passing as the main communication mechanism among capsules instead of shared data in order to minimize the need for concurrency control. Note that even in the native UML-RT model, there are passive objects that are used to encapsulate shared data in addition to the capsules. The number of such passive objects should be minimized relative to the number of capsules.

Compared to CMSP or SMSP, CMCP has a number of advantages from a software engineering perspective, such as modularity, encapsulation, decoupling of interactions, mature tool support, etc. It is also the default runtime model implemented in UML tools, so a lot of legacy applications follow this model, and are not likely to be changed. However, the task model of CMCP does not fit the assumptions of classic RMA. Instead of modifying the runtime model of UML-RT to fit real-time scheduling theory, we believe a better alternative is to adapt real-time scheduling theory to fit the native runtime model of UML-RT. Specifically, we have described real-time scheduling techniques based on the HKL algorithm that are applicable to the CMCP runtime model, which can be used as a subroutine during the design space exploration process for implementation synthesis from UML-RT models.

6   Related Work

Besides the work of Saksena [6] and Kim [7] discussed in detail in Section 2, there has been a lot of work on real-time analysis of component-based embedded software in the CBSE community. Muskens [13] presented a method for predicting runtime resource consumptions in multi-task component-based systems by expressing resource consumption characteristics per component, and combining them to do predictions over compositions of components based on end-to-end scenarios. Their work is targeted towards the Robocop component model. Sandstrom [14] introduced Autocomp, a component technology for safety critical embedded real-time systems, and discussed techniques for component-to-task mapping and task attribute assignment. Wall [15] proposed a method for impact analysis of adding new components to an existing product line based on Prediction-Enabled Component Technology. They considered two properties: end-to-end temporal property and version consistency property. Eskenazi [16] proposed a stepwise approach to predicting the performance of component compositions. Diaz [17] presented a predictable component model and a set of real-time analysis techniques based on mapping from the component model to SDL. Our work is unique in addressing the issue of one component (capsule) participating in multiple end-to-end scenarios, which makes it desirable to adopt concurrency control methods such as Run-To-Completion, and the runtime model of Capsule-Based Multi-threading, Capsule-Based Priority-Assignment (CMCP).

There have been a lot of work in the real-time community on model-based and component-based design tools, conducted concurrently with and in relative isolation from the work of the CBSE community. In the past several years, DARPA has sponsored projects such as *Model-Based Integration of Embedded Software*(MoBIES) and *Program Composition for Embedded Software* (PCES). Representative tools developed include CoSMIC [18], Virginia Embedded Systems Toolkit (VEST) [19], Time Weaver [20], Cadena [21], and the ESML-based Tool-Chain [22][23][24]. CoSMIC [18] uses the *Platform-Independent Modeling Language* (PICML) to enable developers to define component interfaces, QoS parameters and software building rules, and generate descriptor files that facilitate system deployment. PICML is designed to help bridge the gap between design-time tools and the actual deployed component implementations. VEST [19]is an integrated environment for constructing and analyzing component based embedded systems. *Aspect-checks* are used to check for cross-cutting non-functional properties, and *prescriptive aspects* are used to apply cross-cutting advice to design models. Time Weaver [20] is a software-through-models framework that decomposes inter-component relationships with an abstraction named *coupler*. Cadena [21] is an an integrated development, analysis, and verification environment for *CORBA Component Model* (CCM) systems. The ESML-based Tool-Chain [23] provides an open and integrated development environment based on precise meta-modeling and the *Open Tool Integration Framework* (OTIF) [25] for easy plugin and semantic inter-operability of third party tools. All of the above work focus on static offline design and analysis. In contract, Sharma [26] developed component-based dynamic QoS adaptations in distributed real-time and embedded systems by implementing QoS behavior as components that can be assembled with other application components. These projects mainly target the Avionics Mission Computing software [5] from Boeing, which follows the Scenario-Based Multithreading, Scenario-Based Priority assignment (SMSP) approach.

In embedded software development, UML models typically serve in an informal documentation role that the engineer refers to while writing code manually. This is one of the major motivations for developing domain-specific modeling languages and tools to replace UML in both the CBSE and real-time communities, in order to have a more formal, automated and integrated software development process. However, there has been recent progress on making UML more formal and suitable for modeling real-time embedded and component-based software. Some examples include UML-RT, UML 2.0 [27], UML Profile for Scheduability, Performance and Time [28] and the UML Profile for CORBA Component Model [29]. In particular, UML 2.0 has adopted the UML-RT concept of *capsules* communicating with message passing through *ports*. An interesting question to ask is, can we not give up on UML and develop custom, proprietary modeling notations, but leverage the body of work from the UML community to develop tools based on standards? One argument for preferring a custom modeling approach to UML is that we can achieve better domain-specificity by customizing the meta-model, which is more powerful and flexible than the UML profiling mechanism. Another argument is that embedded systems are so diverse that it is next to impossible to have one standard notation that is suitable for all application domains. For example, even though UML-RT is intended to be a general-purpose design tool, it has been mostly used for developing embedded software in the telecommunications domain, which fits well with the interaction style of asynchronous message passing. We plan to investigate these interesting issues in our future work.

7   Conclusions and Future Work

UML-RT is a component-based modeling language. Commercial code generators for UML-RT generate functional code, but do not take into account timing and scheduling issues. The native runtime model of UML-RT does not fit the assumptions of classic real-time scheduling theory, i.e., Rate Monotonic Analysis

(RMA). Some authors have proposed alternative runtime models that can be analyzed with RMA. We take the alternative approach of adapting real-time scheduling theory to fit the native runtime model of UML-RT, instead of adapting the runtime model of UML-RT to fit real-time scheduling theory. This should make our approach more acceptable to industry than previous work in the literature.

We believe our work helps bridge the gap between a logical UML-RT model and its final implementation on the target platform, by giving the engineer real-time scheduling analysis techniques for evaluating different alternatives of generating a multi-threaded implementation from a logical software model. It focuses on the nonfunctional/real-time aspect of implementation synthesis, and is complementary to the existing code generators for UML-RT, which focuses on the functional aspect of implementation synthesis. It is our future work to integrate our analysis techniques with commercial code generators for UML-RT. Even though the discussions in this paper are mainly based on UML-RT, our work has much wider applicability to the general class of component-based software models with interaction style of buffered asynchronous message passing between components with ports.

We have considered the problem of schedulability analysis given a system configuration of capsule-to-thread grouping and thread priority assignment, but it is still an open issue as to how to arrive at such a configuration. We did not deal with the design space exploration issues of how to group capsules into threads or assign priorities to threads. For the CMCP approach, the number of threads needs to be carefully managed. If there are too many threads, the context-switching overheads may be excessive; if there are too few threads, the blocking time may be too much due to insufficient parallelism. Priority assignment is also an important issue that needs to be considered for meeting system timing constraints. Exhaustive search is not feasible in general because the size of design space grows exponentially with the number of capsules or priorities. One possible future work is to apply optimization techniques such as branch-and-bound, simulated annealing and genetic algorithms for design space exploration, in order to optimize design objectives such as minimizing the number of threads or minimizing response time for critical application scenarios.

References

[1] B. Selic, G. Gullekson, and P. T. Ward, *Real-Time Object Oriented Modeling*. Addison Wesley, 1994.
[2] (2004) The IBM Rational website. [Online]. Available: http://www-306.ibm.com/software/rational/
[3] (2004) The Quantum Framework website. [Online]. Available: http://www.quantum-leaps.com/qf.htm
[4] D. Schmidt, D. Levine, and T. Harrison, "The design and performance of a real-time CORBA object event service," in *Proc. ACM Conference on Object-Oriented Programming, Systems, Languages, and Applications*, 1997, pp. 434–445.

[5] Z. Gu, S. Kodase, S. Wang, and K. G. Shin, "A model-based approach to system-level dependency and real-time analysis of embedded software," in *Proc. IEEE Real-Time Technology and Applications Symposium (RTAS)*, 2003, pp. 78–85.

[6] M. Saksena and P. Karvelas, "Designing for schedulability: integrating schedulability analysis with object-oriented design," in *Proc. IEEE Euro-Micro Conference on Real-Time Systems*, 2000, pp. 101–108.

[7] J. Masse, S. Kim, and S. Hong, "Tool set implementation for scenario-based multithreading of uml-rt models and experimental validation," in *Proc. IEEE Real-Time and Embedded Technology and Applications Symposium*, 2003, pp. 70–77.

[8] M. H. Klein, T. Ralya, B. Pollak, and R. Obenza, *A Practitioner's Handbook for Real-Time Analysis: Guide to Rate Monotonic Analysis for Real-Time Systems*. Kluwer Academic Publishers, 1993.

[9] M. Harbour, M. H. Klein, and J. Lehoczky, "Timing analysis for fixed-priority scheduling of hard real-time systems," *IEEE Trans. Software Eng.*, vol. 20, no. 2, pp. 13–28, 1994.

[10] S. Tripakis, "Description and schedulability analysis of the software architecture of an automated vehicle control system," in *Proc. International Workshop on Embedded Software*, 2002, pp. 123–137.

[11] H. Gomaa, *Designing Concurrent, Distributed, and Real-Time Applications with UML*. Addison-Wesley, 2000.

[12] K. Tindell and J. Clark, "Holistic schedulability analysis for distributed hard real-time systems," *Microprocessing and Microprogramming - Euromicro Journal (Special Issue on Parallel Embedded Real-Time Systems)*, vol. 40, pp. 117–134, 1994. [Online]. Available: citeseer.nj.nec.com/tindell94holistic.html

[13] J. Muskens and M. Chaudron, "Prediction of run-time resource consumption in multi-task component-based software systems," in *Proc. International Symposium on Component-Based Software Engineering, LNCS 3054*, 2004, pp. 162–177.

[14] K. Sandstrom, J. Fredriksson, and M. Akerholm, "Introducing a component technology for safety critical embedded real-time systems," in *Proc. International Symposium on Component-Based Software Engineering, LNCS 3054*, 2004, pp. 194–208.

[15] A. Wall, M. Larsson, and C. Norstrom, "Towards an impact analysis for component based real-time product line architectures," in *Proc. Euromicro Conference*, 2002, pp. 81–88.

[16] E. Eskenazi, A. Fioukov, and D. Hammer, "Performance prediction for component compositions," in *Proc. International Symposium on Component-Based Software Engineering, LNCS 3054*, 2004, pp. 280–193.

[17] M. Diaz, D. Garrido, L. M. Llopis, F. Rus, and J. M. Troya, "Integrating real-time analysis in a component model for embedded systems," in *Proc. EUROMICRO Conference*, 2004, pp. 14–21.

[18] K. Balasubramanian, J. Balasubramanian, J. Parsons, A. Gokhale, and D. C. Schmidt, "A platform-independent component modeling language for distributed real-time and embedded systems," in *Proc. IEEE Real-Time and Embedded Technology and Applications Symposium*, 2004.

[19] J. A. Stankovic, R. Zhu, R. Poornalingam, C. Lu, Z. Yu, M. Humphrey, and B. Ellis, "Vest: an aspect-based composition tool for real-time systems," in *Proc. IEEE Real-Time and Embedded Technology and Applications Symposium*, 2003, pp. 58–69.

[20] D. de Niz and R. Rajkumar, "Time weaver: A software-throuhg-models framework for embedded real-time systems," in *Proc. ACM Conference on Languages, Compilers and Tools For Embedded Systems*, 2003, pp. 133–143.

[21] J. Hatcliff, W. Deng, M. Dwyer, G. Jung, and V. Prasad, "Cadena: An integrated development, analysis, and verification environment for component-based systems," in *Proc. IEEE International Conference on Software Engineering*, 2003.

[22] Z. Gu, S. Wang, S. Kodase, and K. G. Shin, "An end-to-end tool chain for multi-view modeling and analysis of avionics mission computing software," in *Proc. IEEE Real-Time Systems Symposium (RTSS)*, 2003, pp. 78–81.

[23] ——, "Multi-view modeling and analysis of embedded real-time software with meta-modeling and model-transformation," in *Proc. IEEE International Symposium on High Assurance Systems Engineering*, 2004, pp. 32–41.

[24] Z. Gu and K. G. Shin, "Model-checking of component-based real-time embedded software based on corba event service," in *Proc. IEEE International Symposium on Object-Oriented Real-Time Distributed Computing (ISORC)*, 2005.

[25] G. Karsai, "Design tool integration: An exercise in semantic interoperability," in *Proc. IEEE Conference on Engineering of Computer Based Systems*, 2000.

[26] P. K. Sharma, J. P. Loyall, G. T. Heineman, R. E. Schantz, R. Shapiro, and G. Duzan, "Component-based dynamic qos adaptations in distributed real-time and embedded systems," in *International Symposium on Distributed Objects and Applications*, 2004, pp. 25–29.

[27] (2004) The Object Management Group website. [Online]. Available: http://www.omg.org

[28] OMG, "Uml profile for schedulability,performance, and time specification," Object Management Group, Tech. Rep., 2003. [Online]. Available: http://www.omg.org/technology/documents/formal/schedulability.htm

[29] ——, "Uml profile for corba components specification," Object Management Group, Tech. Rep., 2004. [Online]. Available: http://www.omg.org/cgi-bin/doc?ptc/2004-03-04

A Component-Oriented Model for the Design of Safe Multi-threaded Applications

Reimer Behrends, R.E. Kurt Stirewalt, and Laura K. Dillon

Dept. of Computer Science and Engineering
Michigan State University

Abstract. We previously developed a component-oriented model that combines ideas from self-organizing architectures and from design by contract to address the complexity of design in multi-threaded systems. Components in our model are cohesive collections of objects that publish contracts declaring the conditions under which they access other components. These contracts localize a component's contextual synchronization dependencies in its interface. Moreover, the resulting systems permit strong guarantees of safety.

This paper reports a case study to validate the efficacy of our model on a realistic design problem: the component-based design of a multi-threaded web server. We first developed a bare-bones web server based on the Apache architecture and then subjected this design to three extension tasks. The study corroborates that our model enables a fine-grain component-based design of multi-threaded applications of realistic complexity, while guaranteeing freedom from certain synchronization errors.

1 Introduction

An essential property of a good component-based design is that component interfaces should make explicit all dependencies between components and the contexts in which they operate [1]. An important class of dependencies for systems in which multiple threads operate over shared objects relates to synchronization. Without thread synchronization, concurrent access to shared objects can lead to race conditions, and incorrect synchronization logic can lead to starvation and deadlock. However, synchronization policies and decisions are difficult to localize into a single software module—it is not uncommon for a module to implement a synchronization policy that satisfies safety and liveness requirements in some usage contexts but that fails to satisfy the same requirements in other contexts. Moreover, these contextual dependencies are difficult to record explicitly in a module's interface. These problems complicate the development of a component model with which to produce clean designs of concurrent systems.

We previously developed a solution that combines ideas from self-organizing architectures [2] and design by contract [3] to overcome these problems [4, 5]. Our *synchronization units model* associates with each module a declarative specification of its contextual synchronization dependencies, effectively localizing these dependencies in the module's interface. We designed these specifications as a non-obtrusive extension to existing object-oriented programming languages and component models, rather than as

G.T. Heineman et al. (Eds.): CBSE 2005, LNCS 3489, pp. 251–266, 2005.

part of a stand-alone component model. Systems produced using this extension permits strong guarantees of safety. This paper presents a case study using this model.

In the synchronization units model, a component is a highly cohesive group of objects, called a *synchronization unit*, and components dynamically assemble and re-assemble into aggregates, called *realms*, that are associated with threads. For brevity, we refer to a synchronization unit as just a *unit*, and we henceforth use the terminology "unit" and "component" interchangeably. Each thread operates exclusively within its own dedicated realm. Inter-component dependencies represent access dependencies between the objects in a *client unit* and those of a *supplier unit*. Client units are *bound* to suppliers when the supplier *migrates* into the realm that hosts the client. Realms are self organizing; their dynamic assembly and evolution is governed by the negotiation of *synchronization contracts*, which a component designer declares as part of the client's interface. The self-organizing nature of this approach relieves the programmer from having to implement complex synchronization logic, and the explicit synchronization contracts declare all contextual dependencies that pertain to concurrency and synchronization.

To date, we have illustrated the theoretical power of the model on standard concurrency problems [4], integrated the model and its declarative contracts into an existing programming language [5], and shown how to safely integrate system libraries and third-party code (which may not be thread safe) with code written using contracts [6]. To validate the efficacy and applicability of our synchronization units model to current software engineering practice, we devised a realistically complex case study, which is the main focus of this paper. The case study involves a component-based design of a multi-threaded web server with database and scripting capabilities. The design is modeled after that of the popular Apache server.

Among the questions we expected to answer by the study are whether the synchronization units model is sufficiently expressive to handle designs of complex systems and how effective it is in localizing synchronization concerns. In an attempt to answer these questions, we subjected an initial design of a bare-bones web server to three maintenance and extension activities. These activities serve to validate that we can add complex new capabilities to the system by adding new units that require synchronization with existing units without modifying existing units. We describe two of these activities below. A description of the third can be found in [6] and is omitted here due to space constraints.

The rest of this paper is structured as follows. We first describe the web-server application that is the subject of our study (Section 2). We then introduce our model of synchronization units (Section 3) and outline the basic architecture of our component-based design of the web server (Section 4). We validate the effectiveness of our model on complex designs and the degree to which it localizes synchronization concerns by extending the bare-bones architecture with new features and assessing the ease with which our model supports the extensions (Sections 5–6). The paper concludes with a comparison of our approach to existing work (Section 7).

2 Rationale for Choosing the Application

The subject of this case study is a component-based design of the popular Apache web server. Apache itself incorporates a modular and extensible architecture in which software modules implement capabilities at many levels of granularity from http-request parsing to PHP scripting. While the Apache architecture was designed for extensibility, the afore-mentioned modules cannot be classified as software components because they fail to externalize all of their contextual dependencies. This deficiency is particularly noticeable as it regards issues of concurrency and synchronization. For example, the authors of the popular PHP scripting engine have warned against its use in the multi-threaded version of Apache [7], because the engine relies on a large number of third-party libraries that may not be thread-safe [8]. Other vulnerabilities have emerged in this multi-threaded version [9, 10]. Our model guarantees freedom from these sorts of synchronization vulnerabilities. This case study aims to demonstrate that our model can also accommodate the major design decisions that have made the Apache architecture so extensible—i.e., that Apache modules can be implemented as components in our model. Given the central importance of web servers in e-commerce applications, such a result could greatly increase the confidence in these applications.

Multi-threaded web servers comprise a rich set of interacting modules with unstructured synchronization dependencies. Many of these dependencies arise from security and efficiency concerns, which justify decisions to introduce shared resources. For example, a URI rewriting module may amortize the cost of translation by caching its results. Such caches must be protected from unsynchronized access by multiple threads. Large modules, e.g., internal scripting engines, are often shared because they are prohibitively expensive to replicate for each thread. Other dependencies arise from the use of non-reentrant third party libraries, such as the POSIX function `crypt`, which is used by an authentication module.

Because these modules contain implicit synchronization dependencies, it is difficult to certify the safety of a given configuration, a problem that is exacerbated by the reconfiguration requirements of modern web servers. Such applications are reconfigured often, e.g., to fix a bug, close a security hole, accommodate the changing requirements of evolving web standards, or service the varying needs of users [11, 12]. New modules may have synchronization needs and resource-access patterns that differ from the needs and patterns of the modules that they replace. Thus, assuring against concurrency flaws during maintenance and extension is a major problem, especially in cases where new modules are developed by third-party vendors. Such a problem begs for a component-based solution, but the component model must guarantee safety in the face of frequent reconfiguration. The remainder of this paper attempts to demonstrate how our model, which provides exactly these guarantees, can support the component-based design of such a large, extensible, and critical application.

3 Synchronization Contracts

This section overviews the key ideas underlying our model of synchronization units. Detailed discussions of the model can be found in [4, 5].

```
1  synchronization class REQUEST_HANDLER inherit PROCESS_BASE

2  feature { NONE } -- instance variables

3     auth_stage, content_stage: BOOLEAN    -- condition variables
4     authenticator: AUTHENTICATOR          -- unit reference
5     connection: INBOUND_SOCKET            -- unit reference
6     dispatcher: CONTENT_DISPATCHER        -- unit reference
7     ...

8  feature { ANY } -- operations (methods)

9     authenticate ( request : REQUEST ) is
10    do
11       auth_stage := true
12       authenticator.validate(request)
13       auth_stage := false
14    end
15    ...

16 concurrency -- concurrency clause follows
17    connection
18    auth_stage => authenticator
19    content_stage => dispatcher

20 end -- class REQUEST_HANDLER
```

Fig. 1. Elided definition of the synchronization class REQUEST_HANDLER

In the synchronization units model, threads operate in disjoint realms that comprise one or more synchronization units. Any attempt by a thread to access a unit while that unit is not in its realm constitutes a *realm violation* and causes a run-time exception to be raised. The designer annotates a synchronization unit that plays a client role in a collaboration with one or more *concurrency constraints*, each of which specifies a condition under which the client requires exclusive access to a supplier. During execution, the run-time system assembles and reassembles realms, schedules threads to execute, and watches for realm violations using algorithms that 1) ensure that the realms are always pairwise disjoint, 2) guarantee that a thread executes only when the thread's realm consists of a *process root* unit and all suppliers required by constraints associated with units in the realm, and 3) avoids starvation and preventable deadlocks. Because realms are disjoint, two threads are assured to never concurrently access the same memory location—shared units migrate from one realm to another, but these units are never accessed simultaneously by different threads.

By way of illustration, we show part of the definition for a synchronization unit from the case study (Figure 1). It is written in an extension of Eiffel [13] with concurrency constraints, which we developed previously [4]. In this extension, the designer designates that certain classes are *synchronization classes* to indicate that they produce synchronization units when instantiated. In our web-server application, incoming web requests are handled and serviced by instances of a REQUEST_HANDLER class. The keyword synchronization (line 1) signifies that instances of this class define synchronization units.

The class declares several instance variables, some of which encode conditions under which a request handler requires exclusive access to a supplier (e.g., auth_stage and content_stage in line 3) and some of which reference the required supplier (e.g., authenticator, connection, and dispatcher in lines 4–6). We call the former *condition variables* and the latter *unit variables*. [1] For example, auth_stage records when a request handler needs to validate that a web request may access protected parts of a website; at such times, it requires the AUTHENTICATOR unit referenced by authenticator to validate that the access is permitted (line 12). A designer introduces condition variables to record the state of a unit's computation for use in concurrency constraints, thereby making the state observable by a run-time system that negotiates and enforces contracts.

Our Eiffel extension provides a *concurrency clause* for declaring contracts. The concurrency clause appears after the keyword concurrency (line 16). It contains three concurrency constraints (lines 17–19). Each concurrency constraint references a supplier unit, and the last two predicate the unit references on *guards*, which reference condition variables. Because it has no guard, the first constraint (line 17) declares an unconditional dependency—whenever a request handler executes, it requires exclusive access to the inbound socket referenced by connection. By contrast, the next two constraints (lines 18 and 19) say that the request handler accesses the unit referenced by authenticator (respectively dispatcher) only when the condition variable auth_stage (respectively content_stage) is true.

The run-time system for the extended language ensures that, when a process executes, its realm contains all the synchronization units that, according to the concurrency constraints, it needs to access. Briefly, the run-time system intercepts assignments to condition variables and unit variables and automatically reassembles so as to comprise only the required synchronization units. Should a process be unable to update its realm, because it requires exclusive access to a unit already in the realm of another process, it will be blocked until it can obtain the required exclusive access. For example, because the concurrency constraint in line 18 indicates that a process needs exclusive access to the unit referenced by authenticator when auth_stage is true, a process blocks if it attempts to execute line 11 (assign auth_stage the value true) when the indicated unit belongs to the realm of some other process. Later, when the indicated unit becomes available, the run-time system migrates the unit into the realm of the blocked process and unblocks the process. We describe algorithms to efficiently and fairly perform such *realm updates* in [5], along with the results of a performance study.

In controlling migration of units and scheduling of threads, the runtime system guarantees the invariance of the concurrency constraints in a program, thereby enforcing the contracts. This functionality is achieved without the programmer needing to write code that explicitly manipulates realm, unit, or thread representations. Instead, the programmer writes code that maintains condition variables to encode and reflect the current state of the computation and constraints that declaratively specify the suppliers that a

---

[1] In our Eiffel extension, a BOOLEAN variable used in a concurrency constraint is inferred to be a condition variable, and an attribute whose declared type is a synchronization class is inferred to reference a synchronization unit. For lack of space, we omit declarations of the synchronization classes AUTHENTICATOR, INBOUND_SOCKET, and CONTENT_DISPATCHER.

unit accesses in each of these states. We contend that such code—by virtue of being local to a single unit—and concurrency constraints—by virtue of being declarative and expressed at appropriately high levels of abstraction—are less susceptible to synchronization errors than the typical code that a programmer writes to explicitly synchronize processes that share data. Moreover, errors due to code that does not conform to the stated contracts are easily detected at run-time by an efficient realm-boundary check. When one unit attempts to access another, the run-time system checks that the units belong to the same realm, allowing the access only if the check succeeds and raising a run-time exception otherwise.

4 Component-Based Design of a Multi-threaded Web Server

Our architecture follows the basic design of the multi-threaded Apache web server, which manages a pool of threads to concurrently process HTTP requests as they arrive. Figure 2 depicts our architecture.[2] Borrowing ideas from [14, 15, 16], we use UML's built-in extension mechanisms to extend the UML class-diagram notation to express the structure of this architecture. Class names rendered in italics denote abstract classes. Our extensions involve three new stereotypes—$\langle\langle$synchronization$\rangle\rangle$, $\langle\langle$process_root$\rangle\rangle$, and $\langle\langle$external$\rangle\rangle$—that denote synchronization, process-root and external unit classes respectively. For brevity in this paper, our architectural drawings show only the synchronization classes; we therefore elide the $\langle\langle$synchronization$\rangle\rangle$ stereotype in diagrams. Condition variables are shown as boolean-valued class attributes and unit variables as directed associations. We express concurrency constraints in curly braces adjacent to their associated synchronization class. For example, the LISTENER_SOCKET class declares the condition variable startup, the unit variable namesvcs, and the concurrency constraint startup => namesvcs.

The application comprises a main thread, called the *web dispatcher*, and a separate *request handler* thread for each incoming HTTP request. The realm of the web dispatcher is rooted by a unit of class WEB_DISPATCHER and includes a unit of class LISTENER_SOCKET, which it uses to monitor a port for connection requests. At times, specifically when the listener socket is "starting up," the realm of the web dispatcher also contains an external unit of class NAME_SERVICES, which is used to lookup IP addresses. The realm of each request handler is rooted by a unit of class REQUEST_HANDLER.

When a connection is requested, the web dispatcher creates an INBOUND_SOCKET unit with which to receive the actual HTTP request and communicate the resulting content. It then dispatches this unit to a new request handler thread. Each request handler thread parses the data sent over its assigned connection into a *request object*, handles the request, as described below, and then terminates. To minimize the overhead of request-handler initialization,[3] REQUEST_HANDLER units are stored in an object pool [17] and

---

[2] Due to space limitations, Figure 2 abstracts away many details of the full case study—e.g. we omit the database capabilities. The actual web server developed for the case study consists of 57 Eiffel classes, of which 31 are synchronization classes, and a total of 3587 lines of code.

[3] For example, each request handler must contain configuration information, such as which extensions are being used, which URIs need to be authenticated, etc. In our implementation, this

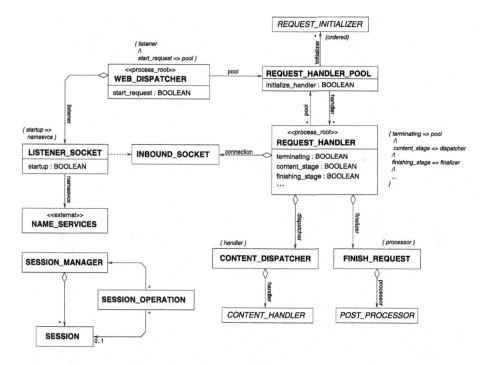

Fig. 2. Basic Web Server Architecture

reused to process different HTTP requests. In our design, the web dispatcher actually dispatches inbound socket units to a unit of class REQUEST_HANDLER_POOL, which then selects or creates a new unit of class REQUEST_HANDLER, and creates a new thread rooted by that unit.

Request handling itself is implemented in stages. For brevity, Figure 2 depicts the components for only three of these stages—request initialization, content generation and request finalization—although our actual architecture supports others, such as authentication. *Request initialization* initializes a request object with attributes prior to parsing the actual request information that is arriving over the inbound socket. The abstract class REQUEST_INITIALIZER declares a method called prepare (not shown), which is parameterized by a reference to a request object. The bare-bones architecture uses a null request initializer, but many extensions need to initialize request objects with attributes before request handing begins in earnest.

Content generation generates the data—e.g., the contents of static web pages, the results of running a script, or an error report—to send back to the requester. This stage is performed by a CONTENT_DISPATCHER unit, which dispatches a request to one of several content handlers. Example handlers (not shown in diagram) include STAT-

---

information is retrieved from a central configuration file that is consulted when the system is initialized.

IC_HANDLER, which is used to serve static web pages, and ERROR_HANDLER, which is used for requests that resulted in an error. Other content handlers can be implemented as extensions to the abstract class CONTENT_HANDLER. The content generation stage uses the *builder* pattern [18], with CONTENT_DISPATCHER in the role of director and CONTENT_HANDLER in the role of the (abstract) builder.

Finalization is responsible for such things as logging and analysis. During this stage, the completed request object is passed to an instance of FINISH_REQUEST, which is responsible for the maintenance of log files, gathering of statistics, and general post-processing of completed requests. The FINISH_REQUEST unit also signals the RE-QUEST_HANDLER_POOL at the end of each request that a request handler is again available. Once the REQUEST_HANDLER unit is returned to the pool, the request handler thread is terminated. The finalization stage can be extended by adding components whose interfaces conform to the POST_PROCESSOR interface. In the bare-bones web server, only a simple logging mechanism is provided (not shown in the diagram).

The basic architecture also provides facilities for tracking and managing *sessions*, which are sequences of connected user-agent requests. The central SESSION_MANA-GER unit controls access to a repository of SESSION units, each of which is identified by a unique session key. In this design, SESSION units comprise sets of key–value pairs that can be queried and set by components in the various stages of request handling. Often, client units do not use SESSION units directly, but instead access them through a SESSION_OPERATION facade, which simplifies access to session information by encapsulating the contract-negotiation and business logic required to locate and manage a session unit by key. SESSION_OPERATION components are constructed with a session key, which may be null. If the key is non-null, the component retrieves the corresponding SESSION from the SESSION_MANAGER; otherwise, it asks the SESSION_MANAGER to create a new session and returns the new session key. Subsequently, the SESSION_OPERATION facade forwards the querying and setting of key–data pairs to the retrieved SESSION. SESSION_OPERATION units encapsulate contract-negotiation logic that would otherwise need to be replicated among all SES-SION clients, and they ensure minimal contention for the singleton SESSION_MANA-GER unit.

As presented thus far, our basic architecture employs a component-based design in order to support extension and to simplify static reconfiguration. However, the loose coupling and fine-grain decomposition of functionality that make the design so extensible is at odds with attempts to make components thread safe and deadlock free. We hypothesize that our synchronization units model enables a fine-grain component-based design (and the concomitant benefits with regard to maintenance and extension/contraction) while guaranteeing freedom from data races [19] and automatically avoiding or recovering from most classes of deadlock. To test this hypothesis, we subjected the basic architecture to three different maintenance tasks, each involving a non-trivial extension comprising one or more component collaborations that interact with existing collaborations in the basic architecture. We describe two of these activities below. For each extension, we document the business logic requirements, provide a design of the extension in our model, and summarize the capabilities demonstrated by the extension.

5   Extension: Dynamic Content

Our first maintenance task extends the web server with a scripting facility for generating dynamic content. Scripts must be able to safely access web-server resources, especially session data. Moreover, scripts typically access such resources according to a two-phase locking protocol, whereby all shared resources are acquired before any are released [20]. Such resources manifest as synchronization units in our basic architecture. Thus, this maintenance task aims to see if we can implement scripting as a set of new components that collaborate and safely synchronize with the existing components without having to modify any of those existing components. A related issue concerns the need for scripts to access standard library functions, such as the POSIX function `crypt` and DNS functions, many of which are not thread safe. In prior work, we showed how multi-threaded accesses to standard libraries can be serialized using wrapper facades that coordinate with external synchronization units [6]. This maintenance task builds upon these prior results.

5.1   Scripting Language and Its Embedding

To explore these issues, we chose to support scripts written in the Lua language [21]. Lua is a small interpreted language with metaprogramming facilities for extending the language with new features and hooks into a host application, such as a web server. We chose Lua over languages such as PHP for purely pragmatic reasons: The Lua integration shares in all of the the essential complexity that would occur in a PHP integration with far less accidental complexity.

Using its metaprogramming facilities, we extended Lua with new primitives for 1) accessing standard libraries and resources in our web-server architecture, and 2) declaring resource needs, as dictated by the two-phase locking protocol. Briefly, we represent each library and each web-server resource as a Lua object, hereafter called a *resource proxy* that is visible to user scripts. For example, we provide a Lua object named my-Session, which represents a SESSION unit in the basic architecture. When a Lua script is executed in response to some http request, mySession is bound to the SESSION component associated with the request. Among others, we also provide the Lua objects myCrypt and myNameservices, which represent CRYPT and NAME_SERVICES units.[4]

In addition to these resource-proxy objects, we extended the Lua language with a new statement called *acquire*, which a script programmer invokes to declare the resources he or she intends to access. The statement takes a variable number of arguments, all of which must be resource proxies, such as mySession or myCrypt. Semantically, we interpret an `acquire` statement as a request to atomically acquire the named resources; a running script blocks on such a statement until all of the named resources have been acquired. Figure 3(a) depicts a small example. Line (1) states the script programmer's intention to access information about the current session and to invoke the crypt function. The session information is queried on line (2) and the crypt function is

---
[4] Note that these components are external synchronization units that serialize accesses to the POSIX function crypt and functions in the DNS library (See [6] for details).

```
(1)  acquire(mySession, myCrypt)
(2)  if not mySession.get("auth_flag")
(3)  then
(4)    if myCrypt.crypt(...) == ...
(5)    then
(6)      ...
(7)    end
(8)  end
(9)  ...
```

```
feature acquire_units(
    use_crypt,
    use_nameservices,
    use_session: BOOLEAN) is
do
    acquire_crypt,
    acquire_nameservices,
    acquire_session :=
        use_crypt,
        use_nameservices,
        use_session
end
```

(a) Example Lua script

(b) LUA_INTERPRETER support function

Fig. 3.

invoked on line (4). All resources acquired by a script are released automatically when the script completes. Thus all Lua scripts conform to the two-phase locking protocol.

5.2 Component-Based Solution

Figure 4 depicts our extension. For brevity, this diagram depicts the unit classes and associations that are new to this extension and only those classes from the basic architecture upon which these new classes depend. Scripting is supported by a new content handler called SCRIPT_HANDLER, which uses a SCRIPT_INTERPRETER component to actually execute a user script. SCRIPT_INTERPRETER is an interface class. Concrete components that conform to this interface implement interpreters for specific scripting languages; the LUA_INTERPRETER component is an example. To support extension, we designed SCRIPT_HANDLER to bind to a particular SCRIPT_INTERPRETER component according to the *abstract factory pattern* [18]. SCRIPT_INTERPRETER_FACTORY plays the abstract-factory role in this design. This abstract class provides a create method (not shown) that is parameterized by a REQUEST object. Concrete factories, such as LUA_INTERPRETER_FACTORY, may then access request-specific information when deciding which interpreter to create or retrieve from a repository.

Class LUA_INTERPRETER has two salient characteristics. First, it is a wrapper-facade [22] that encapsulates the data structures (i.e., C-style structs) that implement a Lua interpreter, and it provides an object-oriented interface to the ANSI C functions that operate over these structures. Second, it is a synchronization class that declares condition variables and parameterized contracts with other components in the architecture. These condition variables are manipulated when the interpreter executes an acquire statement in a Lua script, thereby setting the condition variables that parameterize the relevant contract.

Operations in a Lua script that manipulate resource proxies are connected to operations over synchronization units as follows. LUA_INTERPRETER units link to the units

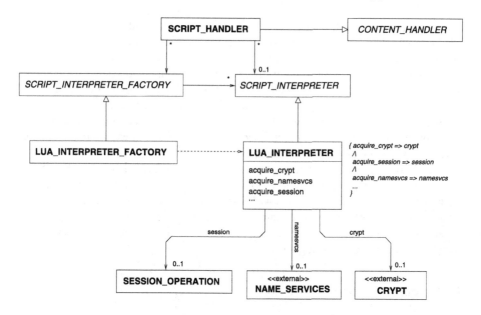

Fig. 4. Dynamic Scripting Extension

that correspond to the resource proxies. Suppose, for brevity, that there are only the three proxies **mySession**, **myCrypt**, and **myNameservices**. Then class LUA_INTERPRET-ER associates to a SESSION_OPERATION unit, a CRYPT unit and a NAME_SERVICES unit, as depicted in Figure 4. Moreover, for each such association, x, class LUA_INTER-PRETER declares a condition variable acquire_x and the contract:

```
acquire_x => x
```

Thus, LUA_INTERPRETER units are able to reflect the resource acquisition needs of Lua programmers, and changes in these acquisition needs trigger a renegotiation of contracts with the corresponding units.

LUA_INTERPRETER implements acquire by atomically setting the appropriate condition variables via a function such as that depicted in Figure 3(b). In our extended version of Eiffel, several variables can be assigned new values atomically, and synchronization contracts are renegotiated only after the entire assignment completes. If these contracts cannot be negotiated, the thread blocks on this statement, thereby providing the expected semantics of the Lua acquire statement. Consider, for example, the call to acquire in line 1 of Figure 3(a). This call produces a call to acquire_units with the value true for the first and third parameters and the value false for the second. Thus, the assignment in acquire_units blocks until the SESSION_OPER-ATION and CRYPT units are migrated into the realm hosting the interpreter.

5.3   Discussion

This task demonstrates that our model supports the safe addition of complex functionality to an existing design without having to modify existing components. We added scripting capabilities to the bare-bones web server without modifying any previously existing components. It is unlikely that we could have added the same capability to the multi-threaded Apache architecture without modifying any existing modules. At a minimum, we would have to carefully analyze the augmented system for potential race conditions and deadlocks, which would involve a detailed analysis of the code for these modules. By contrast, our model guarantees freedom from data races. In ongoing research, we are also developing techniques for analyzing synchronization dependencies between units, as expressed in their concurrency clauses, to expose unpreventable deadlocks or show that no unpreventable deadlocks can occur.

In addition, our implementation allows script writers to reap many of the benefits of the underlying synchronization units model. For example, whereas user scripts may use resources in patterns that we could not anticipate when designing the scripting components, the resulting system is still guaranteed to be free of data races. If a script author forgets to acquire a resource before attempting to use it, the interpreter raises a run-time exception rather than permitting the access.

6   Extension: Load Balancing

Our second maintenance task extended the dynamic content handler with a load balancing mechanism. In this extension, the total number of available script interpreters is capped and adjusted at run time as a function of the server load and static configuration parameters. The extension aims to demonstrate two aspects of the web server design obtained using synchronization contracts: 1) it can accommodate quality-of-service improvements without incurring massive re-design, and 2) it admits replacement of one component with a new one, although the new component and the replaced component have different contextual synchronization dependencies, without requiring changes to other components.

6.1   Number of Scripting Interpreters

The load balancing mechanism automatically estimates the number of interpreters needed according to a heuristic that makes use of a configuration constant M, which is set by the server administrator, and two computed values, the approximate number R of requests for dynamic content per second and the approximate average time T to process a request for dynamic content. The heuristic aims to ensure that, on average, M interpreters are available for each thread. Threads are assigned idle interpreters whenever possible and are randomly assigned a busy interpreter otherwise.

6.2   Component-Based Solution

Figure 5 depicts the new units and collaborations in our extension. The new unit LOAD_BALANCER is a singleton POST_PROCESSOR component that processes each request during the finalization stage of request handling. This new unit computes the approximations R and T and, at regular intervals, initiates a *rebalancing process*, during which it computes a new target number of interpreters and informs the factory (which is

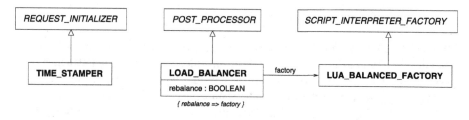

Fig. 5. Load Balancing

used by SCRIPT_HANDLER) of this change. This extension replaces the LUA_INTER-PRETER_FACTORY unit in Figure 4 with a new unit called LUA_BALANCED_FACT-ORY, which contains extra functionality to collaborate with the load-balancing components. During rebalancing, LOAD_BALANCER notifies the LUA_BALANCED_FACTORY unit of changes in the target number of LUA_INTERPRETER units in the repository. In response, LUA_BALANCED_FACTORY creates new interpreter components or deletes superfluous components to achieve the target number.

This extension requires a REQUEST_INITIALIZER called TIME_STAMPER, which augments a REQUEST object with a time stamp that the LOAD_BALANCER consults when finalizing the request object to derive an estimate for T. This new extension involves one new synchronization contract, which specifies that when rebalancing is in progress, LOAD_BALANCER requires exclusive access to LUA_BALANCED_FACTORY.

6.3 Discussion

This task demonstrates two useful aspects of our synchronization units model. First, we showed how a component that participates in one collaboration can be replaced with another component that participates in an additional collaboration without having to modify the synchronization logic in any of the client components in either collaboration. In this case, we swapped out the LUA_INTERPRETER_FACTORY unit for the new LUA_BALANCED_FACTORY unit. This exchange was trivial—we did not alter the factory's client (i.e., SCRIPT_HANDLER) or its interface (i.e., the abstract class SCRIPT_INTERPRETER_FACTORY). This exchange was so trivial because components in our model explicitly represent synchronization dependencies in their interfaces.

Second, and perhaps more interesting, this task demonstrates the improvement of quality of service of an existing design without having to fundamentally alter the design or modify many of its existing components. In fact, the only modification was the component replacement already mentioned. Of course, this is only one example, but it is interesting that a post-hoc quality-of-service optimization was so easy to incorporate into a design that was built upon a component model with support for synchronization. We are currently investigating whether other QoS optimizations are simplified by virtue of our model's ability to deal with synchronization concerns.

7   Conclusions and Future Work

This case study demonstrates our synchronization units model supports the component-based design of a realistically complex multi-threaded system. Our maintenance tasks involved the extension of a component-based design with new features that imposed new synchronization requirements on that existing design. In both cases, the extensions were accommodated by reusing and replacing—but never modifying or redesigning—the existing components in the bare-bones architecture. By virtue of the guarantees inherent to the synchronization units model, the resulting variants are free of data races. Moreover, by virtue of the algorithms used to implement the dynamic assembly and re-assembly of realms, the resulting variants automatically avoid and/or recover from preventable deadlocks. We now discuss the issues that we believe contributed to the ease with which these maintenance tasks were accomplished.

One key question for concurrency management in component-based approaches is how to associate synchronization logic with components. Briefly, synchronization logic can be either associated with the component that is a supplier of services or with the component that is the client of that supplier. Traditionally, it has been held that encapsulating synchronization logic in the supplier leads to the most modular and extensible architecture [23, 24]. Moreover, many of the existing client-side approaches are vulnerable to race conditions [25, 26].

Our model goes against the conventional wisdom by intentionally attaching synchronization logic to the component that plays the role of the client in a client–supplier relationship. Indeed, we believe that this approach enables the development of more extensible component architectures. There are two reasons for this. First, for any component of reasonable size, the component developer may not be able to anticipate all of the patterns of service invocations by clients. The knowledge of how the services are being used—in particular, which sequences of service invocations on a component have to be treated as an atomic operation—resides within the clients that use these services. Second, a client may call upon more than one supplier component in the course of an atomic operation, such as how LUA_INTERPRETER uses a number of formerly unrelated components of our basic server architecture. Naturally, this information is not easily encapsulated in a single supplier component (though Holmes [24] introduces the concept of synchronization rings—wrappers around sets of one or more suppliers—to make this possible). As we have seen in our case study, extensibility seems to benefit rather than suffer from client-side synchronization. Instead of requiring us to add post-hoc extensions to existing components, client-side synchronization allowed us to reuse existing components in formerly unanticipated ways.

The cost of attaching synchronization information to the client component is that synchronization logic may have to be unnecessarily replicated for each client. Our approach combats this risk in two ways. First, we made our contract language compact and declarative; so in most cases there is little or no replication to begin with. Second, we allow the reuse of synchronization logic through the usual techniques, such as aggregation and class extension. Consider, for example, our session-management facilities, in which clients must retrieve SESSION components from a centralized SESSION_MANAGER. If k distinct client components were each to interact directly with SESSIONs and SESSION_MANAGERs, then yes, the synchronization logic would need to be replicated in k different synchronization classes. However, when this occurs, the synchronization logic can be localized and encapsulated within an additional component, such as SESSION_OPERATION. By declaring a contract with these special components, clients may reuse rather than replicate these complex patterns of synchronization logic.

Our future work will focus on stress-testing the extensibility of component architectures designed with our model. Specifically, we will experiment with more sophisticated quality-of-service optimizations that are difficult to localize in a single component or cohesive group of components. For example, the load balancing mechanism presented in Section 6 introduces a potential bottleneck in the request processing pipeline, because each request handler must access the interpreter factory twice. Eliminating this bottleneck means shifting part of the work towards the beginning or the end of the pipeline (where contention already exists and is unavoidable). Such an extension requires adding a set of components at normally unrelated stages of the pipeline.

We are also looking at integrating our contractual approach with existing component models, such as the Corba Component Model (CCM) [27] or Enterprise Java Beans (EJB) [28], with an eye towards automated handling and reasoning of concurrency properties of large component assemblies. Reasoning about such assemblies manually can be overwhelming, if not infeasible [29]. However, synchronization contracts already automate the handling of some synchronization properties, and by virtue of providing a (partial) specification of the concurrent behavior of components, could be leveraged to reason automatically about even more difficult non-local properties, such as liveness issues. To this end, we have conducted some preliminary experiments on finding deadlocks at compile time by analyzing the synchronization contracts of components, with the goal of augmenting our runtime deadlock-avoidance and recovery algorithms. Similarly, synchronization contracts could be used to assist EJB programming by replacing the automated concurrency handling through containers with a contractual approach. Existing research indicates that the use of containers for concurrency control can be a serious performance bottleneck for using entity beans in EJB applications [30]. Providing an explicit concurrency control mechanism with strong guarantees for the avoidance of race conditions and deadlocks such as ours might be able to resolve such bottlenecks.

Acknowledgements. Partial support for this research was provided by the Office of Naval Research grant N00014-01-1-0744 and by NSF grants EIA-0000433 and CCR-9984726.

References

[1] Szyperski, C.: Component software: Beyond object-oriented programming. Addison–Wesley (2002)

[2] Magee, J., Kramer, J.: Dynamic structure in software architectures. In: Proc. of the 4th ACM SIGSOFT Symposium on the Foundations of Software Engineering. (1996)

[3] Meyer, B.: Object-Oriented Software Construction. Prentice Hall (1997)

[4] Behrends, R., Stirewalt, R.E.K.: The universe model: An approach for improving the modularity and reliability of concurrent programs. In: Proc. of ACM SIGSOFT Symp. on the Foundations of Software Engineering (FSE-00). (2000) 20–29

[5] Behrends, R.: Designing and Implementing a Model of Synchronization Contracts in Object-Oriented Languages. PhD thesis, Michigan State University (2003)

[6] Behrends, R., Stirewalt, R.E.K., Dillon, L.K.: Avoiding serialization vulnerabilities through the use of synchronization contracts. In: Proc. of the Workshop on Specification and Automated Processing of Security Requirements. (2004) Held in conjunction with the IEEE Intl. Conf. on Automated Software Engineering.

[7] Lerdorf, R.: PHP and Apache2 (2004) http://news.php.net/php.internals/10491.

[8] The Apache Software Foundation: Apache 2.0 thread safety issues (2005) URL:http://httpd.apache.org/docs-2.0/developer/thread_safety.html.

[9] Common Vulnerabilities and Exposures (CVE) Editorial Board : Candidate number 2003-0189 (2003) URL:http://cve.mitre.org/cgi-bin/cvename.cgi?name=CAN-2003-0189.

[10] Common Vulnerabilities and Exposures (CVE) Editorial Board : Candidate number 2003-0789 (2003) URL:http://cve.mitre.org/cgi-bin/cvename.cgi?name=CAN-2003-0789.

[11] Ricca, F., Tonella, P.: Analysis and testing of web applications. In: Proceedings of the 23rd International Conference on Software Engineering, IEEE (2001)

[12] Sabbah, D.: Software engineering and the internet. In: Proceedings of the 23rd International Conference on Software Engineering, IEEE (2001) Keynote speech.

[13] Meyer, B.: Eiffel: the Language. Prentice Hall (1992)

[14] Abi-Antoun, M., Medvidovic, N.: Enabling the refinement of a software architecture into a design. In: Proc. of 2nd Intl. Conf. on the Unified Modeling Language (UML). (1999)

[15] Kaveh, N., Emmerich, W.: Deadlock detection in distributed object systems. In: Proc. of ESEC/FSE 2001. (2001)

[16] Egyed, A., Medvidovic, N.: Consistent architectural refinement and evolution using the unified modeling language. In: Proc. of the 1st Workshop on Describing Software Architecture with UML. (2001)

[17] Grand, M.: Patterns in Java, Volume 1, A Catalog of Reusable Design Patterns Illustrated with UML. John Wiley and Sons (1998)

[18] Gamma, E., Helm, R., Johnson, R., Vlissides, J.: Design Patterns: Elements of Reusable Object-Oriented Software. Addison–Wesley, Reading, Massachusetts (1995)

[19] Netzer, R.H.B., Miller, B.P.: What are race conditions?: Some issues and formalizations. ACM Letters on Programming Languages and Systems 1 (1992) 74–88

[20] Eswaran, K.P., Gray, J.N., Lorie, R.A., Traiger, I.L.: The notions of consistency and predicate locks in a database system. Communications of the ACM 19 (1976) 624–633

[21] Ierusalimschy, R.: Programming in Lua. Lua.org (2004)

[22] Schmidt, D.C., Stal, M., Rohnert, H., Buschmann, F.: Pattern-Oriented Software Architecture Volume 2 – Networked and Concurrent Objects. John Wiley and Sons (2000)

[23] Bloom, T.: Evaluating synchronisation mechanisms. In: Seventh International Symposium on Operating System Principles. (1979) 24–32

[24] Holmes, D.: Synchronisation Rings - Composable Synchronisation for Object-Oriented Systems. PhD thesis, Macquarie University, Sydney (1999)

[25] Hoare, C.A.R.: Communicating Sequential Processes. Prentice/Hall International, Englewood Cliffs, New Jersey (1985)

[26] Hansen, P.B.: Java's insecure parallelism. ACM SIGPLAN Notices 34 (1999)

[27] Object Management Group: Corba component model, v3.0 (2002) http://www.omg.org/technology/documents/formal/components.htm.

[28] DeMichiel, L., Yalcinalp, L.U., Krishnan, S.: The Enterprise JavaBeans 2.0 specification (2001) http://java.sun.com/products/ejb/docs.html.

[29] Ranganath, V.P., et al.: Cadena: enabling CCM-based application development in Eclipse. In: OOPSLA Workshop on Eclipse Technology eXchange. (2003) 20–24

[30] Cecchet, E., Marguerite, J., Zwaenepoel, W.: Performance and scalability of EJB applications. In: Proc. of ACM SIGPLAN conference on Object-oriented programming, systems, languages, and applications. (2002) 246–261

TeStor: Deriving Test Sequences from Model-Based Specifications

Patrizio Pelliccione[2], Henry Muccini[2], Antonio Bucchiarone[1], and
Fabrizio Facchini[2]

[1] Istituto di Scienza e Tecnologie dell'Informazione "A. Faedo" (ISTI-CNR)
Area della Ricerca CNR di Pisa, 56100 Pisa, Italy
`antonio.bucchiarone@isti.cnr.it`
[2] University of L'Aquila, Computer Science Department
Via Vetoio 1, 67010 L'Aquila, Italy
`{pellicci,muccini}@di.univaq.it`

Abstract. The dependability analysis of a component-based system
may be driven by the components/system implementation or by the
model-based specification provided prior to or together with the implementation. In particular, model-based specifications of a component-
based system allows to explicitly model the structure and behavior of
components and their integration, while model-based testing allows to
derive test sequences which can be successively refined into test cases
and then run onto the system implementation.

Several techniques have been proposed so far to allow model-based testing. However, very few of them show certain characteristics which are
peculiar for use in industrial contexts. We here describe TeStor, a TEst
Sequence generaTOR algorithm which allows to extract test sequences
from both state machine and scenario diagrams. We detail the algorithm,
we apply it to a system study and we provide a link to its implementation.

1 Introduction

Roughly speaking, a component-based software system is an assembly of reusable
components, designed to meet the quality attributes identified during the architecting phase [10]. Components are specified, designed and implemented with
the intention to be reused, and are assembled in various contexts in order to
produce a multitude of software systems.

The dependability of a component-based system strongly depends on both
the quality of the assembled components, and on the quality of the assembly
and its subsumed architecture. While the quality of a single component may
be analyzed in isolation, the quality of the assembly may be verified only after
components integration.

While in the past the verification stage to be properly performed required
the assembly of already developed components, with the advent of the model-
driven development, the models themselves may be analyzed before components

G.T. Heineman et al. (Eds.): CBSE 2005, LNCS 3489, pp. 267–282, 2005.

are developed or bought. The essence of model-driven development is the (very old) idea that a system is incrementally obtained by instantiating and refining a specification of system structure and behavior. The essence of model-driven analysis, instead, is the idea of using such models as representative of the (expected) system structure and behavior in order to predict the achievement of certain qualities, and later on to validate the system implementation.

In this paper, we focus our attention on *model-based testing* of component-based systems, at the integration level. We assume a structural and behavioral specification of the components is available, together with architectural information which allows to specify how such components are supposed to interact when assembled in a component-based system. Goal of our algorithm is to extract test sequences, which can be used to test the conformance of an implemented assembly with respect to the specification, considered as an oracle.

Many different approaches and tools have been proposed so far to extract test cases from system models. (Relevant model-based testing approaches are outlined in Section 2). However, very few of them may be considered applicable in "industrial contexts". Following [7], in fact, a model-based testing approach to be suitable for industrial needs has to comply to some extra requirements and constraints: first of all, we cannot assume that a formal (complete and consistent) modelisation of the software system exists. What we may reasonably assume, instead, is a semi-formal specification in the form of UML diagrams. Moreover, the approach should be *usable* (additional formalisms should not be required), *timeliness* (even incomplete models should allow to start outlining a test plan), and *tool supported* (automated tool support is fundamental for strongly reducing testing costs). Surprisingly, even if many tools have been proposed so far for model-based testing [14, 2, 19], very few of them satisfy such requirements.

We here propose our algorithm, called TEst Sequence generaTOR (TESTOR), which allows to extract test sequences from model-based specifications as produced by practitioners. A behavioral model of each component is provided in the form of UML state diagrams. Such models explicitly specify which components interact and how. Sequence diagrams are used as an abstract or even incomplete ("sketchy") specification of what the test should include. TESTOR takes in input UML state and sequence diagrams and synthesizes more detailed sequence diagrams (conforming to the abstract scenarios) by recovering missing information from state diagrams. The output represents test sequences (which include a sequence of stimuli to the system under test, and the expected responses to those stimuli [14]) specified in the form of more informative scenarios. Differently from other approaches, the test sequence generation process in TESTOR does not compute the parallel composition of the state machine models, it does not require any additional formalism, and it is completely tool supported.

The following of this paper is organized such that in Section 2 we analyze some relevant related work. Section 3 is utilized to describe the TESTOR algorithm. Section 4 describes how the TESTOR has been implemented. Section 5 provides initial evaluations of the proposed algorithm while Section 6 concludes the paper.

2   Related Work

In recent years the use of explicit models in software development (most notably the use of UML for object oriented analysis and design) has expanded greatly. Several researchers have focused their efforts in finding methods and tools for guiding the testing activities by means of system model description [2]. In this section we briefly summarize some of the recent research results which make use of UML-diagrams for testing purposes.

Many model-based testing approaches are *state-machine based*. Initial attempts to use UML state diagrams for testing purposes are presented by Offutt and Abdurazik [21], who translate these diagrams into formal SRC specifications, Liuying and Zhichang [18], who use a formal semantic of state machines to derive the test cases, and Kim et al. [17], who focus on class testing. More recently, Hartmann et al. [15] extended to a component-based paradigm the approach of [21], and Antoniol et al. [5], considered the derivation of test sequences from UML statecharts by covering selected paths in a FSM.

Some relevant proposals for *scenario-based testing* include: the approach of Graubmann and Rudolph [12], in which the Message Sequence Chart (MSC) inline expressions and High Level MSC (hMSC) are included into Sequence Diagrams for the specification of test cases; the methodology of Harel and Marelly [13], which is specifically designed for scenario-based specification of reactive systems; TOTEM (Testing Object-orienTEd systems with the unified Modelling language) [8], which uses sequence or collaboration diagrams associated to each use case for deriving test cases, test oracles and test drivers, and SCENTOR [25], which uses JUnit as a basis for test case derivation. SeDiTeC [11] automatically generates test stubs for the classes and methods whose behaviour is specified in the sequence diagrams. The Cow Suite tools and methodology recently discussed in [6] provide an integrated and practical approach for generating and planning UML-based test suites for industrial contexts.

There are very few approaches, like our, were *both state machines and scenarios* are required for test case generation. UMLAUT (Unified Modelling Language All pUrposes Transformer)[3] is and approach tool supported which translates UML diagrams into an intermediate formal description understandable by the Test Generation and Verification (TGV) tool. AGEDIS (Automated Generation and Execution of Test Suites for DIstributed Component-based Software)[1], generates and executes test cases for application modelled according to the AML (AGEDIS Modelling Language), which is a specialised UML profile. SCENT (SCENario-based validation and Test of software) [24], creates scenarios in a structured way, formalizing them into statecharts.

Our work shares with all of them the idea of guiding the testing activities by means of system models. In particular, we share with UMLAUT, TGV, AGEDIS and SCENT the combined used of state and sequence diagrams. Differently from other approaches which use UML diagrams to model and test use cases or classes, we put ourselves in a component-based context, where state diagrams are used to model how components are supposed to behave in a component-based system.

3   The Test Sequence Generator Algorithm

According to [14], a model based test generator accepts as main inputs a *model of the software under test*, and a set of *test generation directives* which guide the test cases selection (called test purposes in [16]), and outputs a *test specification*, which includes a set of stimuli the tester should introduce in the system together with expected responses.

The model based test sequence generator TESTOR gets in input the behavioral model of the components (in terms of components' state machines) and a sequence diagram (inSD) representing the test directive, and outputs a set of sequence diagrams (outSD) representing the shortest paths which cover the inSD into the state machines. In other terms, each outSD contains the sequence of messages expressed by the inSD, enhanced/completed with information gathered by the components' state machines. It is important to notice that the TESTOR algorithm identifies the different test sequences outSD by individually simulating the different state machines, and without constructing the global automaton, i.e.: without parallel composition of the different behaviors. This important optimization allows to handle the well known state-explosion problem.

In order to help in explaining how TESTOR works, we go through an explanatory example. Figure 1.$a-d$ illustrates the state machines related to the Siemens C.N.X. Optical Session System (OSS) conceptual architecture. Each state machine denotes a component and the labels on the transitions identify exchanged messages, with the assumption that a message can be exchanged only by a pair of components. For each transition an ? or ! operator is defined with the following meaning: ?l[!l] identifies an input [output] of the l message.

The OSS description and its architecture have been presented in [20], and its discussion is out of scope for this paper. (The state machines' labels have been renamed to improve readability). The sequence diagram used as test directive is illustrated in Figure 1.e.

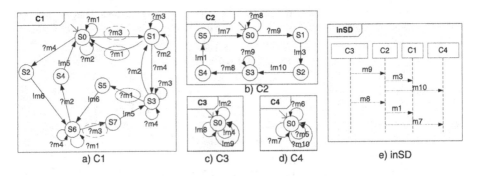

Fig. 1. $a-d$) SA Components Behavior, e) inSD

TESTOR, focussing on the first (not visited) message m in the inSD, and looking inside each state machine, searches a trace which allows to reach m, starting from the current state of the state machine. When such trace is found, TeStor recursively moves to the next (not visited) message m' in inSD, and checks a trace which allows to reach m' starting from the current state. At the end of this process, TeStor tries to merge together the different traces in a unique trace (the outSD) which moves from the initial state and covers any message m in the inSD.

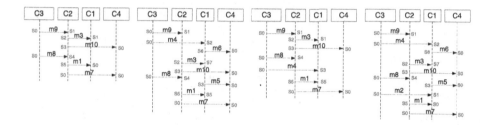

Fig. 2. The four traces generated

Figure 2 shows the four outSD traces generated by applying TeStor to the case study in Figure 1. To increase readability, we report on the outSDs lifeline of each component, the state reached by the component, after having exchanged the message. Following the TeStor algorithm, $m9$ is initially selected in the inSD in Figure 1.e. Starting from the initial state of the four state machines, the components C2 and C3 may exchange $m9$. C2 changes its state to $s1$. Then, $m3$ is selected in inSD. C1 and C2 may reach $m3$ from their current states ($s0$ and $s1$, respectively). Whenever the last message in inSD has been analyzed, a different algorithm, Merge, merges together the different traces, by checking if and when the different components may synchronize.

The TeStor algorithm can be split into two macro-steps:

1. *State machines -sm- Linearization:* instead of traversing sm for identifying a trace which allows to reach m in sm, starting from sm current state s, we initially decompose sm in a set of linear *traces*. In order to limit the number of linearized traces, TeStor avoids loops and repetitions such as each trace is branching free and each pair of traces do not share transitions.

2. *Test Sequence Generation:* the second macro-step involves the test sequence generation. This macro-step looks at each linearized state machine in order to identify the *sup-traces* of the inSD. A sup-trace is *a trace which contains any message contained in the inSD, in the same order they were in inSD, and includes any other message necessary to simulate the inSD trace into the state machines.* Sup-traces generated by TeStor are minimal, since loops are removed. This algorithm is composed by a *Validation* part, which checks when and how sup-traces need to be combined to produce the outSD.

In the following of this section we detail the TeStor algorithm. In Section 3.1 and 3.2 we detail the Linearization and Test Sequence Generation algorithms

used by TESTOR. For the sake of brevity this paper omits algorithm's details
which can be found in [23].

TESTOR makes use of the following methods:
- `MessageSet messages(SD sd)`: is a method that returns the set of messages contained into the sequence diagram sd.
- `boolean isEmpty(Set s)`: is a boolean method that returns true iff the set s is empty.
- `delete(Set s, Element el)`: this method deletes the element el from the set s.
- `add(Set s,Element el)`: this method adds the element el to the set s.
- `updateIs(SD sd)` is a method that updates the initial state for each state machine.

For each state machine (sm), the Linearization algorithm is invoked (lines 2-5).
We suppose that each sm is in its own initial state.

TESTOR Pseudo-Code

```
    TeStor(){
2       SDSet sdSet;
        foreach sm ∈ SM{
4           Linearize(sm);
        }
```

In lines 6-24 the TESTOR algorithm attempts to *construct the sup-traces* for each
message m, and to *concatenate* them in order to obtain the wanted outSD. For
each message m in the inSD, the method `TestSequenceGeneration` is called.
It returns a set of traces, $sdSetMsg$, containing the message m and additionally any other message required to properly exchange m. Each message causes
the construction of a set of traces. In order to produce a unique sup-trace for
inSD, the sup-traces of any message in inSD need to be concatenated. Note
that the `updateIs` method invocation precedes the `TestSequenceGeneration`
method invocation because for each trace we have to set a different initial state.
The errors raised in lines 9 and 17 identify the impossibility to reproduce the
inSD inside the set SM of state machines. When such errors are raised, an inconsistency between inSD and the state machines is identified. The code in lines
19-22 constructs the set of outSD by appending the obtained traces for the current message m to the already stored (partial) outSDs i.e.: the traces built for
messages that precede m in inSD.

```
6       sdSet = TestSequenceGeneration(m,∅,∅);
        if(isEmpty(sdSet)){
8           /* It is not possible to obtain the sequence */
            return Error;
10      }
        foreach m ∈ messages(sd){
12          foreach sd ∈ sdSet{
                updateIs(sd);
14              SDSet sdSetMsg = TestSequenceGeneration(m,∅,∅);
                if(isEmpty(sdSetMsg)){
16                  /* It is not possible to obtain the sequence */
                    return Error;
18              }
                delete(sdSet,sd);
20              foreach sdMsg ∈ sdSetMsg{
                    add(sdSet,sd.sdMsg);
22              }
            }
24      }
    }
```

3.1   Linearization

Starting from the initial state in the components' state diagrams, the Linearization algorithm follows each transition exiting from that state until the start state, or a state with output degree *outDegree* or input degree *inDegree* greater than one is reached. Roughly speaking, the linearization process creates a trace at any time a state with a branch is reached (i.e., a state with outDegree > 1 or inDegree > 1). The algorithm is iterated, starting from the previously reached state, until unvisited states still exist.

The number of linear traces generated can be computed as in the following:

$$\#traces = \mathbf{outDegree}(startState) + \sum \mathbf{outDegree}(s)$$

for each state s so that $(\mathbf{outDegree}(s){>}1) \vee (\mathbf{inDegree}(s){>}1)$

The linearization properties are the following:

1. it partitions states into *intermediate* states (states that are in the middle of a trace) and *exterior* states (states that are the source or the target of a trace).

    - *exterior* states are *i*) all the states with (outDegree > 1) ∨ (inDegree > 1), or *ii*) the start state, or *iii*) each sink state; *intermediates* are the other states.

2. the linearization does not loose information i.e.: it is possible to reconstruct the original state machines starting from the linearized traces.

Linearization Applied to the Optical Session System: in the following we show the results of the linearization algorithm applied on the case study in Figure 1. As an example we explain how the traces for component $C2$ are obtained. The start state of $C2$ is S_0 (as shown in Figure 1.b). Since outDegree(S_0)=2, S_0 is an *exterior* state. The trace 1 is created thanks to the message $m8$. The trace 2 follows the path indicated by $m9$ and ends with the state $S3$ that is a state with outDegree equal to two. While trace 3 is generated by the loop message $m9$, trace 4 is the path that allows to reach state S_0.

C1		C2	C3	C4
1. $S_0 \xrightarrow{m1} S_0$	9. $S_1 \xrightarrow{m4} S_3$			
2. $S_0 \xrightarrow{m2} S_0$	10. $S_3 \xrightarrow{m3} S_3$	**C2**	**C3**	**C4**
3. $S_0 \xrightarrow{m3} S_1$	11. $S_6 \xrightarrow{m4} S_6$	1. $S_0 \xrightarrow{m8} S_0$	1. $S_0 \xrightarrow{m9} S_0$	1. $S_0 \xrightarrow{m7} S_0$
4. $S_1 \xrightarrow{m2} S_1$	12. $S_6 \xrightarrow{m2} S_4 \xrightarrow{m5} S_0$	2. $S_0 \xrightarrow{m9} S_1 \xrightarrow{m3} S_2 \xrightarrow{m10} S_3$	2. $S_0 \xrightarrow{m8} S_0$	2. $S_0 \xrightarrow{m10} S_0$
5. $S_0 \xrightarrow{m4} S_2 \xrightarrow{m6} S_6$	13. $S_6 \xrightarrow{m3} S_7 \xrightarrow{m5} S_3$	3. $S_3 \xrightarrow{m9} S_3$	3. $S_0 \xrightarrow{m4} S_0$	3. $S_0 \xrightarrow{m5} S_0$
6. $S_6 \xrightarrow{m1} S_6$	14. $S_3 \xrightarrow{m4} S_3$	4. $S_3 \xrightarrow{m8} S_4 \xrightarrow{m1} S_5 \xrightarrow{m7} S_0$	4. $S_0 \xrightarrow{m2} S_0$	4. $S_0 \xrightarrow{m6} S_0$
7. $S_1 \xrightarrow{m3} S_1$	15. $S_3 \xrightarrow{m1} S_5 \xrightarrow{m6} S_6$			
8. $S_1 \xrightarrow{m1} S_0$	16. $S_3 \xrightarrow{m2} S_1$			

3.2 Test Sequence Generation

The input of the `TestSequenceGeneration` is a message m and two sets which identify the already explored state machines and related traces, while the output is a set of traces representing the different paths that conduct the system to exchange message m. The second and the third inputs are used for recursive purposes, propagating the state reached for each state machine and the traces under construction. In the first invocation the two sets are empty.

Let C_s (C_r) the component which sends (receives) m. The algorithm initially generates two sets of scenarios from the linearized traces of C_s and C_r, and eventually merges them (through the `merge` method) generating the outSD scenario.

`TestSequenceGeneration` makes use of the linearized state machines and can be synthesized as follow:

1. Let is the state of C when m must be exchanged.

   The `TestSequenceGeneration` method selects the linearized traces containing m. For each selected trace t we check if the trace contains the state is. If it contains it, the trace t is accepted. Otherwise we must check if concatenating several traces it is possible to reach the state is. The selection of those traces uses some rules: i) if a trace contains twice the message m, the trace is rejected. ii) if a trace adds a loop (an already visited state is reached), then it is rejected.

   This procedure is implemented by the `Validation` method and identifies sup-traces which may contain new messages that are required by the system to reach the configuration able to exchange the message m.

2. Any added message to the sup-trace can require the introduction of other messages. In fact, for each new message contained into the sup-trace, the `TestSequenceGeneration` algorithm is invoked with the set of the updated state machine and the already constructed traces as parameters.

For a complete description of the algorithm please refer to Appendix A. In the following, the `Validation` and the `Merge` algorithms are detailed.

Validation: the input of this algorithm are a trace t, a message m, the current state cs for trace t, the initial state is for component C (where component C contains trace t), and a set of traces tr used to avoid infinite loops. The output of the algorithm is a set of sup-traces ST, of a valid trace.

It performs also validity checks in the sense that returns an empty set if it is impossible to reach the initial state is.

In the algorithm we make use of the following methods:

- `append(Trace` $tr1$`,Trace` $tr2$`)`: is a method that assigns $tr2.tr1$ to $tr1$.
- `Trace` `subtrace`(t,s_1,s_2): this method returns the sub-trace of t that starts with s_1 and ends with s_2;
- `tracesSet` `tracesToValidate`(s): this method returns the set of the traces with target state s that must be verified;

- boolean <u>contains</u>(t,m): is a boolean method that returns *true* iff the trace t contains the transition m.
- State <u>initialState</u>(Trace t): this method returns the initial state of the trace t.
- State <u>finalState</u>(Trace t): this method returns the final state of the trace t.

The code for function `Validation` can be divided into three parts: *i*) the current state *cs* coincides with the initial state *is*, lines 5-9, *ii*) we reach the start state of trace t, lines 10-14, *iii*) we iterate on the other traces identified thanks to the function `tracesToValidate`, lines 19-29. In the recursive construction of the sup-trace, traces containing the considered message m, loop generated through nested invocations of validation, and traces with loops on one state are not considered (lines 19-27).

Validation Pseudo-Code

```
ST Validation(Trace t, Transition m, State cs, State is, StateSet sSet){
2      ST Ist = Ø;
       Traces tdv;
4      /* Basic step */
       if (cs == is){
6          st = subtrace(t,is,cs);
           add(Ist ,st);
8          return Ist;
       }
10     if (initialState(t)==is){
           st = subtrace(t,is,cs);
12         add(Ist ,st);
           return Ist;
14     }
       add(sSet,cs);
16     /* If the start state of the trace is not equals to is */
       tdv = tracesToValidate(cs);
18     foreach t' in tdv{
           if (!contains(t' ,m)&&
20             !(initialState(t') ∈ sSet)&&
               !(initialState(t')==finalState(t'))){
22             ST Istc = Validation(t' ,m,cs,is ,sSet);
               foreach st ∈ Istc{
24                 append(st ,subtrace(t,is,cs));
                   add(Ist ,st);
26             }
           }
28     }
       return Ist;
30 }
```

Merge: This method gets in input two sets of sequence diagrams and tries to merge them in order to obtain a single sequence diagram. Each sequence diagram contains the set of messages that are contained into the inSD but each one of them can be enriched with messages required by some components in order to respect the inSD. Then the `Merge` method tries to merge each sequence diagram into the first set with every sequence diagram contained into the second set.

For every message contained into the inSD the following reasoning is iterated: let m the current message and m' its predecessor. We are sure that m and m' (if m' exists) are contained into the pair of sequence diagram. We remember that each one of the sequence is complete, in the sense that no additional messages are required to allow the system to exchange the message m. Then let $setS$ the set of messages contained into the first set, between the message m and m', and $setR$ the set of messages contained into the second set, between the message m and m'. The algorithm checks if there exists an ordering of messages that allows the system to exchange all the messages contained into $setS$ and $setR$ in according to the state machines that dictate the behavior of the system.

Test Sequence Generation Applied to the Optical Session System: in the following, we show how the TESTOR algorithm works by making use of the case study. We take into consideration only few steps in the scenario in Figure 1. As showed in Figure 1.e, the first message in inSD is $m9$. The traces (in Section 3.1) which make use of $m9$ are those related to components C3 and C2 where the sender component is C3 (with associated state machine sm_s) and the receiver component is C2 (with associated state machine sm_r).

Analyzing the traces generated for the sender and the receiver, the traces of interest are $itc_s = \{1\}$ and $itc_r = \{2, 3\}$. Trace 3 in itc_r is not of interest since it does not allow to reach the start state without loops. So far, the obtained $sdSet$ contains only one sequence diagram: by exchanging message $m9$, component C3 reaches state $S0$ and component C2 reaches state $S1$.

The second message in the inSD in Figure 1.e is $m3$. $sm_s = $ C2 and $sm_r = $ C1. $itc_s = \{2\}$ and $itc_r = \{3, 7, 10, 13\}$. The traces that must be considered are: trace 2 for component C2 and traces 3 and 13 for component C1. Trace 3 is selected since allows to reach state $S0$. Trace 7 is not selected for the following reasons: the initial state of trace 7 is $S1$; the traces analyzed to reach state $S0$ are traces 3, 4, and 16, where traces 3 and 4 are deleted because represent a loop (trace 3 contains also the message $m3$) and trace 16 requires to consider traces 9, 10, 13, and 14 which represent a loop or contain message $m3$. Trace 13 is selected since it can be combined with trace 5 to reach state $S0$ obtaining the path $S_0 \xrightarrow{m4} S_2 \xrightarrow{m6} S_6 \xrightarrow{m3} S_7$.

Traces 3 and 13 then cause the construction of two different sequence diagrams. The first scenario simply requires the exchange of message $m3$ that conducts component C2 to state $S2$ and component C1 to state $S1$. The second scenario contains, before the message $m3$, the messages $m4$ and $m6$ as required by the sup-trace obtained concatenating traces 13 and 5.

The states reached are the following: $C1_{is} = S1$, $C2_{is} = S2$, $C3_{is} = S0$, and $C4_{is} = S0$ for the sequence diagram 1 and $C1_{is} = S7$, $C2_{is} = S2$, $C3_{is} = S0$, and $C4_{is} = S0$ for the sequence diagram 2.

The same reasoning is applied to the remaining messages. Only another message, $m1$, causes the generation of two different sequence diagrams. Thus, the obtained sequence diagrams are four, as illustrated in Figure 2.

4   Tool Support

The TESTOR algorithm has been implemented has a plugin component for CHARMY, a validation framework for architectural analysis. A beta version of the TESTOR plugin implementation is currently available in [4].

While the CHARMY (standard) editing capabilities allows to edit the SA topology, the components' behavior and the inSD, the TeStor plugin takes in input such information and produces the outSD scenarios.

Figure 3 shows a couple of screenshots of CHARMY and its TeStor plugin. In Figure 3.a) the *sequence editor* pane is shown which allows to draw inSDs and to show resulting outSDs, while Figure 3.b) graphically depicts the *thread editor* which allows to specify the behavior of each component.

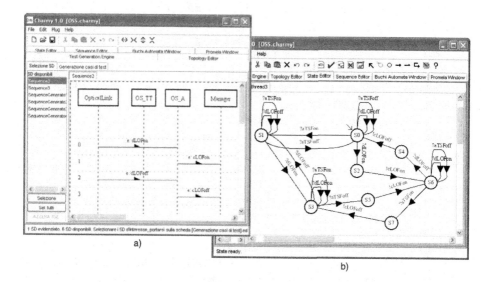

Fig. 3. Some screenshots of TeStor and CHARMY

More details on CHARMY, the TeStor plugin and the CHARMY model of the case study may be found in [4].

5   Some Initial Considerations

As presented in Section 2, there are up to now many model-based testing approaches which make use of UML as the input notation. However, we may distinguish TeStor from such approaches from many reasons: *i)* TeStor does not require the parallel composition of component state machines. While other techniques usually require to create a global model representing the assembled system, TeStor analyzes the components behavior in isolation. The state machine linearization process allows to synthesize traces which are successively traversed in order to reproduce the output scenarios. Since only a subset of the generated traces are traversed by an inSD, this solution allows to strongly reduce the state explosion problem; *ii)* TeStor does not require any formal notation. State machine and scenarios are the only input required by the approach and the tool; *iii*) TeStor is conceived to meet some important (and often conflicting) requirements imposed by industry: low testing effort and high testing accuracy. Effort reduction imposes that models are used as they are, i.e., without requiring extra information and imposing model completeness. Testing accuracy, on the other side, requires to generate test cases from models that are as much informative as possible. The use of both state machine and scenario specifications allows to perceive this goal; *iv*) TeStor is completely tool supported.

Here we report some initial considerations about the proposed algorithm, in terms of *completeness, correctness*, and *complexity*. Future work will improve such informal notes.

Regarding completeness, TeStor does not generate all the possible traces out of the SA behavioral model. In fact, since the `TestSequenceGeneration` algorithm creates loops-free traces, completeness cannot be guaranteed (neither it whould be). However, the TeStor algorithm guarantees to cover at least once any occurrence of inSD messages.

Talking about correctness, instead, we may empirically prove that the TeStor is correct (i.e.: the traces generated from the algorithm are real traces in the state machine models). The linearization algorithm, for definition, contains traces which are contained into the state machines. The `TestSequenceGeneration` algorithm initially selects such linearized traces which allow to reach m, and then combine such traces based on how state machines synchronize. The algorithm `merge` assures, finally, that the traces produced are behaviors contained into the system.

Another important point to be evaluated regards the algorithm computational complexity, in terms of time and space occupied. The linearization algorithm requires to visit each arc of the state machine graph, thus it has a complexity equal to the number of arcs. The `TestSequenceGeneration` algorithm complexity depends on the number of traces generated by the linearization algorithm, on the size of the inSD, and on the "granularity" of the inSD (i.e., how much the inSD scenario is incomplete, with respect to the state machines). In future work we plan to formally discuss the algorithm computational and time complexity.

6   Conclusions and Future Work

TeStor is an algorithm, which taking in input state machines and scenarios, generates test sequences in the form of scenarios. The algorithm poses its basis on the idea that scenarios are usually incomplete specifications and represent important and expected system interaction. Such incomplete specifications may be "completed" by recovering, from state machines, the missing information. TeStor has been implemented as a plugin component of the Charmy analysis framework.

In an ongoing work we are integrating the test case selection approach implemented in TeStor in our model-checking-based testing methodology proposed in [9]. We are starting applying the resulting tool supported methodology to the Siemens C.N.X. system described in [20], and evaluating the efficacy of our approach with respect to Siemens C.N.X. design and analysis processes. Moreover, we are currently analyzing how TeStor generated test sequences can be converted into executable tests.

Another interesting integration we have in mind is to use the TeStor output as input for the Use Interaction Test (UIT) method [6]. Largely inspired to the Category Partition Method [22], UIT systematically constructs and defines a set of test cases for the Integration Testing phase, by using UML sequence diagrams as its exclusive reference model. We believe in this way we may combine the UIT main advantage of effort reduction with a more effective set of derived test cases.

Other improvements we have in mind are to analyze the possibility to produce linear traces and generate test sequences all at once, and to provide a richer formalism to express inSDs. In particular, we may wish to extract all such outSDs which correctly implement inSDs such as those in Figure 4: inSD1 (i.e., any path which includes $m1$ followed by $m3$, excluding $m2$ in between the two) and inSD2 (i.e., any path which includes $m1$ immediatly followed by $m2$, and eventually followed by $m3$).

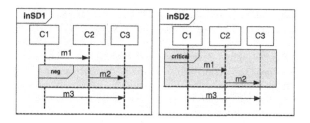

Fig. 4. inSD1 and inSD2 in the UML 2 formalism

Acknowledgment

The authors acknowledge Siemens C.N.X. who provided the case study and supports this research, Pierluigi Pierini for his contribution on a previous version of the paper, and Antonia Bertolino and Eda Marchetti which contributed on a previous paper with similar goals. We are indebted with the anonymous reviewers too which suggested relevant changes.

References

[1] AGEDIS Project. http://www.agedis.de/index.shtml.
[2] Model-based Testing Home Page.http://www.geocities.com/model_based_testing/. Maintained by Harry Robinson.
[3] UMLAUT Project. http://www.irisa.fr/UMLAUT/.

[4] CHARMY Project. Charmy Web Site. http://www.di.univaq.it/charmy, 2004.

[5] G. Antoniol, L. C. Briand, M. Di Penta, and Y. Labiche. A Case Study Using the Round-Trip Strategy for State-Based Class Testing. In *Proc. IEEE ISSRE2002*, 2002.

[6] Francesca Basanieri, Antonia Bertolino, and Eda Marchetti. The Cow_Suite Approach to Planning and Deriving Test Suites in UML Project . In *Fifth International Conference on the Unified Modeling Language - the Language and its applications(UML 2002)*, pages 383–397, Dresden, Germany, September 2002.

[7] Antonia Bertolino, Eda Marchetti, and Henry Muccini. Introducing a Reasonably Complete and Coherent Approach for Model-based Testing. In *In Testing and Analysis of Component-Based Systems Workshop, Tacos 2004*. To be pubblished in Electronic Notes of Theoretical Computer Science, 2004.

[8] L.C. Briand and Y. Labiche. A UML-Based Approach to System Testing. *Journal of Software and System Modelling (SoSyM)*, 1(1):10–42, 2002.

[9] A. Bucchiarone, H. Muccini, P. Pelliccione, and P. Pierini. Model-Checking plus Testing: from Software Architecture Analysis to Code Testing. In *Proc. International Testing Methodology workshop*, Lecture Notes in Computer Science, LNCS, vol. 3236, pp. 351 - 365 (2004), October 2004.

[10] Ivica Crnkovic and Magnus Larsson, editors. *Building Reliable Component-based Software Systems*. Artech House, July 2002.

[11] F. Fraikin and T. Leonhardt. Seditec - testing based on sequence diagrams. In *Proc. IEEE CASE 02*, Edingburgh, September 2002.

[12] P. Graubmann and E. Rudolph. HyperMSCs and Sequence Diagrams for use case modeling and testing. In *Proc. UML 2000*, volume LNCS Vol.1939, pages 32–46, 2000.

[13] D. Harel and R. Marelly. Specifying and Executing Behavioural Requirements: The Play In/Play-Out Approach. *Journal of Software and System Modelling (SoSyM)*, 2003.

[14] Alan Hartman. Model Based Test Generation Tools. Technical report, AGEDIS project Downloads, 2002.

[15] J. Hartmann, C. Imoberdof, and M. Meisenger. UML-Based Integration Testing. In *ACM Proc. ISSTA 2000, Portland*, 2000.

[16] C. Jard and T. Jéron. Tgv: theory, principles and algorithms. In *The Sixth World Conference on Integrated Design & Process Technology (IDPT'02)*, Pasadena, California, USA, June 2002.

[17] G. Kim, H. S. Hong, D. H. Bae, and S.D. Cha. Test Cases Generation from UML State Diagram. *IEEE Proceedings - Software*, 146(4):187–192, August 1999.

[18] L. Liuying and Q. Zhichang. Test Selection from UML Statecharts. In *Proc. of 31st Int. Conf. on Technology of Object-Oriented Language and System*, China, 22-25 September 1999.

[19] Eda Marchetti. *Software Testing in the XXI Century: Methods, Tools and New Approaches to Manage, Control and Evaluate This Critical Phase*. PhD thesis, University of Pisa, September 2003.

[20] Henry Muccini, Patrizio Pelliccione, Antonio Bucchiarone, and Pierluigi Pierini. Software Architecture-driven System Testing through Model-Checking. Technical Report TRCS 035/2004, University of L'Aquila, 2004.

[21] J. Offutt and A. Abdurazik. Generating Test from UML Specifications. In *Proc. UML 99, Fort Collins, CO, October 1999*.

[22] T. J. Ostrand and M. J. Balcer. The category-partition method for specifying and generating functional tests. *Communications of the ACM*, 31(6):676–686, June 1988.

[23] Patrizio Pelliccione, Henry Muccini, Antonio Bucchiarone, and Fabrizio Facchini. Deriving Test Sequences from Model-based Specifications. Technical Report TRCS 002/2005, University of L'Aquila, 2005.

[24] J. Ryser and M. Glinz. Using Dependency Charts to ImproveScenario-Based Testing, 2000.

[25] J. Wittevrongel and F. Maurer. Using UML to Partially Automate Generation of Scenario-Based Test Drivers. In Springer, editor, *OOIS 2001*, 2001.

Appendix A: Test Sequence Generation

In this appendix we report a more complete description of the algorithm Test Sequence Generation, in the form of Pseudo-Code. It makes use of the following methods:

- **TracesSet extractTraces**(SMId sm, Message m): this method extracts all traces containing the message m;
- **SMId senderSM**(Message m): this method returns the ID of the state machine that sends the message m
- **SMId receiverSM**(Message m): this method returns the ID of the state machine that receives the message m
- $SDSet$ **merge**($SDSet$ sdSenderSet, $SDSet$ sdReceiverSet): this method makes the merge of two sets of sequence diagrams. The two sets represent the actions required by the send and receive state machine to reproduce the behavior in the input sequence diagram. The algorithm attempts to construct for each element in the first set and for each element in the second one, a sequence that the system is able to execute. If it is impossible to obtain a correct behavior, the algorithm does not introduce any sequence in the output set. If the resulting set is empty, then it is impossible to obtain a correct behavior starting from the two input sets.
- **msgSet messages**(Trace t): this method returns the set of messages contained into the input trace.
- **State startState**(Trace t, Message m): this method returns the start state for a message contained into a trace.
- **Int size**(Set s): this method returns the size of the set s.

The algorithm starts identifying such component which may send/receive m and selects the linearized traces containing m (lines 2-11). The trace selection is performed by means of the extractTraces method.

Test Sequence Generation Pseudo-Code

```
   SDSet TestSequenceGeneration(Message m, SMSet smSet,
2  TraceSet trSet){
       sm_s = senderSM(m);
4      sm_r = receiverSM(m);
       itc_s = trSet(sm_s, smSet);
6      itc_r = trSet(sm_r, smSet);
       if(isEmpty(itc_s)){
8          itc_s = extractTraces(sm_s,m);
       }
10     if(isEmpty(itc_r)){
           itc_r = extractTraces(sm_r,m);
12     }
```

The next part of algorithm is composed of two equal parts: one for the sender component state machine (lines 13-40) and one for the receiver component state machine (lines 41-68). A sender component is one which may send message m. Symmetrically, a receiver component is one which may receive message m. Each of them constructs the set of traces representing what the system must do to allow the exchanging of the message m. Focusing only on the sender part, we note that the algorithm makes use of the method `Validation` (line 15). This method is detailed in the following and intuitively identifies each trace which allows the system to exchange message m.

For each trace identified and for each new message introduced, a recursive call to `TestSequenceGeneration` is performed (line 23).

The `TestSequenceGeneration` is invoked with the sets $smSet$ and $trSet$ increased with the current state machine sm_s and with the current trace t, respectively. In fact the sense of the recursive invocation is to fill the sequence under construction with details needed for all the SM, except for the already considered ones. At each nested invocation, another SM with the related trace is added.

The rest of the code, lines 13-34, represents the construction of the set of sequence concatenating the results of the recursive invocations.

```
     SDSet sdSet_s;
14   foreach t ∈ itc_s{
        sm_s.cs = startState(t,m);
16      ist = Validation(t,m,sm_s.cs,sm_s.is,_);
        if (!(isEmpty(ist))){
18         foreach el ∈ ist{
              if(size(ist)==1){
20               sdSet_s = ist;
           }else{
22            foreach message m' ∈ messages(el){
                 /* ordered from the first to the last */
24               SDSet sdSetMsg = TestSequenceGeneration(m',smSet+sm_s,trSet+t);
                 foreach sdMsg ∈ sdSetMsg{
26                  SDSet sdSetTmp;
                    if(isEmpty(sdSet_s)){
28                     add(sdSetTmp,sdMsg);
                    }else{
30                     foreach sd ∈ sdSet_s{
                          add(sdSetTmp,sd.sdMsg);
32                     }
                    }
34               }
                 sdSet_s = sdSetTmp;
36            }
           }
38        }
        }
40   }
     /* ... */
42   /* Code for the receiver */
```

The last part of the algorithm is the construction of the output set of sequence diagrams by merging the set of sequence diagrams required by the sender and the receiver state machines.

```
     /* Merge of sdSet_s and sdSet_r */
44   SDSet sdSet = merge(sdSet_s,sdSet_r);
     return sdSet;
46 }
```

A CCA-compliant Nuclear Power Plant Simulator Kernel

Manuel Díaz, Daniel Garrido, Sergio Romero, Bartolomé Rubio, Enrique Soler, and José M. Troya

Dpto. Lenguajes y Ciencias de la Computación. Málaga University
29071 Málaga, SPAIN
{mdr, dgarrido, sromero, tolo, esc, troya}@lcc.uma.es

Abstract. This paper presents a parallel, component-oriented nuclear power plant simulator kernel. It is based on the high-performance computing oriented Common Component Architecture. The approach takes advantage of both the component paradigm and the parallel execution of simulation models. This way, the maintenance, evolution and efficiency of a simulator are improved. The work introduces the main features of the simulator kernel, describing concepts and the model it is based on. Data dependencies among components (simulation models conforming a simulator) are solved in a configuration phase, reducing the execution time of the simulation phase. Some preliminary results are shown, which anticipate the feasibility, suitability and efficiency of the proposal.

1 Introduction

The evolution and growing complexity of modern software systems create the need for new programming paradigms that facilitate the development and maintenance of software applications. Component-Based Software Engineering proposes the development of applications by plugging standalone software components [9]. Based on component interoperability, this programming style allows the creation of more flexible and adaptable software, promoting reusability of components already developed and verified in other projects and increasing, this way, the reliability of the final product.

Initially applied to the business world, component technologies are coming to other areas such as scientific computing. Scientific software frequently demands high performance in order to execute complex mathematical models or simulate physical phenomena in acceptable time. Components standards and implementations, such as OMG CCM [14], Microsoft DCOM [10], Sun Java Beans and Enterprise Java Beans [7] [11], share serious shortcomings for parallel and distributed scientific applications, due to the lack of the abstraction needed by parallel and distributed programming and poor performance. They also have trouble with the mechanism for encapsulating an existing scientific application (which might itself be a parallel-distributed application) into a component.

Recently, some efforts are being carried out in order to incorporate component technologies into high performance computing area. In this sense, AS-SIST [19] is focused on high-level programmability and software productivity

G.T. Heineman et al. (Eds.): CBSE 2005, LNCS 3489, pp. 283–297, 2005.

for complex multidisciplinary applications, including data-intensive and interactive software. SBASCO [6] is oriented to the efficient development of parallel and distributed numerical applications. A large effort is currently devoted by the Common Component Architecture (CCA) forum [18] to define a standard component architecture for high-performance computing.

This work is focused on nuclear power plant simulators. A Pressurized Water Reactor (PWR) plant consist of a vessel, containing the nuclear reactor, steam generators and hydraulic loops made up of pipes and pumps through which water and steam flow. The basic working is simple. The reactor produces heat that is carried by pressurized water to the steam generators. They vaporize the water in a secondary loop to drive the turbine, which produces electricity. In order to simulate the operation of a nuclear power plant in a computer system, we need detailed models of heat transmission, vessel, valves, pipes and pumps, etc. Many simulation codes use a plant nodalization as input, a model built up by interconnecting a set of predefined cells whose state variables are solved every time step.

The use of simulators has special importance in the context of nuclear power plants. On the one hand, they can predict the plant status when facing to different situations that can occur in the daily operation. In this sense, a fast response is required and performance becomes a major factor. On the other hand, they can be used as training tools for future operators, allowing for the practice of normal (temperature monitoring, valve manipulation) and unusual (emergency) situations.

Currently, we are collaborating with Tecnatom S.A. [17] in order to carry out the maintenance of different nuclear power plant simulators [4] [5]. Software architecture of these simulators is organized as a collection of distributed applications that can be executed on any node of a network, setting their communications through CORBA [13]. The *simulator kernel* is the most important application in the simulator context. It carries out the iterative execution of different *simulation models*, which are responsible for the precise simulation of physical components of the real system. There is a wide range of simulation models, from computationally intensive complex models like TRAC (thermo hydraulic model) or NEMO (neutronic model) to simpler ones simulating, for example, the operating of a valve.

Current simulators are programmed in a classical (non component-oriented) style, in such a way that simulation models, coded as sequential Fortran subroutines, are statically linked together into the simulator kernel. This approach, apparently feasible at first, presents serious limitations from the Software Engineering viewpoint. For example, it is very usual for a simulation model to read or update data variables computed by others. In order to resolve data dependencies among models, all shared data are declared as global variables allowing access from any subroutine. Besides that, it is difficult to manage different versions of the same models, and substitution, modification or integration of new models into the simulator turn into tedious tasks. Reusability of these simulation models

in other simulators is also limited due to the used programming techniques and
the coupling among the current models.

An attractive solution for solving all these software maintenance related problems is componentization. In this new approach, a simulator kernel can be constructed by connecting the corresponding simulation models, now encapsuled
into software components, to a central manager component which implements
the runtime system taking care of executing the models in a proper way. Apart
from componentization, an additional aspect can be taken into account in order
to improve the system. In the current simulators, simulation models are implemented using sequential procedures. However, codes from some of these models
can be parallelized by splitting the computation in such a way that they could
be run on multiple processors in order to reduce their execution time. For example, in [2] a parallel version of the thermo hydraulic code encapsulated into the
TRAC simulation model is described. Parallelization of this model is especially
important since it represents about 80% of the total simulation time.

In this paper, we present a parallel, component-oriented version of the simulator kernel of a nuclear power plant simulator. The approach overcomes the
above-described limitations, making the management of simulation models easier and allowing the integration of parallel and sequential models into the same
simulator. This way, the maintenance, evolution and efficiency of a simulator are
improved. We have chosen CCA, a component model specifically designed for
high performance scientific computing, as component technology for programming the simulator kernel. Due to the size and large number of simulation models
that constitute the global system, the human work force necessary to componen-
tize them is large enough to consider the development of a previous prototype,
including some test simulation models, in order to evaluate the feasibility and
suitability of our proposal. The runtime support is based on Ccaffeine [1], a
CCA-compliant framework oriented to high performance parallel computing environments.

The rest of the paper is structured as follows. Section 2 introduces the
software architecture of the simulators. The main features of the CCA component model are presented in section 3. Section 4 describes the proposed CCA-
compliant simulator kernel and the experimental results obtained by using the
prototype. The paper finishes with some conclusions and future work.

2   Simulator Architecture

The simulation projects of Tecnatom S.A. usually include two simulators that
influence on hardware and software architectures. The first one is called Interactive Graphic Simulator (IGS), which through graphic applications (see figure 1,
right) allows operator training. The second one is called Full Scope Simulator
(FSS), which is an exact replica of the power plant control room taking care
of all details, from physical artifacts such as furniture, control panels, etc. to
software simulating the applications running in the room (see figure 1, left).

Fig. 1. Details of *Full Scope Simulator* (left) and *Interactive Graphic Simulator* (right).

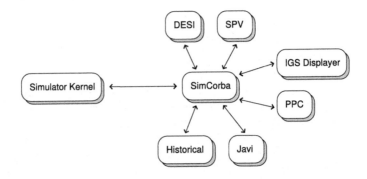

Fig. 2. Main software applications conforming the simulator.

The main high level hardware elements of FSS and IGS are: Simulation computers, Instructor console, Physical panels and Student workstations. Simulation computers are responsible for the simulation process executing the simulation models and providing data to the rest of software and hardware components. The Instructor console is used by the instructor of the simulation sessions and it allows the creation of different scenarios that have to be solved by the students. The Physical panels are exact replicas of those existing in the control room. Operators carry out their actions mainly through these panels, with hundreds of indicators, hardware keyboards, etc. IGS simulators additionally include the hardware needed for Student workstations that basically allow the practice of any simulation area in a comfortable way with graphical applications and several monitors for each student.

The software architecture of the entire simulator is organized as a collection of distributed applications that interact with each other through the high-level communication mechanisms provided by CORBA. Some of the most important applications together with their interactions can be seen in figure 2. The complete software system can be divided into two well differentiated parts. The first one comprises the simulator kernel and SimCorba. These two applications act as a simulation server offering a set of simulation services to the rest of tools and applications, which constitute the second part of the system. The following is a short description of the applications conforming the simulator:

- **Simulator Kernel:** application responsible for computing the simulation of the nuclear power plant by executing the different simulation models. It is the most important application in the simulator context.
- **SimCorba:** a simulation server that offers a set of services such as periodic transfer of variables, actions over the simulator, etc. to the rest of applications. It manages all communications between client applications and the simulator kernel.
- **Client applications:** a wide group of applications that interact with Sim-Corba for different purposes, such as debugging the simulation process, allowing representation and modification of simulation variables, changing simulation aspects like cycling time, recording the simulation state in real-time including all significant variables, etc.

Due to the system size and the heterogeneity of the involved applications, the development of simulators includes different platforms such as Unix, Linux and Windows, with different programming languages such as C++, Java and Fortran.

The work presented in this paper is focussed on one concrete application from the above-described architecture: the simulator kernel. The shortcomings related to the current simulator kernel design, as mentioned before, encouraged us to develop a new version of this application based on component-oriented programming and parallel execution of simulation models. The new simulator kernel, together with SimCorba, must implement the same set of simulation services provided by the current version in order to keep the rest of client applications unchanged.

3   CCA Model

This section describes the main features of the Common Component Architecture (CCA). A more detailed explanation can be found in [18]. CCA provides a means for scientific software developers to build applications by assembling software components in a "plug and play" environment for high performance computing. CCA is a specification developed by the CCA Forum to describe the rules for constructing CCA components, the model for linking them together and the collection of services that frameworks should provide.

Components interact with each other through well-defined *ports* which are the key elements of the connection model representing communication end point for components. A CCA port is described by an interface which declares a collection of methods without revealing implementation details. In this sense, they are similar to interfaces in Java or abstract virtual classes in C++. Components are linked together by connecting their ports following a *provides-uses* interface design pattern similar to that within the OMG CCM proposal. According to this, there are two types of ports: *provides ports*, which represent the services offered by a component and describe its calling interface, and *uses ports*, which describe functionality a component may need and are the stubs that a component uses to invoke services provided by another component. A uses port of a component can be attached to a compatible (same type) provides port of another component. Since this connection is performed, a procedural (not dataflow) relationship is established and any functionality represented by the uses port is obtained by invoking the methods in the connected provides port.

The Scientific Interface Definition Language (SIDL) and the Babel tool [3] have been adopted by CCA in order to make the use of components independent of their implementation languages. SIDL is the high level, object oriented, programming language-neutral IDL used to describe component interfaces. It provides classical abstractions and data types commonly used in scientific computing, such as dynamic multidimensional arrays and complex numbers. It also provides other useful features such as enumerated types, symbol versioning, name space management as well as an object model with partial support for inheritance, polymorphism and method overloading. Using SIDL descriptions, Babel generates the necessary glue code to translate method calls from one language to another, making it possible to connect together into the same application components implemented in different languages.

A framework represents a concrete implementation of the model mechanisms. Component instances are created and managed within a framework, which must provide, according to the CCA specification, a minimal set of services that components use in order to communicate with each other. Currently, different frameworks have been developed to support specific computational environments such as parallel, distributed or multithread. Ccaffeine, the CCA-compliant framework employed in this work, is focused on local and parallel high performance applications. *Single Program Multiple Data* (SPMD) is certainly the most widely used style of parallel computing, where all processes run the same program, although each one has its own data. Ccaffeine uses a trivial extension of this paradigm, referred to as *Single Component Multiple Data* (SCMD), where identical frameworks containing the same set of components wired the same way are instantiated on every process. Inside each process, framework mediates component interactions through a highly efficient port mechanism implementation. Since all components are loaded into the same address space (process), when a component needs to connect a uses port to the provides port of another component for calling a method, the framework returns a direct reference (pointer) to the actual implementation, which causes a minimal latency overhead for component interactions equivalent to a C++ virtual function call. On the other hand, parallel instances of the same component in different processes (referred to as a *cohort*) can communicate with each other through a concrete parallel environment such as MPI [16], PVM [8], Global Arrays [12] or Shared Memory. CCA and Ccaffeine make it possible to construct high performance applications by connecting parallel components which are (possibly) implemented in different programming languages and even making use of distinct parallel communication libraries.

4   CCA-compliant Simulator Kernel

This section presents the main features of the new parallel, component-oriented simulator kernel, describing concepts, execution phases and performance evaluation tests for the implemented prototype.

4.1   Concepts and SIDL Definitions

Simulation models contain the necessary code to simulate specific parts of the system. The execution of a simulation model usually requires reading or updating data variables which are computed by other models (we also refer to these data as *simulation variables*). The previous (classical) version of the simulator kernel resolved these types of inter-model data dependencies by declaring all shared data as global variables allowing access from any subroutine. Since we pursue the encapsulation of simulation models into separated software components, we must adopt a more appropriate mechanism for managing data dependencies. In our proposal, each component must report on:

- *Simulation variables it needs*, for reading or updating, from other models in order to be executed.
- *Simulation variables it provides*, which are computed and offered (exported) to the rest of models.

According to this, the programmer of a concrete simulation model component only has to declare, by implementing the corresponding methods, the simulation variables needed from/provided to the rest of models whereas a *manager component* integrated in the kernel is the one responsible for locating the requested variables (even if they are hosted in different processes) and providing them to the respective models. Specific inter-process communication schemes needed to resolve data dependencies efficiently are established in a configuration phase. This way of managing data dependencies leads to a significant uncoupling among simulation models in both development and execution time. The programmer is not concerned about issues such as knowing the rest of models in the simulator or resolving data dependencies and so, he/she can be focussed on writing scientific code for the simulation model under development.

Simulation models are now encapsulated into (sequential or parallel) independent software components. Since all of them are CCA-compliant components implementing a concrete interface, we make sure they can be integrated into the same simulator, even if they are programmed using different languages or communication libraries. Our proposal makes the construction of different simulator kernels possible. This can be easily achieved by selecting and composing the corresponding simulation models from a component repository. All simulator kernels developed in this way share the same architecture that comprises a central

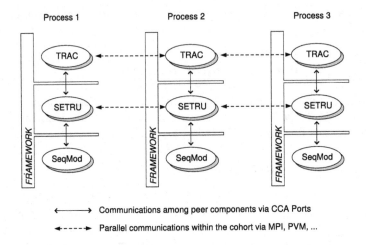

Communications among peer components via CCA Ports

Parallel communications within the cohort via MPI, PVM, ...

Fig. 3. Simulator Kernel implemented as a SCMD-parallel application.

manager component called SETRU and the appropriate collection of simulation models connected to it. SETRU takes care of controlling the simulation by executing the different simulation models in a proper way. In fact, this component plays a major role since it implements the entire runtime system of the simulator kernel. Some of the most important functions carried out by SETRU are:

- To retrieve information from the models connected to it, setting up data structures accessed during the simulation.
- To resolve data dependencies, providing the requested simulation variables to the corresponding models.
- To execute the different simulation models properly.
- To send values of updated simulation variables to the rest of processes for maintaining data consistency.
- To create additional threads for handling communications with SimCorba and executing the simulation commands received from it.

Figure 3 describes the Single Component Multiple Data paradigm used to implement the simulator kernel as a Ccaffeine application. In this paradigm, all components together with the framework are instantiated in every participant process. Different components in the same process communicate among them through the CCA Port mechanism, which occurs, for example, when SETRU needs to call methods on models connected to it.

Simulation models can be programmed using both sequential and parallel programming styles. Instances in different processes of the same parallel component, e.g. TRAC in figure 3, communicate with each other by using a parallel communication library such as MPI or PVM. In this case, all simulation variables computed by the model are distributed across the different processes. On the other hand, instances of a component that represents a sequential simulation model, e.g. SeqMod in figure 3, do not communicate among them and the same whole computation is executed on every process, having their simulation variables replicated on all processes. Other situations can also be considered: for example, a parallel simulation model having both distributed and replicated data variables, or a sequential model being executed on one process only (not replicated). The proposed simulator kernel supports the integration of all these different types of simulation models together, maintaining data consistency for both distributed and replicated data.

Simulation codes model the nuclear power plant as a set of interconnected *nodes* and *cells*. We represent simulation variables, which are used to refer to these nodes and cells, as instances of SIDL classes (figure 4). An instance of class SimReference has a variable name, a number of node and a range of cells over which the particular variable is computed, for example, *pressure calculated on node 2, cells from 1 to 5*. SimVariable class extends SimReference to add the specific real value that the variable takes on each cell. Simulation models use lists of SimReference objects to declare simulation variables needed from other models. The values of these requested variables are provided by SETRU by means of SimVariable objects.

All simulation models are encapsulated into CCA components that implement the ISimModel interface shown in figure 4 and described in next section. Since some methods of ISimModel are independent of the specific simulation model, we offer a base class, called BaseModel, that implements them. Taking advantage of the mechanisms provided by SIDL, classes implementing simulation model components can (optionally) inherit from this base class. In this case, the programmer only needs to code specific methods for configuring, initializing and executing the specific simulation model.

4.2   Execution Phases

The simulator kernel execution is divided into two different phases. In the first one, called the *configuration phase*, both simulation models and communications with SimCorba are properly configured. In the second one, called the *simulation phase*, the execution of the models is carried out according to the simulation commands received from SimCorba.

Configuration Phase. The structure of a concrete simulator kernel, including the simulation models employed, their relative execution order and a set of simulation parameters, is described in a configuration file. SETRU component reads this file and registers a ISimModel *uses port* for each simulation model composing the simulator in order to communicate with them. On the other hand, simulation models only needs to register one ISimModel *provides port* (to provide services to SETRU), besides the proper *uses ports* needed to use functionality offered by other auxiliary components. Port registration procedure is carried out by the *setService()* method, which must be implemented by every component according to the CCA specification. This method is called by the framework when the component is instantiated.

```
package simkernel version 1.0
{
  class SimReference
  {
    void createSimReference(in string name, in int node,
        in int initCell, in int finalCell);

    string getName();
    int getNode();
    ...
  }

  class SimVariable extends SimReference
  {
    void createSimVariable(in string name, in int node,
        in int initCell, in int finalCell);

    double getValue(in int cell);
    void setValue(in int cell, in double value);
    array<double> getAllValues();
    void setAllValues(in array<double> values);

    SimVariable subVar(in int initCell, in int finalCell);
    void assign(in SimVariable variable);
    string toString();
  }

  interface ISimModel extends gov.cca.Port
  {
    string getModelName();
    array<SimReference> getListRefRead();
    array<SimReference> getListRefUpdated();
    array<SimReference> getListRefProvided();
    SimVariable getVar(in SimReference reference);
    void setVar(in SimVariable variable);

    void setup();
    void initialize();
    void execute();
  }

  class Trac extends BaseModel
      implements-all ISimModel, gov.cca.Component
  {}
}
```

Fig. 4. SIDL definitions for SimVariable class and ISimModel component interface.

Once all components are connected together, SETRU calls *setup()* and *initialize()* methods on each simulation model. The former contains the necessary code to create and configure the simulation variables provided (computed) by the model as well as the lists of SimReference objects representing the sets of variables read, updated and provided. The latter initializes the provided variables with correct values. Then, SETRU calls *getListRefRead()*, *getListRefUpdated()* and *getListRefProvided()* methods on the connected models. These methods return the lists of SimReference objects created by *setup()*.

Since information obtained locally from the connected models is sent to all participant processes, SETRU component in each process knows the location (process and model) of simulation variables, which lets it to resolve local and remote data dependencies:

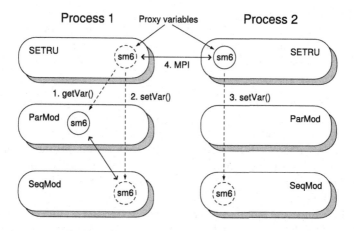

Fig. 5. All instances of *SeqMod* read the simulation variable *sm6* provided by *ParMod* in process 1. *SETRU* uses MPI for updating proxy variables in all processes.

- **Local data dependencies.** When a simulation model needs a variable computed by other model in the same process, SETRU provides it by calling *getVar()* on the "provider" model and *setVar()* on the "requester". An example can be seen in figure 5, where SeqMod in process 1 needs to read the simulation variable *sm6* provided by ParMod in the same process. By calling *getVar()* on ParMod, SETRU obtains a SimVariable object representing the simulation variable, which is passed to SeqMod through *setVar()* method. Since SIDL objects are implemented as references (pointers) by the respective programming languages, SimVariable instances used in both SeqMod and ParMod models make reference to the same physical data.
- **Remote data dependencies.** However, if data dependencies involve different processes, an additional intermediate (proxy) variable is created in every process. When the simulation variable is modified due to the execution of a particular simulation model, its new value is sent to the corresponding processes by using these proxy variables. Figure 5 shows this type of data dependencies as well. SeqMod instance in process 2 is the one that reads variable *sm6* exported by ParMod in process 1. SETRU creates proxy variables on both processes. The SimVariable object representing *sm6* is obtained by calling *getVar()* on ParMod and assigned to the proxy variable in process 1. On the other hand, the proxy created in process 2 is passed to SeqMod instance in the same process by calling *setVar()* method. During the simulation, SETRU uses message passing for updating proxy variables in different processes with the values computed by the provider model ParMod. This way, simulation models can treat proxies as if they were local simulation variables, reading or updating its values, while SETRU takes care of hiding all communication details.

Since the main execution thread carries out the simulation, additional threads are needed in order to communicate with SimCorba application. At the end of the configuration phase, SETRU creates these threads and initialize CORBA communication mechanisms.

Simulation Phase. Each time a simulation model is going to be executed, its required simulation variables must be updated with the latest computed values. By using information obtained in the configuration phase, a specific inter-process communication pattern can be established for each particular model in order to determine the minimal MPI communications needed to resolve its remote data dependencies. By using these fixed communication patterns, message passing is carried out efficiently during the rest of the simulation.

From this point, the simulator kernel is ready to react to different simulation commands received from SimCorba such as *start/stop simulation, start/stop debugging mode, execute n steps, query/modify simulation variable*, etc. Once the proper command has been received, the simulation begins with the execution of the models in the relative order described in the configuration file. The execution of a simulation model involves the following three steps that are carried out by SETRU:

- **Step 1:** Proxy variables are updated with the values of simulation variables hosted in other processes and needed by the model. Values of all simulation variables sent from one process to another are previously packed together in order to minimize message passing.
- **Step 2:** The simulation model is executed by calling its *execute()* method in every process. This method contains the parallel or sequential code implementing the simulation.
- **Step 3:** Once the model is executed, updated values corresponding to simulation variables hosted in other processes are sent to them in order to modify variables in the provider models.

4.3   Performance Evaluation

The use of CCA components together with the Ccaffeine framework, SIDL/Babel tool for language interoperability and (specially) the defined runtime system, which allows the integration and communication of generic simulation models, may affect the efficiency of the system. The purpose of these experiments is to evaluate the efficiency of the mechanisms the described simulator kernel is based on. The developed prototype comprises implementations for SETRU component and some test simulation models programmed in C++ with MPI. We consider appropriate for our test models to implement simple parallel methods for solving partial differential equations (PDEs) based on domain decomposition techniques [15]. We can adjust these numeric methods to demand the same CPU utilization and communications than the real simulation models. The experiments involve comparing the componentized simulator versus a specific direct

Table 1. Execution time (in seconds) and overhead percentage (in brackets) for simulation tests implemented by "classical" C++/MPI program and componentized CCA simulator kernel prototype.

Simulation Test A (Classical vs. CCA)			
	Sequential	2 Processors	4 Processors
Classical	72.34	40.24	26.30
CCA	75.20 (+3.95%)	41.92 (+4.17%)	26.65 (+1.33%)

Simulation Test B (Classical vs. CCA)			
	Sequential	2 Processors	4 Processors
Classical	36.62	26.95	20.15
CCA	37.43 (+2.21%)	28.16 (+4.48%)	20.82 (+3.32%)

implementation made up of a single (non component-oriented) efficiently coded C++/MPI program. We have programmed two different scenarios. The first one (simulation test A) comprises computationally intensive parallel models. Data dependencies among models always occur into the same process (local data dependencies) so message passing is only due to parallel communications within the cohort. The second one (simulation test B) represents a communication intensive scenario in which we reduce CPU demands and add lots of inter-model data dependencies involving different processes (remote data dependencies) in order to make extensive use of SETRU communication mechanisms.

Executions have been carried out in a cluster of Pentium 4, 2.66GHz, 1GB RAM Linux workstations interconnected with a 1Gb/s Myrinet network. Table 1 summarizes the obtained results, which are very similar for the two implementations in both simulation tests. This behavior is due to:

- Component interactions through CCA ports are performed efficiently in the context of Ccaffeine framework.
- Communication schemes, automatically calculated in the configuration phase, are very similar to those coded in the classical approach in order to resolve inter-model remote data dependencies.
- Models use *getAllValues()* method of SimVariable to obtain an array object containing cell values. SIDL array classes have a method which returns a direct pointer to stored data. By calling this method for every simulation variable in the configuration phase, efficient data access is carried out during the simulation.

— When reasonable amounts of computation take place into the models, which is usual for the described simulators, the SETRU runtime system overhead can be accepted.

As a first approach, results reveal the feasibility of our proposal, in the sense that the minimal penalty overhead imposed by the CCA implementation (less than 5% in both simulation tests) is compensated for by the advantages of the component-oriented paradigm together with the developed runtime system.

5   Conclusions and Future Work

A nuclear power plant simulator is a complex, computationally intensive application that can take advantage of component-based software engineering, especially when the used component model allows the execution of parallel components in an efficient way. This paper has presented a CCA-compliant simulator kernel, where simulation models are implemented as both sequential and parallel components. The main characteristics of the used model have been introduced. Simulation models export the variables they own and declare the variables they need. The kernel is in charge of solving data dependencies among components in the configuration phase. This way, the programmer is released from managing inter-model communications and the simulation phase is carried out in a more efficient way. Some preliminary results have shown the suitability of the proposal.

A full scope nuclear power plant simulator needs the integration of hundreds of simulation models. Currently, most of these models are developed by using a graphical tool, which is going to be modified to generate the CCA-compliant models in order to be integrated into the described simulator kernel.

References

1. Allan, B.A., Armstrong, R.C., Wolfe, A.P., Ray, J., Bernholdt, D.E., Kohl, J.A., The CCA Core Specification in a Distributed Memory SPMD Framework, *Concurrency and Computation: Practice and Experience*, **14**, 5 (2002), pp. 323–345.
2. Alvarez, J.M., Díaz, M., Llopis, L., Rus, F., Soler, E., Practical Parallelization Strategies of a Thermohydraulic Code, in *Proceedings of Euroconference in Supercomputation in Non Linear and Disordered Systems*, pp. 254–258, Madrid, Spain, 1996.
3. Components@LLNL: Babel, home page http://www.llnl.gov/CASC/components /babel.html.
4. Díaz, M., Garrido, D., Applying RT-CORBA in Nuclear Power Plant Simulators, in *7th IEEE International Symposium on Object-Oriented Real-Time Distributed Computing (ISORC 2004)*, pp. 7–14, IEEE Computer Society, Vienna, Austria, 2004.
5. Díaz, M., Garrido, D., A Simulation Environment for Nuclear Power Plants, in 8th IEEE International Workshop on Distributed Simulation and Real-Time Applications (DS-RT 2004), pp. 98–105, IEEE Computer Society, Budapest, Hungary, 2004.

6. Díaz, M., Rubio, B., Soler, E., Troya, J.M., SBASCO: Skeleton-Based Scientific Components, in *Proceedings of the 12th Euromicro Conference on Parallel, Distributed and Network-based Processing (PDP 2004)*, pp. 318–324, IEEE Computer Society, A Coruña, Spain, 2004.
7. Englander, R., Developing Java Beans. O'Reilly&Associates, 1997.
8. Geist, A., Beguelin, A., Dongarra, J., Jiang, W., Mancheck, R., Sunderam, V.S., PVM: Parallel Virtual Machine. MIT Press, 1994.
9. Heineman, G.T., Councill, W.T., Component-Based Software Engineering: Putting the Pieces Together. Addision Wesley, 2001.
10. Horsmann, M., Kirtland, M., DCOM Architecture, Microsoft White Paper, 1997. Available from http://www.microsoft.com/com/wpaper.
11. Monson-Haefel, R., Enterprise Java Beans 3th edition, O'Reilly&Associates, 2001.
12. Nieplocha, J., Harrison, R.J., Littlefield, R.J., Global Arrays: a Portable Shared Memory Programming Model for Distributed Memory Computers, in *Supercomputing'94*, pp. 340–349, Los Alamitos, California, USA, 1994.
13. Object Management Group, CORBA home page http://www.corba.org.
14. Object Management Group (OMG), Specification of Corba Component Model (CCM). http://www.omg.org/technology/documents/formal/components.htm.
15. Smith, B., Bjorstad, P., Gropp, W., Domain Decomposition. Parallel Multilevel Methods for Elliptic P.D.E.'s. Cambridge University Press, 1996.
16. Snir, M., Otto, S., Huss-Lederman, S., Walker, D., Dongarra, J., MPI: The Complete Reference, volume 1–The MPI Core. MIT Press, 1998.
17. Tecnatom S.A. home page http://www.tecnatom.es
18. The Common Component Architecture Forum, home page http://www.cca-forum.org.
19. Vanneschi, M., The Programming Model of ASSIST, an Environment for Parallel and Distributed Portable Applications, *Parallel Computing*, **28**, 12 (2002), pp. 1709–1732.

Experience with Component-Based Development of a Telecommunication Service

Gregory W. Bond, Eric Cheung, Healfdene H. Goguen, Karrie J. Hanson,
Don Henderson, Gerald M. Karam, K. Hal Purdy, Thomas M. Smith, and
Pamela Zave

AT&T Laboratories—Research, Florham Park, NJ 07932, USA
{bond,cheung,hhg,karrie,don,karam,khp,tsmith,pamela}@research.att.com

Abstract. AT&T CallVantage^{SM} service is a consumer broadband voice-over-Internet-protocol (VoIP) service. Its feature server has a component-based architecture. This paper is a brief report on our experience with building and deploying advanced telecommunication features using component-based technology.

1 Introduction

Distributed Feature Composition (DFC) is a component-based software architecture for the development of telecommunication services [4]. In AT&T Research we have built an Internet-based implementation of DFC [2]. We have also built the iStudio platform for constructing Web services with an emphasis on reuse [7], and integrated the two service platforms as an application server called V+Plus.

AT&T CallVantage^{SM} service is a consumer broadband voice-over-Internet-protocol (VoIP) service whose advanced features are built and deployed on V+Plus. The service architecture uses the well-known VoIP protocol SIP [5]. V+Plus functions within the service architecture as a SIP application server.

The AT&T CallVantage^{SM} service was launched in March 2004, and is now available in most of the United States. It has received a great deal of favorable press coverage, particularly for its advanced features and voice quality. It has merited a VoIP Service Provider Award from *Internet Telephony* magazine, and *PC Magazine's* Editors' Choice Award.

This paper is a brief overview of our experience with specifying, developing, deploying, and maintaining the service's advanced features, beginning in May 2003. It focuses on the use of components in this software.

2 Components in DFC

In telecommunication software, a *feature* is an increment of functionality added to the basic communication capability. Features are both the work units for software development and the concepts through which a telecommunication service is explained to its users.

G.T. Heineman et al. (Eds.): CBSE 2005, LNCS 3489, pp. 298–305, 2005.

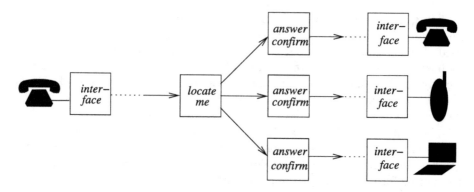

Fig. 1. The Locate Me feature is implemented with two box types.

The telecommunication world has long acknowledged the difficulty and importance of being able to add, delete, and modify the features of a complex telecommunication service. This calls for a style of modularity in which the modules are features. It is also well-understood that features have many interactions, and that managing these interactions is critical to reliability and user satisfaction. This calls for structured composition of feature modules, so that their interactions can be predicted and controlled.

The DFC architecture was designed to provide feature modularity and structured feature composition. It is an adaptation of the idea of *pipes and filters* [6] to the application domain of telecommunications.

In DFC, a request for service is satisfied by a dynamically assembled graph of *boxes* and *internal calls*. A box (filter) is a concurrent process implementing interface or feature functions. An internal call (pipe) is a featureless, point-to-point connection containing a two-way signaling channel and any number of media channels.

In the context of this paper, a DFC internal call is like a plain, old-fashioned telephone call. So the simplest useful graph has two interface boxes, each representing a telephone or other device, connected by one DFC internal call.

More typically, many features apply to each request for service. When features apply, the dynamically assembled graph contains feature boxes implementing these features. Figure 1 shows a fragment of such a graph. Note that a typical connection path between two interface boxes is a chain containing many feature boxes and internal calls.

When a feature box is inactive it behaves transparently. For a feature box between two internal calls, transparent behavior consists simply of connecting their media channels and relaying signals between them. When a feature box is active, on the other hand, it has the autonomy and power to affect communication in any way required. It can place, receive, and tear down internal calls. It can manipulate media channels. It can also absorb, generate, or alter signals as well as propagating them transparently.

The formal definition of DFC [11] falls into three parts. The *protocol* governs how internal calls, signaling channels, and media channels are established and used. The *data model* partitions persistent data, which can be read and written by boxes. The *routing algorithm* controls how boxes of various types are assembled dynamically into connection graphs. The routing algorithm is invoked each time a box places an internal call, and it selects the type of box that will be instantiated or located to receive the call.

The routing algorithm uses data in two categories. *Subscriptions* indicate which addresses (telephone numbers) subscribe to which features. *Precedence* governs the order of features boxes along paths within a graph, and is the primary mechanism for managing feature interactions.

The DFC protocol and routing algorithm are designed so that each feature is optional and each feature box is context-independent—it does not know or need to know which other feature boxes are present. This is the fundamental source of modularity in a pipes-and-filters architecture.

To clarify terminology, a *box* is a dynamically created and assembled component in the architecture. The box's *type* corresponds to a program of which the box is an instantiation.

3   How DFC Boxes Are Used in the Service

3.1   Boxes as Identified Features

Considering all its versions, AT&T CallVantage^{SM} service has 25 features that have been identified and named, either externally (to users) or internally (as units of software development).

Of the 25 features, five (Caller Identification, Caller Identification Blocking, Call Forwarding, Call Waiting, and Three-Way Calling) are basic telecommunication features implemented in a VoIP switch. Two (International Billing, International Call Screening) are implemented in routing components. Three (Phone Book, Simple Reach Numbers, Voicemail eFeatures) are implemented wholly in the Web and data facilities of V+Plus. The remaining 15 are implemented, wholly or in part, by DFC boxes as shown in the table.

Most commonly, there is a one-to-one correspondence between telecommunication features and DFC box types. Occasionally a box type implements more than one feature. For example, a *voice portal* box implements the Personal Call Manager feature. The same box type also implements the Speed Dial function, which is identified to users as a feature.

Also, some features must be implemented using boxes of more than one type. A good example is Locate Me, as shown in Figure 1. An instance of the *locate me* box type can place internal calls—in parallel—to several possible telephones where its subscriber might be located. When one of these attempts succeeds, *locate me* aborts the others and connects the answered telephone with the caller.

DFC Box Type	Features Implemented	Other Purpose
answer confirm	Locate Me	
blind transfer	Add Callers	
call blocking	Call Blocking	
call log	Call Log	
click-to-dial	Click-to-Dial, Record and Send	
conference manager	Personal Conferencing	
de-identification		adaptor
do not disturb	Do Not Disturb	
identification		adaptor
iStudio interface		adaptor
join	Personal Conferencing	
locate me	Locate Me	
mid-call move	Switch Phones^{SM}	
mid-call offer	Switch Phones^{SM}	
phonebook name	Phonebook Name	
rendezvous	Add Callers	
remote identification	Personal Call Manager	
safe forwarding number	Safe Forwarding Number	
send to voicemail	Send to Voicemail	
SIP interface		adaptor
ten-way calling	Add Callers	
tone generator		adaptor
voice mail	Voice Mail	
voice portal	Speed Dial, Personal Call Manager	
voice user interface		adaptor
VoiceXML interface		adaptor

An *answer confirm* box performs another function of the Locate Me feature. If the callee telephone is answered, it prompts for a confirmation that the phone has been answered by the person requested by the caller; if it does not receive a confirming response, it does not propagate a success signal upstream to the *locate me* box. There is an instance of *answer confirm* for each parallel attempt, which is why it must be separated from the *locate me* box.

The *answer confirm* function is particularly valuable when one of the telephones is part of a cellular network with its own Voice Mail feature. Without *answer confirm*, every time the cellphone is unavailable, the call to it will be "answered" by cellphone Voice Mail. This "answer" will probably precede all other answers, aborting the other attempts and subverting the purpose of *locate me*.

3.2   Boxes as Reusable Building Blocks

From another perspective, DFC boxes are reusable building blocks for building telecommunication services. There is reuse at several levels.

At the highest level, we reused whole features from prototype systems we have built in the past. Some required minor modifications to fit into the environment of the new service.

At a lower level, the design of a feature is sometimes influenced by the existence of box types that can be used as generic components to implement it. This is the primary reason why Add Callers—a complex feature that allows the spontaneous formation of conferences of up to ten people—is implemented using three DFC box types.

At a lower level yet, programs are reused to create new box types. We have a "redirect on failure" box program that is used, with modifications for failure type and redirection address, to create the *voice mail* and *safe forwarding number* box types. We have an "address translation" box program that is used, with parameters for regular expression to be matched and string to be substituted, to create any box type that modifies the addresses (telephone numbers) in the signals that initiate internal calls.

At the lowest level, our programming language for boxes [3] allows us to identify and package program fragments for reuse in other box programs. We have amassed a significant collection of such fragments.

3.3   Boxes as Adaptors

The V+Plus application server operates in an environment with many other hardware components such as VoIP switches, gateways, routers, telephone adaptors, and media servers. Despite the fact that SIP is a standardized protocol, all VoIP technology is immature, and integration problems are commonplace.

Given the fact that a DFC box is a filter in a pipes-and-filters architecture, it is not surprising that we find them useful as adaptors. The most important adaptors are *interface* box types. Interface boxes form the periphery of DFC graphs. A *SIP interface* box translates between SIP and the DFC protocol, which is better suited for component composition than SIP. An *iStudio interface* box allows Web services to launch telecommunication activities (see Sections 3.4 and 4). A *VoiceXML interface* allows feature boxes to place calls to media servers capable of running VoiceXML scripts that specify interactive voice-response dialogues.

We put code in interface boxes and other adaptors to solve integration problems as they arise. Modularity is particularly beneficial in this context, because the adaptors represent short-term or localized decisions that we would not wish to embed deeply in feature code.

For example, the *identification* and *de-identification* box types bridge a conceptual gap between DFC and the architecture of the service as a whole. In DFC routing decisions are based strictly on addresses. In the architecture of the service as a whole, routing decisions can also depend on which hardware component originates the routing request. Fortunately, well-placed adaptors can convert from one kind of state to the other.

A *tone generator* box is another kind of adaptor. For the most part, generation of "progress" tones such as busytone and ringback is the responsibility of hardware components independent of V+Plus. However, deficiencies in SIP prevent these components from getting the necessary signals under all circumstances. When SIP cannot carry the necessary signals, a *tone generator* box (with the help of a media server) generates the tone and inserts it into the voice channel.

3.4 Boxes as Interfaces to Web Services

Persistent data is the interface between telecommunication and Web services, as it can be read and written by both. For example, *call log* boxes record history that can be accessed by subscribers via the Web. A *phonebook name* box looks up the name corresponding to a calling telephone number in the callee's phonebook, and substitutes the name for the number in Caller Identification.

Sometimes the interaction between the two aspects of the service is more active. The Click-to-Dial feature is activated by a Web service when a subscriber clicks on a telephone number. The Record and Send feature calls a list of telephone numbers, delivering a prerecorded message to each; it is activated from the Web and implemented by repeated activations of Click-to-Dial.

4 Component-Based Development of Data Views in the Service

Both Web browsers and telephones are end-user interfaces for AT&T CallVantage^{SM} service. Through them, users can enable or disable features, change feature settings, or access personal content such as voicemail messages. The iStudio [7] architecture offers a component-based implementation of these interfaces that is complementary to boxes in the DFC architecture.

Similar to Apache Struts [1] in philosophy, iStudio provides us with a mechanism for supporting software objects that compartmentalize the data for features such as Call Log, Voice Mail, and Locate Me. Each component manages the database tables and operations for its own feature.

iStudio accesses the database on behalf of all other software in V+Plus. It produces HTML for visual Web pages, VoiceXML scripts for interactive voice-response dialogues, and data values for use by DFC boxes. The generators of these data views all share the feature-specific software objects mentioned above.

The Click-to-Dial and Record and Send features are activated by Web services. A user request for one of these features is delivered from the Web application to an *iStudio interface* box that places a DFC internal call to begin assembly of a graph of feature boxes.

5 History and Evaluation of Software Development with V+Plus

We delivered the first 11 features to a test organization two months from the inception of the project. It was possible to fit requirements specification, design, and implementation into this extremely short period only because of much reuse.

Reuse of code, as described in Section 3.2, is obviously important. Equally important is the reuse of domain knowledge based on the DFC architecture.

The DFC architecture constrains how features can interact, and is therefore a foundation for theories of feature interaction. Such theories predict how features *can* interact, justify how they *should* interact, and provide design constraints proven to satisfy correctness in these terms.

These theories are still immature (see [9, 8, 10] for examples). A rudimentary understanding is better than none at all, however, and was extremely helpful to us in predicting feature interactions and in deciding how to manage them. For example, all of Locate Me, Do Not Disturb, Voice Mail, Call Blocking, Send to Voicemail, and Safe Forwarding Number make decisions concerning the disposition of incoming calls. They must interact so that exactly the right features, in the right order, are activated in each situation.

A few feature interactions compromise modularity to the extent that one feature must be programmed with another feature in mind. For example, a *voice mail* box generates a special signal so that a *call log* box knows whether or not a caller recorded a message. This is necessary because the basic DFC protocol does not distinguish these cases. It is always possible, however, to program cooperating feature boxes so that neither breaks if the other is absent.

The implementation of AT&T CallVantage^{SM} features is not a trivial use of components. In the first release of the service a connection path between two subscribers could contain 20 DFC boxes, even without any forwarding (forwarding to other subscribers would increase the number of boxes by seven per forward).

The first release of the service was deployed in a consumer trial which began October 2003. In preparation for the first generally available release in March 2004, we removed a few features from the trial version and made a major change in the media handling. Feature removal was easy due to feature modularity in both DFC and iStudio. The need to change media handling is typical of a rapidly evolving technology, in which the available resources and capabilities can change frequently. The software modification was accomplished quickly, in part because the DFC architecture maintains a separation of concerns between the service layer (features) and the network layer (resources).

Subsequent software development has entailed new feature development, maintenance, and performance optimization. As expected, adding new features to the service is easy. There have been relatively few bugs in feature code.

Most maintenance issues are system-integration problems, arising from the immaturity of VoIP technology. Unfortunately they have arisen frequently and will continue to arise for some time to come; at this point almost every new function added to the service exposes new incompatibilities among the hardware components of the service architecture.

It is inevitable that the modularity of DFC will exact a performance penalty. Our measurements indicate that the penalty is small compared to VoIP performance issues that are independent of feature modularity.

We are working toward accurate performance assessments. Meaningful comparisons between implementation alternatives are difficult to obtain, however, because they require multiple implementations of equivalent feature sets, not to mention adequate time in a laboratory full of expensive test equipment.

6 Conclusion

V+Plus was originally built as a research prototype. Nevertheless, it continues to provide the advanced features of a nationwide consumer telecommunication service built on rapidly evolving technology.

Our experience demonstrates the feasibility and value of a component-based architecture in the area of telecommunications. The experience is particularly interesting because the component model is based on pipes and filters rather than the more common object-oriented programming. Object-oriented programming is also present—most of our infrastructure code is written in Java—but at a lower level of abstraction than the components discussed here.

In the community of researchers concerned with feature interactions and telecommunication software, the DFC component model has been considered interesting but radical and impractical. Our experience demonstrates that it is adoptable and completely practical. None of us would dare to work with a technology as complex and volatile as VoIP without this kind of support for evolution and adaptation.

References

[1] Apache Struts. http://struts.apache.org.
[2] G. W. Bond, E. Cheung, K. H. Purdy, P. Zave, and J. C. Ramming. An open architecture for next-generation telecommunication services. *ACM Transactions on Internet Technology*, 4(1):83–123, February 2004.
[3] G. W. Bond and H. H. Goguen. ECharts: Balancing design and implementation. In *Proceedings of the Sixth IASTED International Conference on Software Engineering and Applications*, pages 149–155. ACTA Press, 2002.
[4] M. Jackson and P. Zave. Distributed Feature Composition: A virtual architecture for telecommunications services. *IEEE Transactions on Software Engineering*, 24(10):831–847, October 1998.
[5] J. Rosenberg, H. Schulzrinne, G. Camarillo, A. Johnston, J. Peterson, R. Sparks, M. Handley, and E. Schooler. SIP: Session Initiation Protocol. IETF Network Working Group Request for Comments 3261, 2002.
[6] M. Shaw and D. Garlan. *Software Architecture*. Prentice-Hall, 1996.
[7] A. H. Skarra, K. J. Hanson, G. M. Karam, and J. S. Elliott. The iStudio environment: An experience report. In *Proceedings of the International Workshop on XML Technologies and Software Engineering*, May 2001.
[8] P. Zave. An experiment in feature engineering. In A. McIver and C. Morgan, editors, *Programming Methodology*, pages 353–377. Springer-Verlag, 2003.
[9] P. Zave. Address translation in telecommunication features. *ACM Transactions on Software Engineering and Methodology*, 13(1):1–36, January 2004.
[10] P. Zave, H. H. Goguen, and T. M. Smith. Component coordination: A telecommunication case study. *Computer Networks*, 45(5):645–664, August 2004.
[11] P. Zave and M. Jackson. *The DFC Manual*. AT&T, 2001. Updated as needed. Available from http://www.research.att.com/projects/dfc.

Reusable Dialog Component Framework for Rapid Voice Application Development

Rahul P. Akolkar[1], Tanveer Faruquie[2], Juan Huerta[1], Pankaj Kankar[2],
Nitendra Rajput[2], T.V. Raman[3], Raghavendra U. Udupa[2], and
Abhishek Verma[2]

[1] IBM T J Watson Research Center, Yorktown Heights NY, 10598, USA
[2] IBM India Research Lab, IIT Campus, Hauz Khas, New Delhi, 110016, INDIA
[3] IBM Almaden Research Center, San Jose CA, 95120, USA

Abstract. Voice application development requires specialized speech related skills besides the general programming ability. Encapsulating the speech specific behavior and complexities in prepackaged, configurable User Interface (UI) components will ease and expedite the voice application development. These components can be used across applications and are called as Reusable Dialog Components (RDCs). In this paper we propose a programming model and the framework for developing reusable dialog components. Our framework facilitates the development of voice applications via the encapsulation of interaction mechanisms, the encapsulation of best-of-breed practices (ie. grammars, prompts, and configuration parameters), a modular design and through pluggable dialog management strategies. The framework extends the standard J2EE/JSP based programming model to make it suitable for voice applications.

1 Introduction

Telephony-based voice applications offer a cost-effective way for enterprises to automate their call centers. Additionally, they provide an alternative user interface to their customers for accessing enterprise services. Through telephony applications, the enterprises gain by increasing the penetration of their services beyond the Web/computer literate world. The first generation of IVR (Interactive Voice Response) applications that capture a user's response through dialing DTMF digits on a telephone keypad are still used widely in banking and travel industries. Enhancements in speech recognition technologies over the past decade has seen the evolution of these IVR applications to conversational systems where a user can speak to the system and the voice is recognized to perform the desired user action. Such conversational systems provide a much more natural interface to the user. 914-945-1800 is an example of an IBM application that uses voice interactions to increase productivity. This conversational system provides the phone number of the person whose name is spoken. Over the last couple of years, conversational systems have matured to handle more complex responses from the users, those that incorporate Natural Language Understanding techniques coupled with the speech recognizers. The DARPA COMMUNICATOR

G.T. Heineman et al. (Eds.): CBSE 2005, LNCS 3489, pp. 306–321, 2005.

application [1] is one such real world example of a complex dialog conversational system.

Due to nature of the communication channel, a voice application results in a sequence of dialog turns with the user. The system carries out these interactions and interprets what the user says in the context in which these utterances occur. The applications developed should have an intuitive interface for the callers and allow them to quickly and dynamically interact with the system. It should also intelligently integrate back-end processes into user driven information flow. In contrast to GUI based applications, which are spatial in nature, voice applications are temporal in nature, hence they need to handle on-the-spot error-control, validation and dialog flow control. The application design should be readily acceptable by developers and be easy to develop and maintain since the end aim is to provide organizations with business benefits of cost-reduction, efficiency and superior interface. The application also needs to handle user commands (like ask for help, ask to start over, or ask to repeat a piece of information) in addition to providing the requested information.

Speech applications are generally specified in interaction flowcharts called callflows. A voice application developer is responsible for authoring the code that carries out the interaction specified in the flowchart. Authoring such applications involves implementing large call flows of the user interaction. Developers also need to provide mechanisms such as confirmation, correction and re-prompting to handle speech recognition errors. The richness of user interaction finally determines the usability of the voice application. Call flows become complex as they have to handle all such speech nuances. Designing such applications not only requires programming expertise, but it also requires familiarity with the behavior of conversational systems. A desirable voice application is one that encapsulates all speech tecnology artifacts, the dialog management nuances and the standard client-server issues and presents a robust and intuitive interface.

The evolution of the voice application development platforms had started with the standardization of the VoiceXML [2], the markup language for voice. Most voice browsers can now execute the voice applications written in this standard language. Additional markups such as SALT [3] have also evolved and matured. Speech applications are beginning to move to the next stage where complex applications are deployed on a standard Web Server and implemented through programs that deliver dynamically generated VoiceXML markup in response to requests from a VoiceXML browser. As in the case of the visual Web, the next step in the mainstreaming of speech Web applications is the adoption of uniform programming models such as the J2EE/JSP framework in the creation and deployment of such applications.

1.1   Componentization in Voice Application Development

Owing to the additional speech specific skills that are required for developing robust and user friendly voice applications, the development process becomes expensive in terms of time and resources. A component based approach to develop voice application by reusing the pre-existing components becomes an attractive feature. Components can help in encapsulating knowledge about the behavior of a speech recognition system, of a speech synthesis system and of the different mechanisms to validate and correct the recognition errors. Components can also be used to encapsulate the different dialog management strategies within the components. By following a component based approach to build voice applications, the level of abstraction can be raised so that development of voice applications does not require a burdensome level of speech specific skills.

Existing research in the component based voice application development was initially focussed on developing static VoiceXML components [4]. Industry products such as Nuance SpeechObjects [5], also provide VoiceXML components that can be plugged in an application development environment to generate voice applications. These components however, leverage client side processing of the components through embedding scripts in the VoiceXML. The mechanism of using client side processing in the components limits the features of the component. Complex validation and disambiguation mechanisms that require back-end information are not possible in such a framework. Additionally, components that restrict the scope of component execution on the client are not scalable in terms of the advancement of processing. For example, using the components mentioned in [6] it is not possible to extend the work to perform credit card validation on the client side, since it requires additional information from the back-end databases. Although these components provide dialog management execution on the server side, the non existence of server side execution of other features is still a hindrance to the power of a component.

Researchers have proposed systems that provide a mechanism to build voice components that can execute on the server [7]. However these efforts have not been carried out in a standardized open-source programming model. For a component based approach to be reusable across different applications, standard programming models need to be followed.

Since the aim of building voice applications using components is to ease the application development skills and time and still build rich interactions, the components need to be designed such that they can be used in a voice application development toolkit. Voice application development platforms such as the IBM Voice Toolkit for Websphere Studio [8], the Avaya Speech Applications Builder [9], the Genesys Voice Platform [10] and the Nuance NLSA provide a platform for plugging such dialog components into their programming interface. With a component based framework, these tools can be made more effective in reducing the complexity involved in developing applications.

1.2   Our Contribution

In this paper we describe a novel approach to voice application development based on Reusable Dialog Components. The proposed RDC framework is based on a J2EE/JSP programming framework. The emphasis in our framework is to reduce the application development cost by allowing the application developer to create voice applications based on *reusable* User Interface *components*. The components provide rich UI techniques of disambiguation, validation and correction, besides being robust. The framework also provides a mechanism to develop more components from the existing set, thus handling scalability of the component model. The framework allows for executing the components on the server side, thus providing a richer exposure to back-end data and processing capabilities for the component. By providing a mechanism to develop voice applications by easily configuring the components and plugging them in an application, the framework ensures that building a J2EE/JSP application constitutes the basic level of skill needed for building a voice application. The development tools used to build voice applications are the same as the ones that are used in building J2EE/JSP applications.

Section 2 describes an RDC at a high level and presents its features. The detailed description of the framework is presented in Section 3. This section also describes the RDC public contract and the RDC execution through a finite state machine. Section 4 describes two voice applications and illustrates how RDCs can be used to build real world voice applications. The analysis and benefits of using RDCs to build a car rental application is also highlighted. Scope for future work and a conclusion of the paper are presented in Section 5.

2   Overview of RDCs

The RDC components encapsulate well-tried elements of speech UI design. A component collects information from the user, ensuring that all the required interactions for guaranteeing the completeness, such as validity and canonicalization format of the data are provided. Based on the type of data they collect, components are classified into *atomic* and *composite*. Atomic components (or atoms) collect simple types, for example, a date, a time, a dollar amount. In contrast, composite components are responsible for complex data types. Examples of composite types are addresses, details of a trip, payment method including credit card number, type and expiration dates etc.

RDC Encapsulations The RDCs encapsualte the following constituents of a speech UI. Thus an application developer does not have to handle these nuances while developing a speech application.

1. Grammar Design: Since the components provide the grammars with respect to the prompts, an application developer is not required to have an understanding of the different gramars that are needed to carry out a particular UI task.
2. Dialog Management Strategies: The RDCs are designed with different dialog management strategies which a UI task can follow. All these are implemented within the component.
3. Error Handling: The RDC is self healing in the sense that it encapsulats the mechanisms to handle a mis-recognized utterance and the mechanism to rectify these errors.
4. Disambiguation and Validation: The RDC also encapsulates the different validation checks that are dequired for a particular data type. The RDC

itself detects ambiguities, or inconsistencies in the data that it gathered, and generates the dialog artifacts necessary to allow the component to handle the disambiguation, clarification or correction states.
Althouth these mechanisms are encapsulated and implemented within a RDC, they can all be configured and overwritten for a specific application.

Features of RDCs Following are the features of an RDC that make it reusable and adaptable to applications.

1. Configurability: An RDC can be configured for a particular application by providing application specific prompts and parameters to the component. For example, the same date RDC can be configured to work as a expiry date UI component in one application and as a date-of-journey in other application.

2. Reuse: Since the RDC can be configured for different applications, the reuse of the same component is extremely useful in building UI components of a voice applications. The reusability ensures the reduction in application development time and effort.
3. Dynamic code generation: Since the RDCs are authored as JSP pages, these generate dynamic VXML at runtime. This provides a richer interface and flexibility as compared to static VXML code components.
4. Composite RDC generation: The RDCs can be used to further build bigger UI components if the application identifies their reusability. The aggregation of components into a composite component extends the use of component based framework beyond the existing set of components.

These features enable RDCs to provide a more modular and reusable approach to building voice applications. Furthermore, they hide the difficulty and complexity of creating high quality voice artifacts, allowing for consistent and highly reusable components.

3   Framework

The RDC framework enables speech developers create and package dialog components which can be used by Web application developers for building speech applications. The framework also supports composition of components in a very simple way wherein a programmer can write new components by composing them from already existing components. The architecture is designed around a JSP-based programming model (JSP2.0) and RDCs are made available as a JSP taglib that can be used within JSP pages. Voice applications authored using RDCs are standard JSP pages that generate VoiceXML 2.0 dialogs.

The design delegates application specific dialog management to authors of the JSP pages, the user interface dialog management to the prepackaged reusable components and finer grained dialog management to the VoiceXML browser by generating the appropriate VoiceXML. By splitting complex voice interaction across one or more JSP pages, and by having these JSP pages dynamically generate VoiceXML pages based on prior user interaction, the framework enables application authors define dialogs that would become hard to maintain if authored as static VoiceXML pages.

Within the framework, applications are authored using one or more RDCs, which are the VUI (Voice User Interface) equivalent of a user interface widget. These encapsulate the finer details of voice interaction, and allow the developer to focus on the overall interaction logic when speech-enabling a given application. They collect user input and publish these values using a data model. While there are two types of RDCs (atomic and composite), both types obey the same public contract with respect to the calling application.

3.1   Public Contract

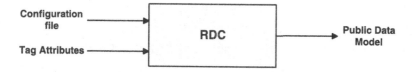

Fig. 1. RDC as Black Box

RDCs provide a consistent interface to the users who can use them to build application or to compose a bigger component. While composing bigger component, the resulting composed RDC also provides the same public interface. Thus, dialog components can be recursively composed. Looking at RDC as a black box (Figure 1), the public contract of an RDC consists of the following:

- Configuration: RDCs expose a set of configurable parameters that are used to define its functional behavior, validation constraints and interaction prompts. These parameters make the RDCs reusable and suited to desired scenario. The configuration consists of following two parts
  - Configuration File This is an XML based file that an application developer uses to provide prompts for various interaction stages with the user like input, confirmation, validation, etc. One can also provide speech specific properties like input timeout, barge-in, etc.
  - Tag attributes The JSP tag attributes are used to control the functional behavior of the RDC like whether to confirm or not, whether to echo the collected input or not, etc. These are also used to provide validation constraints for input verification. For e.g., date RDC can have validation constraints like minDate, say February 12 2004, and maxDate, say Feb 17 2005. The validation constraints come in handy for on-the-spot error checking and validation and rid the application developer of explicit checks after the value is collected.
- Public Data Model: Each RDC returns the collected and canonicalized user input to a pre-defined data structure called the Public Data Model. The type and format of the value of being returned are published by the RDCs so that application developers can use them accordingly.

3.2 Internal Design

The framework defines certain core data structures that are needed for managing the execution of RDCs. It also defines data structures that each RDC much inherit to manage transient data and states necessary for its successful execution. Besides these data structures, each RDC also defines a Finite State Machine (FSM) that is used for dilaog management, and encapsulates necessary validation logic to verify the user input. Figure 2 provides a high-level overview of the framework design through a UML class diagram. The detailed description is presented later in the section.

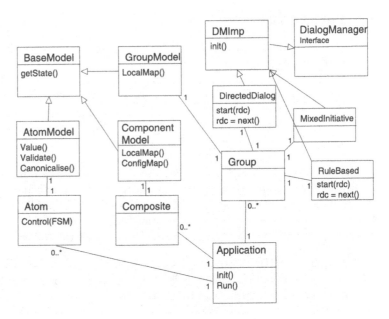

Fig. 2. UML Class diagram of the RDC framework

Data Structures BaseModel is the core data strucuture which forms the basis of the whole framework. It defines key fields which will be needed for execution of any RDC. Each RDC maintains a private data model to hold private interaction state. The private data models of all dialog components directly or indirectly extend the BaseModel class. Dialog Map is a data structure that holds the private data models of all RDCs within the JSP page so that they can be accessed across dialog turns. It is map in which the data models are hashed using RDC id as the key.

Implementation RDCs are themselves implemented as a JSP page. The implementation factors out common data structures such as the Java Beans used to model interaction state into a set of reusable Java classes. Atomic RDCs use a Finite State Machine (FSM) to model the various interaction states attained

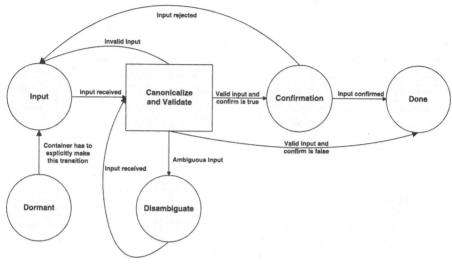

Fig. 3. FSM of Atomic RDC

by the component (Figure 3 illustrates an example of such FSM); the code that implements this FSM is itself factored into a reusable helper tag. This helper tag can be used to advantage in ensuring that all atomic RDCs exhibit a common sound and feel. Similar to atomic RDCs, the composite RDCs must also define their own FSM. Internals of an RDC perform the following steps:

– Initialize private data model for interaction state.
– Implement internal interaction logic as defined by FSM.
– Produce VoiceXML for collecting value.
– Perform validation as needed.
– Canonicalize value.
– Signal completion.

An RDC may carry out one or more dialog turns with the user to complete its execution. For example, a Date component upon receiving a partial date, might generate VXML code to prompt the user for additional information using a disambiguating prompt. Thus execution of a single RDC may involve several round trips between client and server and necessitate RDCs to maintain their state and data across such client-server round trips.

Before an RDC starts executing, it must create an instance of its private data model within the Dialog Map. All RDCs in a JSP page are invoked during the execution of the JSP page. Each RDC looks at their private data model and depending on its state and other data structures decides if it needs to generate code or just remain silent. We describe this mechanism sequence in more detail in the following section.

3.3   Atomic FSM

The FSM of an atomic RDC is shown in Figure 3. The FSM starts in either Dormant or Input state depending upon whether it is inside a container or hosted directly within the JSP page. In Dormant state the atom does nothing. When the atom is in Input state, it generates VoiceXML markup for accepting input from the user. Once the input is received, it is checked for ambiguity, canonicalized and validated against constraints, general as well as user-specified. If the input is valid, then the FSM transitions to Confirmation or Done depending upon whether the confirm attribute of the atomic RDC is true or not. In Confirmation state, appropriate markup to confirm the user input is generated and the user response collected. Done state is the final state of the FSM and the collected input is published through public contract.

3.4   Aggregation

When RDCs are used within a JSP page, the JSP author is responsible for managing the dialog flow among the various atoms hosted within that JSP page. Implementing the dialog management mechanisms across RDCs in the JSPs can constitute quite a substantial task. To handle this repetitive task, the RDC framework provides a generic container tag called **group** whose purpose is to aggregate other components, and to manage the interaction flow among them. The container tag allows use of many pre-designed strategies to move among the various dialog that make up a given interaction. Following snippet shows the structure of the **group** tag. As shown a **group** may contain both RDCs as well as other Groups.

```
<rdc:group id="pickup" strategy="SimpleDirectedDialog">
  <Tag for RDC1>
  <Another Group>
  . . . . .
  <Tag for RDCn>
</rdc:group>
```

Pluggable Dialog Manager Interface Group provides a pluggable interface for including different dialog management strategies for managing the dialog component contained within it. The core of the pluggable dialog manager design is the DialogManager interface which must be implemented by any dialog management strategy to be used with the **group**. DMImp class (as shown in Figure 2) provides a default implementation of the DialogManager interface. Our current implementation provides three pre-built dialog management strategies for managing the dialog flow of a **group**.

- Directed Dialog: Only one dialog components is executed at a time. The components are enabled to conduct their dialogs in the document order. Only when the current component finishes its dialog execution, the strategy moves to the next component.
- Mixed Initiative: More than one dialog components are activated simultaneously to collect multiple pieces of information in a single user interaction turn. The user can specify inputs for one, all or any other combination of components which are currently active. Thus user also has control on the

dialog flow and can direct it. For collecting user inputs for multiple components, the strategy needs mixed-initiative grammar besides grammar for individual components.
- Rule Based: Similar to directed dialog, only one dialog component is active at a time. However, the components are not executed in the document order but in the order which is based on the rules specified by the user in an XML file. Also, depending on the rules and runtime conditions, not all the components may be executed.

The application author can choose the dialog strategy to be used by specifying an appropriate value for "strategy" attribute. As shown in Figure 2, the DirectedDialog, MixedInitiative and the RuleBased classes are derived by extending the DMImp abstract class. The figure also shows that any one of these strategies can be used within the group.

Data Models GroupModel is the private Data Model of the group which extends Base Model, as seen in Figure 2. It adds a new member called *localMap* which acts as a Dialog Map for the RDCs contained within the group and holds their private data models. The public data model of the group is a hashMap. The keys of the hashMap corresponds to the id of the children RDCs and the value is the public data model of the respective child RDC.

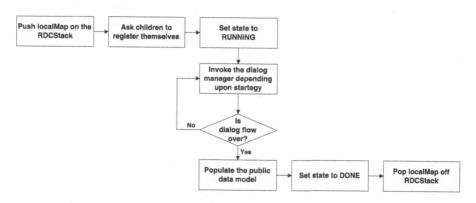

Fig. 4. Execution of group tag

Call Flow of a Container Figure 4 shows the call flow of group. When group is activated for execution, it pushes its localMap on the RDC stack. This acts as the dialogMap for the children RDCs contained within the group and sets the context for their execution. As the group manages the interaction flow among its children, it needs control on their execution. For this group uses two phase execution mechanism. It first enters into the *registration phase* and asks its children for registration. The children RDCs registers themselves by putting an entry of their private data model in the localMap of the group and remain silent by entering into dormant state. group then enters into *execution phase* and based on the value of strategy attribute, invokes appropriate dialog Manager to control the dialog flow of the children. The dialog manager selects the RDCs to be executed in a dialog turn and set their states appropriately. When the dialog flow is complete, group puts the values collected by children RDCs in the return hashMap, sets its state to DONE and pop its local Map from the RDC stack.

3.5   Composite RDCs

Composite components are distinct from atomic components in that they populate complex data structures. Composite components are typically constructed from pre-existing components; however the internal structure of a composite is not visible to the application author. Therefore, in principle one could re-package large VoiceXML applications as an RDC component provided that re-packaged component implements the public contract defined by the framework.

As described in previous section, the container tag group can be used to aggregate other dialog components and manage the interaction flow among those components. Thus, an application author who wishes to collect credit card information, and implements that interaction by using pre-defined CreditCardType, CreditCardNumber and Date components might group these within a group tag for purposes of dialog management. Later on, if collecting credit card information is found to be a common user interaction task that is needed within many applications, this grouping of components may be promoted to a reusable component by defining a new composite that implements a CreditCardInfo component. Notice that the container tag group itself does not create reusable components but is central to the design of composite components.

Anatomy and Design The anatomy of composite is quite similar to that of an atomic RDC. Composites also need to define a Public Contract but their return type is complex data structure. The specific component derives its private data model by extending the ComponentModel which itself extends the BaseModel. Like GroupModel, it also adds a member called localMap which acts as dialogMap during execution of the composite and sets its context.

Composite RDCs are themselves implemented as JSP pages. The composite component implementation uses container tag group to logically group child components and to manage the interaction flow among these children. Composite RDCs can choose among the various pre-defined dialog management strategies provided by container tag group; alternatively, a composite RDC might choose to implement a custom dialog manager, either using JSP control flow tags, or by factoring out the implementation of the dialog management strategy into an appropriate Java class. group constitutes the input state of the composite. Composites may have their own validation, confirmation, disambiguation mechanisms and define any other state. They have their own FSM which manages the composite dialog.

4   Building Application Using RDCs

Voice applications follow the traditional software lifecycle pattern of design, implementation, testing, deployment followed by iterations of maintenance and enhancements and finally gets retired. Traditional IVR applications were built on specialized hardware using vendor specific API and each application was a specialized project. Today voice applications use the much established client server architecture shown in Figure 5. The users use a telephone interface through a voice gateway or a desktop interface to ask a VoiceXML client to request data from a VoiceXML server using the HTTP protocol. The client browser interprets the returned document and may make further request to the same or different server. As we have mentioned, VoiceXML has its own dialog control; we choose to control dialog on the server side using VoiceXML for its standardized portable speech interface. The applications are hosted on a web server such as Tomcat with speech recognition and synthesis handled at the client side. The intention is to benefit the voice application developer from the powerful middleware components that automatically take care of various artifacts of voice application development like speech recognition knowledge, speech synthesis knowledge, voice dialog design, and database coding while making use of the familiar web application server infrastructure and the associated business rule in the enterprise back-end systems.

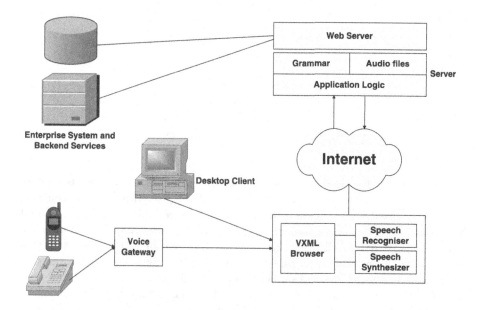

Fig. 5. Client Server configuration for RDC based voice applications

The applications consists of Java beans, JSPs and servlets provided in a web archive format (WAR) and developed based on the MVC paradigm. The application control is managed by the struts controller servlet. Access to business logic and enterprise databases is handled by the application beans and the presentation layer is a set of JSP pages. The configuration of controller servlet and the management of applications beans is the same as traditional web-based applications however authoring JSPs is different. Each RDC within the JSP is configured using a set of configuration file to suit the needs for that particular application. The validation constraints are provided up-front as attributes while associated prompts for input, confirmation, reprompting and help is provided in the configuration file. The JSP author is responsible for managing the dialog flow among the different RDCs used within the page. Here we present two applications to demonstrate how RDCs are used to build applications.

Bill Payment Application: This application is an integrated service that can be used by organizations to accelerate their bill presentation and collection process. Figure 6 shows the application flow. The transition between one JSP to another JSP is controlled by the struts layer.

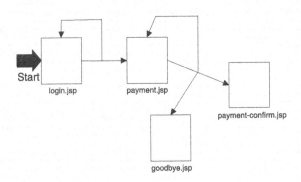

Fig. 6. Bill Payment Application Call Flow

As shown in Figure 6, on first visiting the application the user is greeted and then authenticated with his customer id (login.jsp). If authentication fails the user is asked to try again, otherwise the balance information is prompted to the user and the user is asked to specify the amount and the pay-by date (payment.jsp). After collecting the required information the system validates the payment information and on successful validation updates the information in the back-end using application beans and a confirmation number is prompted back to the user (payment-confirm.jsp). If the payment information cannot be verified the user is asked to give the information again. After certain number of unsuccessful attempts the system exists (goodbye.jsp). The following sample code in Figure 7 from payment.jsp shows how simple it is to configure different RDC, provide validation constraints and use existing built-in dialog management strategies.

```
<%@ taglib prefix="c" uri="http://java.sun.com/jsp/jstl/core" %>
<%@ taglib prefix="rdc" uri="http://rdc-1.0"%>
\vspace{-0.1in}
<jsp:useBean id="taskmap" class="java.util.LinkedHashMap"
 scope="session" />

<rdc:task map="${taskmap}">
 <rdc:group id="pay" strategy="MixedInitiative">
  <rdc:select1 id="billAmt" config="config/bill-amount.xml"
   optionList="config/amount-options.xml"/>
  <rdc:date id="payOn" config="config/pay-on-date.xml"
   minDate="today" confirm="true"/>
 </rdc:group>

 <c:if test="${!(empty pay)}">
  <rdc:struts-submit submit="payment.do" context="${pageContext}"
   namelist="billAmt payOn"/>
 </c:if>
</rdc:task>
```

Fig. 7. Bill payment application code authored using RDCs

The dialog flow among RDCs is controlled using the JSTL tags. Only when the billAmt and payOn date values are collected the values are submitted to the application beans. The pre-built dialog strategy MixedInitiative is used to control the dialogflow between the select1 and date RDCs. The select1 RDC is used to prompt the user for the amount using natural language key words like "full balance", "minimum balance" or "maximum amount". The canonicalized value is submitted to the system. The date RDC cannot accept any date in the past hence the minimum acceptable date is "today". The select1 and date RDCs are configured using the bill-amount.xml and pay-on-date.xml configuration files respectively.

Mortgage Application: In this application the user is first greeted and then authenticated using his member number. He is then prompted for the MLS number he is interested in. The system retrieves the property price and establishes the down payment amount and the duration and interest rate of the loan and computes the monthly payments. Then the system proceeds to the banking portion in which the user is again authenticated by a PIN, and the user funds the new account by means of a transfer transaction. At the end the application provides a transaction number. Figure 8 shows the code sample from the login page. It demonstrates the reuse of digits RDC to gather member number as well as the mls-number. The member number can be of any length greater then 5 whereas the mls-number is of length between 6 and 12. Here the RDCs are controlled using the built-in SimpleDirectedDialog strategy.

```
<%@ taglib prefix="c" uri="http://java.sun.com/jsp/jstl/core" %>
<%@ taglib prefix="rdc" uri="http://rdc-1.0"%>

<jsp:useBean id="taskmap" class="java.util.LinkedHashMap"
 scope="session" />

<rdc:task map="${taskmap}">
 <rdc:group id="login" strategy="SimpleDirectedDialog">
  <rdc:digits id="memNum" config="config/member-number.xml"
   minLength="5"/>
  <rdc:digits id="mlsNum" config="config/mls-number.xml"
   minLength="6" maxLength="12"/>
 </rdc:group>

 <c:if test="${!(empty login)}">
  <rdc:struts-submit submit="login.do" context="${pageContext}"
   namelist="memNum mlsNum"/>
 </c:if>
</rdc:task>
```

Fig. 8. Mortgage application code authored using RDCs

The above two examples demonstrate the effectiveness in building powerful, flexible and user friendly voice applications using the RDC library. The examples substantiate the claim that encapsulating best practices and voice-only channel artifacts into RDC layer while providing flexibility to configure the component and constrain the collected values help in providing dynamic and personalized voice applications which are easily portable.

5   Conclusion and Future Work

In this paper, we have presented a standard-based framework for building reusable components for development of voice applications. We have presented the motivation for developing a component based approach for dynamic VoiceXML generation. We have defined the public contract, the internal data structure and the implementation of an RDC cycle. The concepts of *atomic* and *composite* RDC have been provided and the aggregation constructs to develop composite RDCs have been presented. We have also presented two case studies that describe the use of RDCs in voice application development for practical solutions. The application deployment environment has also been presented.

Near term efforts in improving the framework would involve support for more global navigation commands such as *go-back* and *repeat* into the existing component based approach. The present work concentrates on developing components for the UI parts of a voice application. These components can be made even more powerful by providing a mechanism of integrating the backend logic within the component framework. This would ensure end-to-end development of a voice portal using a component based model. Providing backend integration while maintaining reusability is an interesting and important problem to be solved in the voice programming model area. Encapsulation of the voice application best-practices in the RDCs will further enhance the richness of these components. The success of such a component based approach will finally be governed by the adoption of the framework by the applicaton developer community.

Acknowledgements

The authors would like to thank Charles F Wiecha and Roberto Pieraccini (IBM Watson Research Center, NY) for their valuable suggestions and interactions during the design of the framework architecture. The authors are also thankful to Sindhu Unnikrishnan (IBM Watson Research Center, NY) for providing expertise in the implementation and testing during the course of the project.

References

1. Walker, M.A., et.al.: DARPA Communicator: Cross-system results for the 2001 evaluation. International Conference on Spoken Language Processing, vol 1, 269–272, Denver, USA, 2002
2. http://www.w3.org/TR/voicexml20/
3. http://www.saltforum.org
4. Maes, S.H.: A VoiceXML framework for reusable dialog components. Symposium on Applications and the Internet, 2002. SAINT 2002,28–30.
5. http://www.nuance.com/prodserv/proddevtools.html
6. Pieraccini, R., Caskey, S., Dayanidhi, K., Carpenter, B., Phillips, M.: ETUDE, a recursive dialog manager with embedded user interface patterns. IEEE Workshop on Automatic Speech Recognition and Understanding, 2001. ASRU '01.c, 244–247
7. Obuchi, Y.,Nyberg, E., Mitamura, T., Duggan, M., Juddy, S., and Hataoka, N.: Robust Dialog Management Architecture Using VoiceXML for Car Telematics Systems. Proc. Workshop on DSP in Mobile and Vehicular Systems, 1.5, Nagoya, Japan 2003
8. http://www-306.ibm.com/software/pervasive/voice_toolkit/
9. http://www1.avaya.com/enterprise/whitepapers/lb2432.pdf
10. www.genesyslab.com/contact_center/products/interactions/voice_platform.asp

Unlocking the Grid

Chris A. Mattmann[1,2], Nenad Medvidovic[2], Paul M. Ramirez[1,2] and
Vladimir Jakobac[2]

[1]Jet Propulsion Laboratory, 4800 Oak Grove Drive, M/S 171-264
Pasadena, CA 91109, USA
`{chris.mattmann,paul.ramirez}@jpl.nasa.gov`
[2]University of Southern California
Los Angeles, CA 90089, USA,
`{mattmann,neno,pmramire,jakobac}@usc.edu`

Abstract. The grid has emerged as a novel paradigm that supports seamless cooperation of distributed, heterogeneous computing resources in addressing highly complex computing and data management tasks. A number of software technologies have emerged to enable "grid computing". However, their exact nature, underlying principles, requirements, and architecture are still not fully understood and remain under-specified. In this paper, we present the results of a study whose goal was to try to identify the key underlying requirements and shared architectural traits of grid technologies. We then used these requirements and architecture in assessing five existing, representative grid technologies. Our studies show a fair amount of deviation by the individual technologies from the widely cited baseline grid architecture. Our studies also suggest a core set of critical requirements that must be satisfied by grid technologies, and highlight a key distinction between "computational" and "data" grids in terms of the identified requirements.

1 Introduction

The *grid* is an emerging paradigm concerned with enabling heterogeneous organizational entities to share computing resources (both hardware and software), data, security infrastructure, and the like [4]. Additionally, the grid's goal is to allow such organizations to operate in a coordinated fashion to solve very complex scientific and information management problems [4,14]. Because of this, the grid has become an area of significant interest to computing researchers and practitioners, and a number of open source and standards-based grid infrastructure implementations exist and have commercial backing.[1]

Recently, in collaboration with NASA's Jet Propulsion Laboratory (JPL) our research group decided to port JPL's OODT grid technology [6] onto our Prism-MW middleware platform for mobile and resource constrained devices [25]. The goal was to significantly reduce OODT's footprint and "bring the grid into one's pocket". The ex-

---

1. For exposition purposes, we will use the phrases "grid infrastructure", "grid technology", "grid solution", "grid platform", and "grid system" interchangeably in this paper

G.T. Heineman et al. (Eds.): CBSE 2005, LNCS 3489, pp. 322–336, 2005.
© Springer-Verlag Berlin Heidelberg 2005

ercise was successful, JPL deemed our prototype, GLIDE, quite promising, and we decided to document the experience in a research paper [5], which we submitted to a workshop on middleware technologies.

When we received the reviews for the paper, one particular comment caught our attention. One reviewer was unimpressed with what we had done in part because, in the reviewer's words, OODT "is in itself a very simple class framework"; another reviewer also alluded to this! This was very surprising, given that OODT has been a highly successful grid technology, deployed both within NASA and externally with the National Cancer Institute, and was the runner-up for NASA's Software System of the Year award in 2003.

The grid literature is very rich in general ("reference") requirements a grid platform should satisfy [3, 14, 13], and also details its target ("reference") architecture [15, 21]. Based on this, we had gone with the assumption that a grid technology can be relatively easily distinguished from "something else". However, a review of the OODT documentation revealed that no such distinguishing features were obviously stated. We then studied the documentation accompanying several other grid solutions and found that the same holds for them. Thus, the comment we received, from experts in the area, raised three questions that directly motivated the study on which we will report in this paper:

1. What, in fact, makes a software system a grid technology?
2. What, if any, is the difference between a grid technology, a middleware platform, a software library, and a class framework?
3. Are existing systems that claim to enable grid computing *bona fide* grid technologies?

In order to answer these questions, we decided to recover, study, and compare the architectures of a number of existing grid technologies. Specifically, we chose five such technologies, including Globus, the most widely used grid system, as well as OODT and GLIDE, the two systems that prompted our study in the first place. In principle, the only requirement in selecting the candidate grid technologies was that they be open source. Since OODT was compared to a class framework, we also decided to restrict our study to object-oriented grids. While we decided to apply a particular software architecture recovery technique in our study [23], the technique is representative of a number of architectural recovery approaches, and we do not believe that it significantly influenced our results. The recovered architectures were "interpreted" with the help of the reference requirements and reference architecture for grid systems we gathered from existing literature.

In this paper, we present the details of this study, and the lessons we learned in the process. The overall conclusion of our work has been that grid technologies, including OODT and GLIDE, do in fact adhere to a specific architecture and are thus quite different from software libraries and class frameworks. At the same time, our study also revealed that several aspects of the published grid reference requirements and architecture are overly general and open ended, so much so that it was at times difficult to imagine what a given grid solution would have to do to deviate from them. Based on this, we suggest some improvements to the current state of the practice in grid computing infrastructures.

The remainder of the paper is organized as follows. Section 2 outlines our background research which resulted in reference requirements and a reference architecture for grid systems, and discusses related work in the area of architectural recovery. Section 3 describes the approach we have taken in our study, while Section 4 summarizes the results of applying the approach on five off-the-shelf (OTS) grid technologies. Section 5 highlights the lessons we have learned in the process and suggests possible future work in the area of grids. We then conclude the paper in Section 6.

2   Background and Related Work

In order to effectively study grid technologies, we needed to identify their overarching requirements and shared architectural traits. The existing grid literature contains four separate studies that attempt to provide such information [3, 4, 14, 18]. However, in addition to being dispersed, this information was presented in widely differing ways, at times ambiguous, influenced or obscured by details of particular grid solutions, and even contradictory. Our task thus consisted of locating, compiling, rephrasing (if necessary), and consolidating the requirements.

Particularly helpful in this task was the seminal study of grids by Kesselman et al. [4]. This study provides a rich target set of requirements by exploring a suggested five-layer grid reference architecture. Each layer in the architecture defines services (i.e., software components) that should satisfy particular requirements (including QoS, characteristics, and capabilities) mentioned in the description of the layer. However, many of these requirements are not explicitly called out and had to be "distilled" from the text. In addition, some requirements overlap, while others span architectural layers.

A particular class of grid solutions, called data grids, provides services primarily targeted at managing data and metadata resources. Chervenak et al. [3] identify four guiding principles for data grids: *mechanism neutrality*, *policy neutrality*, *compatibility with grid infrastructure*, and *uniformity of information infrastructure*. However, we found the natural language presentation of these principles ambiguous, especially when we initially tried to assess the conformance of grid solutions to them. Moreover, there is no mapping of the principles to constituent architectural components in grid solutions. We thus had to rephrase and interpret them. Our further research also identified additional requirements for data grids involving replica management, metadata management, and interfaces to heterogeneous storage systems [2, 10].

A significant aspect of our work is the recovery of grid platforms' architectures from their implementations. A number of architecture recovery approaches have been developed in the past decade (e.g. [7, 9, 11, 12, 29]). They typically analyze dependencies among a system's implementation modules (e.g., procedures or classes) to cluster them into higher-level components. A more detailed overview of these approaches can be found in [23].

Recently, a series of studies has been undertaken by Holt et al. to recover the architectures of several open-source applications [15, 19]. Similarly to our approach, the approach taken in these studies has been to come up with an "as-intended" (i.e., reference) architecture by consulting a system's designers and its documentation, and use it as the basis for understanding the system's "as-implemented" architecture recovered from the source code.

Table 1: Reference Requirements for Grids

Requirement		Impacted Layer
1	Share resources across dynamic and geographically dispered organizations	Collective
2	Enable single sign-on	Connectivity
3	Delegate and authorize	Connectivity
4	Ensure access control	Connectivity
5	Ensure application of local and global policies	Fabric
6	Control shared resources	Collective
7	Coordinate shared resources	Collective
8	Ensure "exactly once" level of reliability service	Connectivity, Application Resource
9	Use standard, "open" protocols and interfaces	Collective, Resource, Connectivity
10	Provide ability to achieve non-trivial QoS	Application, Resource, Collective
11	Ensure neutrality of data sharing mechanism	All layer's implementation
12	Ensure neutrality of data sharing policy	Collective, Resource, Connectivity, Fabric
13	Ensure compatibility with Grid infrastructure	Possibly all layers
14	Provide uniform information infrastructure	Application, Resource, Collective
15	Support metadata management	Resource
16	Interface with heterogeneous storage systems	Fabric
17	Provide the management of data replicas	Fabric, Resource, Collective

Another related architecture recovery approach is Dynamo-1 [20], which focuses on middleware-based software applications. It combines the use-case modeling aspect of Focus [23], the approach we have adopted in this work, with the filtering and clustering approach of PBS [26]. Dynamo-1 differs from our approach in that its goal is only to recover the architectures of the *applications* hosted on top of the given middleware infrastructure, while our goal is to analyze and recover the architecture of the grid infrastructure itself.

3   Approach

The approach that we used in our case studies is depicted in Figure 1. It involves three high-level activities. The first activity has two sub tasks (1a and 1b) that were conducted only once, and independently of the other activities. The remaining activities (and their subtasks) were conducted iteratively in each grid technology we studied. We detail our approach below.

3.1   Reference Architecture and Requirements

After studying the available grid literature as outlined in Section 2, we identified the *de facto* reference architecture for grid systems [4] (Step 1a in Figure 1). The architecture consists of five layers, each of which relies on the services of its subordinate layer(s).

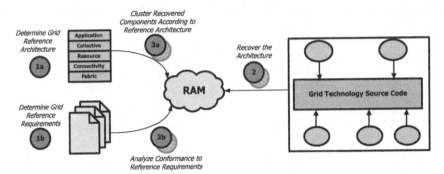

Figure 1 Our approach to studying grid technologies.

The *application layer* represents the software system built using the grid technology, and it relies on the functionality for coordinating system resources available via the *collective layer*. The collective layer coordinates and manages resources exposed at the *resource layer*. The top three layers directly rely on the *connectivity layer* for secure and distributed communication. The bottom layer is the *fabric layer*, providing standard interfaces to heterogeneous system resources, such as file systems and device drivers.

In addition to the reference architecture, we also identified a representative set of high-level requirements for grids (Step 1b in Figure 1) in the manner outlined in Section 2. Due to space restrictions, these requirements are only briefly summarized in Table 1. We have also identified the reference architecture layer(s) that are likely impacted by each requirement.

Both the reference architecture and reference requirements formulate the targets for our study and are used to inform our architecture recovery efforts which we describe below.

3.2   Architecture Recovery

Architectural recovery (Step 2 in Figure 1) involves automated examination of the source code to extract an "as-implemented" architectural model for each grid technology. We refer to this model as the *recovered architectural model*, or RAM. We used the Focus architectural recovery approach [23] in this step. Focus was selected because it is specifically geared to object-oriented systems, while it has been shown to produce comparable results to other recovery approaches. The key steps of Focus are briefly summarized below. Additional details may be found in [23].

Focus relies on an OTS source code extraction tool (we used Rational Rose in our study) to generate class diagrams from the given grid technology's code. Once a class diagram has been extracted from the code, a set of automatable clustering rules are applied iteratively to group individual classes into higher-level components. These rules include grouping classes that share aggregation, generalization, and two-way relationships, grouping clusters of classes that are isolated from the rest of the system, identifying "important" classes that have many incoming and outgoing links, and so forth. Focus identifies two kinds of components: processing and data. It also attempts to identify the key communication elements in a system.

Once these rules cannot be applied on the system's (clustered) class diagram any longer, Focus has produced the RAM. It is important to acknowledge that this architectural model may have several limiting properties:

- *The RAM may not be complete* - Any clustering-based approach may fail to identify all system components. The RAM may also ignore component interaction characteristics (i.e., connectors). Further, the RAM may not provide any insight into the system's legal configurations.

- *The RAM may not conform to the system's intended architecture* - Over time, the system's implementation may have (significantly) deviated from the designers' original intentions. This is referred to as architectural drift or erosion [27].

- *There is no obvious relationship between the RAM and the system's requirements* - The only input to Focus (and many other architectural recovery approaches) is the source code. As such, the recovered architecture does not identify the requirements each component is intended to fulfill.

3.3   RAM Reconciliation

At this point, we have the reference requirements and architecture for grid technologies, as well as the RAM for the particular grid system. Since the RAM may deviate from the reference architecture, the next step in our approach is to reconcile the RAM and the reference architecture, i.e., to place the components identified in the RAM into specific layers of the architecture (Step 3a in Figure 1).

For each RAM component, we try to identify its counterpart in the reference architecture. To do so, we examine (1) any information about the component's functionality from the documentation of the grid system under study, (2) the component's relationships with other components, and possibly (3) the description of similar components in the grid literature.

Once the decision is made to place a component in a given architectural layer, the relationships among the components are examined more closely to identify two types of inconsistencies: (1) the grid reference architecture [4] implies that, with one exception, the layers are opaque, such that components in a given layer can only access services of the layer immediately below; and (2) the layered architectural style prohibits components from making "up-calls". At this point we also note any additional discrepancies, such as our inability to assign a component to any layers, "invalid" or unexpected dependencies among components, and so on.

Finally, since different grid technologies may have different foci (e.g., computational vs. data grids, or high-performance computing vs. pervasive grids) and may approach the problem differently, another relevant piece of information is the degree to which the reconciled RAM adheres to the reference requirements (Step 3b in Figure 1). The goal of this activity is to identify the requirement(s) satisfied by each component, including the components we were unable to fit into the reconciled RAM. We again try to identify any discrepancies in the placement of components in the architectural layers based on the location guidelines shown in the right-hand column of Table 1.

4   Case Studies

We have used the approach detailed above to study five different grid technologies, selected based on the following criteria. First, the technology should be open-source because we needed the ability to perform architectural recovery from the source code. Second, the technology should be object-oriented because, as discussed in the Introduction, one of our objectives was to discover the relationship of grid solutions and class frameworks. Third, we required at least some level of documentation to aid us in determining the functionality of the recovered grid components. We do not feel this requirement to be particularly limiting since the documentation could be as simple as an HTML page (as was indeed the case with the JCGrid study discussed below). Fourth, we wanted to study grid technologies that are used in "legitimate" industrial and/or academic projects in order to ensure the relevance of our results. Finally, we wanted the set of studied systems to include OODT and GLIDE because, as discussed in the Introduction, they were the direct motivators for this study. It should be noted that OODT does satisfy all of our criteria; however, GLIDE is currently being evaluated and thus can be argued not to satisfy the fourth criterion at this time.

In this section, we detail our studies of OODT and Globus, and summarize the results of the remaining three studies. Additional details on all five studies can be found in [22].

4.1   OODT

OODT [6] is a grid infrastructure developed at JPL in support of scientific, data-intensive grid systems. OODT's implementation consists of approximately 14,000 SLOC. The initially recovered OODT class diagram, shown in Figure 2, contained 320 classes. For the most part, it was a densely connected graph, but it also contained approximately 40 classes with no recognized relationships to other classes in the system (shown isolated in the bottom-left portion of Figure 2). UML generalization and interface relationships were most prevalent, with many classes implementing at most one interface.

We applied the iterative clustering rules of Focus on the class diagram to arrive at the OODT RAM. The RAM comprised 38 processing and data components, along with the identified relationships (i.e., connectors) between each component pair. With the help of the component descriptions in OODT's conceptual architecture [6], we were able to place 24 of the 38 RAM components into the layered grid reference architecture with relative ease. The remaining components had to be "shoehorned" by examining ad-

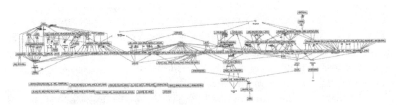

Figure 2   Initial class diagram of OODT. Due to its size and complexity, at this magnification the diagram is shown only for illustration

ditional OODT documentation [21] and, in a few cases, the OODT source code. The final result of this process is shown in Figure 3.

Of note is the fact that only one component was placed in the connectivity layer of the reference architecture. The reason is that OODT leverages third-party middleware platforms (CORBA and RMI) to support distribution, and those are considered external to its code base. There are also several deviations from the reference architecture:

1. Several components in the fabric layer (*ProductServicePOA*, *ProductServiceAdaptor*, and *CORBA_Archive_ServicePOA*) communicate with the *ExecServer* component in the resource layer. The fabric layer components not only cross two layer boundaries, but also make up-calls to perform this communication.

2. Components in the application layer (*ConfiguraitonBean* and *SearchBean*) communicate with the *Configuration* component in the connectivity layer, crossing three layer boundaries. Similarly, the *ProfileClient* and *ProductClient* components in the application layer traverse two and four layer boundaries, respectively, to communicate with their server components.

3. The *Utilities* component (shown in the upper-right of Figure 3) was identified by Focus as comprising classes with no recognizable relationships with other classes. We were unable to determine its correct placement in the reference architecture.

Our analysis of the architecture shown in Figure 3 suggests that OODT satisfies most of the reference requirements specific to data grids[1]. The lone exception is its lack of

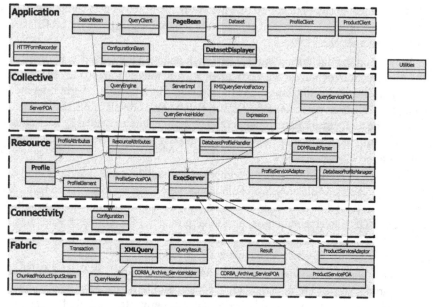

Figure 3   Mapping OODT's RAM onto the grid reference architecture

---

1. Recall the discussion in Section 2 and corresponding requirements 11-17 in Table 1.

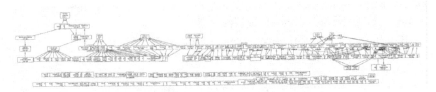

Figure 4 Initial class diagram of Globus.

support for replica management (requirement 17 in Table 1). In addition, OODT fails to address two other reference requirements: single sign-on (requirement 2) and "exactly once" level of reliability service (requirement 8). It appears that this stems from OODT's reliance on CORBA and RMI for such basic services.

4.2   Globus

The Globus toolkit [14] has been used successfully across a number of projects [2, 4, 8, 10, 16], and can be considered to be the *de facto* standard for grid implementations. The initially recovered class diagram of Globus is shown in Figure 4 for illustration. Globus consists of 864 classes and approximately 55,000 SLOC; it was the largest and most complex grid technology that we studied. Similarly to OODT, Globus also has a set of classes (around 60) that share no recognizable relationship with any other classes (appearing at the bottom of Figure 4).

After applying Focus on Globus' source code, we arrived at the Globus RAM. The RAM contained 86 components, 50 of which were identified as data components. Most processing components contained at least one relationship, typically a UML association, with another class.

Relying on the documentation that was included with the Globus core distribution [28], along with our study of the existing Globus literature [2, 4, 10, 13, 14], we were able to place 81 of the 86 Globus RAM components into the layered grid reference architecture. This high percentage was unsurprising since Globus is the realization, and served as the direct inspiration, of the reference architecture presented by Kesselman et al. in [4]. Still, the architecture we recovered did deviate from the proposed reference architecture as discussed below.

As shown in Figure 5 most of the components found their way into the resource and connectivity layers, while only two components were assigned to the fabric layer. Similarly to OODT, Globus also relies on a third-party distributed communication solution: Apache's AXIS implementation of the SOAP protocol. The Globus release includes AXIS; hence the large number of components in the connectivity layer. Globus' major deviations from the reference architecture are as follows:

1. The *Logging* component appears to have a home in both the collective and resource layers of the reference architecture. Similarly, the *Map* data component that we placed in the collective layer actually permeates several of the other layers, and may in fact belong somewhere else. Given that it is a basic data compo-

nent (indeed, implemented as a *Hashtable*), we could not confidently discern its requisite architectural layer.

2. The *JavaClassWriter* component in the fabric layer appears to be making an up-call two layers above to the *ServiceEntry* component in the resource layer. Similarly, the *Java2WSDL* component in the resource layer is making a two-layer up-call to the *CLOptionDescripton* component in the application layer.

3. There were five components, including a *Utilities* processing component and an *Exception* data component, which we were unable to assign to any layers of the reference architecture. This was because the given component appeared to belong to more than one layer, we could not find sufficient documentation for it, and/or it did not have enough relationships in the RAM to positively classify it to a particular layer.

Globus addresses the first 10 grid reference requirements identified in Table 1; however, it does not satisfy all of the remaining requirements, which are specific to data grids. In particular, we discovered that Globus does not natively support requirements 14-16. These capabilities are provided by components built on top of the Globus grid infrastructure, such as the Metadata Catalog Service [10], and the Replica Location Service [2] components.

4.3   Summary of Remaining Studies

Due to space limitations, we only summarize the remaining three case studies here; their complete treatment is provided in [22].

GLIDE [5] is the grid technology that directly motivated our work presented in this paper. It is a lightweight grid infrastructure for data-intensive environments. GLIDE's goal is to extend the grid paradigm to the emerging decentralized, resource-constrained, embedded, autonomic and mobile environments.

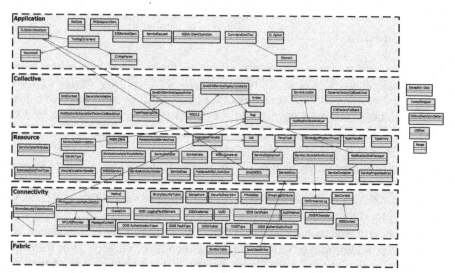

Figure 5   Mapping Globus's RAM onto the grid reference architecture

Dspace [1] is an open source grid system, jointly developed by MIT Libraries and Hewlett-Packard. It is a distributed digital repository system that captures, stores, indexes, preserves, and redistributes the research material of a university in digital formats.

Finally, JCGrid is a computational grid platform developed in Java and available via open source on SourceForge [30]. JCGrid allows one to split CPU-intensive tasks among multiple workstations. It has been used in several significant applications to date.

The implementation sizes of the three technologies ranged from 2,100 SLOC distributed over 61 classes in GLIDE, to 24,000 SLOC and 217 classes in DSpace. All three technologies violated the reference architecture. Some discrepancies include communication spanning the application and connectivity layers in GLIDE, communication across all five layer boundaries in JCGrid (the most significant such deviation observed in the five case studies), and a component (*WorkflowManager*) spanning both the collective and resource layers in DSpace.

The task of mapping the components to the reference architecture was relatively straight forward in the cases of GLIDE and JCGrid: GLIDE's components were similar to OODT's, while JCGrid RAM's 37 components nicely conformed to different architectural layers. DSpace was much more challenging in this regard: many of its components appeared to span several architectural layers and we could not confidently ascertain their appropriate "homes".

In terms of the reference requirements, one observation was that neither GLIDE nor DSpace supports replica management (requirement 17 from Table 1), even though they claim to be data grid solutions. Finally, JCGrid's reliance on a *GridServer* component to manage policy and access control does not bode well for its ability to support application of local and global policies (requirements 3-5).

5   Discussion

Our objective in conducting this study was to clearly identify what distinguishes a *bona fide* grid technology from other utility software, such as "ordinary" middleware platforms, software libraries, and frameworks. We believe that we have achieved a qualified success in this endeavor, but that we have also identified several deficiencies in the current level of understanding of the grid. These deficiencies can, in turn, form a coherent research agenda for the grid community.

Grid technologies can be thought of most appropriately as specialized middleware platforms that share a reasonably well defined reference architecture. In other words, grid technologies are an example of domain-specific software architectures [17], for the domain of grid computing.

As such, grid systems have little in common with software libraries, although they may indeed provide useful services in the form of libraries. Similarly, while the implementation of each of the five technologies we studied may be looked at as a framework of object-oriented classes that is specialized and instantiated to solve a particular problem, we believe that to be the wrong abstraction in this case. The fact that a given technology is designed and implemented in, say, Java is incidental; a number of successful grid technologies have in fact been designed and implemented using the procedural paradigm and languages (e.g., C). The key property of a grid technology is its satisfaction of a well defined set of requirements via functional services that are distributed across five well defined architectural layers.

Of course, as can be gleaned from Section 4, the preceding statement is only partially true. The existing grid technologies vary widely in the selection of requirements they choose to satisfy, as well as in the functional services they provide in the form of components. If we consider the five grid technologies we studied in depth, they covered a very broad range in terms of source code size and implementation class complexity. For example, GLIDE was implemented in slightly over 2,000 SLOC, while the current implementation of Globus is at about 55,000 SLOC. Likewise, GLIDE's entire implementation comprises 61 classes, while Globus has over 14 times as many.

This discrepancy can be partly attributed to the differences in the design choices and foci of the different grid technologies. For example, Globus subsumes a relatively large third-party middleware platform (AXIS) and provides numerous utilities to its users; on the other hand, GLIDE leverages a much smaller middleware platform and provides only basic grid services. Furthermore, each grid technology we studied differs in the adopted distributed communication mechanism, and the type and degree of support provided to application developers, as summarized in the below table.

	Communication Mechanism	Application Development Support
OODT	Remote method invocation	Object-Oriented
Globus	SOAP Publish and Subscribe	Web-services based
GLIDE	Event-based and publish-subscribe	Software architectural style-based
DSpace	Client-server over HTTP	Object-Oriented
JCGrid	Client-server with asynchronous invocation	Object-Oriented

In addition to the above, at least to some extent the discrepancies found across the grid technologies are a by-product of the reference requirements each development group has chosen to satisfy. There are currently no guidelines for which requirements are mandatory and which are optional. Based on our study, it appears that requirements numbered 1, 5-7, and 9-10 in Table 1 are mandatory (i.e., every grid technology must satisfy those), while the rest are optional. Moreover, if we consider more carefully the intended uses of the grid systems, we can identify a finer distinction, one that pinpoints the difference between "computational grid" and "data grid" systems. As indicated in Section 2, this distinction has been widely used in literature (e.g., [3, 4, 10, 18]), but has not been carefully explained or justified to date. DSpace's, OODT's, and GLIDE's primary stated objective is, in fact, to support data grids. Then, based on the results of our studies we hypothesize that requirements numbered 11-12 and 14-17 must be satisfied in addition to the above set of mandatory grid requirements in order to support data grids.

If we shift our focus more toward the architectures of the studied grid systems, again some interesting observations emerge. Even though these systems vary widely in their size, complexity, and specific focus, for the most part their components map rather nicely to the five-layer reference architecture. Upon closer inspection, we believe this to be true for several reasons that must be addressed by the grid community.

First, *the requirements for grid systems are very broad*, and generally applicable to a number of middleware solutions. Several of the grid requirements involve basic middleware QoS requirements such as security, dependability, marshalling of data, and the use of standard, open interfaces. These requirements give little help in distinguishing a grid solution from "something else"; alternatively, given such generally applicable requirements, it is difficult *not* to provide at least some grid capabilities.

Secondly, *there is overlap between grid layers*. An example is the difference between the resource and collective layers, where one layer coordinates individual resources and the other layer multiple resources. In practice, it has been difficult to determine the layer to which a given component belongs. For example, if only a single resource of a given kind exists, in which layer should the corresponding component be placed, or do there still need to be two separate components, one in each layer?

Third, *grid technologies regularly violate the reference architecture*. Specifically, nearly all of the grid systems that we studied fail to conform to the restrictions of the layered architecture style. Violations include component communication spanning multiple layers, up-calls, and dependencies between layers that were not specified in the reference architecture. This is at least in part caused by the haphazard way in which the requirements and architectures of existing grid systems are captured. We believe that appropriate use of architectural formalisms, such as architecture description languages [24], would provide the needed descriptive power as well as rigor to support the validation of each of these systems against the constraints specified in their reference architecture.

Finally, it is also evident that, due to the broad definition of what constitutes a grid technology, *interoperability between grid solutions poses a key challenge*. Even conformance to the recently adopted Open Grid Services Architecture (OGSA) [14] does not guarantee interoperability between grid middleware systems. This is in part evidenced by OGSA's lack of backward compatibility with previous Globus systems, which directly influenced OGSA. Many questions still remain, such as, what data do the grid services exchange and how is it described? OGSA and the recently announced Web Service Resource Framework (WS-RF) represent initial steps towards remedying this problem, but the problem remains wide open.

6   Conclusion

Our study of grid technologies has corroborated some of the claims made in grid literature, while suggesting refinements to others. In particular, we found the reference grid architecture [4] a useful baseline for comparing disparate grid solutions, especially since their recovered architectures (i.e., RAMs) were quite divergent. Furthermore, the reference requirements we distilled from literature certainly helped to improve our understanding of the grid. Together, the architecture and requirements suggest a tangible distinction between grid technologies on the one hand, and commonly used software notions such as middleware, libraries, and frameworks on the other. Another distinction rendered more concrete by our study is between computational and data grids.

At the same time, one conclusion of our study is clear: the answer to the question "what makes a grid system a grid system?" has many possible answers. This is not necessarily a drawback, as it allows developers of a given grid platform to tailor its functionality, and to some extent its architecture, to the needs at hand. At the same time, we argue that this open-endedness may become an impediment to the on-going standardization efforts and the claimed goal of grid platform interoperability.

7 References

[1]   DSpace at MIT. DSpace: An Open Source Dynamic Digital Repository. *D-Lib Magazine*, 9(1), January 2003.

[2]   A. Chervenak et al. Giggle: A Framework for Constructing Scalable Replica Location Services. In *Proc. of IEEE Supercomputing Conference*, pp. 1-17, 2002.

[3]   A. L. Chervenak et al. The Data Grid: Towards an Architecture for the Distributed management and analysis of Large Scientifc Datasets. *Journal of Network and Computer Applications*, pp. 1-12, 2000.

[4]   C. Kesselman et al. The Anatomy of the Grid: Enabling Scalable Virtual Organizations. *International Journal of Supercomputing Applications*, pages 1-25, 2001.

[5]   C. Mattmann et al. GLIDE: A Grid-based, Lightweight Infrastructure for Data-intensive Environments. *Technical Report* USC-CSE-2004-509, University of Southern California, June 2004.

[6]   D. Crichton et al. A Science Data System Architecture for Information Retrieval, in *Clustering and Information Retrieval*, W. Wu, H. Xiong, S. Shekhar (Eds.):pages 261-298. Kluwer Academic Pubishers, December 2003.

[7]   D. R. Harris et al. Extracting Architecture Features from Source Code. *Automated Software Engineering*, vol. 3, no. 1/2, pp.109-138, 1996.

[8]   E. Deelman et al. Grid-Based Galaxy Morphology Analysis for the National Virtual Observatory. In *Proc. of IEEE Supercomputing Conference*, p. 47, 2003.

[9]   G. Murphy et al. Software Refection Models: Bridging the Gap between Design and Implementation. *IEEE Transactions on Software Engineering*, 27(4):364-380, 2001.

[10]   G. Singh et al. A Metadata Catalog Service for Data-intensive applications. In *Proc. of IEEE Supercomputing Conference*, pg. 33, 2003.

[11]   G.Y. Guo et al. A Software Architecture Reconstruction Method. In *Proc. of First Working IFIP Conference on Software Architecture*, pp. 15-34, 1999.

[12]   H. Gall et al. Object-Oriented Re-Architecting. In *Proc. of 5th European Software Engineering Conference*, pp. 499-519, 1995.

[13]   I. Foster et al. Grid services for Distributed Systems Integration. *IEEE Computer*, pp. 37-46, June 2002.

[14] I. Foster et al. The Physiology of the Grid: An Open Grid Services Architecture for Distributed Systems Integration. *Work in progress*, Globus Research, 2002.

[15] I. T. Bowman et al. Linux as a Case Study: Its Extracted Software Architecture. In *Proc. of International Conference on Software Engineering*, pp. 555-563, 1999.

[16] J. Blythe et al. Transparent Grid Computing: A Knowledge-Based Approach. In *Proc. of Innovative Applications of Artificial Intelligence (IAAI)*, pp. 57-64, 2003.

[17] W. Tracz et al. Software development using domain-specific software architectures. *ACM Software Engineering Notes*, pages 27-38, 1995.

[18] I. Foster. What is the Grid?: A three point checklist. *GridToday*, 1(6), 2002.

[19] A.E. Hassan and R.C. Holt. A Reference Architecture for Web Servers. In *Proc. of Working Conference on Reverse Engineering*, pg. 150, 2000.

[20] I. Ivkovic and M.W. Godfrey. Architecture Recovery of Dynamically Linked Applications: A Case Study. In *Proc. of IEEE International Workshop on Program Comprehension*, pp. 178-186, 2002.

[21] S. Kelly. OODT Web Documentation. web site: http://oodt.jpl.nasa.gov, 2004.

[22] C. Mattmann. Recovering the Architectures of Grid-based Software Systems. web site: http://www-scf.usc.edu/~mattmann/GridMiddlewares/, 2004.

[23] N. Medvidovic and V. Jakobac. Using Software Evolution to Focus Architectural Recovery. *Automated Software Engineering*, to appear.

[24] N. Medvidovic and R. N. Taylor. A Classification and Comparison Framework for Software Architecture Description Languages. *IEEE Transactions on Software Engineering*, 26(1):70-93, 2000.

[25] M. Mikic-Rakic and N. Medvidovic. Adaptable Architectural Middleware for Programming-in-the-Small-and-Many. In *Proc. of ACM/IFIP/USENIX International Middleware Conference*, pp. 162-181, 2003.

[26] Univ. of Waterloo. PBS: Portable Bookshelf. web site: http://swag.uwaterloo.ca/pbs/intro.html, 2004.

[27] D. E. Perry and A. L. Wolf. Foundations for the Study of Software Architecture. *ACM Software Engineering Notes*, 17:4, 1992.

[28] T. Sandholm and J. Gawor. Globus Toolkit 3 Core - A Grid Service Container Framework. *Technical report*, Argonne National Laboratory, 2003.

[29] K. Sartipi and K. Kontogiannis. Pattern-based Software Architecture Recovery. In *Proc. of 2nd ASERC Workshop on Software Architecture*, 7 pages, 2003.

[30] Sourceforget.net: Project Info - Java Grid Computing. web site: http://sourceforge.net/projects/jcgrid, 2004.

Experience Report: Design and Implementation of a Component-Based Protection Architecture for ASP.NET Web Services

Konstantin Beznosov

Laboratory for Education and Research in Secure Systems Engineering,
University of British Columbia
beznosov@ece.ubc.ca

Abstract. This report reflects, from a software engineering perspective, on the experience of designing and implementing protection mechanisms for ASP.NET Web services. The limitations of Microsoft ASP.NET container security mechanisms render them inadequate for hosting enterprise-scale applications that have to be protected according to diverse and/or complex application-specific security policies. In this paper we report on our experience of designing and implementing a component-based architecture for protecting enterprise-grade Web service applications hosted by ASP.NET. Due to its flexibility and extensibility, this architecture enables the integration of ASP.NET into the organizational security infrastructure with less effort by Web service developers. The architecture has been implemented in a real-world security solution. This paper also contributes a best practice on constructing flexible and extensible authentication and authorization logic for Web services by using Resource Access Decision and Attribute Function (AF) architectural styles. Furthermore, the lessons learned from our design and implementation experiences are discussed throughout the paper.

1 Introduction

ASP.NET container is a popular hosting environment for Web services built and run atop Microsoft Windows and .NET platforms. However, the ASP.NET security architecture [11, 13], as provided "out-of-the-box," is not sufficiently scalable, flexible, and easily extensible to be adequate for enterprise applications [3]. As we describe in [8], ASP.NET supports limited authentication and group/user-based authorization, both bound to Microsoft proprietary technologies (Windows domains and Passport [12]). If a Web service application needs to be protected via third-party authentication or authorization services available in the enterprise security infrastructure, the real-world developers have two options. The first is to develop homegrown container security extensions, which are hard for average application developers to get right. The second is to program the security logic into the Web service business logic, making the resulting application costly to change and support. In both cases, the development of security-specific parts by average application developers is commonly believed to result in high vulnerability rates due to hard-to-avoid security-related

G.T. Heineman et al. (Eds.): CBSE 2005, LNCS 3489, pp. 337–352, 2005.

bugs. Because our architecture achieves fine-grain flexible decomposition of the security logic into components, the design allows a higher degree of security logic reuse whilst supporting application-specific security policies and the separation between business and security logic. We expect the reuse will lead to fewer errors by developers.

Due to its flexibility and extensibility, our component-based protection architecture enables the integration of ASP.NET into the organizational security infrastructure with less effort by Web service developers. The architecture is flexible because it allows for the configuring of machine-wide authentication and authorization functions, and for their overriding for a sub-tree of the Web services (up to an individual application) in the directory-based ASP.NET hierarchy. Its extensibility is revealed through the support of a wide variety of authentication and authorization (A&A) logic, as long as the logic can be translated into a .NET component and/or accessed (possibly via a proxy) through a predefined .NET API. Furthermore, one can reuse those components by combining authorization decisions from them according to predefined or customized rules.

These properties were achieved via

1. separating custom SOAP [21] extension modules, which act as ASP.NET-specific A&A enforcement logic, from the A&A decision logic;
2. following Resource Access Decision (RAD) architecture style [4, 5, 17], which, through the decomposition of the authorization engine into components, makes the customization of access control decision logic easier and avoids the need for a generic policy evaluation engine;
3. taking advantage of the extensibility, inheritance, and caching features of ASP.NET *web.config* configuration mechanism; and
4. separating the logic of retrieving attributes from the authorization and business logic by following the Attribute Function (AF) approach [2].

Although this paper discusses the design of a protection architecture for Web services, we believe that our approach and design decisions could be useful in a broader context of component-based protection sub-systems for distributed applications.

This paper is organized as follows. The next section reviews ASP.NET Web services. Section 3 discusses the requirements for the design. Intertwined with the discussion of the design decisions and lessons learned, an architecture description follows in Section 4. To illustrate the architecture capabilities, we present two examples of policies and corresponding configurations in Section 5. We conclude in Section 6.

2   Overview of ASP.NET Web Services

This section provides background information on ASP.NET Web services technology for the uninformed reader to aid with understanding the rest of the paper. Those familiar with the technology can skip to Section 3.

A Web service is an XML-based messaging interface to computing resources that is accessible via Internet protocols. A Web service front end can be added to an existing information-processing infrastructure. Alternately, applications can be engineered to use a consistent Web services model in all tiers, from data stores and back-ends to middle and presentation tiers. A key Web services technology, SOAP [21] is a unidirectional XML-based protocol for passing structured information.

ASP.NET is the most popular platform among Microsoft technologies for engineering Web services. ASP.NET Web Services rely upon ASP.NET, .NET Framework, IIS, and, underneath them all, the Windows OS platform. ASP.NET can be viewed as a middleware container, similar to J2EE, for hosting components of .NET-based distributed applications accessible via Microsoft's Internet Information Server (IIS). Since ASP.NET runs in .NET's virtual machine, common language runtime (CLR)—whereas IIS is a regular Windows executable—ASP.NET_ISAPI dynamically linked library (DLL) acts as a bridge between the two, as shown in Figure 1. The DLL receives HTTP requests for URLs ending with specific extensions, the one for ASP.NET Web Services being .asmx.

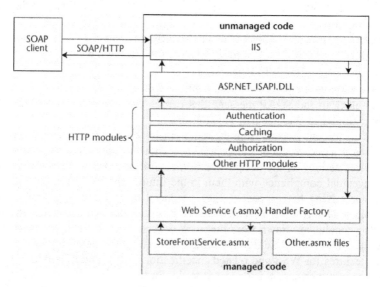

Fig. 1. Request handling by ASP.NET Web services

While running in unmanaged code, IIS forwards a request to the ASP.NET_ISAPL.DLL first. The DLL passes the request to ASP.NET, where the request passes through registered HTTP modules acting as invocation interceptors and reaches the Web Service Handler Factory. The factory uses the information in the URL to determine which Web service implementation should handle the request. ASP.NET dispatches the request to the implementation on demand of the factory. Not used only for performing security functions, the HTTP modules are also used for protecting ASP.NET Web services "out-of-the-box."

Discussed in detail in [8], the ASP.NET Web services preinstalled security mechanisms consist of the security available for the building blocks of these services and SOAP security. Overall, Microsoft products provide a convenient family of technologies to support the security of modest-sized applications with little effort. However, when the security requirements reach the enterprise scale, one needs either significant amounts of in-house development or additional third-party products and services to fill the gap. Fortunately, .NET in general and ASP.NET in particular have architectures that accommodate various security extensions. We designed our protection architecture as an extension to a typical ASP.NET installation.

3 Requirements

The design of the architecture was driven by its requirements and the underlying technology, ASP.NET. The functional objectives of the architecture were to allow flexible authentication and authorization for ASP.NET Web service applications. It was required to support "out-of-the-box" the following types of data (a.k.a. security tokens) for client and message authentication:

- user name and password from the HTTP header, a.k.a. HTTP Basic Authentication (HTTP-BA),
- ASP.NET Session state object with a pre-configured name,
- "stringified" credentials token found in any of the following:
- the custom field of the HTTP header, and/or
- HTTP cookie with a pre-configured name, and/or
- header block of the SOAP message that carries the request to the ASP.NET Web service, similar to WS-Security [15] (WSS).

One of the lessons learned from the requirements engineering exercise was that the end users did not care about the compliance with the security standards related to Web services as long as the design was in the spirit of those standards and therefore enabled eventual compliance with them in the future. The likely reason was the lack of plans for mixing heterogeneous (i.e., produced by different development teams) Web services. That is, no cross-enterprise Web service deployments were envisioned.

Another conclusion drawn from the work concerns the difficulty of determining a practical set of compliance criteria. Taking into account the flexibility of the information architectures for WSS and related specifications, we found it hard to define what a compliant implementation is expected to do. Furthermore, without prior agreement between application owners about the WSS profiles, two compliant applications would not necessarily interoperate in a useful manner.

In regards to authorization, the architecture was required to support a) third-party enterprise-wide A&A products, such as Policy Director [9], SiteMinder [14], getAccess [7], etc., b) selective availability of some service methods for public (i.e., anonymous) access, and c) simple variations of authorization logic.

The architecture was also required to be extensible enough to accommodate new types of A&A logic, e.g., access restriction based on the IP addresses of the Web service clients or the access day and time. Since it was impossible to envision all probable instances of A&A policies, the extension mechanisms had to be sufficiently generic. We also anticipated the need to compose new authorization policies out of existing ones (where developers could re-use much of the existing A&A logic).[1] Because this paper focuses on A&A, we do not discuss other requirements such as audit.

---

[1] For example, some publicly accessible methods with the remaining methods controlled by the enterprise-wide authorization.

4 Architecture Overview

To integrate with ASP.NET run-time, the architecture takes advantage of the ASP.NET generic interception mechanism, *SOAPExtension* [10], intended for additional processing of SOAP messages. As shown in Figure 2, our custom version of SOAPExtension (labeled "interceptor") performs the initial extraction, formatting, and other preparation of HTTP requests and, contained in them, SOAP messages, passing the data to the decision A&A logic and enforcing authorization decisions.

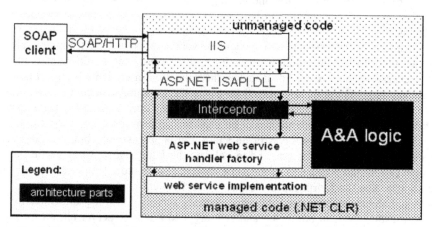

Fig. 2. General organization of the architecture into an interceptor and A&A logic

Since the purpose of the architecture is A&A, SOAP messages are processed on their way in and only after ASP.NET run-time has successfully parsed all SOAP-specific XML and HTTP formatting. If the protection of data in transit were a requirement, then the additional processing of the SOAP messages on their way out would be necessary. Since we did not anticipate it to undergo future changes, the interceptor has been designed with no extension or modification points. On the other hand, its design and implementation were optimized for performance since it was the most frequently used component in the architecture, invoked each time a protected Web service is accessed. Design for change [19], however, was a major goal for the decision part of the architecture, labeled as "A&A logic" in Figure 2. This part is composed of several other elements as described in the following sections.

4.1 Authentication

Authentication is commonly divided into two phases: retrieving authentication data and validating it. Following the same division, our *CredentialsRetriever* objects specialize in retrieving authentication data. Each retriever implementation is responsible for extracting particular data types (e.g., user name and password encoded as HTTP-BA, credentials token found in the SOAP message header, etc.) from the appropriate locations and encapsulating them in *Credential* objects. In the design of the authentication-related components, we wanted to isolate anticipated changes due to variations in authentication policies ("What data is acceptable for authentication?") from the rest of the architecture. For this purpose, retrieved authentication data and retrievers themselves are represented as implementations of *Credential* and *CredentialsRetreiver* interfaces. This approach allows for adding new modules of retrieving logic to the architecture by application developers, owners, or third-party vendors. For instance, the use of new types of authentication data, such as a client's public key certificate in requests over HTTPS, could be accommodated by developers by creating a new implementation of *CredentialsRetreiver* that retrieves the corresponding attributes of the HTTPS connection and packages them into a new instance of *Credential*. Before retrieved credentials can be used in authorization decisions, they need to be validated.

There are several reasons why credentials validation is separated from the retrieval phase and delayed until authorization. First, some credentials could be computationally expensive to validate. For instance, the validation of credentials signed by a private key requires public key operations as well as potentially unbound delays due to the checking certificate revocation lists. Second, only during the authorization step is it determined which credentials will be used for authorization. For example, if a request is accompanied by a certificate and a username-password but only the certificate is used, then there is no need to validate the latter. Third, some useful policies might call for the evaluation of the same credential with more than one authentication authority. Yet the fourth reason is due to the frequent co-location of authentication and authorization services in enterprise security servers. Lumping authentication and authorization steps in one batch and sending it to a remote server allows for a substantial reduction of the communication overhead in such cases.

Delaying credentials validation until the authorization phase, however, turns out to have a disadvantage as well. Those authorization components that implement the *PolicyEvaluator* interface have to contain credential-specific validation logic. In retrospect, a better design could be to encapsulate such validation logic into objects as parts of the credentials and configure binding between validators with the credentials.

4.2 Authorization

An authorization decision is reached in a three-step process, which is supported by the structure based on RAD and AF architectural styles. Initial decisions are made by zero or more predefined or custom authorization modules referred to as *PolicyEvaluator* (PE). The simplest PE is one that always returns the same decision, e.g., "deny," "permit," depending on its static configuration. Clearly, it ignores any credentials or other attributes of the request or target in question, environment, or the history about the previous requests. Despite its dullness, such a PE turns out to be very handy for testing, debugging, and deploying Web service applications and the architecture itself. More interesting PEs, supplied with the architecture implementation, grant access based on the IP address of the request sender, the name of the Web service target and its methods, and the decisions provided by an enterprise authorization server. The strength of RAD architectural style is in the support of fairly sophisticated authorization policies (see [1] for an example) without the need for complex authorization engines. This support is achieved by combining run-time decisions from several simple PEs into one at the second step, performed by a *DecisionCombinator* (DC).

Another reason for dividing the authorization process into the phases of evaluating (possibly several) policies and combining evaluation results, i.e., decisions, is to enable a high degree of authorization components reuse. Based on prior experience with protection for enterprise applications, we expected that, on the one hand, authorization policies would vary not only from organization to organization but also from application to application. On the other hand, common elements of authorization logic (e.g., decisions based on the roles, groups, and other attributes of the users) recur in most policies, making them perfect candidates for reusable components.

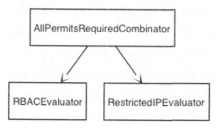

Fig. 3. Resulting configuration with the PE restricting access based on the sender's IP address

To appreciate the power of DC&PEs approach, consider a composition of "All Permits Required" DC with a role-based access control (RBAC) [20] PE. They implement authorization based on user roles and their hierarchies. If the application owners decide to restrict access further to a particular range of IP addresses, they can do so by adding a PE that authorizes IP addresses, instead of modifying the fairly complex logic of the RBAC PE. The result is shown in Figure 3. Support for policies in which PEs might have different priorities is enabled through the use of (unique) PE names so that custom DC logic can discriminate between them.

The authorization process continues to its third stage. This stage is important for achieving *fail-safe defaults* in those cases when a DC experiences a failure due to a design or implementation error and does not come to a binary decision. During this stage, the interceptor renders any decision, except "permit," received from the DC to "deny" and thus reaches authorization verdict. If access has been denied, the corresponding exception with the configurable explanation message is thrown to the ASP.NET run time, which translates it into an appropriate SOAP exception message.

Besides credentials—obtained from the SOAP message, the corresponding HTTP request, or the underlying communication channel—PEs are supplied with other information related to the request: name and attributes of the Web service, its policy domain, and the method to be invoked. All this information is constructed into a *permission*. Thus, the authorization process results in a decision on whether a given permission should be granted to a given subject (represented by its credentials). If so, the interceptor passes control to ASP.NET, which activates the corresponding Web service implementation and passes to it the request contained in the SOAP message. It is the construction of the permission that furthers the flexibility and extensibility of the architecture.

4.3 Permission Construction

To support the flexibility and extensibility of the architecture, we designed permission construction out of four distinct elements, as shown in Figure 4.

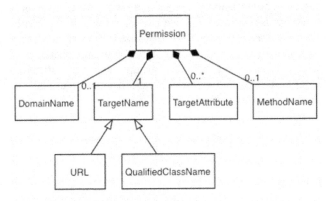

Fig. 4. Elements of the permission generated by the default permission factory

1. *TargetName*—the name of the target Web service can be represented by either a URL or the .NET class name of the service implementation. The URL represents the web server's interpretation of the URL from the corresponding HTTP request. The use of URLs for naming Web services is less attractive in ASP.NET because the same .NET class can be reused to create separate instances of Web services. In the ASP.NET environment, a single file hosts each target Web service. Different URLs can be used to invoke the same implementation class. The presence of these synonyms can pose a challenge to the security administrator's primary goal— maintaining proper security policy for Web services. The use of the .NET class name instead of the URL means that all instances of a Web service application can share the same authorization policy rules. This reduces the cost of maintenance and allows the same application logic to be protected no matter how many names under which it is deployed. When used together with the domain capability, several instances of the same Web service can be treated the same, or distinctly, as appropriate for the application structure.
2. *DomainName*—the use of a domain classifier is borrowed from CORBA Security [6, 16] architecture, whose policy domains support different security requirements for implementations of the same interfaces. In our architecture, optional domains allow discrimination between those same implementations of a Web service that have different access control requirements. Another purpose of domains is to allow for a logical grouping of several Web services, perhaps so that they can share an authorization server or its policy database. Since the means of determining the domain of a Web service is highly specific to the application and its authorization policies, our architecture provides a simple version of a domain retriever and a means for replacing it with custom implementations.
3. *Target attributes*—further differentiation among Web service instances is achieved through an optional list of one or more name-value pairs holding target attributes. For example, a Web service representing a bank account manager could have at-

tributes that identify the branch to which all the managed accounts belong, provided the division of the accounts among such managers is based on the branches. As it was argued in [2], the use of target attributes reduces the need for mixing authorization and other security logic with business logic. These application-specific attributes and the mechanism for obtaining them at run time are directly based on the prior work on Attribute Function [2, 18]. The extensible retrieval mechanism is designed as a replaceable *TargetAttributeRetriever* interface, with a simple implementation provided by the architecture implementation.

4. *Method*—since ASP.NET, at the time of this work, supported only RPC semantics for interactions with hosted Web service implementations, acceptable SOAP messages had to specify the method of the .NET implementation class responsible for processing the request. As with other RPC-based middleware technologies, it was important to support these authorization decisions based on method name. The method name is optional in the constructed permission to support types of applications that do not require authorization policy granularity at the method level.

Table 1 shows examples of permissions:

Table 1. Examples of permissions

Permission Example	Explanation
http://foobank.com/bar.asmx	Only the URL is used
com.foobank.ws.Sbar/m1	Class and method names
D1/com.foobank.ws.Sbar /m1	Same but in domain "D1"
com.foobank.ws.Sbar/owner=smith	Class name and attribute
D1/com.foobank.ws.Sbar/owner=smith/m1	Domain, class, attribute, method

The construction of permissions is done by a default permission factory, which can be replaced by a custom implementation possibly producing permissions of other format and content. The configuration, described below, determines which permission factory, DC&PEs, credential retrievers, and other replaceable parts of the architecture are used for serving requests for each Web service instance.

4.4 Replaceable Parts

As stated before, the flexibility and extensibility of the architecture is achieved via designing most of its elements to be replaceable. Any of the black boxes in Figure 5 can be replaced by a version that comes with the implementation or by a version produced by Web service developers or owners. Custom versions of the grey boxes are subject to the control by those modules that create them. Other architectures, e.g., CORBA Security [6, 16], also make some of their parts replaceable. The novelty of our approach is the level of replaceable parts' granularity. In CORBA Security, for instance, authorization logic (encapsulated in *AccessDecision* interface) has to be replaced as a whole, whereas in our architecture, one can selectively replace specific PEs and/or a DC. Furthermore, each Web service in the same container can be protected by a different set of replaceable elements, which is not the case with CORBA Security, COM+, or EJB implementations. Flexible and manageable configuration turns out to be critical for making fine-grain and yet scalable replaceability workable.

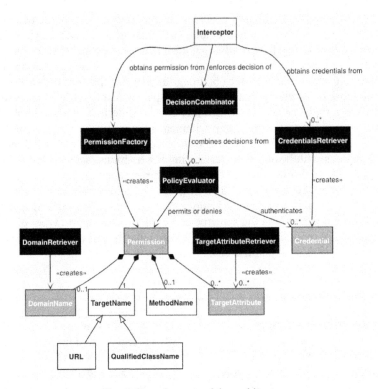

Fig. 5. Key elements of the architecture

4.5 Configuration

Flexible and scalable configuration is critical in order for our architecture to be extensible and, at the same time, carry low administration or run-time overhead. Since an ASP.NET container might host many Web services, each with its own security requirements, and deployment and maintenance life cycles, the run-time changes to the configuration should not result in the restart of the container or its lasting performance degradation. It turns out that ASP.NET configuration architecture, with settings defined in *web.config* files, had most features we were looking for.

The use of simplified XML in web.config files enables a flexible hierarchy of configuration elements, as shown in Figure **6**. By leveraging the web.config ability to delegate the handling of new configuration sections to custom handling logic, we developed a simple hierarchical language to define and configure various elements of the A&A decision logic as well as the protection policies that comprise them.

A protection policy can simply be viewed as a collection of specific credential retrievers, PEs, DC, as well as of attribute and domain retrievers, and permission factory. They are defined in other sections of the configuration and the policy only refers to them by name (and possibly re-configures them), thus enabling reuse.

Since all of these elements are defined independently of the policies and have unique names, they can be referenced by more than one protection policy. A singleton in the scope of a web.config instance, *Governing Policy* (GP) specifies which particular policy is used for controlling access to the Web service in question. Thus, one can prepare and test a protection policy, and perform a quick switch to the new policy by just changing the *name* attribute of a GP, a reference to specific protection policy. Multiple policies can be prepackaged and used to alter the behavior of the protection mechanisms in response, for example, to the changes in the threat level.

The hierarchal nature of web.config parsing semantics enables good scalability without losing a fine level of granularity in the control over sub-sets of (or individual) Web services. The GP defined in the root web.config determines the protection of all those Web services, for which no web.config file between the service and the root directory overrides it. Thus, developers can deploy their Web services, which can be administered by changes to the root web.config file. This approach, though, does not address the question of scalable administration for multiple ASP.NET containers, which is an issue for COM+ and standard EJB containers as well. Similar to product-specific solutions on the EJB market, one could remedy the problem by synchronizing web.config files or their specific sections across multiple containers.

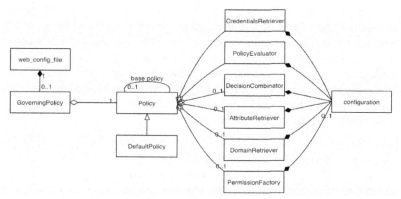

Fig. 6. Simplified model of the configuration elements with default cardinality "0..*"

The configuration flexibility is achieved through two design decisions. First, any web.config file down in the ASP.NET directory hierarchy can override GP, or define any new element, including new policies, as long as the name of this element has not been used in an ascendant web.config (i.e., one down in the directory hierarchy). Unfortunately, the freedom of overriding GP means the loss of control over GPs used for protecting the Web services located down in the directory hierarchy. However, this loss can be remedied by the use of OS file system controls, if necessary, by the Windows administrator restricting the rights of other users to modify web.config files down the directory hierarchy. Second, to reduce the effort required for creating policy variations, we also implemented a single inheritance mechanism for protection policy definitions. Thus, a policy could reuse most of the other policy's definition and override just a few elements, such as a *DomainRetriever* or a specific PE.

The performance overhead from storing all configuration information in web.config seems to be relatively small because ASP.NET caches read web.config files and invalidates the cache when the OS detects any changes to the file. Since the behavior or cache of our protection mechanisms is not affected by the changes to descendent web.config files, the goal of isolating Web services that are developed independently but co-hosted by one instance of an ASP.NET container is half-reached. The other half, eliminating the possibility of undesirable effects from changes in the higher levels of the hierarchy, can be achieved by allocating separate directory sub-trees to independent applications and sharing little or no settings through the web.config mechanism. Even though this solution is far from perfect, we believe it is good enough for most environments.

Adding a new component to the protection sub-system requires the simple step of adding an entry with the information about the corresponding .NET assembly, class name, and the name of the component into the web.config file. Afterwards, this component can be referenced in the corresponding sections of web.config. Removing a component involves the same steps but in reverse order. The above steps do not even require stopping the protection sub-system.

5 Examples

To demonstrate the ability of our architecture to be customized through different compositions of replaceable components, we provide hypothetical examples of implementing two different policies. These examples also illustrate the high degree of security logic reuse that, we expect, could reduce the error rate in the corresponding parts of the applications and their supporting infrastructure. Real commercial applications and policies that have used our implementation cannot be discussed due to the lack of permissions from the application owners.

5.1 Example 1: University Course Web Service

Consider a simplified application that provides online access to university courses as Web services. Let us assume that the following is a relevant fragment of the application security policy to be enforced:

Policy 1

1. All users should authenticate using user name and password in HTTP header (HTTP-BA).
2. **Anybody** can *look up* course descriptions.
3. **Registration clerks** can *list students* registered for the course and *(un)register* students.
4. The **course instructor** can *list registered students, manage course assignments* and *course material*.
5. **Registered** for the course **students** can *get assignments* and *course material*, and *submit assignments*.

Given that each course is represented by a separate instance of a web service, the following is a configuration of our architecture that enables the enforcement of **Policy 1**. It is illustrated in Figure **7** with custom-built modules in black.

Configuration 1:

- An HTTP-BA *CredentialRetriever* CR_1 extracts the user name and password from the HTTP request that carried the corresponding SOAP request.

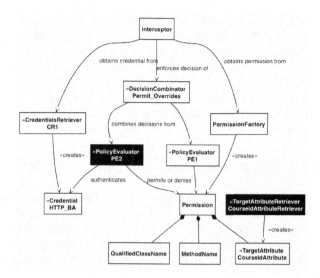

Fig. 7. Configuration 1. Custom-built components appear in the black boxes

- A custom *TargetAttributeRetriever* provides the course number in a form of an attribute, e.g. CourseId=EECE412.
- The default *PermissionFactory* is configured to compose permissions with the qualified class name of the .NET class, as a *TargetName*, the corresponding method name, and the attributes provided by the custom retriever. No domain name is used in this configuration. Here is an example: "ca.ubc.CourseMngmnt.SimpleCourse/CourseId=EECE412/GetDescription".
- A pre-built *PolicyEvaluator* PE₁ grants permissions to any request on publicly accessible methods. In the case of Policy 1, there is one public method, Get-CourseDescription.
- A custom *PolicyEvaluator* PE₂ is programmed and configured to make authorization decisions according to the rules informally described as follows:
  1. Permit users in role "registration clerk" to access methods "ListStudents", "RegisterStudent" and "UnregisterStudent".
  2. Permit users in role "instructor" whose attribute "CourseTaught" contains the course listed in Permission.TargetAttributes.CourseId to list registered students, manage course assignments and material.
  3. Permit users in role "student" whose attribute "RegisteredCourses" contains the course listed in Permission.TargetAttributes.CourseId to list registered students, manage course assignments and material.

  User roles and other attributes are retrieved by the PE during or after it validates the credential received from HTTP-BA *CredentialRetriever*. We refrain from discussing this step since it is very specific to the particular student and employee databases used by the university and is irrelevant to the discussion.
- A pre-built *DecisionCombinator* of type *Permit Overrides* grants access if either PE grants access.

This example also illustrates one specific issue with any component-based design: even when each component satisfies its specification, there is no inherent guarantee that the assembled system also does. For instance, PE$_2$ (which assumes the presence of a *CourseId* attribute in the permission passed to it) depends on the *TargetAttributeRetriever* to retrieve such an attribute and on the *PermissionFactory* to insert the attribute into the permission. All three have to function together for the protection sub-system to function as expected. In our solution, we have not addressed this issue, leaving developers to ensure the consistency of the assembled protection mechanisms manually. The development of a specific automated solution for consistency verification is a potent topic for future research on component-based security subsystems.

5.2   Example 2: Human Resource Web Service for International Organization

Now consider a multinational company that has divisions in Japan, Canada, the USA, and Russia. Each division has its own department of human resources (HR). The company rolls out a Web service application in all of its divisions to provide online access to employee information. Each division has one or more Web services providing HR information for that division. The company establishes the following security policy for accessing this application.

Policy 2
1. Only users within the *company's intranet* or those who access the service over SSL and have valid X.509 certificates issued by the company should be able to access the application.
2. **Anybody** in the company can *look up* any employee and *get essential information* about her/him (e.g., contact information, title, and names of the manager and supervised employees).
3. **Employees of HR** departments can *modify contact information* and *review salary information* for any employee from the same division.
4. **Managers of HR** departments can *modify any information* about the employees of the same department.

Configuration 2:
- Same *CredentialsRetriever* CR$_1$ is used as in Example 1.
- Another *CredentialRetriever* CR$_2$ obtains an SSL client certificate from the HTTPS connection.
- A pre-built simple *DomainRetriever* always returns the same statically configured domain name. The domain name designates the division for which HR information is served by the web service instance, e.g., "Japan".
- The default *PermissionFactory* is configured to compose permissions with the domain name, qualified class name of the .NET class, as a target name, and the corresponding method name. No target attributes are used in this case. Here is an example: "Japan/com.mega-foo.EmployeeInfo/GetContactInfo".
- Same pre-built *PolicyEvaluator* PE$_1$ as in Example 1 is used. This time, there are four public methods: FindEmployee, GetEmployeeInformation, GetEmployeeManager, GetSupervisedEmployees.
- A pre-built *PolicyEvaluator* PE$_3$ permits access to any request made from a machine with an IP address in the range of the company's intranet addresses.
- A custom-built *PolicyEvaluator* PE$_4$ permits access to any request made by a user with a valid X.509 certificate (retrieved by CR$_2$) issued by the company.

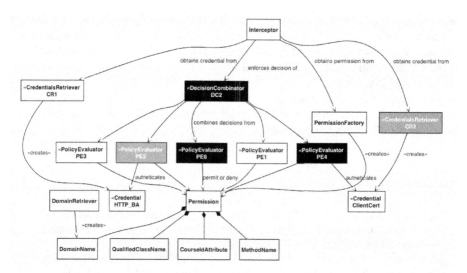

Fig. 8. Configuration 2. Custom-built components appear in black boxes. Generic ones supplied by vendors appear in gray boxes

- A generic RBAC *PolicyEvaluator* PE$_5$ permits the invocation of different methods based on the role of the user:
  1. Any user with the role "hr employee" can invoke methods that modify contact information and review salary.
  2. Any user with the role "hr manager" can invoke methods permitted to users with role "hr employee" as well as methods that modify an employee's salary, title, and the names of the manager and supervised employees.
- A custom-built *PolicyEvaluator* PE$_6$ permits access to any authenticated user, whose attribute "Division" has the same value as the domain in the permission.
- A custom-built *DecisionCombinator* DC$_2$ grants access according to the following formula: (PE$_3$ ∨ PE$_4$) ∧ (PE$_1$ ∨ (PE$_5$ ∧ PE$_6$)). That is, a request is permitted only to intranet users or those with a valid company certificate (PE$_3$ ∨ PE$_4$), provided that either the requested method is public (PE$_1$) or an authorized HR person is accessing a record for the employee from the same division (PE$_5$ ∧ PE$_6$).

The high degree of the architecture composability allows for re-using two pre-built (PE$_1$ & PE$_3$) from configuration 1. Even though configuration 2 has three more PEs and one more *CredentialRetriever* than configuration 1, as shown in Figure **8**, there are only three components (DC$_2$, PE$_4$, and PE$_6$) that have to be custom-built. Among them, PE$_4$ is simple to build with certificate validation tools and libraries, and PE$_6$ requires marginal effort. DC$_2$ can be implemented in one 'if' structure. Two other (PE$_5$ and CR$_2$) are generic and can be supplied by third-party vendors.

6 Conclusions and Acknowledgement

This paper reports an experience of designing a flexible and extensible architecture for protecting enterprise-grade ASP.NET Web services. The architecture's flexibility and extensibility have been achieved through a component-based design that follows the architectural styles of RAD [4, 5, 17] and Attribute Function [2]. This architecture has been implemented in a real-world security solution. We described requirements, presented the architecture, and explained the design decisions along with the lessons learned from this work.

The author thanks the anonymous reviewers for their insightful comments that helped to improve this paper. ICICS editorial assistant Ben D'Andrea was instrumental in making this paper more readable.

References

1. Barkley, J., Beznosov, K. and Uppal, J., "Supporting Relationships in Access Control Using Role Based Access Control," in Proceedings of the Fourth ACM Role-based Access Control Workshop, (Fairfax, Virginia, USA, 1999), pp. 55-65.
2. Beznosov, K., Object Security Attributes: Enabling Application-specific Access Control in Middleware. in 4th International Symposium on Distributed Objects & Applications (DOA), (Irvine, California, USA, 2002), Springer-Verlag, pp. 693-710.
3. Beznosov, K. Overview of .NET Web Services Security, presented at Distributed Object Computing Security Workshop, Baltimore, MD, USA, 2002.
4. Beznosov, K., Deng, Y., Blakley, B., Burt, C. and Barkley, J., A Resource Access Decision Service for CORBA-based Distributed Systems. in Proceedings of the Annual Computer Security Applications Conference (ACSAC), (Phoenix, Arizona, USA, 1999), pp. 310-319.
5. Beznosov, K., Espinal, L. and Deng, Y., "Performance Considerations for CORBA-based Application Authorization Service," in Proceedings of the Fourth IASTED International Conference Software Engineering and Applications, (Las Vegas, Nevada, USA, 2000).
6. Blakley, B. CORBA Security: an Introduction to Safe Computing with Objects. Addison-Wesley, Reading, MA, 1999.
7. Entrust. getAccess Design and Administration Guide, Encommerce, 1999, 182p.
8. Hartman, B., Flinn, D.J., Beznosov, K. and Kawamoto, S. Mastering Web Services Security. John Wiley & Sons, New York, 2003.
9. Karjoth, G., "The Authorization Service of Tivoli Policy Director," in Proceedings ACSAC, (New Orleans, Louisiana, 2001), pp.319-328.
10. Microsoft. "Altering the SOAP Message Using SOAP Extensions," 2002.
11. Microsoft Building Secure ASP.NET Applications: Authentication, Authorization, and Secure Communication. Microsoft Press, 2002.
12. Microsoft. Microsoft .NET Passport, 2001.
13. Microsoft. "Securing XML Web Services Created Using ASP.NET" in .NET Framework Developer's Guide, 2001.
14. Netegrity. SiteMinder Concepts Guide, Waltham, MA, 2000, 78p.
15. OASIS. Web Services Security: SOAP Message Security 1.0 (WS-Security 2004), 2004.
16. OMG. CORBAservices: Security Service Specification v1.7, formal/01-03-08, 2001.
17. OMG. Resource Access Decision Facility, formal/2001-04-01, 2001.
18. OMG. Security Domain Membership Management Service, Final Submission, 2001.
19. Parnas, D.L. "Designing Software for Ease of Extension and Contraction," IEEE Transactions on Software Engineering, SE-5(2):128-137, 1979.
20. Sandhu, R. et al. "Role-Based Access Control Models," IEEE Computer, 29(2):38-47, 1996.
21. W3C. SOAP Version 1.2 Part 1: Messaging Framework, W3C, 2002.

Concept Index

Author Index

Lecture Notes in Computer Science

For information about Vols. 1–3399

please contact your bookseller or Springer